Ideological Fixation

Ideological Fixation

From the Stone Age to Today's Culture Wars

AZAR GAT

OXFORD
UNIVERSITY PRESS

Oxford University Press is a department of the University of Oxford. It furthers
the University's objective of excellence in research, scholarship, and education
by publishing worldwide. Oxford is a registered trade mark of Oxford University
Press in the UK and certain other countries.

Published in the United States of America by Oxford University Press
198 Madison Avenue, New York, NY 10016, United States of America.

Library of Congress Cataloging-in-Publication Data
Names: Gat, Azar, author.
Title: Ideological fixation : from the Stone Age to today's culture wars /Azar Gat.
Description: New York, NY : Oxford University Press, [2022] |
Includes bibliographical references and index.
Identifiers: LCCN 2022010848 (print) | LCCN 2022010849 (ebook) |
ISBN 9780197646700 (hardback) | ISBN 9780197646724 (epub)
Subjects: LCSH: Ideology—History.
Classification: LCC B823.3 .G38 2022 (print) | LCC B823.3 (ebook) |
DDC 145—dc23/eng/20220610
LC record available at https://lccn.loc.gov/2022010848
LC ebook record available at https://lccn.loc.gov/2022010849

DOI: 10.1093/oso/9780197646700.001.0001

1 3 5 7 9 8 6 4 2

Printed by Sheridan Books, Inc., United States of America

CONTENTS

PREFACE

I began writing this book before the 2016 US presidential elections, before the terms "fake news" and "alternative facts" were coined, and before the further, ever-continuing escalation of America's ideological civil war. What prompted the book was not any particular political development but, as all intellectual ventures should ideally be, a deep sense of wonderment; wonderment at the way people tend to be wholly enclosed within their ideological frames and entirely deaf—indeed, react with total rejection and hostility—to arguments and claims about the world that come from the opposite camp, no matter how valid they might be. Ideology consists of cherished normative prescriptions as to what is just and how social reality should accordingly be shaped, together with an interpretive roadmap indicating how these normative prescriptions can be implemented in the real world. Ideological fixation is the result of the ever-present tensions and conflicts between our normative wishes and interpretation of reality. I have always been intrigued by this phenomenon and by the built-in biases and gross errors in the understanding of reality it breeds.

I am an Israeli, a citizen of a country that since its inception has experienced profound existential concerns and ideological divides. More remarkably, after social theorists around 1960 proclaimed the "death of ideology", ideological divides and clashes have re-emerged with renewed intensity throughout the world. Currently, they include not only the challenges to liberal democracy presented by illiberal and non-democratic China and Russia or by fundamentalist and jihadist Islam, but also deep cleavages and all-pervasive antagonisms in the liberal democracies themselves. In the United States they have become particularly acute and venomous. The zeal of the opposing sides is often scarcely less than that which characterized the religious ideologies of old, or that which prevailed between the great rival ideologies of the nineteenth and twentieth centuries: liberalism, socialism, and fascism. The other side is widely viewed as malicious, irrational, or downright stupid and, often, as barely legitimate.

People are strongly predisposed to regard their own camp as both patently right and righteous, while viewing the other side as malevolent and willfully wrong. In my experience, the prospects of bringing even the best and the brightest— *particularly* the best and the brightest—on either side of an ideological divide to critically examine their camp's dogmas or consider the possibility of even a partial validity of some of the other side's arguments are very slim indeed. That those who express the opposite claims are identified with the other side is enough to close ears and minds. In this dialogue of the deaf, the arguments simply do not register and are received with a mixture of contempt and rage.

Ideologies, and hence ideological clashes, antagonism, and fixations, are as old as civilization itself. During most of history, ideologies were mainly religious, whereas during modern times they have taken the form often described as "secular religions" or "religion substitutes". They have always served to legitimize socioeconomic and political orders, or have projected alternatives to them. The ideological mode of interpreting and relating to the world, as well as ideological fixations, seem to be intrinsic features of the human mind. In his book *Thinking, Fast and Slow* (2011), psychologist Daniel Kahneman has suggested that the human mind has two basic systems of operation: the first and more common relying on simple cues and heuristics used to arrive at split-second decisions; the second, far slower and more deliberate, is occasionally resorted to when a more systematic analysis of complex problems is called for. The ideological mode of thinking may belong to a third category. It involves highly complex interpretations of and emotional-behavioral reactions to the world, for which we rely on ready-made and deeply internalized templates to produce instant, reflex-like attitudes and propositions.

This book is not a survey of past and present ideologies. There are many such excellent surveys on the market. Instead, it is an attempt to understand the cognitive, emotional, and social roots of the ideological phenomenon: why we are so prone to—indeed, are captive of—the ideological mode of thinking. To find the answer to this riddle, the book combines insights from evolutionary theory regarding the nature of some of our deepest proclivities with a sweep through the great drama of history, from the Stone Age, to the rise of civilization, to the present. Ideology has been the subject of prodigious study over the past century or so. Scholars and publicists have emphasized both ideology's indispensable role as a compass guiding large-scale action and the application of social visions in the public arena *and* built-in biases and dogmatic, zealous rigidity in the interpretation of reality. We hope to take the inquiry of both these aspects a step further. Reversing Marx's famous saying (himself both a pioneering theorist and victim of ideological fixation): I have little faith in the ability to change this deep human propensity—my aim is to understand it.

In the first part of the book we lay the groundwork by undertaking to decipher, first, what truth is—does this concept have a meaning, or is everybody equally entitled to his or her facts; and, second, how we are to understand morality, our vivid and deeply emotive normative coloring of the social world. Both questions have been the source of profound confusion, resurfacing with great public fanfare in the intellectual discourse of the last decades. I think you may learn from, and enjoy, this part a lot. However, if you are less interested in these profound questions that have preoccupied both philosophers and ordinary people throughout the ages, you can safely skip these preliminaries and jump right to the second and third parts of the book and into the great ideological divides and fixations of the past and present.

ACKNOWLEDGMENTS

Friends, colleagues, and other dear ones read parts or all of the manuscript and made very helpful suggestions. Alex Yakobson and Peter Berkowitz stand out in their dedication and contribution. Innumerable corrections and improvements were offered by Uriel Abulof, Yitzhak Benbaji, Eyal Chowers, Julie Cooper, Tomer Fadlon, Daniel Finkelshtein, Jonathan Gat, Meir Litvak, Udi Manor, Yotam Margalit, Tamar Meisels, Dan Schueftan, Yossi Shain, Uriya Shavit, Omer Solodoch, Alberto Spektorowski, Daniel Statman, Asher Susser, and Yoav Tenenbaum. My editor Dave McBride excelled in navigating the book through the process at Oxford University Press. I am grateful to them all. Needless to add, I alone am responsible for the faults of this book and for the views expressed in it.

PART I

GROUNDWORK

What Is True?

(*Though Never the Whole Truth*)

When I originally wrote this chapter, the phrase "alternative facts" did not yet exist. However, the questions underlying it—what is true, is there truth—are among the most profound questions that have preoccupied humanity since the dawn of civilization. The nature of truth needs to be clarified prior to any discussion of ideology, ideological differences, and ideological fixation. In this opening chapter we argue that while the skeptical tradition concerning the existence of truth, from antiquity to present-day "postmodernists", has a point, and a highly significant one, this point has been vastly overdrawn. Truth about reality—properly understood—is a very meaningful notion, and not everything is equally true, or true at all. We begin with some elementary and familiar stuff, at least to those with a little knowledge of the history of thought. So the more informed readers are asked to exercise some patience as we progress in this chapter from the basic to the more advanced.

In a very deep sense, we live in a world of our own making—the world that exists in our mind is largely a product of that mind. This is the conclusion reached by millennia of philosophical reflection and centuries of modern scientific discovery. Thus, people see only a limited section of the spectrum of colors, from red to violet, and are blind to anything on the infrared and ultraviolet spectra. Our hearing is similarly restricted to a limited tonal range on the spectrum of vibrations, roughly between 20 Hz and 20 kHz. Moreover, color and sound themselves are regarded within our current understanding of the world as mental renderings that exist only in the mind, of physical properties of the world (waves, particles) that impact our sense organs. The seventeenth-century philosopher John Locke called such mental representations of reality, which also include products of our other senses such as smell, taste, touch, and heat-chill "secondary qualities". If a tree falls in a forest and no one is around to hear it, does it make a sound, or only create vibrations? Much the same applies to objects'

Ideological Fixation. Azar Gat, Oxford University Press. © Oxford University Press 2022.
DOI: 10.1093/oso/9780197646700.003.0001

physical extension and solidity, Locke's "primary qualities" that supposedly belong directly to the objects themselves, irrespective of our sense perception. We inhabit a perceived world of solid objects of roughly our own size range, and become aware of the infinitesimal world of elementary particles and the vast spaces that separate them, as well as of the imperceptible size of the universe beyond the observable heavens, only by means of instruments that extend our senses' reach and by inferences beyond sense perceptions.

Different organisms have different senses and sense perceptions, tuned to the different physical features that constitute their relationship with their environment. Hence they experience different images of the world. Selecting an especially alien example, philosopher Thomas Nagel has illustrated this point in an article that stimulates the imagination: "What Is It Like to Be a Bat?"[1] The ancient Greeks, who almost miraculously raised all the big questions that would preoccupy humanity through the ages, made pretty much the same point millennia ago. The Greek school of skeptics, confounded by the elusiveness of our sense perceptions and the limitations of our concepts, cited as examples the differences in their inner experience between men and a variety of more or less alien creatures, from frogs to bees to shellfish.[2]

If our perception of the outside world turns out upon reflection to be different from the transparent one-to-one mirror that we instinctively feel it is, what then *is* the relationship between reality and our mental representations of it? What part of the picture of the world that we carry in our heads comes from reality itself and what part is contributed by our own sense organs and mental processes? How can we separate the two, the "objective" from the "subjective", and tell what the world is really like? Aristotle defined error and truth in the following commonsensical way: "To say of what is that it is not, or of what is not that it is, is false, while to say of what is that it is, and of what is not that it is not, is true."[3] Plato had articulated a similar definition.[4] This is known as the correspondence theory of truth: a correspondence between our ideas and realities in the world. But in what way do ideas, which are mental phenomena in the mind, correspond to real things outside? What barriers exist between the two, and what kind of bridges allow us to cross between them? Each of these questions has turned out to be a monumental puzzle and the subject of intense contemplation from the ancient Greeks on, as well as outside the Western tradition, to the present.

We shall touch on some of the main points in this intellectual journey as succinctly as possible. First, how do we know that the image of the world in our mind actually represents a reality outside? In dreams, we get along pretty well in an imagined reality. Maybe our lives are similarly just a dreamlike illusion. Plato thought that the connection between the world of our senses and reality is so distorted that we are like people eternally locked in a cave with only faint shadows of reality projected on the wall opposite them.[5] From antiquity on, some Buddhist schools have taught that reality is an illusion, something like a big dream. In the seventeenth century, René Descartes, setting in motion the train of modern philosophy, focused his search for secure knowledge of the world on this fundamental problem. He concluded that God, whose existence he thought he had proved a step earlier, would not conceivably play such a dirty trick as to deceive people that they lived in a real world rather than in a dream.[6] Unfortunately, we tend to regard both the existence and benevolence of God as less straightforward than did Descartes. Indeed, in the early eighteenth century, philosopher George Berkeley, an Anglican bishop, evidently viewed God's work very differently from Descartes. He argued that there was no material reality and that the world actually existed only as ideas in the minds, a view known as idealism.[7] In his *Critique of Pure Reason* (1781), philosopher Immanuel Kant conceded that we could not really know the world "in itself", beyond what our senses and perceptual tools presented to us. He consoled himself with the view that knowledge and certainty are at least secured in the world of phenomena as experienced in our mind, precisely by virtue of the fixed features of the mind's sensual and perceptual apparatus that imprint all experience. This line of thought has been taken up by the philosophical school known as phenomenalism from the late nineteenth century on. After all, there appears to be no conceivable way that we can step outside ourselves to check what reality is beyond our inner world of sense perceptions.

Ordinarily, we find doubts regarding the reality of the world futile. In the eighteenth century, Dr. Samuel Johnson, famous, among other things, for his wittiness and commonsense wisdom, responded to Berkeley's denial of the existence of a material world by vigorously kicking a stone, saying: "I refute it thus."[8] Our world seems very real and solid to us—most of the time. But how can we tell for sure? Who has not felt sometimes that the reality we live in is elusive and perhaps deceptive? The hugely successful Hollywood movie *The Matrix* (1999), which portrays a simulated world created by artificial intelligence to deceive the people who are locked in it, has become an often-invoked metaphor, a modern equivalent of Descartes's problem, Plato's cave, and the Buddhist world as an illusion. Thus, the often-made claim, amusingly illustrated by Dr. Johnson, that nobody truly believes—let alone actually *acts* on the belief—that the outside world is not real may be generally correct; and yet it is not a refutation of the skeptics' fundamental doubt, because it is precisely the vividness and cage-like nature of the world as a possible illusion that is the issue. "Commonsense" and our immediate sense perception are no help either, because even seemingly self-evident sense perceptions, such as the apparent flatness of the earth, the movement of the sun around it, and, indeed, colors, turn out to involve perceptual illusions of some sort.[9] On the other hand, empirically well-supported scientific theories can be so counterintuitive and non-commonsensical as to cause Albert

Einstein (whose own relativity theory is far from intuitive) to rebel against the implications of quantum mechanics, despite its huge predictive success. Nor do the amazing achievements of science and technology constitute, in and of themselves, a refutation of the skeptic position, as they too apply to the world of phenomena that we perceive—the world as it appears to us. The laws of nature themselves may be part of a dreamlike illusion of an outside world.

Thus, as almost everybody who has concerned himself with this problem agrees, it is not possible to refute the skeptical doubt regarding the foundations of our entire picture of the world. In a strict sense, the overwhelming majority of humanity holding that the world outside us actually exists—a view known as "realism"—assumes or believes this proposition because, given the world's concreteness in our mind and our existential need to live and survive in it, it is more natural and it appears more plausible to take that position where no substantial evidence for the opposite view exists. The formal systems of logic and mathematics enjoy a higher level of certainty only because they are taken to reflect forms of the mind rather than beings in the world.

Therefore, contra Descartes, our knowledge of the world rests from its very foundations not on certainties but on assumptions or beliefs that seem more plausible given the other elements of our worldview. The same applies at every stage up the edifice of our knowledge, as more and more assumptions are added, based on the same criteria. Indeed, the problem of reality and of our comprehension of it concerns not only the actual existence and nature of the world but also the status of every individual statement about it.

The intrinsic interdependence of the various elements of our worldview was first pointed out by the Greek skeptics. It puzzled them because it suggested that there were no foundational, self-evident facts on which everything else we think we know about the world could be securely based.[10] This may be taken to mean that human knowledge is arbitrary, circular, and relative—as to some degree it is. In the spirit of Greek philosophy in which the Roman elite were schooled, Pontius Pilate sophisticatedly responded to Jesus' profession of truth with the words: "What is truth?" (John 18:38). And the Roman philosopher-emperor Marcus Aurelius wrote skeptically, albeit less cynically: "Remember that all is opinion."[11]

The view that our knowledge of the world is not certain in any absolute sense has become commonplace from the second half of the twentieth century. Some of the period's most influential analytical philosophers, such as Willard Quine, Wilfrid Sellars, Donald Davidson, and Hilary Putnam, incorporating older philosophical traditions, have argued that our picture of the world is based on beliefs that are judged more plausible given the weight of the evidence and all the other interrelated elements of our worldview, a view known as "holism". These include the best methods of observation and more persuasive explanatory theories available at the time. This conceptual framework involves a more conditional, tentative, and fluid understanding of what should qualify as true given the intrinsic limitations of the connection between mind and reality.[12] I share this view (indeed, I held it before I ever heard the names of any of these philosophers) and wish to develop it, generally and as concerns social and historical realities.

Framing and Tagging—Concepts and Conceptual Grids

We comprehend the world through a grid of concepts that relate to each other. (The terms "scheme", "web", "net", "cluster", and "fabric" have all been interchangeably used.) This means that we issue a label—a code symbol—for any feature of the world that is of interest to us. We tag it, attach a "signifier" to something that is signified, in the terminology of pioneering linguist Ferdinand de Saussure. The tagged features often do not fully overlap in different conceptual grids and they obviously have different names (words) in different languages, which also use somewhat different syntactical rules to arrange and manipulate them. But the cognitive mechanism involved is basically the same. We are able to issue any number of such labels to tag features of the world in greater detail or to cover new features that have come to attract our attention. We group concepts that we find similar in some way into more general concepts; coin abstract concepts that do not seem to have obvious tangible objects in reality, such as capitalism, government, or Christianity; and for various purposes invent imagined concepts that may or may not exist. We combine concepts into meaningful narratives woven into our conceptual grids, and we are able to imagine actual and potential scenarios, past and future. This is an amazing mental process, responsible for humankind's exceptional cognitive capabilities and ability to deal with the world. It is also very natural and intuitive to us, so we do not easily comprehend what the process entails, or its limitations.

Consider ostensibly simple concepts, such as a tree or a chicken. Their meaning and, moreover, their tangibility are very obvious to us, as they are also to animals. Yet not one tree, even from the same species, is identical to any other tree; nor is any particular tree similar to what it was a moment ago or to what it will be in the next moment. The same applies to chickens, and to all other ostensibly simple concepts. Realizing that "everything flows and nothing stays", the ancient Greek philosopher Heraclitus famously stated that "you could not step twice into the same river."[13] Furthermore, on what grounds do we distinguish between the group of atoms and molecules that we identify as a "tree" from those we call "soil", "air", "water", or "moss" surrounding it (each of which is also an ostensibly simple concept that actually covers great internal diversity)? Moreover, how do we distinguish them from the entirety and continuum of being? As "holistic" philosophers have argued, all our concepts of "objects" are only partial abstractions extracted from their innumerable deep connections with the rest of the universe.

Indeed, many of the questions that we have seen with respect to "objects" extend to what we perceive as "actions" and other "connections" and "relationships" between "objects". We focus on, and in this way isolate, particular connections that we perceive as "causation" and other relationships that are of interest to us. But as the Greek skeptics long noted, in this process we do not notice, or we set aside, the innumerable connections and interactions existing between the things that are irrelevant to our particular interest or perspective at a given moment, or ever.[14] This is despite the fact that ultimately everything is supposedly connected to everything else in infinite ways.

The realization of these sorts of puzzles drove the Greek philosopher Cratylus to a desperate conclusion, which he allegedly adopted in practice. He felt that, given the unresolvable limitations of our conceptual tools and comprehension of the world, one best serves the truth by keeping silence and not uttering a word, as any speech is necessarily inaccurate and incomplete and therefore distorts reality.[15] We find Cratylus' plight and existential decision amusing, not only because we do not ordinarily pay much attention to the constraints of our strongly intuitive system of concepts, but also, or mainly, because we give practical life and the needs of human communication a vastly greater priority over the idealistic quest for an unattainable absolute accuracy and comprehensiveness. Furthermore, in a more reflective mode, we look at the full half of the glass and are in awe at the magical stuff that fills it and serves us so amazingly in comprehending and coping with the world. Rather than keeping silent, we may better serve our understanding of what is truth by paying the closest attention to how our cognitive and conceptual system works.

Assuming that the world outside us does exist and that we need to live and survive in it, it is not possible for our necessarily finite cognitive system to comprehend reality in its entirety or totality. Such an ability was traditionally reserved to God in the Western tradition, and has survived in some strands of metaphysics in what philosopher Hilary Putnam—echoing Friedrich Nietzsche's famous "death of God"—has called (and dismissed as) "God's eye view of the world".[16] As already mentioned, in the absence of infinite comprehension, we use an ingenious shortcut by focusing on and conceptualizing features of reality—objects, actions, connections, and relationships—that best serve our more general or momentary needs and interests. Our conceptual tagging system functions as a shorthand or translation code that converts the infinity of the world into finite concepts and conceptual grids. Every ostensibly simple concept, such as a tree or a chicken, despite its concreteness in our minds, is actually a general concept that singles out, frames together and tags a group of features on the basis some "family resemblance" that we see between them.

The term "family resemblance" was coined by twentieth-century philosopher Ludwig Wittgenstein. In his early work *Tractatus Logico-Philosophicus* (1921) he championed the view that there were elementary observable facts out there that could be captured by picture-concepts in the mind on a one-to-one basis if only we rigorously adhered to a clear and coherent symbolic-linguistic system. However, Wittgenstein later changed his mind completely. He spent the rest of his life developing the view, presented in his posthumous *Philosophical Investigations* (1953), that our conceptual-linguistic terms were constructs created to cope with the world and communicate with other people in the service of life's many and diverse practical needs, functions, and purposes. He called this variety of uses and modes of expression "language games". His concept of "family resemblance", the basis for the grouping together of items into general concepts or categories, is widely cited, but needs some further exploration.

By its very nature, family resemblance is (partly) in the eye of the beholder, while, however, being established on the basis of some meaningful criteria. In some cases, the chosen resemblance can actually be reduced to the molecular level: no piece of flint is identical with any other (or is not alloyed), but they are more similar to one another than to non-flints. They form a close cluster in terms of their physical traits. Sometimes, an organic element is added. No pine is identical to any other pine, but pines are closer to each other on the molecular level than to any non-pine. And this resemblance, which extends to the molecules of the pines' genome, guarantees that pines will produce only pines and will be produced from pines only. (We noticed these facts long before we knew anything about molecules or genes.) Moreover, a pine constitutes a biological system in which the parts are bound together by functional interdependence. The same applies to chickens, with an added twist: the combination of features that constitute chickens as separate from their environment stay, or run, more or less together, as chickens move against their background. Furthermore, as a practical rule, chickens are good to eat, they are potential "food", and, with obvious qualifications, can be counted to taste more or less the same. Indeed, with some objects no physical resemblance on the molecular level underlies our conceptual groupings, and the "family resemblance" that we assign is more functional, most often in relation to us. "Desks" (or "tables") can be made of different materials (molecules), but we tag them as similar based on their physical form (that is, a flat plane on the top) and function: writing, eating, etc. In yet other cases, not even physical resemblance is involved—only the concept's function in relation to us. Concepts such as "tools" or "dwellings" (from caves, to straw, wooden or stone huts, to steel and glass high-rises) are of such nature, to say nothing of even more abstract concepts such as "threats", "dangers", or "opportunities". There are many criteria of "family resemblance", and mixtures of criteria, that our cognitive system uses in producing conceptual groupings.

What this means is that the groups of things that are framed together in our concepts have no essence—if what is understood by essence is a shared element that is actually *identical* in the things themselves. The "essence" is assigned by us to a group of things that we find similar enough on the basis of criteria such as the above. This is far from a new idea. For millennia, there was a debate between so-called realists and nominalists on the question of whether universals, and thus essences, actually existed, while "conceptualists" took an intermediate position that they existed only in our minds. Like many other questions in the history of thought, the matter is worth returning to because it is still very much alive and kicking in today's intellectual discourse. Many arguments still revolve around semantics, as though words and concepts have fixed meanings directly associated with things. This brings to mind Humpty Dumpty's lesson to Alice in Lewis Carroll's *Through the Looking-Glass*: "'When *I* use a word', Humpty Dumpty said, in rather a scornful tone, 'it means just what I choose it to mean—neither more nor less.'" Semantic arguments often occur on the border of conceptual frames, as in: Are "French windows" windows or doors, but most typically on questions that stir greater public interest and are often charged: "Are movies an art form or a business?" (a false dichotomy as the two are not mutually exclusive, but the question obviously relates to the frame deemed most relevant from some chosen perspective); or "What Islam truly is?"

Indeed, at an ostensibly higher intellectual level, the charge of "essentialism" (or "reification")—ascribing fixed qualities to a diverse and changing category—has become the stock-in-trade of polemics in recent times. This charge is sometimes invoked as a much necessary correction to crude generalizations, and all the more so when they are used in the service of social and political bigotry. However, no less often "essentialism" has become a worn-out shibboleth or cultural cliché. *Both* generalization and specification are the two indispensable and complementary devices of our cognitive system. The one, categorization, or "lumping", is necessary for our ability to understand and cope with the world by placing a modicum of manageable order on its infinite diversity. Social thinker Max Weber—who concerned himself with many of the questions discussed in this chapter, and came up with pretty similar answers—coined another much-cited concept, "ideal type", to describe such categorization.[17] The opposite cognitive device, "splitting", is equally indispensable to achieve greater resolution or focus on differences when such discerning is appropriate. While it is generally in keeping with our practical and intellectual needs to regard each plural such as flints, pines, chickens, and, moreover, churches, billionaires, and sovereignties as a single concept, we focus our attention on the sometimes enormous differences that exist within each concept when such differences become relevant. Human history can be regarded as a process in which we develop increasingly abstract conceptual symbols and grids that appear more distant from the "tangibility" of objects, but at the same time enable us to condense and simplify a complex reality and in this way also manipulate it more effectively.

Therefore, unlike the greater certainty, precision, internal coherence, and comprehensiveness of the abstract, empty frames of logic and mathematics that our mind projects onto the world, our concepts of reality cannot presume to capture the fullness or totality of the objects to which they refer. Instead, concepts are usefully used as frames or boxes in which we arrange in an orderly manner features that are similar enough according to some intellectual or practical criteria. Concepts abstract, in effect flatten, differences and diversity. They cover, encompass, a range—coding infinity into finite forms.

Limits of Realism and of Skepticism

It was the late nineteenth-century philosopher Friedrich Nietzsche who most forcefully expressed what such a realization meant. He poured scorn on mainstream Western metaphysics for its false pretense of capturing reality within a comprehensive, certain, and finite intellectual system. He argued that all of our claims about the world represented partial, particular points of view, projections, or perspectives—a view known as "perspectivism". It is not clear from Nietzsche's numerous, aphorismic, and idiosyncratic writings if he believed truth was a meaningless concept (which would make his own claims meaningless); or, if not, what meaning should be assigned to it.[18] His self-proclaimed disciples, the "postmodernists" and "deconstructionists", the school of skeptics and relativists who sensationally captured the headlines from the 1960s to the 1980s, have been similarly obscure on this question. At the same time, they left the impression—much accentuated, as is so often the case, by their host of epigones—that they lean toward the first option. Unlike the ancient skeptic tradition, humbled by the puzzles of cognition and reality and advocating a suspension of judgment and intellectual restraint (*epochē*), many of the postmodernists have adopted flamboyant rhetoric and extravagant, sometimes frivolous, claims. However, as the critics of postmodernism and deconstruction have pointed out, the claim that there is no truth, only points of view, contradicts itself, as it claims to be true rather than merely a point of view.

It is not that the skeptic tradition—from ancient times to Nietzsche and the postmodernists—does not have a point, and a very significant one. They all highlight the irreducibly partial, subjective, and context-dependent element of our projections of reality. As this realization is far from being intuitive or trivial, it is understandable that it has been developed in all directions to call into question metaphysical and metahistorical "grand narratives"; undermine other cherished narratives of all sorts; expose subjective tendencies behind them, including the "hegemonic" interests of the powerful in society; and claim validity for a diversity of points of view. It has thus spread like fire in the humanities and social sciences and has been celebrated, sometimes excessively. For unless one adopts the belief that reality is all in the mind, the world we experience is a composite of our subjective mental apparatus and input from the objective world outside. While the two are difficult to isolate and separate, the latter is as present as the former. Therefore, although Nietzsche famously wrote that "There are no facts, only interpretations",[19] perspectivism cannot mean that everything is equally true, or true at all. Indeed, the concept of truth is perhaps better clarified through the concept of error. Simon Blackburn's *Truth: A Guide* (2005), one of the best introductions to the subject, takes this line, which I wish to develop further.

We begin with an example. The answer to the question of what and who caused World War I remains contentious and problematic to this day. When asked what he thought the judgment of future generations on this question would be, the indomitable French prime minister during that war Georges Clemenceau reportedly retorted: "They will not say that Belgium invaded Germany." As long as we assume that there is no devil or illusion that confuses us on this point—a preliminary assumption we always need to make—Clemenceau's statement is obviously true. But is it the whole truth, and does it exhaust the subject?

In my earlier books on war I happened to deal with this particular question, so here are a few relevant propositions. First, Britain and France created vast colonial empires in Africa in the decades before 1914, and Germany, a leading industrial power, felt that if colonial empires were the way of the future, then it, too, was entitled to one of its own. As most potential territories were already taken, this necessitated accommodation by the other powers, which they were not in a hurry to offer. Second, given the system of rival great-power alliances in Europe, Germany, which was by no means keen on war, felt driven into it as a measure of self-defense. Its leaders considered that if there were to be a war, then it had better come early rather than late, as they feared that a fast-industrializing Russia would become too powerful to cope with. It is not our business here to delve into these and other long-discussed questions, as this is not a history book. They are presented here as an example of how our comprehension of reality works (assuming we are after understanding and have no particular axe to grind). Within an infinitesimally complex reality, we focus on some features and connections/lines of causation that we regard as most pertinent to the question at hand and weave them into a causal-narrative sketch. Narratives are the format whereby we order the facts in a way that makes sense of complexity. Detailed as we may strive to make them, such pictures of reality are necessarily a simplified model, in which we ideally seek to incorporate and assign relative weight to events and angles of view or perspectives that best serve as a representation of the situation that draws our attention.

Truth as a Spectrum: Zooming In and Out

This is where we come to the crux of my argument. As already mentioned, ostensibly simple facts are also a shorthand. There is no question that the German army invaded Belgium on August 4, 1914. But one can be more accurate by citing, for example, the exact time of the crossing of the border by the German troops, or by every German formation or even individual—ad infinitum on this aspect alone. We judge whether or not, or when, such a thickening of the fact is necessary according to the question that interests us. To give a more mundane example, suppose the fact that Dan lives in a house in California corresponds with reality and is evidently as true as can be. Yet we might also mention that he owns the house, that the house has three bedrooms and a double car park, that it is painted white, that it has a garden of a certain size, with certain plants, that it has solar panels, and so on, endlessly. Supposing that all these claims are true, they do not make our first proposition, that Dan lives in a house in California, less true, but only demonstrate that it, like all the additional details, is a shorthand. Whether or not we choose to delve into such further elaborations depends on our particular frame of relevance: we might want to buy the house, we are interested in the domestic use of renewable energies, etc. As with Google maps, we zoom in and out.

Cartographic maps are a commonly used analogy for and illustration of our cognitive maps or grids, as are also drawings and, indeed, pictures. Maps can have different scales, focus on different features (roads, cities, climate, various aspects of the economy, and so on), or make various uses of color—all as code symbols of genuine features of the world. They can also wholly or partly err in presenting features that are not there or by putting them at a distance from their correct place. Much the same applies to drawings and pictures. Despite our inclination to view pictures in particular as one-to-one representations of reality, they have different resolutions, cut out only a framed section of reality and present it from a particular angle, are two-dimensional, can be black-and-white, and so forth. Maps, drawings, and pictures can give downright false information about reality or provide various degrees of correct information about it, from the fuzziest to a most detailed and accurate, but they can never capture its infinite content in full. They can distort by selection and by omission.

Therefore, if we make the preliminary assumption that the world is not a complete illusion that may disintegrate like a dream upon awakening, there are such things as truth and error: Germany invaded Belgium (given our generalized tagging for these aggregate human collectives), not the other way around; the invasion was launched in 1914, not in 1915 (using our conventional yardstick for the division of time); Dan lives in a house in California, not in New York (using our standard geographical framing). Each of the concepts here is a shorthand or a frame that covers an infinite internal diversity and can therefore always be refined by elaborating our conceptual grid and making it denser. However, if we do not judge this as necessary under the circumstances, such further elaboration will not be pursued, first, because our cognitive machinery is inherently limited and needs to prioritize its tasks; and, second, because more information may not always improve our judgment of a situation. As absolutely complete information is unattainable, more information may tilt our picture of a situation in a particular direction, thereby cluttering and throwing our simplified model of reality off balance. There is some cognitive trade-off here, in which reduced "noise" and "keeping it simple" are sometimes preferable.

Crude and Complex Modeling of Reality

An error occurs when our conceptual frame does not correspond to the piece of reality it is supposed to cover. Sometimes the pieces of reality or facts concerned are relatively clear-cut, and verification or falsification are quite straightforward: Belgium did not invade Germany in 1914; Dan does not live in New York. However, the truth value of many other concepts and conceptual arrays is more ambiguous or is a matter of degree. First, consider concepts that have become quite crude by our standards. Concepts such as the four basic elements of the world—air, water, earth, and fire—have been found to have scant truth value. But what about other traditional concepts, such as Yin and Yang, masculinity and femininity, understood more or less metaphorically? Or the concept of the soul or, more palatably, the mind, a concept that is indeed still very much in use in mainstream scientific discourse? Such past and present concepts are crude in the sense that their resolution in terms of distinctiveness, precision, and elaboration is quite low. Nonetheless, they can be considered to refer to genuine features of reality, and be useful as such. Another example: we now know that the earth revolves around the sun, rather than the other way around. At the same time, the notion that the sun rises in the east and sets in the west was and is true in a very specific sense, and indeed was (and still is) valuable information about the world for people. To complicate things further: entire thought systems, such as astrology and numerology, are now judged to be pseudo-sciences, as they lack empirical corroboration, underlying logic and truth value.[20] By contrast, acupuncture may still be a useful medical technique (pending further research) even if the traditional Chinese theory and map of the human body that accompany it turn out to be not merely indistinct and inaccurate by modern scientific standards but perhaps largely or wholly bogus.

Verification or falsification can be quite ambiguous not only in relation to "crude" concepts, but also, at the opposite end of the spectrum, with respect to complex and highly abstract models of reality. As many features of reality are involved and interact with one another, the truth may be more elusive in such cases because our simplified model raises doubts as to whether we have not omitted certain aspects, considerations, perspectives, and broader contexts that we may judge relevant to the question at hand. This is what habitually occurs with respect to propositions such as: Whatever its shortcomings, the market economy is by far the most effective system of wealth creation the world has known; or, democracy is the type of regime most in tune with modern conditions and is likely to spread across the globe as modernization advances in less-developed regions of the world. Our judgment in weighing the evidence for such propositions tends to be more qualified and tentative, or it should be.

Furthermore, we have seen that our shorthand system for coping with the infinite complexity of the world is based on the generalization of diversity into a simpler finite order. This also applies to our constant search for regularities, patterns of causation, relationships, and other connections and dynamics between things, where we again count on proximate similarities. We are ever on the lookout for, ceaselessly hypothesize about, and test any trace of regularity—more rigorous or sufficiently probabilistic—in our natural and social surroundings that will make our dealing with these surroundings cognitively more economical and practically more effective. This strong propensity extends from the instinctive heuristic rules of thumb we formulate in everyday life, to more abstract precepts and principles of various applications used to decipher and make sense of the world, to the yet more fundamental and ideally more rigorous theorizing of "science". It involves constant revisions based on trial and error, but also exhibits a great deal of conformity, so as to reduce and economize our cognitive load.

On the whole, this pattern-detecting and ordering system has been tremendously successful. At the same time, given the mind-boggling complexity of reality and the vast array of the conceptual schemes that we interweave to reflect it, it is easy to understand why we err so often. Furthermore, our pattern-detecting cognitive system is prone to misfire, regularly producing false signals of imagined patterns—"faces in the clouds"—to which, among other things, the human addiction to "superstitious" beliefs and practices is widely attributed. We can be suckers for regularities.

A detection of error or at least of some problem with a proposition's truth value often occurs when we become aware that some scraps of our conceptual grid do not align or accord with other scraps of that grid; that is, that which we hold to be true in one part of our mind does not cohere with what we believe in another part. In such a case, some adjustments to one or both of them and, potentially, also to much else in the conceptual grids in which they are imbedded, are called for. This is known as the coherence theory of truth. It emerged as a rival to the naive notion of a transparent correspondence between ideas and objects, but more recently has become part of the more sophisticated, "holistic" notion of correspondence as conditioned on, and interdependent with, everything else we hold to be true.[21] Of course, we know that in the real world, people regularly live with any number of contradictions and tensions in their conceptual representations of the world. Because of both subjective and objective reasons relating to the limits and functional utility of our cognitive system, absolute coherence or consistency is not within our grasp more than absolute accuracy or comprehensiveness is. Moreover, it is time to note that the term "conceptual grid" itself involves a very considerable simplification. It should more accurately be described as pieces or scraps of grid relating to various aspects of the world that attract our attention, pieces which are more or less tenuously, loosely, and coherently stitched together in our minds.

We saw that the more complex and abstract the issues, the more difficult it is to determine whether our propositions are true or not—that is, correspond to reality—and, indeed, *how* true they are. We need only the most basic assumptions regarding the non-illusionary nature of the world to determine that Germany invaded Belgium in 1914, and not the other way around. But answering the question of what brought about World War I requires a selection and ordering of facts and perspectives within an explanatory model or representation to which high truth value may or may not be attributed. And while World War I belongs mainly in the past, and the reality surrounding it can only be reconstructed in our minds, a question such as the merits and demerits of the market economy is highly relevant to current realities and their potential future trajectories. It concerns very practical decisions that will need to be made and that will deeply affect the life of people. Setting aside the value questions involved (values are discussed in the next chapter), it is crucial to get the models of reality we construct in relation to such questions as right as we can if we want a valid picture of the world to base our actions on.

The cognitive scientist Terrence Deacon has described the seemingly magical process involved thus: "The ability to use virtual reference to build up elaborate internal models of possible futures, and to hold these complex visions in mind with the force of the mnemonic glue of symbolic inference and descriptive shorthands, gives us unprecedented capacity to generate independent adaptive behaviors. Remarkable abstraction from indexically bound experiences is further enhanced by the ability of symbolic reference to pick out tiny fragments of real world processes and arrange them as buoys to chart an inferential course that predicts physical and social events."[22]

Multiple Perspectives and Reality Checks

Clearly, an irreducible element of selection takes place with respect to both features of and perspectives on the world when constructing cognitive models of complex realities, past and future. People tend to focus on features and perspectives that best serve their particular interests—in both senses of this word. As Weber, for one, has pointed out, there is no objective criterion for what is important in history.[23] We choose different factual projections and cross-sections of reality, depending on our purpose and the goals we pursue, and we regularly switch them when our purpose and goals change. Given the infinite complexity of the world and both the intrinsic limitations and practical orientation of our cognitive system, this is inevitable. Furthermore, as with the question of what brought about World War I, each of these different and seemingly conflicting factual projections of reality can be true to some degree—capturing genuine aspects of the world and, hence, having some truth value—without this necessarily violating the logical law of non-contradiction already formulated by the ancient Greeks. An old Jewish joke makes this point. It tells of a rabbi who receives two people for judgment over a dispute between them. After hearing one of them the rabbi says: you are right. After hearing the other, he says: you are also right. The rabbi's wife, listening to the proceeding, then tells her husband: how can they both be right? To which the rabbi replies: you are also right.

At the same time, it is again wrong to hold, as some postmodernist rhetoric has led its followers to believe, that *any* chosen factual feature or perspective is as valid as any other. Selecting some features of reality and blocking out others, indeed, even downright errors, may serve us well in many cases—cognitively and, most conspicuously, in situations of social bargaining. However, just as often, not only factual errors but also selection biases can distort our reading of reality in a way that defeats our purpose, whatever it may be. Earlier we mentioned the possibility that too much information can tilt our simplified model of reality in a particular direction or become "noise". On the other hand, too little information can be an even greater problem, and distortion by omission can have a particularly disruptive effect. Objectivity is a notoriously illusive concept, because any construction of facts and perspectives relating to the world inevitably involves selection and interests (again in both senses of the word). Still, although, like all concepts, the meaning of objectivity can never be absolute, we employ this concept to denote a conscientious effort, first to establish the facts and avoid downright falsehood; and, second, to take account of conflicting considerations and perspectives, irrespective of one's particular motivations and involvement in the situation in question.

No claim can be proven or disproven in the absolute, conventional, and intuitive strict sense of these words. As I write this chapter, there are half-amused/half-bemused media reports on the renewed Flat Earth Society whose adherents claim that all the evidence that the earth is a sphere is an elaborate conspiratorial hoax. There is no way to disprove this claim, or the belief that Elvis is alive or innumerable other claims we regard as absurd, unless basic assumptions that underlie the debate are shared (which obviously they are not in these cases). Most of us do not waste too much time on such claims, except for nodding our heads in marvel at human eccentricity. Still, note that any particular experience can potentially be explained, or explained away, by an infinite number of theories, and the only question is what explanations we find plausible and reasonable given everything else we know. Indeed, the view that the earth is flat used to be eminently rational at the time. We apply various heuristic principles and rules of thumb to decide between alternative explanations. One of the most famous of them is Occam's razor: that, other things being equal, the simpler explanation, calling for fewer assumptions and variables, should have preference. However, there is no guarantee that the simpler explanation is the right one, generally or in any particular case. Strictly speaking, there is no way to refute the suggestion that capricious genies in the wings are responsible for the flight of airplanes. Nonetheless, a physical force of "lift" appears to most of us as a far more valid explanation. This is so not because of an empty tautology, as in Molière's famous quip: "Why opium produces sleep: Because there is in it a dormitive power";[24] rather, it is due to the concept of lift's mathematical precision, close correspondence with observed realities, integration within our more general theories of physical matter, and, not least, its usefulness for actually building planes. This has been the practical criterion for truth advanced by the philosophical school of "pragmatism", to which we shall get shortly.

Paper is tolerant, as the German proverb goes. But reality is sometimes less so, and a reality check is in some cases quicker and less ambiguous than in other cases. It is a cruel irony that Michel Foucault, the most flamboyant and most iconic postmodernist, should have died from AIDS, which he implied was a social ploy to oppress gay men.[25] As Putnam has suggested, if someone believes that he can fly and chooses to leave a high-rise building by jumping through a window, we have pretty good reasons to regard this belief as irrational.[26] Yet this is an easy case, whereas the irrationality—espousing mental processes and conclusions judged as starkly divorced from reality—of other beliefs and actions is less clear-cut. In the spirit of what we have already seen, Putnam has argued that what is considered true and rational depends on the context of the overall picture of the world given to us at the time. The Copernican revolution is a much-cited example of a radical change in our worldview that transformed our entire belief system. When it was discovered that the earth and the other planets circle the sun, rather than the sun and the planets circling the earth, this did not only dispel one of our most elementary sense perceptions, previously regarded as self-evident, and has cast the view based on this sense perception as irrational; it has also removed the earth from the center of the universe. Together with later discoveries about the immense size of the universe and the nature of the celestial bodies, this cognitive revolution rendered the previous picture of an intimate world centering on the earth and designed for man appear decreasingly credible. This, in turn, has profoundly affected many aspects of people's worldview, including, famously, those fostered by the biblical tradition.[27]

In my view, Putnam was not sufficiently consistent on this important point. He argued that the belief in the divine right of kings was irrational even when the god-centered view of the world prevailed.[28] However, basically the ancients had two main options to explain the existence of the world: that the world had always existed or that it had come into being at some point, perhaps by a creator. The existence of a creator was deemed even more necessary to explain the world's dazzling marvels of design, evident most conspicuously in even the smallest of organisms and their relation to one another. This was the famous argument from design for the existence of God. Now, in the context of a worldview in which God played the dominant role as the world's creator, designer, and regulator, it was only natural that He took on many other functions, as in the crucial realm of morality, and much else. Within this worldview, the notion that kings ruled by divine right made a lot of sense and has a very good claim to be regarded as rational for its time, depending, again, on the exact content one puts into the concept of the rational. All this does not mean that other and different worldviews did not exist at the time, espoused, for example, by the ancient Greeks, by Buddhists, or by Confucians (who also believed in the Mandate of Heaven to rulers), each with its own explanatory framework, internal coherence, and particular conceptual and logical vulnerabilities.

Foucault celebrated the point that the concept of madness was a social construct that was perceived differently under different historical mindsets.[29] Traditional societies often regarded the seemingly confused utterances of people who appeared to be estranged from reality as transmissions that conveyed deep truths, prophesies, or powers from supernatural beings. They sometimes conferred holiness on these people. This view has changed radically with the adoption of a very different picture of the world during modern times. Further stretching Putnam's conundrum: was the traditional view of the madman rational within the overall picture of the world that prevailed at the time? And, more significant, relating to Foucault's implicit elusion, was rationality itself, and perhaps also sanity, merely a sociohistorical construct that was context-dependent and inherently subjective? We are quick to define present-day believers that the earth is flat or that Elvis is alive as irrational, if not somewhat insane. Many attribute similar irrationality to a variety of religious beliefs that seem to be absurd, delusional, or even crazy within the overall framework of our prevailing picture of the world. Freud, for one, framed religious belief as a kind of neurosis. Others may be less quick to extend the label of insanity, and perhaps also of absurdity or irrationality, to religious beliefs—for various intellectual and practical reasons. We shall look at religion more closely later in this book.

Much of mainstream philosophy has rightly stepped away from the notion that there are definitive meanings or criteria to rationality, truth, and objectivity. This, more or less, is the gap in which the postmodernists, deconstructionists, and other contemporary skeptics have established a firm foothold. Thinkers such as Jacques Derrida have left an enormous impression on their contemporaries by arguing that the meaning of words and concepts is ceaselessly created and shifting, largely open, illusive, and elusive, because of their irreducible context dependence.[30] On the other hand, it is equally necessary to get away from the view that since meaning and rationality, like all concepts, cannot be fully determined—they entail intellectual construction and hence are partly subjective—they are therefore *entirely* constructed and *wholly* subjective. This intellectual misstep has all too often led the social sciences astray over the last decades. The intrinsic flexibility of our concepts does not make the world itself infinitely flexible. A more relativist and qualified view of our cognition does not mean infinite relativity and an absence of the objective.

Growing Approximation to, Interface, and Correspondence with Reality

Therefore, although we cannot achieve absolute certainty, we have very strong reasons to hold that our picture of the world—its web of features, connections, and relationships—has become exponentially more precise, elaborate, and comprehensive over the past centuries. This has been most conspicuously so in the spheres of knowledge that have a greater claim to be included under the label "science", for several reasons. In the first place, such spheres, most notably the natural sciences, deal with parts of reality that are beyond our immediate sense perception and normal experience. The more the techniques and technologies to observe these phenomena develop, the more the scope of our world expands in both space and time, and into both the infinitesimally small and large. The natural sciences also happen to deal with elementary phenomena that exhibit greater regularities that are subject to mathematical conceptualization.[31] Furthermore, the label "science" suggests the establishment and institutionalization of more rigorous standards of observation, verification, and falsification, regulated by the community of experts on each subject. Philosophers of science such as Thomas Kuhn and Paul Feyerabend have undermined the earlier ideal notion of a unified, regular, and clearly defined Scientific Method or Procedure that supposedly guides the process of scientific discovery and vouches for its progressive advance.[32] Still, scientific methods and procedures, with small letters and in plural, more diverse and less systematic than previously posited, are much more conducive to a greater truth value—a greater scope and depth and a higher level of precision and certainty of knowledge—than the sporadic, unsystematic observations and insights of our ordinary interaction with experience.

The pragmatist school has made significant contributions on this subject, from various angles. It was developed in the late nineteenth-century and early twentieth-century United States by philosophers Charles Peirce, William James, and John Dewey. Although they differed among them on some matters, the pragmatists took as their point of departure the irreducible gaps between the reality outside us, our experience of that reality, and our theories for explaining the world of experience. They argued that since in the strict sense there was no way to close these gaps, we need to eschew the futile quest for an absolute, definitive criterion for truth and certainty. At the same time, they held that our knowledge, and science in particular, were so tremendously useful, productive, and predictive in our struggle to cope with the world that this criterion alone should be practically adopted as a sufficient justification for espousing whatever our observations, methods of verifications, and theorizing suggested was the best knowledge we could achieve at any given time. Thus, pragmatists have been strongly committed to knowledge and science, while professing agnosticism, a non-committal attitude, toward the question whether, or to what degree, that knowledge actually corresponds to and describes the world "as it is".

Some pragmatists and neo-pragmatists have tended to emphasize the latter, more skeptical, aspect of this double-edge doctrine, as the view that there has been a massive advance in our genuine knowledge of reality has been the subject of an intense debate. Our vastly greater ability to control and manipulate the world through the application of knowledge and knowledge-based technology is the standard argument in support of the view that we actually know progressively more about the world. It is difficult to understand how this vastly greater ability to control and manipulate reality can be *entirely* disassociated from a better understanding of that reality. As Putnam has put it, holding the opposite view would make the success of science a miracle.[33] Indeed, the Kantian gulf between our perceptual-cognitive apparatus and reality "in itself", the basis for much of later philosophy, including the phenomenalist and pragmatist schools, is unlikely to be as unbridgeable as Kant's metaphysics made it to be; that is, if we assume that our perceptual-cognitive apparatus and the world need to be sufficiently in accord for them to actually interface in experienced reality and make it possible for us to act and survive in the world.

From the other, skeptical side of the debate, several arguments have been made. Most significant, it has been argued that the history of science reveals a march of false theories and imaginary beings, some of which were actually pretty good at explaining, predicting, and manipulating the realities they purported to cover. Among the most famous examples are Ptolemaic astronomy, substances such as phlogiston and ether, and even Newtonian physics, superseded by Einstein's relativity. All of these have been thrown to the scrapyard of our attempts to objectivize the world, and much the same is likely to occur with many of our currently held theories.[34] This, however, does not mean that we have not become far better in developing observation-based theories that approximate reality ever more closely and, indeed, foster a vastly expanding sphere of knowledge.[35] There is every reason to hold that the earth revolving around the sun has a very high objective truth value in describing reality, rather than being merely a pragmatic claim that conveniently accords with observed experience and is the most useful in serving our practical purposes.

Precisely this point has been contested by the brilliant and most influential philosopher Richard Rorty, a neo-pragmatist of the more skeptical vein, who was closer and sympathetic to the postmodernists. Rorty accepts that there is a reality outside of us. However, he argues that, as it impossible to grasp what reality "in itself" is, separate and distinct from our cognitive input, any attempt to regard our knowledge of the world as real rather than "useful" is futile and needs to be discarded. No proposition about the world can be held true, or truer than another one, except in this sense of being useful. As Rorty repeatedly stresses, it is the notion of "correspondence" to or "representation" of reality, which he wholly rejects, that is the root of the debate. He perceives it as a one-to-one correspondence between words, parts of sentences and beliefs, on the one hand, and bits of the world or "facts", on the other. This is known as the "isometric" view of correspondence, now mostly discredited as naive. Indeed, having assigned such an unrealistic high standard for correspondence truth, as a "mirror of nature" (the title of his signature book)—a standard it necessarily fails—Rorty falls back on an unrealistically *too low* standard of truth, which, however, also fails.

As Rorty puts it: "To say that the parts of properly analyzed true sentences are arranged in a way isomorphic to the parts of the world paired with them sounds plausible if one thinks of a sentence like 'Jupiter has moons.' It sounds slightly less plausible for 'The earth goes round the sun,' less still for 'There is no such thing as natural motion,' and not plausible at all for 'The universe is infinite.' . . . they resemble such sentences as 'Love is the only law' and 'History is the story of class struggle.' The whole vocabulary of isomorphism, picturing, and mapping is out of place here, as indeed is the notion of being true of *objects*."[36]

However, to begin with, Rorty never explains why it is that certain scientific facts and theories are more useful than others if they do not correspond to reality in *some* way. He asks: "in what sense Pasteur's views of disease picture the world accurately and Paracelsus' inaccurately."[37] One cannot help thinking that this is simply silly. The discovery of germs and of their role in causing disease was a huge advance in understanding the world by way of approximation to reality. By the same standard, older notions that bad air caused disease or that worms emerged spontaneously from muck can be judged to be either extremely crude or entirely wrong. Indeed, while the catalogue of past historical errors is long and seemingly impressive, can it seriously be doubted that modern scientific study has made our understanding of both the human body and disease immeasurably vaster? And that this knowledge is directly associated with and responsible for the great advances in medicine and the huge improvement in our health and longevity?

Moreover, because of his all-or-nothing conception of correspondence and representation as an "isometric" relationship between beliefs and facts, rather than a simplified code shorthand to be understood in terms of more or less elaborate and accurate map or model, Rorty is bound to regard all statements about reality as equally "unrepresentative". And yet he must concede that the statement "Jupiter has moons" does in fact correspond to reality in a way he argues "Love is the only law" or "History is the story of class struggle" are not. And he must accept that the same distinction also applies elsewhere: "Can true beliefs or sentences be treated on the model of realistic portraiture? Obviously some sentences can, at least *prima facie*, be so treated—for example, 'The cat is on the mat'. There are many other cases, such as the sentence 'Neutrinos have no mass' or 'The pursuit of scholarly truth requires academic freedom', to which the notion of 'parts of the world' has no evident application. We philosophers haggle endlessly about whether the notions of 'correspondence' and 'representation' can be extended to these harder cases."[38] What Rorty (and perhaps also his many critics) do not seem to notice is that such a distinction between easy and hard cases—indeed, allowing the status of correspondence to the world to *any* statement—undermines his fundamental position.[39]

The difficult problem of empirically verifying the existence of elementary particles (like the neutrino) aside, the propositions that Rorty cites as examples actually suggest—demonstrate—that there are vastly different levels of modeling in terms of crudeness and metaphoric abstraction, which cannot be squeezed into his one-size, all-or-nothing, conception of correspondence. Rorty's "isometric" conception of correspondence is a straw man that, paradoxically, deceives him above all. The symbols of our conceptual grid correspond to reality as simplified code abstractions, by framing and tagging aspects of it. "Correspondence" means sufficiently representative code symbolization, not "mirror" imaging.[40] Thus, correspondence with reality is intrinsically cumulative, is a matter of degree, as concepts and conceptual grids are always a simplified model. They can be relatively crude and yet constitute real knowledge about the world, albeit of a hazy, indistinct and imprecise nature. And they can be made ever truer, in terms of precision, distinctiveness, elaboration, and scope. Correspondence involves cognitive artifacts that nonetheless relate to things in the world, with the world's objective input imposing a reality check on the subjective elements of our cognition. Again, too many in the humanities and social sciences have sensationally interpreted the proposition that we live in imagined worlds as if it meant imaginary.

Pragmatists have been correct to focus on the most fertile interpretation of observed phenomena and practical usefulness as criteria for what is to be regarded as knowledge. They have been equally correct to insist on the flexibility and fluidity of what should be taken as true and of the vocabulary (i.e., conceptual grid) that serves to express it. At the same time, again, it seems implausible to hold that the practical workability of knowledge in dealing with the world is—can be—*entirely* disassociated from any correspondence with reality. Crude as concepts such as the soul or the sky are, they were and still are representations of real features of the world as refracted through and shaped by our cognitive prisms. Our knowledge of the world is not only continuously discarded and replaced, as the more radical overtones in Kuhn and Feyerabend have been interpreted by some;[41] it is also being increasingly refined, as our conceptual grid becomes vastly more precise, discriminating, extensive, and elaborate. Pragmatic coherence should better be viewed as an aspect, rather than a rival, of the correspondence conception of truth, properly understood.[42]

Conclusion: Thinking Inside the Boxes

The main point of this chapter may narrow the gap between skeptic-relativist and more realist views of the world. Truth as correspondence to reality is a valid notion, but as a vastly simplified and finite code representations of features of the world that cannot fully encompass reality's infinite diversity and are intrinsically partial and incomplete. Thus, "approximation" is an infinite process. A proposition is true when the fact described falls within the particular conceptual frame issued to cover it; it is false when it falls outside it. That said, the conceptual frame itself is a loose range. The point that is not easily grasped is that propositions can be perfectly true, while never being the whole truth, as our conceptual grid of reality can always be further refined, elaborated, and contextualized. We zoom in (and sometimes out). While statements can be untrue, the truth value of true statements has a vast spectrum. This is different from the classical notion of statements as either true or false. Our map of true statements about the world consists of "crude" and less "crude" facts. Truth value, correspondence with the world, increases as we think inside the boxes, while progressively adjusting and tightening their framing of reality.

On the one hand, this goes against our strongly intuitive sense of the immediate transparency and tangibility or our interface with the world while, on the other, it belies the suggestion that all perspectives are equally valid. Concepts and conceptual grids, including narrative structures, pattern-based rules, and imagined situations, past and future, can be entirely fictional or simply wrong, in the sense that the feature of the world they purport to cover is not there. At the same time, what is or is not there—say, unicorns, fairies, the gods, you choose— is problematic to ascertain. Even seemingly self-evident sense perceptions have been revealed to be preconditioned by our prior conceptions about the shape of the world, as well as often being deeply misleading. Moreover, inferences about the less immediate features of the world are held or withheld to the extent that they agree, integrate, with basic assumptions that shape our conceptual grid or the scattered pieces that constitute it. Worldviews are more important than "facts", or, less provocatively, they fixate as well as being fixated by them.

Coda: Evolution and the Coded Framing of Reality

A series of scientific revolutions during the modern period have each transformed the dominant worldview whereby the elements of reality are perceived and interpreted. We have already mentioned some of the most prominent of these revolutions, such as those generated by Copernican cosmology, Newtonian physics, Einstein's relativity, and quantum theory. Darwin's natural selection has been as profoundly revolutionary. It has thoroughly transformed our understanding of the origin and design of all organic phenomena—of life—with profound implications for the understanding of everything human. During the last decades, the rapid ascent of evolutionary theory in the study of humans has gone hand in hand with the fast expansion of cognitive science. This combines experimental techniques for the study of the brain and of human perception with the evolutionary perspective on why and how our cognitive functions came into being. The evolutionary perspective recasts the static, seemingly context-less, and in a way arbitrary image of our cognitive apparatus, as classically portrayed by Kant (and more recently in Noam Chomsky's linguistics). It places our cognitive apparatus within the documented sequence and naturalistic logic of living creatures' evolving, adaptive capacities for coping with the world.

This new, revolutionary perspective for understanding all things human encountered enormous resistance during the "sociobiology" debate of the late 1970s and early 1980s. However, since then it has become increasingly commonplace, with the most persistent resistance currently confined to parts of the so-called cultural studies. In addition, the age-old discipline of philosophy has yet to fully digest the far-reaching implications of the Darwinian revolution. Schooled in pre-Darwinian concepts and habits of mind, philosophers have generally been hostile toward the idea that long-accepted abstractions of traditional philosophical discourse are brought down to earth and recast in the naturalistic language of the evolutionary logic of life.

Paradoxically, some of the philosophers mentioned in this chapter have traded places on this question. Rorty, true to the pragmatist tradition, professes to espouse the Darwinian evolutionary picture of the world, but draws the wrong conclusions from it. He writes: "Since the pragmatists . . . took Darwin and biology seriously, they had an additional reason for distrusting the idea that true beliefs are accurate representations. For representation, as opposed to increasingly complex adaptive behavior, is hard to integrate into an evolutionary story."[43] Once again, Rorty's straw man of "*accurate* representation" deceives him. Indeed, what those who recognize the compelling logic of evolutionary theory are obliged to accept is that an adaptive correspondence between our system of concepts and the world outside must exist in a very meaningful way, or we would not have been able to act and survive in the world. On the other hand, some of Rorty's chief critics in the debate about reality and truth, such as Putnam and Blackburn, champion the validity of science, the naturalistic picture of the world, and the paramount significance of the scholarly most authoritative worldview. And yet they appear on the opposite side with respect to the significance of that recent and tremendously transformative scientific revolution, the evolutionary perspective for the understanding of human reality. Their opposition extends above all to the human perception of what proper social behavior is, the field of morality, to which we now turn.

Before we proceed into this, and to everything that follows, it may be worthwhile at this junction to cite Ernst Cassirer, the well-known philosopher whose concept of *homo symbolicus*, the symbol-creating human, anticipated much of what we have seen in this chapter, but whose work has nonetheless largely fallen out of the philosophical discourse. Writing in the first half of the twentieth century, Cassirer maintained that Darwin had placed philosophical anthropology on new grounds. The Aristotelian, teleological interpretation of humankind and nature in general had been discarded. The complex design of organic life was now accounted for by the process of natural selection advancing on the basis of what are otherwise blind accidents. In this evolutionary context, symbolism was the new and uniquely human form of adaptation. Thus, "Man cannot escape from his achievement . . . man lives in a symbolic universe. Language, myth, art and religion are part of this universe. They are the varied threads that weave the symbolic net, the tangled web of human experience. All human progress in thought and experience refines upon and strengthens this net. . . . [Man] has so enveloped himself in linguistic forms, in artistic images, in mythical symbols or religious rites that he cannot see or know anything except by the interpretation of this artificial medium."[44]

What Is Right?

How Morality Should Be Conceived

Morality, what is the proper behavior toward others and in the social context, is the second element of ideology that needs our prior attention. It is widely agreed that we are moral creatures, not in the sense that we act morally all or most of the time, but in that we have a strong and deep proclivity to issue moral judgments and experience feelings of condemnation or approbation—often intense—in response to human behavior. Other questions are more in dispute: Do our moral percepts resonate in some way with the deep structure of the universe or are "true" or "objective" in any other sense? Or are they pure projections of our inner attitudes, feelings, and emotions onto the world, and are therefore "subjective" or even "relative" to the individuals or societies that hold them? This is how the question is typically presented and the battle lines drawn. Indeed, they have been drawn so for millennia, which may raise the question of whether this dispute can ever be resolved. As we have seen in the previous chapter, no question can ever be resolved in the strict sense, and no answer, however absurd or fatuous we judge it to be, can be refuted conclusively. Nonetheless, we form our views of what is true in the context of everything else we take to be the most plausible explanation of the evidence. So has anything substantial changed in the cognitive constellation that shapes our understanding of morality?

From ancient through medieval to modern times, moral philosophy has been influenced by changes in people's cosmological worldviews—regarding man, God, and the universe. However, in recent decades, philosophers have failed to recognize the major contribution that the Darwinian revolution and the evolutionary perspective have made to the understanding of major questions for which there were previously no satisfactory answers: how morality came into being, what sustains it, and perhaps also, to some degree, what can be expected of people morally. Thus, this chapter seeks to clarify the implications of the naturalistic perspective, immensely enhanced by evolutionary theory, for moral

Ideological Fixation. Azar Gat, Oxford University Press. © Oxford University Press 2022.
DOI: 10.1093/oso/9780197646700.003.0002

philosophy. Rather than dealing with moral questions per se, we shall try to advance our understanding of what morality is.

Some Background: From Plato to Modern Times

We begin, again, with an overview of the debate, so those familiar with it are asked to exercise some patience. Here, too, the ancient Greeks almost said it all millennia ago. Plato regarded the world that people experience as a faint and illusive image of a pure, immutable, and certain cosmic order, or *logos*. This also extended to our notions of the beautiful, the good, the moral, and the just, which in his view mirrored the underlying Forms and eternal harmonies of the cosmos, of which, he increasingly came to argue, they partook via an immortal soul.[1] However, many, perhaps the majority, of the Greek philosophers of the time viewed morality and its sources in more down-to-earth anthropocentric terms. They explained the moral notions and precepts as emanating from, and serving, human and social functions, while differing on whether and to what degree these notions and precepts were deep-seated and universal or more diverse and expressing social conventions.

Aristotle—in many ways more naturalistic than his teacher Plato—viewed morality as the practical and fundamentally universal principles of virtuous behavior that best served the aim of human well-being.[2] Protagoras, Socrates' philosophical opponent in the Platonic dialogue that bears his name, leaned toward a more relativist view when positing man as the measure of all things. Thrasymachus, another of Socrates-Plato's debating rivals, went further in contending that "justice is the advantage of the stronger"—the group that happened to wield power in any particular society shaped moral standards to suit its interests.[3] (This was pretty much the doctrine that Marx and, later, Foucault would recreate.) Conversely, Epicurus, similarly naturalistic and anthropocentric, held that morality was a cooperative means in the service of people's collective life: "Justice was not a thing in its own right, but [existed] in mutual dealings in whatever places there [was] a pact about neither harming one another nor being harmed."[4]

For the Greeks, the good consisted of happiness, well-being, and the prosperity of the spirit (*eudaimonia*), which they regarded as the goal in life. Ethical inquiry, guided by reason, was intended to identify what the right conduct, virtue (*aretê*), for man to achieve the good life was. Plato, Aristotle, and latter-day Greek philosophers of all schools took it as a matter of course that behaving well toward others, being "good", served and was inseparable from achieving one's own good. They argued that a careful analysis by reason revealed that harming others would ultimately boomerang and cause harm to oneself. Other major traditions in the developed civilizations of Eurasia shared a more or less similar view regarding the fundamental affinity between individual and collective interests as recognized by the wise. With greater or lesser supernatural underpinning, this applied, for example, to the Hindu and Buddhist concept of *Dharma*, somewhat akin to the Greek *logos* and *aretê*, as well as to the Confucian doctrine of a harmonious life in a harmonious society.

It was, however, Christianity, with its non-naturalistic, God-centered, Jewish heritage and the mantle of the neo-Platonic and Aristotelean conceptions of God, that dominated the Western tradition from late antiquity until (at least) the early modern period. Its adherents, and those of the other monotheistic religions, did not fully share the comfortable view that in and of itself it paid for individuals to behave well toward others—to cause them no harm and to extend to them some helping hand. They were not entirely sure that in the final analysis individual and collective interests aligned, so that it would not be advantageous for an individual to pursue his selfish interests at the expense of the collective and by doing harm. "Why does the way of the wicked prosper?" asked the biblical prophet Jeremiah (12:1). Nor were the adherents of the monotheistic religions as confident as the Greeks, Buddhists, and Confucians that the unbridled, "excessive" "indulgence" of sensual pleasures was intrinsically harmful to oneself. In short, they did not quite trust morality to successfully stand on its own feet. There were various conceptions, of course, but it was now largely the role of God, and of His divine sanction—in this or the next world—to deter people from doing "evil". (True, both Plato and the believers in *karma* also partly relied on harm to evil-doers in the next reincarnations of the soul.)

During the early modern period, God was in retreat among European intellectuals, or at least His role was being redefined and vastly contracting, as His traditional conceptual framing did not sit well with the new cosmological outlook and philosophical standards of ontological and moral coherence. Anthropocentric and naturalistic conceptions of the sources and nature of morality were back, most notably with Benedict Spinoza and Thomas Hobbes in the seventeenth century, and with the British school of moral sentiments—Lord Shaftesbury, Francis Hutchinson, David Hume, and Adam Smith—in the eighteenth century. They regarded morality as a human creation in the service of social life and believed it functioned quite successfully on this naturalistic-social basis. However, in a Western world steeped in the Christian tradition, even among those who reacted against it, many were far less sanguine.

Among the philosophers of the Enlightenment—a few of them atheists and the majority deists who did not believe that God intervened in the world—it was nonetheless widely held that a God that vouched for morality was a vital illusion. Voltaire stated that "if God didn't exist, it would be necessary to invent him. Let the wise proclaim him, and kings fear him".[5] He was reportedly even more apprehensive of the people than he believed in the kings' piety, suspecting that without God and the fear of hell people would have no inhibitions against cutting each other's throat when nobody watched. A profound, widespread sense of crisis regarding the Death of God, in Nietzsche's famous phrase, most notably concerning His role as the guarantor of morality, spread in the late nineteenth century. The statement by Fyodor Dostoevsky's Ivan Karamazov that "if God does not exist, everything is permitted" and the murder committed by Dostoevsky's other literary character Raskolnikov in *Crime and Punishment* typified the bewilderment about and apprehension of what the people of the time termed "nihilism"—the collapse of all transcendent guarantees and customary standards for value and the good.

Philosophers, most typically of the so-called existentialist school, rushed in to fill the void. Announcing the death of God and all the metaphysics—moral and otherwise—that depended on Him, Nietzsche cast himself in the role of a prophet of a new self-centered ethics of the Will to Power. One may suggest that, by his own standards, Nietzsche fell victim to the very same ill he criticized: his projected super-man may be regarded as merely a more advanced stage of what Nietzsche ridiculed as the illusions of the God-centered world, which he tried to replace with something of almost similar mythical magnitude—fictitious and metaphorical-poetic or not. Nietzsche, too, could not really stand the void and embrace morality on a human scale with little supra-human heroic aura.

Half a century later, the existentialist Jean-Paul Sartre similarly rejected God, and all external authority, as bygone illusions, skyhooks to hang morality on. Instead, he proclaimed the free, autonomous, and self-creating individual as the agent whose moral choices and actions were responsible for shaping the kind of world he or she and all of humanity would live in. As suggested by the title of his 1946 pamphlet "Existentialism Is Humanism", Sartre could not quite avoid the connotation that some moral choices were good and some bad. In a famous example, he presented the options of joining the Resistance against the Nazis or staying at home to care for an ailing mother as equally autonomous and self-creating moral choices. Yet he did not mention the option of joining the Nazis, autonomous and self-creating as it may be, as a moral choice on quite the same footing. His was an uplifting message about man (and woman) pursuing their "authentic" choices. As it surfed on the crest of a generational rebellion against what came to be viewed as the petty, narrow-minded conventions, constraints and prejudices associated with traditional "bourgeois" society, it was received with great popular fanfare in his time.

Philosophers of the analytical school active during the early and mid-twentieth century were more prosaic than the existentialists, whose lofty musings they often regarded with suspicion and scorn as romantic mumbo-jumbo. Nonetheless, they held a view not dissimilar to that of the existentialists regarding human preferences as the source of morality. Interested almost exclusively in the logical and linguistic status of moral statements, they emphasized the distinction already made by Hume: that moral statements are not descriptions of facts in the world but expressions of our emotions, attitudes, and wishes with respect to such facts, particularly those relating to human and social behavior. Moral judgments are expressively "emotive" and "prescriptive" with respect to the above.[6] Thus, rather than being objective in the sense that they captured truths about the world, moral judgments are subjective or, at most, intersubjective, that is, they come from us and reflect the inner emotions and expectations that people have and, to some degree, tend to share with other people.

This view of the nature of morality has been the subject of intense controversy. Although I generally agree with "emotivism"-"prescriptivism", some of the criticism directed at these views reveal genuine shortcomings in them. Most notably, they tell us little about the *content* of the moral judgments people tend to have and on *why* they have them. In the eighteenth century, Hume had already made all the major points of "emotivism"-"prescriptivism", while offering a much more complete picture of the nature and sources of morality. Indeed, I share the view that the philosophical discussion of morality has made very little progress since Hume—if anything, it has periodically retreated. This high evaluation of his moral philosophy may raise the question of whether there is any purpose to dwelling further on a subject he has already illuminated. But, as suggested here, Hume was missing one huge piece of the puzzle, and, moreover, *recognized* that such a piece may be missing. We shall get to this after reviewing his ideas of what morality is and is about.

David Hume on the Nature of Morality

Like other naturalistic thinkers of antiquity and of his own times, Hume argues that the root of all moral notions and percepts is in us—that they are a human creation projected onto the world. He makes the point that "the mind has a great propensity to spread itself on external objects",[7] and that this propensity misleads people, confuses them into regarding their own mental processes as things that exist in the world outside us. In a present-day metaphor, we view the world through glasses of augmented reality and often regard the head-on images projected on our lenses as belonging to the outside reality itself. Turning to the content of the moral notions and precepts, Hume holds that what we regard as morally good are the qualities, attitudes, and behaviors that benefit society at large. While moral values and norms vary between societies, sometimes greatly, they nonetheless tend to converge on the same broad rationale of upholding the communal good as the generally perceived standard of morality.[8] As Hume claims, such a moral standard prevails even within a group of robbers, among themselves, of course.[9]

Moreover, Hume argues that this shared moral standard is not merely a cultural invention by communities and rulers to regulate social dealings by a kind of social contract, as both the Epicureans and Hobbes believed. Rather, he insists that the viewing of morality in terms of the communal benefit is rooted in our nature, and that our emotional inner world is tuned to this rationale and tends to produce positive feelings when it is met and negative feelings when it is not.[10] We experience such moral sentiments in reference to the behavior of others, but also to our own behavior. Even though people habitually behave selfishly against the common good, they often experience pangs of conscience—feel shame and guilt—on that account. Hume rejects the view he finds in the Epicureans and Hobbes that human motivations are entirely selfish, based on self-interest alone, and argues that people also have genuine altruistic sentiments toward others.[11]

To clarify: Hume does not argue that individuals *should* act in a way that advances the benefit to society. (Unlike the Greek philosophers, nor does he claim that it is necessarily, or always, in their best interest to do so.) His account is descriptive: he portrays how things are, what he holds to be people's innate perception of the standard of morality and the intense feelings that they experience in relation to its actual practice. His discussion is what is known as meta-ethical, that is, he is interested not in justifying or advancing certain moral views, but in the question of what morality is. Thus, he famously advances a fundamental distinction between *is* and *ought*. The former describes objective things about the world, the latter refers to subjective—individual or shared—human wishes as to how we want things to be. Hume expresses his surprise as to how easily people confuse the two.[12] He insists that what ought to be done can never be deduced purely from the facts of the world alone, that the facts necessitate no particular behavior in and of themselves, without the addition of the subjective element of our wishes or preferences.

Correspondingly, Hume argues that the motivation for action is our desires—the "passions", in the language of the time—in effect, what we want. Reason is not the source of volition, action, or morality, but only a calculating device that estimates the possibilities of realizing our desires in the specific conditions of the world that we happen to face at any given moment and assesses the likely consequences and the costs and benefits involved.[13] Hume argues that, rather than being the master that the Greeks portrayed it to be, reason is the slave of the passions.[14] Thus, in and of itself, no human choice is more or less rational than another. Rationality refers only to the availability of the means to achieve our chosen aims. As Hume puts it: "Tis is no less rational to prefer the tip of my finger to the whole of humanity."[15]

The distinctions that Hume draws between is and ought and between the respective functions of the desires and reason is often contested.[16] One is almost tempted to comment that suggestions as to how these distinctions can be overcome are as recurring as the never-ceasing designs for *perpetuum mobile*. Most of these objections are based on misunderstandings of Hume's exact views. He does not argue that what *is*, the facts of the world—as assessed by reason—do not influence our decisions and actions as to what *ought* to be done.[17] As we learn how things are and the likely or potential consequences of the attempt to fulfill our desires under the circumstances at hand, we adjust or change our choice of desires, and reorder our priorities of them, so as to best achieve these desires and the combination of them that reason assesses to be attainable. Thus, while what ought to be done can never be deduced purely from the facts of the world *alone*, the facts affect our decisions on the goals that ought to be pursued by the constraints they impose on our desires in terms of feasibility and compatibility with the world and with one another. Max Weber was to emphasize precisely this distinction, arguing that rationality pertains only to the assessment of the means to an end, and not to the choice of the ends themselves.

Thus, according to Hume, facts very much matter with respect to our decisions as to what ought to be done, even if they cannot be the ultimate justification for our choices. Indeed, he places a special emphasis on the facts of our nature, including what he regards as the facts about our natural sentiments and shared innate criterion of morality. As already noted, he claimed that, in addition to self-interest or self-love, we are endowed with natural sentiments of sympathy toward others that are manifested in both our feelings and behavior. Hume derives all these claims from what he believes an observation of human nature reveals.[18] In this, he addresses the actual *content* of the moral precepts, which, as noted, is largely missing in twentieth-century emotive-prescriptive philosophy. The mystery that remains unanswered is *why* we have such natural moral criteria, emotions and propensities? How is it that they became such an intrinsic part of human nature? This question appears all the more pertinent if one accepts neither that the moral precepts are merely a social convention agreed upon in a social contract of sorts, nor that they were planted in our nature by God. While Hume rejects both of these options, he regards what he sees as our natural propensities as a fact of life, simply the way things are, to which he offers no further explanation. And yet he is not entirely unaware that there may be some deeper answer to the mystery. This comes up most notably with respect to the question of why we have feelings of sympathy toward others that are not reduced to "self-love", egotistic self-interest.

As Hume writes, in rejection of the ideas of the Epicureans and Hobbes: "To the most careless observer there appear to be such dispositions as benevolence and generosity; such affections as love, friendship, compassion, gratitude. These sentiments [. . . are] plainly distinguished from those of the selfish passions. And as this is the obvious appearance of things, it must be admitted, *till some hypothesis be discovered, which by penetrating deeper into human nature,* may prove the former affections to be nothing but modifications of the latter."[19] Still, Hume remains highly skeptical of such a future discovery. As he writes: "All attempts of this kind have hitherto proved fruitless . . . the nature of the subject furnishes the strongest presumption, that no better system will ever, for the future, be invented, in order to account for the origin of the benevolent from the selfish affections."[20]

As it turned out, Hume was prophetic about the possibility that a future discovery would shed new light on human nature and morality. At the same time, he was wrong in his prediction that the natural human propensities for self-love and benevolence toward others would forever remain distinct from each other and lacking a common ground and explanatory rationale. As mentioned, if the moral notions and precepts are embedded in human nature, as Hume insisted, the question of how they got there becomes overwhelming. And yet Hume, despite all his erudition and wisdom, had no way of answering it, as nothing in any existing "system" of human thought (to use his language) in or before his time offered an answer that squared with his naturalistic approach. This is the big piece of the puzzle Hume was missing and, indeed, could not have possessed.

The Darwinian Revolution

Darwin's theory of evolution by natural selection is revolutionary in providing an explanation, massively supported by the evidence, for how the amazingly complex functional design of all organic creatures, of life, came into being. His explanation is simple: tiny modifications that occur in organic creatures are naturally selected by the test of survival in a difficult and competitive natural environment; and the accumulation of the surviving traits, passed on to offspring, results in better adaptation, more complex design, and increased speciation. For the first time, there was now an explanation that did not rely on an intelligent creator for the complexity and diversity of life's design and for the compatibility of the designs with the functions they were required to perform. Indeed, the evolutionary explanation was far more in tune with both traditional philosophical queries and modern empirical data: postulating a creator of the world only regressed the question a step backward, as it raised the question of who or what created the creator; the imperfections of the world and, most notably, the existence of misery and "evil" traditionally remained with a few satisfactory answers; the fossil record of life on earth unequivocally shows the evolution from very simple designs to ever more complex living creatures—and such a haphazard process of natural trial and error does not sit well with design by an omniscient and omnipotent creator who could have gotten things right in the first place. Pre-Darwinian thinkers like Hume, who were deeply skeptical about, if they did not outright reject, the God hypothesis,[21] would for the first time have a systematic alternative and an empirically far superior explanation for life's design.

In effect, Darwin picked up the subject of morality where Hume had left it and took it a crucial step further. He was able to offer a naturalistic answer to the mystery of how socially beneficial moral sentiments had become part and parcel of human nature and elucidated the way they related to and fitted together with egotistic self-interest. In his *The Descent of Man* (1871), Darwin put forward the line of argument the evolutionary investigation of morality would develop. Human beings, and other social animals, profited as individuals from the pulling together of the group's resources, for example in hunting and fighting. This was so because on average the synergic outcome of their efforts divided among them promised greater benefit to each of them than their independent efforts could. By a process of natural selection—the survival and inheritance of biological traits—the qualities that fostered mutually beneficial group cooperation became increasingly entrenched in our nature. As Darwin wrote: "All animals living in a body, which defend themselves or attack their enemies in concert, must indeed be in some degree faithful to each other".[22] Thus, "any animal whatever, endowed with well-marked social instincts, the parental and filial affections being here included, would inevitably acquire a moral sense or conscience".[23] "Besides love and sympathy, animals exhibit other qualities connected with the social instincts, which in us would be called moral."[24]

This evolutionary explanation of the roots of morality was still rudimentary. Nonetheless, evolutionists are often struck by how much Darwin got right in his pioneering work—in our subject, with respect to both animal and human prosocial behavior. We shall see more about this and the exact mechanisms that have supported the evolution of morality later on. But first, we need to mention the hiatus into which Darwin's influence fell during the early to mid-twentieth century, most notably with respect to the study of the human species. Popular social-Darwinist theories that attributed all racial and social differences to biological factors and, moreover, celebrated the necessary elimination of the weak in the social competition resulted in a backlash in the humanities, social sciences, and among intellectuals at large. There was a swing in the opposite direction toward the view that human beings were "all-culture", a "blank slate" entirely shaped by their socio-historical surroundings.[25] Humans were supposed to have no nature worth speaking of. In actuality, both nature and nurture are crucial for explaining our behavior, of course, and they are deeply interconnected and mutually affect one another. Indeed, by the last third of the twentieth century, evolutionary theory in the study of humans was making a sweeping comeback, much enriched by new scientific breakthroughs: Gregor Mendel had come up with the biological mechanism of inheritance that Darwin had lacked; population genetics developed sophisticated mathematical modeling of how traits spread; and the deciphering of the genome has vastly extended our understanding of evolution and inheritance all the way down to the molecular level.

As already mentioned in the previous chapter, the return of the evolutionary perspective in the study of humans came as a shock to generations of scholars in the humanities and social sciences who had been schooled on the supreme premise that human nature was a discredited, misleading, and, not least, politically reactionary concept. For all that, the evolutionary perspective has become increasingly commonplace, fostered by its progressively demonstrated explanatory power, by its intrinsic logic, and, ultimately, by generational change. There is an insightful joke that science progresses from funeral to funeral—a lighthearted version of Thomas Kuhn's explanation for scientific "paradigm shifts". Nonetheless, the age-old discipline of philosophy remains pretty much a bastion of resistance, not to evolutionary theory itself, but to its implications for, and encroachment on, philosophy's domain and traditional preoccupations.

Not by everybody in philosophy, though. John Mackie's *Ethics: Inventing Right and Wrong* (1977) is widely regarded by philosophers as one of the major contributions to the philosophy of morality in the twentieth century, even if the majority of philosophers do not to accept his position. Mackie is a modern-day Hume with respect to morality, regarding its precepts as a human creation projected onto the world while they appear to us as binding objective universals. He argues that human attitudes reveal, in Hume's term, "confined generosity" toward others in addition to self-interest, with emotions to match. All of these emanate from life in society: "We need morality to regulate interpersonal relations, to control some of the ways in which people behave toward one another, often in opposition to contrary inclinations."[26] Where Mackie advances beyond Hume is precisely where Hume lacked the necessary intellectual tools. As Mackie writes: "Why we are like this is in the first place a psychological question, to be answered, perhaps, as Hutcheson, Hume, and Adam Smith suggested, by reference to 'sympathy'; but more fundamentally it is a sociological and biological question to be answered, as I have said, by an evolutionary explanation."[27]

This was a remarkable statement, given that the two books that brought the neo-Darwinian synthesis to the public attention, Edward Wilson's *Sociobiology* (1975) and Richard Dawkins's *The Selfish Gene* (1976), appeared only one and two years respectively before Mackie's book. At the same time, while Mackie clearly understood the role of evolution in explaining morality, he did not go much beyond this fundamental recognition in his book, as it came out too early to be able to profit from the wealth of ideas that the burgeoning literature on the evolution of morality would produce in the following years.[28]

The Philosophers' Regression: Is Morality Objective?

From the 1970s onward, the study of morality has divided along two entirely separate paths. On the one hand, the evolutionary study of the mechanisms that underpin and explain human prosocial, altruistic, and moral behavior has resulted in pathbreaking insights, which were not quite possible before. We shall learn more about them later on. On the other hand, the philosophical discourse on morality has stagnated, if not regressed. The general trend in this discourse has turned against the emotive-prescriptive position, already articulated by Hume and repeated by Mackie, that values are subjective or "constructed" rather than objective, in the sense that they reside in our minds rather than in the outside world and express our feeling and attitudes with respect to social behavior. Instead, moral philosophy has been largely preoccupied with what is, in my view, insignificant distinctions and inconsequential terminology. I shall therefore discuss them only very briefly.

The objective versus subjective-constructivist positions in this debate are also known as realism and anti-realism, respectively. Historically, the objectivist or realist position held that the moral values were beings in the world—that they existed in the cosmos or were imbedded in its *logos*, irrespective of us. One dissenting voice among the philosophers has reportedly dismissed the whole point of the current debate with the witty comment that "the question of moral realism seemed to him to be the question whether the universe cares what we do. Since we have long since given up believing that the cosmos pays us any mind, he thought we should long since have given up moral realism."[29] Indeed, very few realists still hold such a metaphysical view of morality. Instead, the objectivity of values is now chiefly defined as the question of whether statements about them are actually statements about fact, which can be judged to be true or false; for example, that the statement "killing babies for fun is wrong" is objectively true as the statement "this is a house". The main question that this position raises is that if moral facts are not beings in the world, what are they and how can they be true or not?[30] In the current debate, there are three main lines of realist argument, and combinations of them, that purport to demonstrate that values are objectively true without being out there in the world.

One line of argument is the intersubjective-interpersonal argument: we all share a common core of moral values, so we can attribute truth or falsehood to a certain value by reference to this shared core. However, what if people are divided on this or that value within the supposed shared core? Realists argue that the shared core of values is far more substantial than the much-heralded differences. They invoke an analogy to Noam Chomsky's "deep grammar" that supposedly underlies all natural human languages.[31] The existence and scope of deep grammar is itself in dispute among linguists, and Chomsky himself has loosened his criteria for it.[32] Indeed, what if the shared moral core, which, like Hume, I think exists, is actually less clear-cut and more diffused? This after all is precisely the reason why irreconcilable moral disputes about values occur.

A second line of objectivist-realist argument in today's philosophical discourse equates moral facts with the "secondary qualities" of our world of perception. As mentioned in the previous chapter, sensations such as color, sound, taste, smell, touch, and hot-cold are regarded within our current understanding of the world as mental translations of physical properties of the world (such as waves and particles) that impact our sense organs. They exist only in the mind, and yet they are inextricably linked to real (primary) qualities of the outside world. They can therefore be regarded as objective in the sense that we can meaningfully ask and get an answer to the question if this shirt is red or blue; this, under specified conditions of light and given that the sense organs of the great majority of us (not everybody, of course) distinguish between the two wavelengths. Now, might the same not apply to assertions about moral values? It has been suggested that although values are indeed in our mind, they are so inextricably linked to, so directly and immediately activated by, behaviors in the world that they can be regarded as an inseparable part of our objective world of experience in the same way that colors and sounds are.[33]

Hume was actually the first to make the analogy between our enduring attitudes and "secondary qualities". As he wrote: "Vice and virtue may be compar'd to sounds, colours, heat and cold, which, according to modern philosophy, are not qualities in objects but perceptions in the mind."[34] And yet Hume was not a realist-objectivist with respect to morality. For while the analogy between colors and moral values is not groundless, the difference between the two is still significant, and crucial to the subject of morality. Realists of the secondary qualities brand in effect accept that moral values are a mental reaction to, rather than a perceptual translation of, things in the world. Yet the subjective element in our moral reactions is much greater than it is in our perceptual translations, because the latter are ultimately tied to an objective feature that can be determined (such as wavelength).[35] This, precisely, is the reason for the endemic debates about moral values, which realists try to circumvent. Thus, our disagreements about the values we ought to uphold are not only much greater than, but are also of a different *kind* from, those we have with respect to colors we see in the world. They cannot be settled by reference to features of the outside reality. Hence the difference between people who are "color blind" and the much discussed category of "sociopaths" or "psychopaths", people who do not care about the feelings of others. The former are unable to detect some objective features of the world, whereas attributing the same quality to so-called sociopaths is merely metaphorical, as what they supposedly "lack" is an attitude. Nor, as tests show, do they lack rationality.[36]

Here also lies the main weakness of the third realist line of argument in the current debate. It takes its cue from the developments in the philosophy of mind during the second half of the twentieth century and is mostly represented by one of its chief protagonists, Hilary Putnam. The threshold to what is considered an objective truth about the world has been lowered in the philosophy of the mind, as it has been recognized that there is no secure, undisputed foundation for the structure of our knowledge other than plausibility and coherence given everything we think we know about the world. Putnam has argued in a pragmatist vein (following Dewey), that the same criterion of plausibility that we apply to what we believe to be true applies equally to our beliefs as to what is right. He argues that our disagreements on moral values are no different from the disagreement we see on scientific facts and theories.[37]

But does this analogy hold?[38] While our beliefs about the facts of the world may indeed be less rigorously and definitively substantiated than previously thought, they are still beliefs about facts in the world that are independent of us. What is in dispute about them is which fact actually exists. By contrast, if one does not think, as Putnam does not think, that moral values are metaphysically embedded in the universe, then moral values are feelings and attitudes. The dispute about them is not on whether this or that value exists, but which of them should be upheld. The subjective and indeterminate element here is of a different kind than it is in scientific questions of fact. Thus, there is every reason for one (like myself) to be a realist about things outside us, to hold that the world exists independent of our perception, while rejecting moral realism, however construed.

A small number of philosophers still espouse a metaphysical, "transcendental", conception of objective moral values—the view that the moral values exist as part of the order or *logos* of the cosmos, irrespective of us. According to this conception, moral values would indeed be facts in the world, which means that it can be argued that some claimed values are true and some false. As we have seen in the previous chapter, no view, including that of metaphysical moral values, can be refuted in the strict sense of the word. Historically, the metaphysical-transcendental view of morality was much more widespread than it is today, because it was integral to an overall picture of an intimate, earth-centered cosmos, in which God and man held the supreme position. This cosmological picture is no longer accepted as plausible as widely as it used to be, given everything else we have come to know about the world. Notably, the majority of philosophy professors have declared themselves moral realists in a recent poll (which has not prevented the largest number of them to name Hume as the philosopher with whom they most identify themselves!).[39] However, the great majority of them are not metaphysically realists in the sense described. Rather, they subscribe to the softer versions of realism that have developed since the 1970s. As I have been arguing here, these softer versions are difficult to make sense of, because their main claim, that statements of value can be true or false, that they have the same status as facts in the world, cannot be rationalized. Thus, I argue that if metaphysical moral realism is not claimed, the softer versions of realism are not very different from versions of subjectivism-constructivism.

Simon Blackburn, a staunch Humean, has chosen to label his version of moral philosophy "quasi-realism", partly because realism is so deeply entrenched in people's minds.[40] I call the softer versions of realism "quasi-metaphysical". Representing not much more than semantics, they also, in not a few cases I suspect, express philosophers' self-definitions or self-identifications—more of a declared attitude toward the subject of morality than truly substantial differences.

The Evolutionary Rationale: What Are the Natural Source and Underpinning of Morality?

During the decades when philosophers of what morality is have largely confined themselves to an argument within a narrow field of concepts and definitions, rather than seek to break away from—and transcend—them, evolutionary theory has been advancing by leaps and bounds, including in our subject. Remember that Darwin pointed at the key to explaining the mystery to which Hume had had no answer: why naturally selfish human beings exhibit equally natural prosocial, altruistic, and moral behavior. This question has become even more pertinent as the evolutionary logic makes it all the clearer why organisms that compete to outdo one another in the struggle for survival and reproduction should behave in a way that advances their own interests. As we have seen, Darwin argued that people's prosocial behavior—with sentiments to match—stems from the benefits they derive from group cooperation. This does not eliminate the strong tension that exists between selfish and prosocial behaviors. On the contrary, there is a balancing act between contributing to a mutually rewarding group effort and hurting one's own prospects. During the last decades, evolutionary theorists have elucidated the rationale and evolution-shaped mechanisms that underpin and explain this balancing act. There are now many hundreds and thousands of articles and books that describe these findings, which I shall present here as briefly and as simply as possible, without getting into the intricacies. Some readers may already be more or less familiar with the evolutionary account of these matters, and to those who are not I recommend that they familiarize themselves. This is one of the most significant scientific developments of our times.[41]

Modern evolutionary theory is famously based on the "gene's eye" view of natural selection, popularly dubbed the "selfish gene", in the title of Dawkins's highly influential book. However, the genes-centered perspective explains not only selfish behavior but also how genes for altruism toward others have been selected and have proliferated on the logic of self-preservation. Several evolutionary mechanisms have been at work here. The most basic is parental care for offspring, long noted by moral philosophers and highlighted by Hume as an example of unselfish behavior.[42] However, there was no explanation for this behavior until Darwin, except that is was deeply sensed to be, and taken for granted as, most natural. We now understand this natural propensity. While organisms die, their genes survive in their offspring. Those animals who care for their offspring enhance the prospects of the offspring to survive, and thus the trait itself of caring for the offspring survives and proliferates. As Hume has brilliantly seen, caring for the offspring is all the more pronounced among humans, because human offspring have a longer period of childhood before they can become independent and cease to be in need of vital help. Hume has also noted that the institution of matrimony and the virtue of matrimonial modesty, in his language (pair bonding and loyalty, in ours), stemmed naturally from this human reality of protracted childhood and the need for joint parental care. He has even argued that this virtue is more demanded of the women, because their role in the raising of the offspring tends to be more vital.[43]

In addition to offspring, people tend to exhibit greater generosity toward other kin than they do toward the vast majority of those who are not close kin. While family bonds have also been regarded as a natural fact of life in all cultures throughout history, we now understand the evolutionary logic that explains these natural affinities. People share on average 50 percent of their genes with their siblings, 25 percent with their niece-nephews, and 12.5 percent with their cousins. Those who supported their kin increased the representation of their own genes in the next generation, including the genes for helping kin. On this logic, pioneering evolutionist J. B. S. Haldane half-whimsically suggested that he would be prepared to sacrifice his life for two siblings or eight cousins. Of course, rivalry between kin is also common, and is explained by the same evolutionary rationale: one is doubly closer to oneself than to a sibling, and to one's own children than to a sibling's children.

As Hume saw, people exhibit prosocial and altruistic behavior not only toward kin but also toward non-kin—in modern evolutionary parlance, toward people who are not closely related to them genetically. However, as mentioned earlier, he was wrong to think that such behavior was not motivated by the same principle as self-interest and in his expectation that no future, deeper, understanding of human nature was likely to show otherwise. The logic behind supportive behavior toward non-kin is the benefit of cooperation, and the mechanism that secures it is the promise of reciprocity: I help you under the assumption that you do the same, now or in the future. Bonds of friendship cement a reciprocal relationship by creating both familiarity and emotional ties of fondness and trust. If the other fails to reciprocate, we tend to feel moral indignation or outrage, cease to cooperate, and even actively punish those who fail us. We are very good in detecting "cheaters" and constantly look for signs of whether or not the other can be trusted. Inter alia, we infer a "good character" from observing a person's general behavior toward others, in the social milieu in general. Indeed, reciprocity extends beyond bilateral relations to the group level at large. Individuals are judged, rewarded, or punished (subtly or even brutally) by the collective for their keeping with the group's general division of contributions and benefits.

Of course, the other side of the same logic is that individuals are disinclined to pay more than the benefits of cooperation promise—they tend to exhibit, as Hume noted, only "confined generosity". Moreover, they have an incentive to cheat without being detected, so as to "free-ride" the system, reaping the benefits of cooperation without contributing to it and paying its costs. Thus, behaving immorally is evolutionarily as natural as a moral behavior.[44] Hence the intrinsic gap that exists between the moral ideal (and often pretense) and actual human behavior that falls far short of it. This does not mean that people are thoroughly cynical, hypocritical, or consciously calculating and manipulating. Although to some degree we obviously are—some more than others—much of our prosocial behaviors are spontaneous and involve a very real sense of good will and altruism toward others. "Good character" is genuine. Indeed, the above-described evolutionary rationale accounts for the process by which prosocial behaviors have been selected, so as to become internalized in human nature and be buttressed by feelings such as duty, guilt, and shame—the so-called human conscience. Experimental psychology has shown that moral notions can already be detected in small infants; that, as with language and other cognitive and emotional human traits, they are innate propensities developed in early life.[45]

Experimental moral psychologist Jonathan Haidt, author of an important book, *The Righteous Mind: Why Good People Are Divided by Politics and Religion* (2012), has called attention to the fact that morality as actually conceived and practiced in past and present societies around the world consists not only of the precepts of doing no harm to others but also of norms regarding what is socially perceived as sanctified and degraded, pure and impure. Partly, this notion is evolutionarily rooted in the feeling of disgust and revulsion at foods and other objects that may be unclean, contaminated, or poisonous and therefore harmful to us. This elementary emotional reaction takes the form of particular taboos in different societies, socially sanctified by custom and religion. Morality as an adaptation to social life and social cooperation has always incorporated such communal features.

We can only very briefly refer to a number of often-made objections to the evolutionary explanation for the origin and nature of human morality and human conscience. Some would argue that this explanation is cynical and an affront to human dignity.[46] However, rather than being a transcendental metaphysical value or entity, dignity itself is a moral notion whose roots, I argue, are explained—and reconfigured—within the evolved rationale of human social interactions. In response to another common misconception, it is crucial to understand that no teleological logic or intentions by genes or by individuals is involved in evolution's blind algorithm. This is the revolutionary reversed perspective that evolutionary theory has introduced. What turns out to promote survival survives, and therefore is increasingly represented in the next generation. The trait in question thereby proliferates.

But if so, is evolutionary theory not tautological and its logic circular and seemingly irrefutable? How can it explain both moral and immoral behavior as natural? On the contrary, being the regulatory mechanism that accounts for the emergence of all natural traits, evolution *must* be able to explain all major features of observed phenomena. Consider that gravitation explains why bodies move toward, keep their distance between, or move away from each other. Evolution is nature's immanent principle. The only relevant question is whether or not this explanation withstands the tests of logic and the evidence. Evolution-shaped mechanisms, no different from man-made designs, can "malfunction" under certain conditions and occasionally "fail". But the logic of natural selection can only be refuted if major evidence that contradicts it as the regulative principle of nature ever arises. As of now, in the famous words of one evolutionary biologist: "nothing in biology makes sense except in the light of evolution."[47]

As Darwin foresaw, modern researchers of animal behavior detect basic traits of moral behavior in social animals other than human.[48] It is just that humans took group life and group cooperation to a new level in terms of scale, complexity, and sophistication. Stone Age *Homo sapiens* already lived in tribal groups of hundreds and had evolved language and other mechanisms of social cooperation—including morality—as adaptations that made large-scale social life possible. These traits are still with us today as part of human nature.

All this is a very brief outline of scholarly literature, intended to bring out the logic of the evolutionary account of the origins of morality, the mechanisms that brought morality into being, and the natural propensities and sentiments that continue to sustain it. Where this chapter aims to make a contribution is in elucidating some of the implications of the naturalistic evolutionary understanding of morality for the philosophical discourse on the subject. Except for very few, the great majority of philosophers have fiercely opposed the suggestion that the evolutionary perspective offers anything that is significantly relevant to the philosophy of morality.[49]

The Naturalistic vs. Quasi-Metaphysical Understanding of Morality

As already noted, the evolutionary and philosophical discourses on morality have been traveling along two almost entirely separate roads since the 1970s. Two separate scholarly communities have consolidated, which are not on speaking terms with each other. Evolutionary biologist David Lahti has described the situation as follows:

> Academia is currently in an awkward transitional period where pairs of fields with identical subject matter share little else but a mutual disdain. There are essentially two kinds of anthropology, two kinds of psychology, and two kinds of sociology. There are two general approaches to the study of behavior, and to the human mind and culture. The rivalry in each case can be described very simply: one field is rooted in an evolutionary framework, and the other ignores evolution as a matter of principle. The study of morality can be divided along the same fault line. Consider one person who self-identifies as "an evolutionary biologist interested in morality" and another who self-identifies as "a moral philosopher." In my experience, there can hardly be two people with such similar interests who are typically so committed to the idea that the other has nothing to offer. I once introduced such a pair to each other and received an identical look from each of them within the space of a minute or two when the other wasn't looking—the look that said, What do you expect me to do with this person?"[50]

Lahti continues: "The vast majority of professional philosophy is pre-Darwinian, by which I mean pre-Darwinian in its level of understanding of life, whether the ideas themselves date from before 1859 or today. We should not rely on pre-Darwinian philosophy to understand human nature, ethics, beliefs, emotions, and attitudes, any more than we would rely on Aristotle's physics or Galen's medicine in the respective fields today."[51]

An attempt to bring together the two scholarly communities dealing with morality in the framework of a Harvard symposium, published under the hopeful title *Understanding Moral Sentiments from a Darwinian Perspective,* has failed miserably. The philosophers' reaction to the advent of the evolutionary perspective, which necessitates a thorough revision of the entire philosophical tradition—the whole discourse philosophers have been brought up on—has been totally negative and dismissive. Mackie's 1977 book remains an exception, and the evolutionary logic as applied to morality is accepted by very few philosophers.[52]

Strangely, the most ardent philosophical advocates of the primacy of science in shaping what we should regard as a valid conception of the world, such as Putnam and Blackburn, fail to apply this view to the Darwinian revolution. One cannot but suggest a parallel here with the total rejection, by the established Aristotelian-Thomistic schoolmen philosophers who ruled at the universities, of the seventeenth century's New Philosophy, which drew on the new, revolutionary, scientific discoveries in cosmology and physics. Because of this, university philosophy remained largely irrelevant to the development of modern philosophy for the space of a century. By the end of this period, the old scholastic philosophy itself, the questions that preoccupied it, and its answers increasingly ceased to be regarded as relevant to the way people perceived the world.

Lahti has offered some constructive recommendations to narrow the gap between the two antagonistic scholarly communities currently dealing with morality. He has recommended to philosophers that they acquaint themselves with the fundamentals of evolutionary theory, and he has suggested that evolutionists pay greater attention to the questions that preoccupy philosophers. In applying myself to this task, I seek above all to address the question that, I believe, represents much of the skepticism among philosophers. Putnam has conceded that the evolutionary perspective can shed light on the origins of human propensities that underlie morality, such as altruism and sympathy (not a small feat!). However, he and other philosophers have been skeptical that these insights (when recognized at all) are actually helpful for capturing, let alone adding to, the subtleties of positions and propositions developed over centuries and millennia of philosophical moral discourse; moreover, that they can contribute to the task that philosophers have resumed over the last decades of actually resolving moral questions and offering guidance for moral behavior.[53] The remainder of this chapter, although mainly concerned with meta-ethics—what morality is—is intended to shed some light also on the moral questions themselves. It will ask how the naturalistic evolutionary understanding of morality impinges, if not directly on our answers to the moral questions per se, then at least on our approach to them.

Naturalism has long been a highly suspect position in the philosophy of morality. What is known as the "naturalistic fallacy" is the view that the values that should be upheld can be deduced from the facts of the world or of our nature. Remember that Hume has rejected such attempts, insisting that what "is" has no compelling status, in and of itself, with respect to what "ought" to be done. I share this view, and it applies equally to the facts of evolution. The fact that the blind algorithm of evolution has predisposed us toward these or other behaviors is not—in and of itself—an argument why we should follow a certain course of action. Even less does it make this course of action morally binding. However, as we have seen with respect to Hume himself, all this does not mean that the facts of the world and of our nature cannot help to explain the *facts* about why we tend to make these or other choices. They reveal not only the source but also the rationale behind our moral sentiments, notions, and precepts. Furthermore, such facts may shape—and perhaps alter—our perspective as to what we can expect from moral discussions.

The view of morality as a natural phenomenon, the product of social life—a view greatly enhanced by the evolutionary perspective—is an antidote to what I shall call the "metaphysication" of the moral discussion. As already noted, very few philosophers nowadays hold a metaphysical-transcendental realist position of morality: the belief that moral values are in the world or are imbedded in its *logos*, irrespective of us. Still, as Nietzsche famously charged, metaphysical modes of thinking linger on in philosophy long after their metaphysical underpinnings have been discarded and proclaimed dead. Nietzsche himself rejected Darwin's evolutionary theory (showing poor understanding of it, one must add) and, in the mold of nineteenth-century German philosophy, cited it as yet another example of the mediocrity of the British spirit.[54] Furthermore, as mentioned earlier, his own claimed elementary force—the "will to power"—remains couched in the kind of superhuman imagery and rhetoric he scorned. Still, his criticism of the vestiges of bygone metaphysics in philosophy stands.

What I mean by "metaphysication" is the tendency to look for a complete, abstract system of principles—often of an absolutist-exclusivist claim—that will describe and typically also prescribe moral behavior. To be sure, thinking in terms of general principles is natural to us, as it is a vital and highly useful cognitive and behavioral shortcut. It is even more natural to philosophy, because of its age-old identification with abstract reflection on general concepts. True, from Aristotle to this day, there have been philosophers who have ostensibly eschewed an abstract moral system and have described morality as an essentially practical field that can only be approached with accumulated insights and practical wisdom. Some of them have also proclaimed freedom from metaphysical assumptions.[55] And yet, more often than not, they too reveal some forms of "metaphysication". This would seem to be an occupational hazard.

Some would reply that the evolutionary perspective itself is a metaphysical presupposition; indeed, that we always, necessarily, hold some metaphysical assumptions, the underlying basis of any view of the world. Put that way, this claim is certainly true. However, note that I have no argument with the objectivist metaphysical view of morality, except for suggesting to its adherents and to others that this view is implausible given everything else we have come to hold as true about the world. Rather, the problem of "metaphysication" applies to those who, in my view, are inconsistent and incoherent in clinging to metaphysical forms of moral philosophizing even though they no longer espouse its objectivist metaphysical base.

By all this I do not mean that there is no broad common denominator to what we understand by moral behavior. On the contrary, there is. From the ancient Greeks to Hobbes and Hume, philosophers rightly traced moral sentiments and behavior to the demands of social life and to people's need to get along together and cooperate. The socially oriented prescriptions of the Ten Commandments are an example of a codification of such widely held moral notions that have always been around, however they have been interpreted and implemented in different cultures and societies: Honor thy father and thy mother; Thou shalt not kill; Thou shalt not commit adultery; Thou shalt not steal; Thou shalt not bear false witness; Thou shalt not covet. As people searched for a more general, abstract, formulation of the principle involved, they came up with the so-called Golden Rule, independently formulated by many cultures: "don't do to others what is hateful to you", or "treat others in the way you would want to be treated".

Like all conceptual frames, this most successful one is open to all sorts of questions and criticisms. For example, is the Golden Rule enough, or should we not be more active in pursuing the benefit to others, especially if they are in distress, and perhaps even if they are not? The Jewish Torah's command "Love your neighbor as yourself" (Leviticus 19:18) was echoed by Jesus (Mark 12:28–31). Is such an extended effort a moral obligation, or should it be considered an extra virtue beyond the call of duty? In my view, such a question is largely a matter of the semantic lines we draw between various conceptions and degrees of morality. However, many believe that a question of this kind has a principled, abstract answer.

Challenging the Golden Rule from the opposite direction, some values we hold dear are abhorrent to others. So do holding and practicing them qualify as harm to these others? Again, while some philosophers recognize the diversity of, and a certain fundamental incommensurability between, values that different people and cultures hold, others contend that there are actually definitive and binding answers to such questions and to conflicts of value. They claim or imply that the answers can be deduced from the intrinsic logic of morality, on whatever they base its authority.

As members of the same species, human beings broadly share notions and precepts of morality, of what is socially regarded as a proper conduct. But again, there is no reason to think that these notions and precepts should fully converge and cohere between different people and different communities, or even in the minds of the individuals themselves. The naturalistic rather than the meta-physical or "quasi-metaphysical" perspective on the origin and function of mo-rality helps us realize why the bundle of our moral precepts and common moral denominators, while existing, are actually too diffuse and diverse to meet such an abstract requirement. The ancient Greeks, attempting to reconcile what they observed as our common moral denominators with the apparent considerable diversity of human values, suggested a distinction between *logos*, the deep moral structure that we all supposedly share, and *nomos*, the different and often conflicting customs, and values, that different cultures practice and cherish. This distinction was a significant insight at the time and is still often invoked. But its dichotomist character obscures the actual untidiness and diversity of even the more central elements of our moral core. Again, it is not that they do not exist at all. It is just that they are fuzzy enough to never fully be captured by the abstract webs of the conceptual net that the metaphysical or quasi-metaphysical moral mind throws on the world and postulates as binding.

One might respond that there is nothing unusual about this because, as we have argued in the previous chapter, our conceptual frames *never* capture reality in full. However, to repeat, there is a difference in kind between factual claims about the world and claims about what our attitudes and behaviors ought to be. Furthermore, I am not at all arguing that there is something wrong with suggesting abstract schemes of what our moral precepts are like, or, moreover, offering guidelines as to what our moral behavior should be. Quite the opposite, such projects are most useful and are inseparable from our nature as moral creatures who are highly sensitive to moral issues. What I am suggesting is only that *philosophically* we should not approach such projects with the (quasi-)metaphysical assumption—explicitly held or unwittingly lingering on—that there is a definitive and compelling moral *logos*, either written in the heavens or set in stone in human hearts and minds.

One might protest that what I have presented here is a straw man or caricature. After all, there are many stripes of moral philosophy—pragmatist, skeptic, relativist, postmodernist—that explicitly reject the quasi-metaphysical approach to morality. And still, if anything, mainstream moral philosophy has pretty much resumed that approach, which goes hand in hand with philosophers' return to address, and quest to solve, practical moral questions. The quasi-metaphysical frame of mind can be detected, for example, in the ongoing debate between what is currently regarded as the three main schools or systems of moral evaluation and conduct, based on: motives and rule-based principles; consequences; and virtue. Their respective proponents advocate the merits of their chosen system of morality and point out the flaws in the other systems, in what tends to be a rather exclusionary discourse. By contrast, a naturalistic understanding of morality shows each and all of these evaluative moral systems to represent distinct, interchanging, and complementary cross-perspectives and sets of criteria through which we judge complex real-life situations. Being particular perspectives and frames of mind as they are, it is only to be expected that each of them would have its limitations and shortcomings as a guide for our moral evaluation and conduct. At the same time, they can all be useful and helpful to us in performing this task. No single cognitive moral algorithm holds.

The False Contest between Motives, Consequences, and Virtue

Of the above, the most common standard of moral evaluation that people employ is that of motives and intentions. This is clearly shown by experiments in the new field of cognitive moral psychology.[56] It should be quite obvious why this is so. When we judge other people for their behavior toward us and toward the collective at large, their benevolent motives and intentions are the best, and most reassuring, indication, first, that they would actually act upon these motives—unhindered by selfish, apathetic, or hostile attitudes—and, second, that their action is likely to yield the desired result.

In philosophy, Kant is the strictest and most influential proponent of the purity of motives—good will and a strict adherence to the moral duty—as the only criterion of moral action. Rejecting the naturalistic approach to morality, his *Groundwork of the Metaphysics of Morals* (1785) and *Critique of Practical Reason* (1788) rooted morality in what Kant posited as the universalistic legislation of an autonomous reason, guided by moral duty alone. It was this kind of "metaphysication" or abstractions that would provoke Nietzsche's scorn. Stripped from its quasi-metaphysical elements, Kant's concept is best viewed as an analytical attempt to define the essence of how we ideally understand morality: a selfless obligation acted upon out of purely benevolent intentions. In his Categorical Imperative, Kant postulated that in adopting moral norms and taking moral action we ought to regard it as their standard that they should be able to serve as a universal law for humanity. In part, this meant a version of the Golden Rule: treat others as you would want to be treated yourself. Kant was so strict in his moral concept (he was a Prussian, after all) that he forbade lies under any circumstances as violating a universally useful law, including "white lies", even if this meant unnecessarily hurting other people's feelings. Unlike Kant, we do not tend to be so strict, but the morality of motives and intentions has other problems as well.

The main problem is captured by the old proverb—actually an observation— that the road to hell is paved with good intentions. People have long noticed that actions taken out of the most charitable motives and according to the best of moral principles may sometimes result in very undesirable, even catastrophic, results. The opposite is also true: ostensibly immoral actions can successfully achieve a moral good. This goes against our deep feeling that as long as we do the "right thing" everything will be all right, and is the cause of a most common moral dissonance. Problems of this and of similar nature have given rise to so-called consequentialist approaches to moral action, which focus on the likely outcomes of our action rather than on our motives. The best known consequentialist approach is utilitarianism. This doctrine was already put forward by Epicurus and his disciples in antiquity and was developed by Jeremy Bentham and John Stuart Mill in the late eighteenth and nineteenth centuries, respectively.[57] Its proponents posit the greatest happiness to the largest number of people as the goal of moral action.

Critics of utilitarianism have argued that utilitarian morality is immoral. For one thing, they ask if happiness, or the satisfaction of people's desires, can really be regarded as the goal of moral action. Is it really the "good"?[58] Secondly, and most famously, they pose the question whether the killing of one person in order to maximize the happiness of ten, for example, qualifies as a moral act. Some things, they argue, are simply not done. Again, experiments by cognitive psychologists of morality show that people recoil from and tend to reject such acts as immoral.[59] They go against our gut instincts. However, the same experiments, and daily life, reveal that in some circumstances we accept such actions as the lesser of evils, say, in order to save the lives of many from a natural or man-caused disaster. In such circumstances and when giving the situation an extended consideration, we often bring in the factor of consequences, which is less instinctive and natural in our moral evaluation.

People are regularly confounded in real-life situations when confronting the sometimes conflicting precepts of the above approaches to morality. This may result in swings of mood toward one or the other approach. For example, during the middle part of the twentieth century, many intellectuals—most famously Sartre—justified brutal means taken by the communist regimes as necessary for the advancement of the supremely just objectives of communism. There followed a disillusionment and a swing in the other direction. Albert Camus was among the earliest to so react, rejecting the view that the ends justified the means and upholding "human rights"—in practice, the principle of doing no harm—as the overriding moral guide for action. From the late 1970s onward, the moral discourse of human rights has become hegemonic in the West. However, adherence to this standard, worthy as it is, has seen the old problems of the morality of good intentions resurface.

For example, the practicing of the moral imperative to intervene to free people from tyranny, oppression, and killings has often resulted in even greater mayhem. One recent instance is the destructive anarchy in Libya following the European intervention in 2011 to topple Muammar Gaddafi, a venture championed on purely humanitarian grounds. To clarify: I am not attempting to issue judgment on this affair, either moral or political. As Zhou Enlai, the communist leader of China, reportedly replied in 1972 when asked about his opinion on the French Revolution: "it is too early to say." (He actually referred to the events in Paris 1968 rather than 1789, but his saying is too precious to give up on historical technicalities.) This example is intended only to bring out the moral tensions involved. Note that Libya was not a case of pitting other interests, so-called *Realpolitik*, against morality, but of a clash between two criteria for taking moral action: moral intentions and moral outcomes. Consider also the morality of cooperating with brutal dictatorships for the supposed greater good of winning the Cold War against communist oppression. Everyday politics is full of such examples, which place people on the horns of a dilemma between a sense of moral duty and the expected moral utility. Machiavelli highlighted this point, and his message remains embarrassing and disquieting to this day.

Weaknesses and problematic test case examples such as the above in the various approaches to morality are typically treated in the "metaphysication" of the moral discourse as fatal deficiencies that are sufficient to disqualify a "system" and leave the field free for the critic's favorite approach. By contrast, the various approaches are naturalistically understood as alternative and complementary cognitive sets of criteria we formulate in order to evaluate real-life situations that carry a moral dimension in our eyes. None of these perspectives is free from weaknesses, and there is no reason to assume that they are, or could be. Nor can any of them serve as an exclusive or superior set of criteria. Nor, again, is there anything inconsistent about alternating between or combining them, as may be called for by the situation. They are no different in this respect from the various, alternative, and complementary standards and indicators we use, say, for assessing the strength of the stock market or the prosperity and well-being of a society. None of these criteria is fool-proof or exclusive, while they can each be relevant and useful in throwing light on significant aspects of the phenomena we wish to evaluate.

A third approach to morality in the current philosophical discourse is what is known as the morality of virtue. Its leading proponent is philosopher Alasdair MacIntyre, whose book *After Virtue* (1981) has revived the Aristotelian approach to the subject. This approach is fundamentally naturalistic, and MacIntyre has plenty of wise things to say. He criticizes analytical philosophy for its blindness to history (i.e., to real life) and, as a result, for overlooking the diversity of moral traditions and the considerable incommensurability of moral values between these traditions. He rejects the view that any universal moral rule, allegedly deduced from or by reason, can settle such differences. He makes the long-familiar point that both the concepts of human rights ("natural" or otherwise) and utilitarianism are moral fictions, in the sense that they are postulates of our mind typically confused for objective entities (which does not mean that they cannot be very useful and important morally). At the same time, he argues that the debate between moral traditions and systems is worthwhile, as the sides try to convince each other of their superior position by elucidating the theoretical and practical advantages of their particular approach.

MacIntyre is naturalistic in holding, like Aristotle (and the Stoics), that the virtues that are most conducive to human happiness and prosperity—the "good life", as the Greek philosophers called it—are embedded in human nature. Like Aristotle and the other ancient schools, he argues that this applies to both the individual and communal levels, and, like them, he has no explanation for the fact that caring for the communal good is in our nature. His claim regarding a basic compatibility and convergence of the egotistic and prosocial motives remains rudimentary and somewhat naive. That aside, "well-being" has been variably described since antiquity as a kind of optimal, desired combination and balance between happiness, self-fulfillment, peace of mind, freedom from pain and frustration, and, indeed, also from guilt and shame.

The ancient Greek philosophers, being philosophers, were convinced that a calm life of contemplation is the truly "good life".[60] Other ancient schools of wisdom such as Buddhism and Confucianism held more or less similar views. The preference for a life of contemplation seems to be an occupational bias. It is good to know that philosophers like what they do. But other people might regard, say, a life of action as the good life, even if it regularly involves setbacks, failures, and frustrations—one of the main reasons the ancient philosophers opted for a quieter life. In modern times, Mill demonstrated a similar bias, recommending that the "superior" pleasures, deriving from the "higher faculties", be given precedence in the calculation of social utility over the "lower", "beastly" pleasures.[61] MacIntyre, closer to the spirit of our times, seems careful to avoid what can be regarded as the bias of elite preferences. However, as a result, his account of the good life in accordance with human nature—the cornerstone of his philosophy—is disappointedly (or predictably) vague and dull: "the good life for man is the life spent in seeking for the good life for man, and the virtues necessary for the seeking are those which will enable us to understand what more and what else the good life for man is."[62] All this is done with the view to helping the community as a whole, however the particular society in question perceives the common good.[63]

The ancient schools of thought had an important point to make. They highlighted some general notions people tend to have about life, such as that the "excessive" pursuit or "indulgence" of sensual pleasures often results in negative aftereffects. These include feelings of nausea, sensual hangover, emotional emptiness, and sometimes ill-health. The naturalistic perspective explains how some consumptions—such as alcohol, drugs, smoking, or overeating—riding on our limbic system of pleasures, create addictions that run counter to the system's evolutionary "function", and therefore often spark an emotional dissonance. Furthermore, the relentless pursuit of some pleasures, such as the sexual, may create a frustrating sense of Sisyphean un-fulfillment. This is most typically so when this pursuit stands in the way of forming stable, deeper relationships.

Evolutionarily, a stable relationship has been advantageous (mostly for women but also for men) for successful childrearing and, hence, is embedded in our natural emotional makeup in the form of romantic love and sense of commitment.

To be sure, there are conflicting natural drives in all of this. Here is one example that is more directly relevant to our subject. It is clear why young people are predisposed to get more involved in sexual exploration and in the highly elaborate social activities surrounding it. They are in greater need to gain more experience, find out about their options, and become better positioned to make their choices before settling down (if they do). Thus, Aristotle, who held that morality, the way to the good life, should be taught to mature people who had largely curbed their youthful passions, mixed things up.[64] He had a point in that experience, and the wisdom of older age that comes with it, tells us useful things about what is worth pursuing in terms of our emotional well-being. At the same time, despite his naturalistic and practical approach to morality, he did not see that the natural rationale for young people might be different from what he thought applied to older people. This is the same as faulting young people, say, for their typical preference for high-energy foods, and more of them, or for milk chocolate rather than for the dark variety. Such preferences are a consequence of their faster metabolism, more intense activity, and need to grow. It is not that their taste about food is not yet fully "developed" or "mature" as that of older people.

The ancient schools also held that prosocial virtues and behaviors were inseparable from one's well-being. They supported this claim by a variety of arguments: some of them metaphysical (karma); some, as with Socrates in Crito—where he explains why he will not try to escape Athens and the death penalty issued against him—are predicated on the notion of fairness to the laws, which is, however, precisely one of the virtues whose claim on our behavior we seek to explain; some, again as in Crito, amounting to the utilitarian benefit of social cooperation—which still leaves the option of successful free-riding; and some boiling down to the negative (psychological) effects of a guilty conscience, assuming of course that one is significantly susceptible to pangs of conscience. The naturalistic evolutionary understanding of morality regards only the last two factors as real, and, moreover, explains how they are connected. To repeat: the social pressures on individuals to contribute their share to a mutually rewarding cooperation selected for individuals' prosocial psychological traits such as a sense of duty, guilt, and shame.

The cues for virtuous well-being that the ancient schools put forward are best viewed as accumulated insights from the wisdom of the ages. They suggest some behavioral observations, signposts, warning signs, reminders, and rules of thumb that deserve our attention as we navigate our way in life within a social context. There are principles such as Aristotle's Golden Middle Way[65] or the Buddhist Middle Path. At the same time, running in the opposite direction, there is, for example, a prevalent notion that devotion to a great passion, be it artistic or true love, should win, including against some otherwise ordinarily held moral precepts. The American public, in keeping with American public morality, is often variably surprised, shocked, and entertained by the news that French public morality is more tuned with this precept, expressed in the proverb that "all is fair in love and war". Something similar may apply to great feats of egotistic action, à la Nietzsche, as opposed to the "middle way", if the latter is perceived as a recipe for mediocre compromising. What such examples show is that not only are there different criteria for judging moral action, but also that the moral perspective is only one postulate through which we judge the propriety of human action and measure the good life.

Some of today's leading moral philosophers declare themselves as Aristotelian—searching for practical virtues that are in accord with human nature and therefore recommend themselves on the strong claim that they promote human prosperity and well-being.[66] At the same time, some of these philosophers are staunch opponents of the intrusion of evolutionary theory into the sphere of morality. This makes little sense, as the evolutionary understanding of human behavior and morality is rooted in human nature and in utility and could have been embraced by neo-Aristotelian philosophers of natural virtue. It is true, however, that this would have made it necessary for them to loosen some of their rigid conceptions of the good, the vestiges of the metaphysical frame of mind, and make their naturalistic approach somewhat more flexible.

How Does All This Matter?

We now get to the questions that most people are interested in above all: If morality is not anchored in some objective, "metaphysical" basis, can it hold? And how does the naturalistic understanding of morality enlighten and perhaps assist us with respect to the practical moral questions to which we seek answers? Remember that the generation that proclaimed the Death of God feared the consequences of "nihilism" for morality. Dostoevsky was so obsessed with this concern as to be preoccupied in his novels with little else. Indeed, he unwittingly answered his question of what was keeping morality alive if God was dead. The godless heroes of his novels, the perpetrators of near perfect crimes, ultimately succumbed to excruciating torments of conscience. As Hume had already seen, we have a strong (confined) propensity to behave morally because moral sentiments are in our nature. Of course, there is no need to hold naively that this factor is invariably so strong as to deter all or most crimes. The answer to why people have a significant, albeit limited, propensity to act morally is that they are pressured to do so by the evolutionarily interconnected pincers of social sanction coupled with positive inducement, on the one hand, and the resulting natural propensity we have to feel and act prosocially, on the other.[67] The fact that we may be aware of this natural rationale does not significantly change either of these motivating factors. Traditionalist moralists who doubt that these are sufficiently resilient to keep us fully in line are correct. But they should equally remember that no other spiritual envelope, be it the command of God or any alleged dictate of reason, has been sufficient to achieve this moral ideal either—which only highlights the underlying natural rationale that buttresses moral behavior, and its limits.

How does the naturalistic evolutionary perspective inform our approach to the moral questions and dilemmas themselves? Clearly, it cannot "resolve" them. At the same time, the de-metaphysication and demystification of morality may contribute to the reconfiguration of our understanding of differences of value and of what can be expected from moral discussions. I write "contribute" because some of the ideas discussed below are already variably represented in philosophy.

Among the less represented is the view that moral notions and precepts are neither universally shared nor entirely relative. This false dichotomy has been the cause of endless and fruitless debates in philosophy, ultimately as pointless as the debates between moralists of good intentions and utilitarians. There is a growing realization among some philosophers that morality should be understood as a largely construed, self-supporting edifice, built on broader underlying natural sentiments of benevolence toward others.[68] Some philosophers have redefined—narrowed—the claim of a truth value to moral sentences precisely to their validity within such a projected framework.[69] However, quite apart from the evident disputes over moral values, is this bounded, closed definition of moral truth really worth the huge amount of effort invested in defending the label "realism"? Can't we leave it behind and move on?

Systems of morality are ideal postulates that we project as summaries of our notions of the right and the just, which people ought to adopt from the social perspective. There are broadly shared core elements to such systems, such as the Golden Rule, good will, reciprocity, loyalty, fair distribution, charity, truth telling, and more. But the relative weight, concrete forms, and the overall cultural traditions and worldviews within which such notions are expressed are "irreducibly" diffused and diverse. Such differences, conflicts, and clashes of values cannot be settled by an appeal to some fundamental, compelling moral rationale, because no such Archimedean point exists in the structure of the cosmos, in the human soul, or in the intrinsic logic of morality itself, a concept which is itself a reification of our emotional and behavioral prosocial propensities.

Some philosophers still cling to such ambitions. John Maynard Keynes, the great economist, tells about his experience from his university days in the early years of the twentieth century, in the circle of the leading moral philosopher G. E. Moore, author of the then famous *Principia Ethica* (1903). Moore believed that the "good" was an elementary quality of things, directly perceived by our moral intuition. (I avoid using the term "intuition" myself and use moral notions instead, precisely to avoid the connotation that the "good" exists out there, to be recognized by our senses.) Keynes humorously reports that when arguing for the immediate, undisputed morality of something, "victory was with those who could speak with the greatest appearance of clear, undoubting conviction and could best use the accents of infallibility. Moore at this time was a master of this method—greeting one's remarks with a gasp of incredulity—*do* you *really* think *that*, an expression of face as if to hear such a thing said reduced him to a state of wonder verging on imbecility, with his mouth wide open and wagging his head in the negative so violently that his hair shook. *Oh!* he would say, goggling at you as if either you or he must be mad; and so no reply was possible."[70] Most moral debaters and some of today's moral philosophers still seem to adopt this attitude.

To be sure, many contemporary philosophers reject "metaphysication" as groundless. John Rawls's *A Theory of Justice* (1971) has returned philosophy to the business of proposing moral principles and systems based on the claim that the principles put forward would best advance people's interests. Still, Rawls did not quite shake off the claim that all rational people would adopt the principles he believed they should adopt behind his proposed "veil of ignorance" (basically a rationale for the welfare state). Nor did he forsake the concept of "inviolable rights". Rawls's book has created a great stir among philosophers (much less have his very general principles influenced practical politics). Some of them have advanced different principles of moral obligation, opposing Rawls's, often with the tacit assumption that their particular principles and the concepts that support them should be accepted as self-evident.[71] By contrast, in the nineteenth century, Mill had gone much further. Rejecting concepts such as "natural rights" as metaphysical fictions, he based his political and moral proposals on nothing more than the suggestion that people would find the liberal principles worthwhile given the evident success of the societies based on these principles. This way of moral philosophizing is conditional—that is, wholly relying on other people accepting the proposed moral principles as a beneficial guide for action by these people's own standards.

Indeed, as not a few philosophers have argued, there is no ultimate, superior, or "foundational" moral truth—objective or otherwise perceived—that can decide on contested moral questions and resolve conflicts of value. Although people are predisposed to hold that such a standard exists, and attempt to persuade or are being persuaded on this basis, the actual process by which we try to make someone else view a moral question our way is different.[72] We look for a shared underlying moral view, a common moral denominator, with the target of our efforts—in the hope that such common ground exists—which we argue invites or compels the claimed moral inference. This amounts to convincing others that their set of moral beliefs is incoherent or inconsistent—that given what they hold as moral in other parts of their moral outlook, they need to adjust their views on the moral question at hand. Similarly, we try to convince other people that our moral view is going to produce better results by their *own* moral standards. In other cases, we simply convert them to our view, change their moral standards, by the sheer force of our personality and authority or by the weight of the communal creed into which we are socialized. Sometimes the contested moral issues themselves die away or lose most of their relevance as the entire social outlook undergoes change. Thus, if a common moral denominator exists, we share similar enough standards of worth, possess a strong charisma or compelling formal authority, or belong to a sufficiently close community of creed, the chances of moral persuasion or mediation between values are stronger. If these conditions are not met—and often they are not—moral disagreements and conflicts of value are likely to remain, and they tend to be extremely jarring and emotionally charged.

Semi-Floating, Partly Anchored Towers

People find the view that there is no objective arbiter between moral values, that there are no objectively right values, very difficult to accept. But as I have already noted, the objective-subjective distinction with respect to morality is a false dichotomy. This is because our core moral notions and precepts are sufficiently entrenched in and common to human nature to invite and expect agreement, while at the same time they are diverse and diffused enough to defy agreement to a still very significant degree. Many people are concerned that such a realization implies moral relativism and prescribes toleration toward values and practices in other cultures or in their own societies that they regard as totally abhorrent. However, as philosophers have pointed out in response to other philosophers, the demand for toleration in the name of moral relativism is self-negating, as toleration is relative and unbinding within a relativistic frame.[73]

True, liberal societies may still be asked to practice toleration by reference to their own standards. They have espoused toleration as a norm and value, initially as a prudent alternative to bloody struggles and later out of respect for the diversity of moral views and, indeed, also due to a creeping suspicion that there is no ultimate, "foundational" argument for deciding between values. At the same time, it is also in line with the liberal creed to eschew toleration when confronting values and practices that are starkly at odds with the liberal creed. In a famous historical incident, the British commander-in-chief in India in the mid-nineteenth century, Charles Napier, prohibited the burning of widows in funerals to accompany their husbands in the afterlife. A delegation of Hindu priests came to complain about this prohibition on the grounds that this was their age-old sacred custom. To which Napier replied: "Be it so. This burning of widows is your custom; prepare the funeral pile. But my nation has also a custom. When men burn women alive we hang them, and confiscate all their property. My carpenters shall therefore erect gibbets on which to hang all concerned when the widow is consumed. Let us all act according to national customs."[74]

Sometimes, a conflict of values, rather than being about the imposition of the liberal values on others, actually entails the survival of the liberal moral creed itself. This was the case with the struggle of the liberal democracies against Nazism and, somewhat less horrendously, against communism. More generally, Nazism figures as an emblematic symbol that raises some fundamental questions with respect to our subject and has served as an extreme test case in moral philosophy. It signifies the ultimate evil. However, is this not the view of the victors rather than that of the Nazis? Is there an objective criterion for regarding Nazism as immoral? Indeed, does Nazism qualify as a system of morality? I am Jewish of East European descent, my family on all sides are Holocaust survivors and the great majority of their dear ones did not survive, so I am anything but indifferent to Nazism. Our goal here is to clarify the nature of what we mean by morality.

Nazism was clearly a system of values, with its own particular definitions of good and evil. Whether it is conceived as a system of morality depends, as with all things, on our semantic framing. Nazism may even be claimed to meet some of the formal requirements of Kant's Categorical Imperative, as the Nazis not only regarded but also approved of the struggle of all against all as a universal rule of conduct. Furthermore, they regarded the merciless racial war in the service of their country as a moral duty and obligation. Adolf Eichmann, the administrator of the Final Solution, specifically claimed in his trial in Jerusalem that he had followed the Categorical Imperative.[75] Kant obviously would not have accepted the validity of this application, but this only highlights a weakness in his system.[76] It has long been noted that Kant's formal frame, like the Golden Rule itself, being nonspecific and "empty", might be filled with content that is very vicious indeed.

Furthermore, loyalty to the point of self-sacrifice to one's kin-culture group in a life-and-death conflict with other groups was part and parcel of morality in ancestral human societies, for obvious reasons, and it is still widely regarded as a virtue. For this reason, authorized killing for one's country in war is starkly distinguished morally from unauthorized killing, known as murder. Moreover, in the past, total annihilation of the enemy group—men, women, and children (except for young women taken as trophy)—so as to eliminate the threat once and for all, was the goal among warring tribal groups, and was fully sanctioned by their moral standards after the right purification ceremonies were taken.[77] A favorite example of a supreme moral truth in today's philosophical discourse is that killing babies for fun is wrong. I don't know how much fun was involved is such acts in tribal societies, and wonder what is to be made of the moral precept if no fun but only utility was involved on their part.

On the other hand, the notion that morality was about doing no harm, and fairness and benevolence toward others, always partly extended and has increasingly spilled over to members of outgroups. As forms of peaceful relations alternated with war in the interactions between tribal groups, it is understandable why this was so, at least to a limited degree. Norms such as the Roman *jus gentium*, a customary Law of Nations, crystallized in the ancient civilizations. Even war had to be just, although this moral requirement was easily met given group bias toward itself. At the same time, warrior societies throughout history regarded the subjugation or destruction of others and the spoils of war as the victor's legitimate right.

So what are the implications of all this? First, whether Nazism is perceived as a system of morality is a matter of definition. That said, its values and practices ran contrary to a very deep notion of morality as benevolence toward others. Such a notion has always been intrinsic in morality and has been increasingly developed and projected as an ideal in settled civilizations to all of humanity, almost in direct proportion to the greater benefits they saw from peaceful relations. The deep sense of moral revulsion and shock many (not all!) of us feel toward Nazism is based on both these intrinsic and developed cannons of morality. This is not a metaphysical, "objective" rejection of the Nazi system of values because, despite our strong sense to the contrary, no such leverage point exists beyond these intrinsic and developed notions. If Mill's efforts fail to persuade adherents of other creeds that liberal societies have proved the most successful in providing the goods they want, there is no other argument left to settle the clash of values that people hold dear and regard as being beyond compromise—except for the gun. This is not an original argument, as it is the conclusion widely reached by non-metaphysical, non-objectivist philosophers of morality.[78]

Vexing Moral Questions Reconfigured

If we cannot rely on an objective moral standard to judge moral values against, where does this leave the notion of moral progress? Like many other notions people have, it need not be dropped but ought to be reinterpreted non-metaphysically. Again, we should eschew the false objective-subjective dichotomy. Morality is a very real and extremely potent human postulate projected onto the world. It includes broadly shared common denominators, evolutionarily engraved in human nature by the logic and adaptive pressures of social life and social cooperation. It consists of a bundle of attitudes and precepts that serve this logic, which takes different and sometimes incommensurable forms between people and between different cultural traditions. At the same time, morality generally centers on the notions of fairness, justice, and benevolence toward members of the ingroup and, to a much more limited degree, also toward members of the outgroup. Furthermore, morality incorporates a most powerful psychological urge to see its rule established and its reign expanded as much as possible (particularly if one's own interests are not adversely affected).

From this perspective, morality can be perceived as an expanding project, an ever deepening effort to extend the application of our moral notions onto the social world.[79] Such notions and yearning became central to the ancient systems of morality, yet remained largely marginal to the harsh realities of society and politics. However, the more successful modern affluent societies have become in releasing people from the pressing, desperate pursuit of the basic needs of life and in advancing prosperity on the basis of peaceful relations, the larger the space that has been created in the public mind and in the political arena for demanding a greater implementation of the notions of fair sharing, or social justice, however conceived.[80] Rather than being "discovered" or "revealed", morality is a historically developing human creation in the service of social needs. In developed societies, moral notions and yearning now mainly take the form of liberal norms and the question of how they should be interpreted. Liberalism has acquired this dominant role because its precepts have been the underlying economic and political rationale of the successes of modernity. I hasten to clarify that what I mean is liberalism broadly understood, including, as we shall see, the two scions of classical liberalism—progressivism and conservativism—as well as modern forms of social democracy.

Hence the arguments on what exactly morality prescribes with respect to the social distribution of wealth, opportunity, and support for the needy. Does morality prescribe nothing more than doing no direct harm? Does it further require a safety net for the poor against hunger and ill-health? Or does it demand equal opportunity in terms of a starting point in life, or, indeed, perhaps a concerted effort to increase equality in the possession of property? Moreover, should similar standards be applied to foreign people, and to what degree? Is more not better by moral standards? There are conflicting values and concepts of moral obligations in such debates. Furthermore, there is a tension between good motives and the actual social consequences or results of the policies based on them. An age-old example, already highlighted by both Aristotle and Hume,[81] is the tension between the abolition of private property, and hence of property-based inequality, and the resulting loss of incentive to work and create wealth. Whatever position we hold on these and other questions, it is typical of our moral nature that we are inclined to regard them as rooted in a principled conception of what the range and limits of the moral obligation are. And yet there is no objective standard to decide between these competing notions. Each of them has roots in our psyche, shaped by the tension between egotistic and prosocial propensities, and the only general thing that might be ventured on this point is that it may perhaps be prudent to expect much, but not too much, from human benevolence. This still leaves quite a wide range within which debates on social policy, under any particular socio-economic conditions, take place.

Another, interesting, "expansion" of the moral realm is toward non-human animals. This is interesting because the evolutionary rationale that accounts for the emergence of morality is life and cooperation with other human beings, not with animals, and a major field of this cooperation was in hunting. Indeed, we are biologically adapted meat eaters—especially men with their higher muscle mass in relation to body weight and greater energy expenditure—a fact that, in and of itself, has no moral status, of course. Thus, the attitude guiding human relation to animals has generally been one of utilitarian exploitation. For all that, it would seem that a general compassion and sensitivity to suffering in human relations spilled over to form a moral notion that animals should at least not suffer unnecessary pains. This notion has expanded in traditional schools of morality such as Buddhism into a moral precept that living creatures ought not be killed for food or to serve any other human objective. At present, affluence, the increasing availability of substitutes, including, around the corner, artificially grown meat, and environmental considerations are increasingly impactful in the advancement of vegetarianism. With the dominant moral discourse in liberal countries now revolving around the concept of "rights", the question of whether animals, like humans, are entitled to rights has evolved into a subject of a moral debate.

The human-projected, rather than metaphysical or quasi-metaphysical, nature of morality and of moral progress impinges on other questions that have preoccupied philosophers of what morality is. One of these questions concerns our attitude to moral issues in history. In what way should we approach historical events that infringe our moral notions and sensibilities? Putnam, for instance, who proclaims a pragmatic, non-metaphysical conception of morality, has at the same time insisted that the fifteenth-century Prince of Wallachia (today's Romania) Vlad the Impaler (Dracula), who used to impale his enemies alive on a sharp stick (he is merely an example in the gruesome annals of history), is to be regarded as simply and objectively cruel.[82] It is difficult, however, to understand what the philosophical meaning of this statement is. People obviously have a deep and widely held notion that such acts are cruel, and most of them tend to shudder and feel deep feelings of revulsion and compassion when visualizing past horrors. Remember, though, that crowds, including women with their knitting, used to assemble to watch public spectacles of horrific punishment. More to the point, I submit that we tend to find questions such as the following as somewhat awkward and out of place: Was Alexander the Great unjust in conquering the Persian Empire or Persia itself? Were the Romans morally wrong to build their empire? After all, nowadays we tend to reject imperial rule as immoral. Similarly, should we not denounce as criminal the Mongols' practice of massacring everybody who resisted them as a warning for others not to resist?

Some moralists would state with conviction that we should, and of course sometimes we do. And yet why do we feel this sense of awkwardness when confronting such questions regarding the distant past? A number of philosophers who are skeptical about the stretching of our moral norms and precepts into the distant past have suggested that we ought to take into account the different conditions of past societies, which make the application of our own standards of morality unrealistic. As Bernard Williams writes: "The outlook of liberal universalism holds that if certain human rights exist, they have always existed, and if societies in the past did not recognize them, then that is because either those in charge were wicked, or the society did not, for some reason, understand the existence of these rights." Williams thus suggests a "relativism of distance", which he claims should not hold with respect to judgements concerning contemporary societies, which we can actually influence.[83] While somewhat contrived to my taste, this concept comes close to the view suggested here of moral progress as a human constructed project.

I suggest that since the logic of our moral precepts and judgments revolves around the practical realities of social life, we are highly agitated by questions that still impinge on issues that are in the heat of public debate. For the same reason, we tend to lose interest in moral issues that no longer seem to be of living relevance to present concerns and sensibilities. Thus, Nazism, Adolf Hitler, and the Holocaust, or the experience of slavery, or current cases of mass killings and torture, or questions regarding capitalism or communism are deep moral issues in our minds, while ancient Roman imperialism or Genghis Khan scarcely are. It is within this framework that a debate is currently raging in the United States on whether historical figures such as Woodrow Wilson, Robert E. Lee, and Christopher Columbus should be deposed from the country's hall of fame, or should be judged by the standards of their times and benefit from the "relativism of distance".

Conclusion: The Naturalistic De-metaphysication and Demystification of Morality

From ancient times onward, philosophy has been preoccupied with the question of morality. It has been influenced by changes in cosmological worldviews—regarding man, God, and the universe—because what we hold to be true depends on everything else we hold to be true given the evidence at hand. And yet, in recent decades, philosophers have failed to comprehend and assimilate the major contribution that the Darwinian revolution and the evolutionary perspective have for understanding major questions for which there were previously no answers: how morality came into being, what sustains it and perhaps also, to some degree, what can be expected of people morally. Philosophers of morality are in danger of backing themselves into the same corner as their seventeenth-century schoolmen predecessors facing the New Science and New Philosophy. Nearly two decades after the publication of his influential *After Virtue*, MacIntyre stated in a later book that he sees a need to correct his earlier work because he now understands the importance to moral inquiry of biology and of the behavior of other animal species. He criticizes philosophers for their failure in this regard. He cites Darwin, though it is necessary to comment that his application of the evolutionary rationale remains poor.[84] That aside, in nearly all of the books on moral philosophy that have come out during recent decades, Darwin and evolutionary theory are simply not even mentioned.

Partly, this is an understandable reaction when established disciplinary modes of discussion and intellectual premises are challenged. A guild resistance comes into effect. Over the last centuries, philosophy has had to give up on spheres of inquiry previously regarded as part of its domain of abstract reflection but later established as more empirical disciplines, such as psychology, economics, sociology, and even physics, earlier known as natural philosophy. Mackie has argued that moral questions are more fruitfully approached with the tools of psychology, sociology, and biology—indeed, of evolutionary theory—than by the traditional cannons of philosophy. Revealingly, Blackburn, who initially rejected the significance of evolutionary theory to moral philosophy, a few years later wrote that "There are no trade-union barriers in the pursuit of knowledge." Moreover, he expressed the hope that, given the developments in evolutionary theory, cognitive psychology, and other sciences, philosophers and their traditions would still have a role to play in the understanding of morality.[85] I think they will, but only after the whole field of moral philosophy adjusts itself to the new, revolutionary perspectives—and a profound change this is inevitably going to be.

Of course, no theory is immune to refinement, amendment, or replacement. That said, evolutionary theory is the most persuasive, incontestable, general framework we have for explaining the evidence regarding the sequence, diversity, and complex design of life. Quite apart from its contribution to the understanding of how morality came into being and what sustains it, the naturalistic approach to morality counters the "metaphysication" of the moral discourse. This point is not new. Nietzsche has already criticized the reliance on the lingering relics of a metaphysical—God-centered—cosmology that is no longer held. A more or less similar criticism was central to pragmatism and to logical positivism in the late nineteenth century and first half of the twentieth century. In recent decades, the philosophical reaction against logical positivism has greatly eroded the standing of the de-metaphysication argument. However, as suggested here, the reinforcement of the naturalist approach by the evolutionary perspective vastly enhances this argument. The discussion of moral norms and precepts as if they were inscribed in the heavens or set in stone on the human heart is itself a natural proclivity, a product of our mind's propensity to spread itself on the world, as Hume has put it. Furthermore, the tendency to believe that there are binding moral conclusions to moral debates is similarly a natural human propensity, to be understood by the social function of morality. Indeed, the expectation of agreement can serve us well in the social moral discourse. And yet, *philosophically*, such an abstract, "quasi-metaphysical" view of morality cannot be sustained by those who no longer hold that morality is embedded in the *logos* of the cosmos. There are still a few philosophers who so hold, and, as already noted, the plausibility of their claims should be judged in the context of everything else we hold to be true about the world.[86]

Thus, rather than constituting a skeptical rejection of the realist claims regarding the validity of the moral notions,[87] or imply moral nihilism, evolutionary theory challenges the realist "metaphysication" of morality. The insistence by most present-day philosophers on defining moral norms and precepts as objective, instead of allowing for a more flexible understanding of this evolved phenomenon—an understanding that would transcend the traditional objective-subjective dichotomy—has outlived its usefulness. Conceived nonmetaphysically, this means that our species shares enough of morality's naturally evolved logic of group cooperation to allow a discussion of morality as a universally familiar phenomenon, while also exhibiting deep, sometimes irreducible, differences. The shortcomings of the quasi-metaphysical view are similarly revealed in the endless haggling between moralists of motives, utility, and virtue.

Philosophers, and others—often poorly informed about the fundamentals of evolutionary theory—have made many false assumptions and misplaced objections with respect to the theory's claims and supposed pretenses. For example, evolutionists do not ignore the cardinal role of culture in human affairs.

Quite the opposite, they are the ones who seriously work to understand the intricate relationship between nature and nurture. They explore how cultural evolution has emerged from our naturally evolved traits and, indeed, in turn, has decisively affected our natural traits in what is known as gene-culture coevolution.[88] Consider, for example, the cultural invention of fire and its massive effect in reducing our biological machinery in the chewing and digestive systems. This made more room for the brain and freed much time, paving the way for further cultural inventions.[89] Or consider the cultural invention of tools that made our body build much lighter than that of our ape ancestors and cousins. In the same way, the natural evolution of morality has driven, and, in turn, has been driven by, the evolution of our species' social nature—in a mutually effecting, snowball process that made possible cooperation on a large scale. Furthermore, the interplay between nature and nurture continues, as cultural norms undergo constant transformation. It would be wrong to belittle the significance of either nature or nurture in this compound.[90]

The ancients believed, somewhat naively, that moral behavior ultimately coincided with one's own good. The adherents of the monotheistic religions were not as sure about this and enlisted divine punishment to buttress morality. As the belief in God's judgment increasingly faded away during the modern period, the question of what should compel people to behave morally came to the fore. Hobbes held that we behave so out of fear of social sanction. Hume had a rosier explanation, insisting that behaving morally was in our nature. Darwin closed the circle, providing a naturalistic evolutionary rationale that explained how the benefits and pressures of group life, which had become one of the chief traits of human adaptation during geological times, selected for prosocial behavior. At the same time, the evolutionary rationale explains why the incentive to cheat and free-ride the system of social cooperation is as deeply embedded in our nature. People constantly steer their way between these two behavioral strategies. This makes people both sincere and hypocritical in their relation to morality, with individual differences of course. Although morality, and "evil", are not etched in the heavens, and despite the fear of "nihilism", morality survives the Death of God, resting as it is on the twin Hobbesian-Humean pillars—interwoven together by the evolutionary process—of fear of social punishment and natural prosocial sentiments.

Are there no differences at all between the naturalistic and metaphysical or quasi-metaphysical view of morality in terms of our psychology and resulting moral behavior? This is not an easy question to answer, but my view is that such differences, even if they exist, are not great. Evidently, people have a strong tendency to project morality onto the cosmic order. Reasoned arguments about morality tend to take the form of deductive logic and claims of axiomatic validity. Testifying about myself and the mundane view of morality presented here, the sentiment of causing no actual and concrete harm and showing (confined) benevolence toward deserving people is a substantial emotional force in my psychological constitution and behavioral conduct. This also involves a concern for fairness, an eye for reciprocity, and a sense of duty that, like the rest, is (contra Kant) psychological rather than "reasoned". At the same time, I regard general abstract moral precepts somewhat less seriously and more flexibly than many people do, or profess to do, while I am fully aware that rule-based conceptualization is a necessary shorthand the human species has evolved to order and cope with the world.

Having laid the groundwork by clarifying the nature of both truth and morality, we can now approach the subject of ideology and ideological fixation, the sphere in which people's views concerning what is true and what is right about the world merge.

PART II

THE CLASSICAL IDEOLOGIES

Religious Ideological Fixation

Examined by a Non-Hostile Atheist

Ideology is the broadest framework our mind produces in which a picture of reality—propositions of facts—is weaved together with a prescription of values and norms, providing a manual for how society should be organized and conduct itself. It is a modern word, coined during the French Revolution, so some scholars reserve its use solely for the secular ideologies that have emerged from the eighteenth century onward. By contrast, anthropologists, sociologists, and historians of earlier times regularly use the concept in reference to the overall factual cum normative outlook on public life and politics that every premodern society, no less than modern ones, possessed. The premodern varieties were predominantly "religious". Indeed, viewed from the opposite direction, modern ideologies have been famously referred to as secular religions.

I have put "religion" within quotation marks because its exact meaning is one of many cardinal questions that have intrigued people throughout the ages and continues to do so. As two of the greatest, broad-minded scholarly works on religion, William James's *Varieties of Religious Experience* (1902) and Max Weber's *The Sociology of Religion* (1920), have noted, the diversity of the assorted phenomena that come under this heading defy a clear-cut definition. Rather than representing a fully distinct "module" in our mind, the phenomena and concept of religion have been recognized to be fluid, with various major elements of our evolved psyche going in and out of it, expanding and contracting in response to the changing realities of the far-reaching historical-cultural transformations of humanity.

In recent decades there has been a new wave of writings on the sources and nature of religion, informed by fresh insights and findings emanating from the fields of evolutionary theory and experimental cognitive psychology. Some of the most heated debates on the subject of religion have centered on its relationship with other major spheres of the human mind, particularly science

Ideological Fixation. Azar Gat, Oxford University Press. © Oxford University Press 2022.
DOI: 10.1093/oso/9780197646700.003.0003

and morality. We shall explore these questions, striving to combine the biological and historical-cultural perspectives on the evolution of the religious phenomena. We again seek to advance from a broad survey of familiar materials into
an attempt to sort out what in my view are the more valid and significant points
concerning the religious phenomena, with special reference to our subject—
ideological fixation.

Ritual and Magic as Primitive Science

The notion that the cluster of the somewhat shifting phenomena that are conventionally designated religion poses a problem and an enigma for the inquisitive
mind—moreover, that the religious phenomena conflict with it—emerged late
in the long time span of our species' history. Religious beliefs and practices have
been ubiquitous in all known societies, and they raised little doubts until the
advent of literate civilizations. Even then, skepticism mostly prevailed among a
relatively small minority of people. Indeed, some recent studies in experimental
cognitive psychology have elicited evidence that the religious modes of thinking
are natural for us.[1]

Correspondingly, the famous secularization of modern societies (more am-
bivalent in the United States) has been called into question. It has been argued
that this development mostly reflects a decline in traditional institutionalized
religions, which are, however, replaced by a whole new galaxy of "New Age"
cults, beliefs, and practices. Furthermore, polls show that the majority of people,
even in developed societies, continue to believe in God or in some "superior
cosmic force".[2] Most intriguingly perhaps, it has been widely observed that ostensibly non-religious people turn to all sorts of self-made rituals in high-stake
situations, from sports matches to more serious matters. They keep their fingers
crossed, or might wear the same (unwashed) shirt that they wore in a previous
match that ended in victory, or turn their cap in a particular direction, or otherwise repeat a series of actions and gestures they believe might positively affect
the outcome. People also resort to private prayers and vows, all in the hope of
recreating and securing success. I do not engage in any of these practices myself,
but, although a lifetime atheist, I recall I was not immune to them during childhood and adolescence. As there is no evidence that such practices change the
outcome of world events, at least not those which are independent of us—it is
pretty clear that they do not—all these acts are labeled as "superstitions". And yet
they are very common even among people who do not attend places of worship
or participate in the rituals of established religions.

So what is it that supposedly makes such beliefs and practices natural for
us? In modern times, from the seventeenth century onward, religion has been

embroiled in an often bitter conflict with science, and has become strongly associated with this conflict. However, as one of the pioneers of modern anthropology in the nineteenth century, Edward Tylor, has argued, the source of the
beliefs and practices that he and other anthropologists identified as religion in
pre-state and often pre-agricultural societies around the world was fundamentally akin to the quest for explaining the world that gave birth to science.[3] Extant
or recently extinct pre-agricultural, hunter-gatherer societies in particular are
the closest thing there is to the distant past of our species *Homo sapiens*—people
who are biologically us—stretching back tens of thousands and hundreds of
thousands years. It was during this long time span, the 95 percent of our species'
history that constitutes the human evolutionary state of nature, that our natural propensities took shape. In all hunter-gatherer societies (and later), people
believed in hidden forces that operated behind the phenomena. And they were
looking for and practicing techniques—activities called "ritual" and "magic",
with their appropriate instruments and props—intended to manipulate these
forces to their advantage.

In our vocabulary, the forces in question are labeled "supernatural", as opposed to "natural". Such a distinction was already becoming accepted in literate civilizations of antiquity. There was a tendency in them to distinguish
between the regular, natural, ways the world seemed to follow and the more
mysterious underlying forces, supposedly also responsible for the exceptional occurrences habitually attributed to and celebrated as divine, "supernatural", intervention or "miracles". At the same time, ancient researches of
the hidden patterns and mathematical order behind the perceived phenomena
were often, for this very reason, also mystics who engaged in mystery rituals.
The Pythagoreans, who influenced Plato, are a well-known example. Indeed,
it was precisely this quest for deciphering and controlling the "occult", the
hidden forces and order behind the phenomena, that historians, to their
surprise, have revealed motivated the Renaissance alchemists, astrologists,
and cabbalistic precursors and pioneers of what would become modern science. Most famously, in the late seventeenth century, no lesser a figure than
Isaac Newton was still preoccupied with the attempt to decipher the hidden
prophesies of the Scriptures and immersed in complex eschatological and millenarian calculations.[4] He did not see them as fundamentally different from his
mathematical calculations concerning the forces and harmonies of nature. It
was only during the Enlightenment, in the eighteenth century, that the effort
to distinguish between valid and fanciful claims of underlying hidden forces
that explain perceived reality—between science and "superstition"—became
the center of attention. This effort has been continuing ever since, essentially
predicated on the application of rigorous, collective, and institutionalized
standards of empirical evidence and verification.[5]

Tylor, endorsed by Darwin and followed by some other leading anthropologists, has suggested that Stone Age people engaged in a kind of primitive science. Clearly, they had an astonishing amount of knowledge about their natural environment and they developed elaborate techniques for coping with it. Going beyond more mundane activities such as hunting, gathering, and food processing, these techniques also extended to the attempt to decipher and control the underlying forces of nature and life, such as those involving the elements, fertility, sickness, and death. Humans are programmed to look for underlying causes, recurring patterns, and effective techniques, and this proclivity—a chief element of our success—knows no stopping. What we label ritual and magic were the main instruments of these attempts at control and manipulation. Ritual is the carrying out of a mostly collective, very strict order of actions, intended to effect cosmic forces. In a famous experiment, behaviorist psychologist B. F. Skinner demonstrated that this sort of behavior was older than humanity. He showed that pigeons that were given a signal followed by food at random timing looked for a connection between their pattern of movement and the arrival of the food. They began to perform a "ritualistic" dance to prompt the delivery of the food—became "superstitious".[6] Compared to ritual, magic is more associated with the active work of an individual endowed with secret knowledge and special powers, who in agricultural societies would become a professional shaman. Both ritual and magic were universal among human societies.

Quite a few present-day studies argue, mistakenly in my opinion, that what characterizes religion is that it is intrinsically counterintuitive, and that it has always been so.[7] However, science is also deeply counterintuitive, and its major twentieth century theories—the theory of relativity and quantum mechanics—are famously even more so. Moreover, absent the means of controlled experiments, people over our immense ancestral time span (and later) had no reason to think that the practices of ritual and magic failed to do their work. Like any other investigative and intentional human activity, they supposedly increased the prospects of success: rain often did come, the sick often recovered, women often got pregnant, and enemies often suffered misfortune. Under these circumstances, a difference between "rational" and "superstitious" practices, techniques, and instruments was scarcely felt. A long line of researchers have come to this conclusion. As Weber has put it: "religious or magical action or thinking must not be set apart from the range of everyday purposive action. . . . Only we, judging from the standpoint of our modern views of nature, can distinguish objectively in such behavior those attributions of causality which are 'correct' from those which are 'incorrect,' and then designate the incorrect attributions of causality as irrational, and the corresponding acts as 'magic.'"[8]

Furthermore, all "practical" measures—those whose effects are more clearly recognized in daily life—were taken side by side with the resort to the hidden forces of the environment and cosmos. By and large, with some exceptions, a similar non-neglect of earthly means also prevailed in historical societies, even in those whose religious concepts tended toward the fatalistic. Indeed, special theological explanations were called for to justify why people should not rely solely on heavenly deliverance.

The hidden forces that permeated nature in the eyes of prehistoric (and historical) societies came in various forms. Some of them were blind powerful effects or qualities of things that could be unleashed spontaneously or by human action, intentional or unintentional. Such forces were widely associated with taboos, "pollution", or, on the opposite side, with benevolent *mana*. As the world was full of dangerous forces and effects, and the need to avoid spoiled and poisonous food or a contaminated environment was a top priority, ultra-sensitivity and overreaction to such hazards was an extension of normal behavior and is evolutionarily accounted for by the behavioral rule of "better safe than sorry". Other hidden forces were supposedly animate and deemed as conscious and intentional agencies. These traits were attributed not only to animals but also to plants and to what we regard as inanimate matter: to distinctive objects in the environment such as the sun and rain, winds, mountains, or imposing rocks. "Spirits" is the common designation for these supposed agencies, not all of them assuming a religious significance. Indeed, a whole array of elusive animate agencies—benevolent, malevolent, or just willful and capricious—lurked in the surrounding environment: deceased ancestors, demons, fairies, dwarves, nymphs, crosses between humans and animals, magical animals, the list goes on. People widely believed they existed and occasionally reported encountering them. They still do. And it was practically impossible to prove or disprove their existence, given the supposed shyness of these twilight creatures.

As Hume noted in his *The Natural History of Religion* (1757) (sect. iii): "We find human faces in the moon, armies in the clouds". Like Hobbes in *Leviathan* (1651), chap. 12, he believed that religion was rooted in the existential fears and anxieties of human life, as people—unlike other animals—were deeply conscious of the suffering, other misfortunes, and ultimate death awaiting them. Evolutionary and cognitive psychologists have recently developed these ideas. As people's greatest threats during our long evolutionary history were other, hostile, people and animals of prey, we have become particularly conscious of their presence and hyper-sensitive to detecting them in the surrounding environment, above all movement and faces, even when they are not really there. Again, the evolutionary logic behind this so-called hypersensitive agency detection device (HADD) is that it is far better to be safe than sorry—better to err repeatedly on the side of caution than to fall victim to one fatal instance of neglect. Cognitive experiments with babies and small children confirm this innate natural sensitivity and hypersensitivity to anything that can be interpreted as facial and animate.[9] Our brain appears to possess special, highly developed, and overactive "module" or "modules" for these cognitive categories.

While ritual and magic were in a significant way no different from ordinary knowledge and techniques for coping with the world, they were still endowed with a special quality. As the cosmic and more local forces and agencies—lurking on the hills, behind the rocks, and in and among the trees—were powerful, mysterious, and often capricious, attitudes toward them were markedly different from, for example, those toward human agencies with whom people interacted. Relations with them were unequal, with people as the vulnerable side. They thus incited fear and respect, attitudes reflected in the solemn seriousness of the rituals and magic designed to cope with such forces and agencies and of everything surrounding them. This is the source of the strong sense of the "sacred" that is closely associated with the religious experience—deep awe toward the out-of-the-ordinary, superior, and powerful that needs to be handled with great care. The Aborigines of Australia, the world's largest, oldest, and purest concentration of hunter-gatherers to survive practically intact up until the arrival of the Europeans, inhabited what has been described as a "sacred landscape", permeated with hidden forces and alive with willful agencies.

In his *Meditations on First Philosophy in Which the Existence of God and the Immortality of the Soul Are Demonstrated* (1641), Descartes, following a long accepted distinction, stipulated that there were two different kinds of substance in the world: human souls and inanimate matter. Curiously, he even held that animals had no inner life or consciousness, that they were clocklike automata. The distinction between mind and matter has served science well, even though it has always been fraught with profound problems, most notably concerning the relationship and interaction between these two very different substances. Intriguingly, there has recently been a lot of research on the inner life of plants. The view that the dichotomy between the conscious and the inanimate—the mind-body rift—cannot be rationalized has been expressed by distinctively secular contemporary philosophers and, one may speculate, might still await a revolution in our understanding of the world.[10]

To remove any possible misunderstanding, all this is not to suggest that ritual and magic are tantamount, let alone equal, to science. Not even close. It is only to argue, as Tylor did, that, in a deep sense, the two phenomena, which have branched out in two different directions in modern times, are rooted in a similar proclivity of our mind: its drive to identify and control the hidden forces behind the perceived reality. Moreover, it is argued here that Stone Age people had no real means of determining that the properties and spirits they deemed to see around them in the forces of nature and life were imagined, or that the techniques and instruments of ritual and magic employed to manipulate them were ineffective. We shall return to examine the gap that has opened up between science and religion later in this chapter. But before that, we need to broaden our perspective, for "religion" during our long prehistoric past, and later, consisted of much more than primitive science.

Religion: Adaptive or a "Bug" in Our Software?

Another interpretation of the sources and nature of prehistoric religions was advanced in the early twentieth century by Émile Durkheim, one of the founders of modern sociology. Studying the large amount of evidence from Aboriginal Australia, he concluded that, rather than being predominantly about beliefs and deities, ancestral religion, centering on communal rituals, functioned primarily as an instrument of social cohesion among tribal group members. Some later leading anthropologists have expressed a similar view.[11]

This view has recently been given a new twist. Evolutionary theorists have been grappling with the enigma of religion, given that it appears to be patently maladaptive, supposedly consisting of both false beliefs about the world and costly investments of time and resources in futile activities: from the offering of sacrifices to the building of cathedrals. A widely held answer to this enigma in the evolutionary literature is that religion is an unintended byproduct of, a "bug" or a "virus" in, our sophisticated intellectual software.[12] It allegedly rides on our propensity to look for ultimate causes and the work of agencies. Like "bugs" or "viruses"—be they biological or digital—religious beliefs and practices are, according to this explanation, harmful for us. And yet the infected carrier—in this case humankind—might live with the error in, or parasite on, the system, albeit at a cost, sometimes heavy.

Some evolutionary theorists have advanced a different explanation, updating Durkheim with a Darwinian rationale. They argue that religion during our ancestral past was actually adaptive, in that communal rituals, a major element of the tribal group's shared culture, fostered social cohesion among its members. Supposedly, this led to enhanced social cooperation, as well as giving the group an advantage in competition with other groups, including war. Thus, according to this view, the investment in what seems to be senseless activities actually paid off in evolutionary terms, accounting for religion's survival and strong presence in our psyche.[13]

It is not (yet?) clear how it could be decided which of these two diverging evolutionary explanations for religion—maladaptive or adaptive—is closer to the truth. My own contribution to this particular question is to suggest that the alleged costs of ancestral religious practices among hunter-gatherers scarcely existed at all, or at least were far less than has been recognized by both sides to the debate. The examples that have been cited as a matter of course for the heavy costs of religion were not actually there for hunter-gatherers. Sacrifices of pro-duce to the gods came only after the advent of agriculture. The super-heavy costs in labor and resources of monumental religious construction—from megaliths to temples and cathedrals—as well as the maintenance of a specialized clergy, also came only after the coming of agriculture and the rise of states. Most people are not used to thinking in this way, but these two momentous transformative historical developments—taking off, respectively, from 10,000 and 5,000 years ago onward, the last 5 percent of our species' history—are only the tip of the iceberg of the vast time span of *Homo sapiens*. The overwhelming bulk of our natural propensities was shaped during our long past, the tens of thousands and hundreds of thousands of years of our "evolutionary state of nature", in which our species lived as hunter-gatherers. The revolutions of the more recent past, such as those generated by agriculture and by state societies, constitute historical-cultural changes. They represent cultural, not biological, evolution. While deeply interacting with our biological inheritance, they have introduced only a few significant changes to our biology.

Thus, what we identify as ancestral religious beliefs and practices were not only an extension of human cognitive probing and manipulative techniques; they were also not distinctively costly or harmful, and therefore not maladap-tive, during the long human ancestral past, when our natural propensities were shaped. Hunter-gatherers' rain dance ritual or the exorcism of evil spirits in-volved no special spending of resources, nor did these practices come at the expense of productive occupations, for they were mainly pastime activities performed in societies that enjoyed an abundance of free time. If so, there is no mystery to explain as to how religious beliefs and practices became integral to our psyche, irrespective of whether or not one holds that their galvanizing social effects were in any case beneficial and adaptive. Furthermore, as already noted, nor did hunter-gatherer (and later) societies neglect all "practical", mundane, measures alongside their appeals to superior forces. Thus, there seems to be little that was maladaptive in their conduct from this perspective as well.

The costs of religion have indeed mounted and have become very substantial during the recent past, in evolutionary terms, after the spread of agriculture and of states. As mentioned, they have ranged from the sacrifice of produce (and some-times children—even, rarely, one's own!) to the labor and resources invested in monumental religious construction, to the upkeep of a specialized clergy. It can plausibly be argued that religion may still have been adaptive under these changed conditions for a variety of reasons: religious practices may have had a galvanizing social effect in peace and in war; and/or they may have contributed to human health or higher fertility. (Remember: biological adaptiveness means reproductive success, the proliferation of genes, and those who carry them, through surviving offspring and other kin.) Note that there should not necessarily be a general answer to the question of religion's adaptiveness in agricultural and state societies—some religions and some religious practices may have been adaptive, while others might have been maladaptive. For example, religion is now largely identified with high fertility, but until recent times high birth rates were the norm irrespective of religion, whereas the greatest religious devoutness sometimes meant celibacy, as in Catholic Christianity or Buddhism. Moreover, a religion could spread even if it reduced fertility and survival if it was contagious enough to enlist new recruits. The bottom line, however, is that no matter how religion has changed under the altered conditions of historical societies, the roots of its strong presence in the human psyche may be explained by its negligible cost and supposed utility during the long "evolutionary state of nature", when our natural propensities were shaped.

People's desire for sweetness serves to illustrate originally adaptive natural propensities that have gone astray in altered cultural conditions. Indicative of ripeness and high nutritious value in fruits, sweetness is now artificially produced and harmful. Obesity, when appetite that was adaptive in an environment of food scarcity is indulged in a society of plenty, is another illustration. On a happier note, people continue to intensely pursue sexual gratification, even though effective contraception has made most of this obsessive activity irrelevant in terms of the reproductive success it originally evolved to achieve. Looked from the opposite direction, high fertility itself was hugely adaptive under the conditions of very high mortality prevailing up until only a few generations ago. Yet it has become, if not biologically maladaptive, then certainly a grave threat to human well-being after mortality has fallen, with the ensuing demographic explosion and given both the limited space and resources of our planet and the life options offered by modern society in terms of education, good health, and economic prosperity.

Such examples are a reminder that the blind evolutionary algorithm of survival and reproduction, maximizing the propagation of genes, has no normative status—moral or behavioral—independent of our considerations and choices; nor is it tantamount to human well-being, which we may judge by a variety of criteria. The evolutionary logic can inform us about natural human propensities, whose often ignored effects in the "everything is cultural conditioning" scholarly and public discourse we would be wise to bear in mind, but which are varied and often conflicting. While following natural propensities, we constantly adjust and choose from them, so that our choices better suit our changed circumstances, as well as, of course, our individual traits. Religion might originally have been either adaptive or a maladaptive "bug". It might have remained adaptive in agricultural and state societies, because of its galvanizing effects, or it might have become maladaptive, because of its spiraling costs. It might have remained "good for us" under modern conditions, because of its claimed collective and personal effects, or be judged harmful, because of its allegedly false concepts, emotional abuse, bad guidance, and sometimes bigotry and bloody fanaticism. Therefore, the question of how religion evolved as a bundle of natural propensities during our species' ancestral past, and whether or not it was adaptive then, is highly significant for our understanding of the deep roots of the religious phenomena. Equally, however, the religious phenomena need to be considered in the context of humanity's cultural evolution, the revolutionary historical-cultural changes that have transformed religion in many crucial ways, altered its costs and benefits (judged in terms of adaptiveness or by other criteria of the good), and, indeed, changed perceptions as to the truth of religious propositions.

There is a vast literature on the transformation of the religious phenomena through history.[14] While this is not a study of comparative historical religions, we shall dwell on some of the changes, as various threads of our evolved psyche have been weaved in and out of—have thickened, withered away, or changed their color within—what people have conceived and practiced as religion. However, before embarking on this voyage through history, we yet again need to broaden our perspective on the nature of the religious phenomena, past and present.

Ecstatic Elation and Transcendence

Together with both the quest to exercise a measure of control over cosmic and more local forces and spirits and the reinforcement of communal cohesion, rituals have incorporated other activities and experiences of high emotional intensity, including, very prominently, those involving ecstatic arousal. Ecstasy is a feeling of elation and transcendence produced by an increased flow of hormones like adrenaline, serotonin, and dopamine. It reduces the body's sensitivity to pain and fatigue, raises its energy to a high pitch, and lowers normal inhibitions. Such a hormone rush is produced naturally during outstanding bodily exertion, associated with, and intended to support, high-stake activities such as fighting and hunting. However, very early on humans found ways to produce it artificially, for the euphoric feel-good effect itself, through activities such as rhythmic dance and singing or by the use of narcotic substances—all of which are widely attested to in hunger-gatherers societies, as later.

Of course, dancing, singing, and narcotic consumption existed and continue to exist independently of religion. It is not within our scope here to explore the deeper sources of activities like singing and dancing, such as our special attentiveness to telltale orderly patterns of voice and rhythm or the demonstration of superior physique, coolness, and charisma in the mating game, in humans as among other singing and dancing animals.[15] All the same, in societies steeped in religious beliefs and practices, various behaviors, emanating from different sources, have joined hands and interacted with religion. Our natural propensities are not compartmentalized, but variably merge into one another in the complex test of life. The integration of rhythmic movement and singing into religious rituals, from Stone Age societies to the present, has reinforced the sense of spiritual, sometimes ecstatic, elation and transcendence of daily troubles and sorrows that has been widely associated with the religious experience.

Transcendence has (at least) two meanings that have been highly relevant to the religious experience. First, religion is supposed to transcend, reach out to beyond the perceived world. Second, it involves a flight from and above the troubles, anxieties, and sufferings of life and death, including the pains of frustrated desires (pains that are evolutionarily calibrated to push us into action) and the clashes and constant bickering of social bargaining. Partly, this latter element corresponds with the social interpretation of religious rituals, as people enter a state of consciousness in which they supposedly put their frictions and animosities aside, even if momentarily, and celebrate a spirit of togetherness and desire for communal harmony. It is impossible to miss these highly visible and very potent emotions in any communal religious gathering, among hunter-gatherers as later. Tellingly, singing and dancing in religious rituals are performed collectively, in unison.[16] Of course, in some cases, the experiences of religious emotional elation and spiritual transcendence can be very individual, even solitary. Either way, the quest for transcendence has been another major source of the sense of the "sacred", as distinct from the "profane"—the distinction Durkheim has postulated as the basis of religion. Some experiences of life and being have been set apart and elevated as qualitatively different from and superior to the mundane. Art, with its sense of the "sublime", has performed a similar role in human consciousness, often in conjunction with and in the service of religion. Love, sex, and eroticism, with their hormone rush and idealized images, on the one hand, and deep frustrations, on the other, have been variably perceived as either a major source of transcendence or the nadir of the profane.

The quest to transcend life's pains would become far more central to the religious experience as human societies expanded dramatically, beyond the small-scale kin communities of prehistory, with the advent of agriculture, the rise of state societies, and the coming of modernity.

Historical Times: Social Alienation, Religious Morality and the Quest for Consolation and Salvation

One prominent explanation for religion in the evolutionary literature of recent decades has been its association with morality. According to this view, religion was positively selected because it promoted moral behavior within the group by enlisting the overwhelming threat of divine punishment to offenders, thereby fostering mutually beneficial social cooperation.[17] However, unlike other strands of the social cohesion interpretation of religion's natural adaptiveness, this ostensibly plausible view cannot be sustained. The reason for this is that the association of religion with morality is quite recent. It scarcely existed during our long "evolutionary state of nature", when the natural adaptiveness of the religious phenomena (if such is assumed) should have evolved. For hunter-gatherers, the hidden forces and spirits around them could be willful and capricious, vindictive, or otherwise dangerous, and they needed to be handled with great care, but they carried little by way of social morality.[18] If anything, they tended to be extremely self-centered. Sentiments and notions of social morality were very strong among hunter-gatherers, as with all human societies. But they were underpinned, as we have seen in the previous chapter, by the logic of reciprocity and by the threat and actuality of sanction, imposed by either the offended side or the wider group. Purification rituals after killing, common among hunter-gatherers, is the closest thing I can think of for a relationship between acts of moral significance and the spirits.[19]

A significant connection between morality and religion began to form only with the advent of agriculture and the spread of state societies during the last millennia. And it has become deeply entrenched only with the growth of more developed civilizations and the corresponding rise of religions of morality and salvation ever since the so-called Axial Age of the mid-first millennium BCE. This latter development is widely familiar in the comparative historical study of religions.[20] The gods of early agricultural and state societies were still themselves immoral, as well as exhibiting the full range of human negative emotions and character flaws. What the philosopher Xenophanes wrote at the dawn of Greek philosophy with respect to the ancient Greek gods applied everywhere: "Homer and Hesiod have attributed to the gods all sorts of things which are matters of reproach and censure among men: theft, adultery and mutual deceit."[21] Indeed, reflecting the new sensitivities and intellectual unease, Plato went as far as suggesting that the poets be banished from his ideal state because they propagated such harmful "lies".[22]

People's relationship with the gods revolved around the rituals, offerings, and other forms of negotiation needed to avoid the gods' wrath and court their favors. Increasingly, however, among the human behaviors the gods might choose to punish, such as disrespect for them and hubris (wishing to be like the gods), immoral behavior began to creep in. The gods' accounting of such offenses was still haphazard and capricious, but it was beginning to appear as part of what could be expected from them and functioned as a deterrent. Scholars have noted that as societies grew in size and became more anonymous, the social surveillance that had buttressed morality in the intimate, face-to-face hunter-gatherer tribe of hundreds was no longer sufficient.[23]

Further historical developments would interweave morality and religion much closer together. State societies became highly stratified, with huge gaps opening between people in terms of wealth, power, and status. Emergent urban centers in particular saw the disintegration of the close kin networks that had supported people in the prehistoric past and still did so in the rural countryside. There grew the proverbial sense of social "alienation": of being alone in an indifferent society and of social injustices resulting from social inequality and abuse by the socially powerful.

The spread of literacy from a small group of clerics and scribes to broader (albeit still minority) circles had a tremendous effect. Literacy was the quintessential sphere of transcendence. It offered an imagined, rich, and boundless inner world into which people could withdraw and in which they could lose themselves in escape from life's daily stresses and frustrations. In addition, the written medium was a stable storage and sphere of communication in which the intrinsic problems of human existence—the inevitable pains and sufferings, unsatisfied and insatiable desires, and ultimate death—were articulated and pondered, and creeds of social justice to correct social evils were put forward and disseminated widely. The vague catchphrase the "Axial Age", when a spiritual transformation along these lines became evident throughout the civilizations of Eurasia, was the product of parallel developments on this landmass, the spearhead of human cultural development.[24] Around the middle of the first millennium BCE, the prophets of the Hebrew Bible, Greek philosophers, Zoroastrianism in Persia, post-Vedic Hinduism of the Upanishads, Buddhism and Jainism in India, and Confucianism and Daoism in China all projected quests for and articulated systems of social justice, personal ethics, and individual and communal salvation.

Some of the new spiritual and ethical systems were not religions, and the application of the designation religion to some others is questionable. At the same time, they were all variably, often closely, associated with the religious phenomena. Thus, the Greek philosophies were not religions in any accepted sense of the word, and their proponents were skeptical and critical of the Greek religion of their time. In the first century BCE, Cicero summarized these skeptical philosophical traditions in his *De natura deorum* (On the Nature of the Gods), on which Hume would heavily rely. However, partly the product of their scrutiny of the logical and moral failings of the accepted attributes of the gods, Plato's and Aristotle's projections of a perfect God would later be seized upon—amended and adjusted—by the rising monotheistic religions of the West.[25] By comparison, the emerging spiritual systems of South and East Asia were neither monotheistic nor religiously exclusivist. Moreover, they were primarily creeds, ethical systems, or "philosophies" of individual and communal conduct, whose status as religions is questionable, as they ostensibly did not involve deities. Nonetheless, as scholars have noted, the mass followers of each of these spiritual and ethical systems would in practice surround them with a host of folk deities, demons, and ancestral spirits; deify the great founders of the systems themselves; and intensively engage in rituals, including offerings, both in respect for these minor and major deities and to court their favor.

While differing widely from each other, the new systems of morality and salvation shared some broad concerns and emphases. Above all, they each put forward a comprehensive doctrine, manual, or code of behavior for individual and communal conduct toward the self, others, and the cosmos. This was a vast expansion of the religious sphere compared to earlier times, generated by people seeking guidance as to how to steer their way in a society and world that had become vastly larger and more complex, more baffling, more intimidating, and more alienating than before. Elaborated and codified through the medium of writing, the new systems took the form of full-blown ideologies, combining a projected picture of reality—here and beyond—with normative prescriptions as to how people should conduct themselves. People were called upon to curtail their behavior in compliance with these ideological systems and regimes. Islam literally means submission, but the same notion applied to all of these ideological systems—whether promoted by a benign promise of a greater good or, additionally, by the threat of divine punishment to offenders against the good.

Within the frames and boundaries set by the new ideological systems, they have all, in various degrees, advocated emotional and sensual restraint. Explicitly or implicitly, this has been advanced as the best strategy to cope with inevitable frustrations—aggravated by both the new dazzling temptations and social constraints of large-scale societies—and achieve individual peace of mind and social harmony. Some of these systems have preached full asceticism, universally or to the chosen few, a suppression of desires in a quest to achieve transcendence.[26] Although ecstatic elation—most notably through the use of collective singing and dancing, sometimes reaching a semi-hypnotic pitch—has remained prominent in the religious repertoire, it has tended to assume more tranquil forms. Sexual ecstasy in particular, formerly often part of religious experience, in forms such as Bacchanalias, fertility rituals, and official temple prostitution, has now tended to be eschewed and highly regulated in the cause of sensual and moral transcendence. Modesty in the relations between the sexes, applied to both men and women—albeit differentially—has been emphasized as a prominent aspect of virtue, the harmonious tuning to the deeper callings of our nature. Sexual ecstasy has continued to creep in, sometimes powerfully, only in some, usually minority and often persecuted cults. More conventionally, ecstatic arousal has often been embraced by mystic currents and cults and presented as a means for direct contact and unity with the divine.

Unlike morality, art was not a new recruit to religion, but its richness and sophistication increased enormously in state societies and civilizations. It was expressed in the religious sphere in pictorial and sculptural images, decoration and architecture, dancing and singing. Art's emotionally arousing and up-lifting powers elicited a wide range of affects co-opted by religion—the sublime, solemn, awe-inspiring, tantalizing, mesmerizing, humbling, and fear-striking are among the most prominent on the list. Even special scents were enlisted for effect. Suggestive language, oral and literary, most notably enticing fables, hymns, verses, and proverbs of wisdom, as well as personal charisma, were highly evocative. The artistic emotional repertoire, too, tended to gravitate toward more tranquil and reflective forms in the religions of the Axial Age, although dazzling impressions and "warm" sensations remained very much of the essence. Acceptance of, consolation for, and salvation from life's ills became central to the religious phenomena. A spirit of brotherhood was promoted, as well as, in various forms, the notion of an afterlife: as a means to transcend death, promise of a future better than this world, and medium of ultimate justice.

Marx, who more than anybody else introduced the term ideology into currency, regarded religion as the chief original ideology. He famously referred to the historical religions of consolation and salvation with which he was familiar as "the sigh of the oppressed creature . . . the opium of the masses".[27] Marxists have suggested that rulers and the socially powerful cultivated religion to numb the oppressed masses. However, the consolation and salvation religions grew equally from below and typically incorporated strong criticism of both social injustice and the abuse of power. Moreover, rulers and elites were as addicted as the masses to the opium, and, even when cynical, they were more often than not "superstitious" cynics.

Why So Potent?

A brief recapitulation of why religion is such a potent phenomenon is in order at this stage. While the elements of the proposed answer have long been suggested, it is important to note how they have gravitated in and out of the religious constellation and have changed and reassembled in the course of the human historical-cultural evolution. The "family resemblance" shared by the religious phenomena is sufficient for rendering useful our treatment of them as a distinct, albeit highly diverse, concept.

The oldest and most enduring element of the religious phenomena is probably the existence of hidden, mysterious, and powerful forces and agencies in the world around us, which are feared, handled with care, and negotiated with. Although they and their actions are concealed, they are allegedly vividly manifested. Indeed, their presence or lack thereof is intrinsically difficult to determine with certainty. They can be evolutionarily accounted for by the oversensitivity of our cognitive systems in detecting ordinary hazards and agencies on the principle of better safe than sorry, or be regarded as genuine, depending on people's overall assessment of what is plausible given the weight of the evidence and everything else they take to be true. Within the framework of the cosmological picture held by pre-state societies and early civilizations, the existence of such occult forces and agencies was a plausible assumption and highly potent reality, with major consequences for human conduct.

Thus, archaic cosmologies, which we term mythic, were everywhere alive with hidden forces and willful agencies, and projected intentional meaning onto the world. (If you think these cosmologies were implausible for their times, or, more likely, that they have become implausible given what we now know, first make sure you do not regard morality or beauty as metaphysically anchored in the cosmic order, along the lines we saw in the previous chapter.[28]) The search for purpose and meaning in the universe, for an explanation of what brought the world into being (philosophically: "first cause") and where it is heading, reflects natural human thought categories and processes. In the spirit of Hume and Kant (followed by Ludwig Feuerbach's sensational *The Essence of Christianity*, 1841), they can be regarded as part of the mind's tendency to spread its perceptual and conceptual forms onto the world. Nonetheless, they remain legitimate questions of paramount significance. The concept of a designer who would account for the apparent design complexity of much of reality responded to a genuine ontological puzzle. Historically, all these questions were more systematically pursued on the western side of Eurasia, whereas lack of purpose, chaos, and perceptual illusion were more assumed by the spiritual systems that came out of India.

Answers to all such questions were expressed in the narrative format, the unique cognitive device that has made it possible for humans to impose order on, and come to grips with, an infinitely complex reality. The prominence of this cognitive tool in arranging our impressions of the world into highly simplified yet very meaningful and easily memorable conceptual grids has attracted special attention in several fields of knowledge over the last decades: history, anthropology, literature, linguistics, philosophy, and cognitive science.[29] Correspondingly, there has been a heightened awareness of the strong biases in terms of content and form that characterize these meta-narratives. Contrary to the impression created by some writers, not any story, to be cultivated at will, can fill the function of an organizing narrative myth. To fulfill this function, the narrative needs to both address questions of fundamental significance to people and respond to some of our deepest natural proclivities. Heroes and heroism, love and romance, moral tales—these are among the universal themes that dominate the most popular narratives. The funny, tragic, thrilling, solemn, up-lifting, and epic are among the affects that most potently push the buttons of our attention and emotional responses. Therefore, our grand narratives tend to be cast in the form of these themes and literary genres, as Aristotle saw millennia ago in his *Poetics*. Indeed, recent studies have shown that "genres" feature not only in artistic works of fiction but are also all-pervasive in our supposedly non-fiction interpretations of reality. And the more remote from experience the human conceptual-narrative grids weaved to explain reality, the more they took the form of myths, with images and themes of "archetypal" nature playing a cen-tral role in them.

"Archetypes" is a somewhat hazy but still significant concept, which was popularized by Carl Jung and has been accorded a somewhat clearer rationale by evolutionary psychology. It refers to images, themes, and entities that are strongly imprinted in our innate psyche because of their universal significance. Our instinctive fear of snakes is an often cited example. Even chimpanzees that have never seen snakes react with terror when encountering them. Similarly, children's (and some adults') fear of darkness, or of monsters, is biologically embedded in us for adaptive reasons. In the human state of nature in particular, darkness harbored great dangers, and children more than others must not have strayed away from the campfires. Monsters are an imagined composite arche-type of all the features that we had to be beware of in animals of prey: sharp teeth and claws, imposing bodies, staring eyes, and often scales and wings. As Jung has argued, archetypes play a prominent role in our shared twilight sphere of reli-gious images and notions. He therefore suggested that religion was an intrinsic and a highly significant element of human psychology, which, for this reason, should be treated seriously and respectfully, even if it consisted of imagined objects of the mind alone.

Concerning myths, it is only in hindsight and given better empirical evidence and higher critical standards that they can be defined as such. For their time, they are better viewed as archaic expressions of the relentless, intrinsic human urge to account for the world around us, including cosmological and meta-physical questions that still lie far beyond the possible grasp of human under-standing. Furthermore, narrative myths relate to these questions in a language of stories that is naturally and popularly attuned to the inner grooves of the human psyche. Their great power is derived from their being easily understood by, and highly evocative for, everybody. When this is added to our bias for detecting agencies, we arrive at Robert McCauley's provocative but suggestive argument, based on psychological experiments, that for us "religion is natural and science is not". Ironically, Sigmund Freud, who regarded religion as a kind of compulsive neurosis and illusion, may serve to demonstrate the power of the myth. His own writings on religion involved stories that were as mythical and wildly fanciful as anything he attributed to religion, which, indeed, may partly account for their sensational public and cultural resonance.[30]

As old and fundamental as a cosmology teeming with powerful elusive agencies and occult forces has been the search for techniques that would appease, control, and manipulate them in people's favor. With this in mind, the meticulous execution of rituals, using the appropriate instruments and other paraphernalia, lest the rituals lose their efficacy or even become blasphemous, has been perceived as *practical* concerns of the first order. The same applies to strict adherence to rules and taboos, and, later, to more abstract points of doctrine. All these supposedly affect life on earth crucially and, where it exists, the afterlife. Moreover, as divine agencies have been perceived as so much more powerful than the human, while also being less easy to fool (although people have continued to try), it has been that much more vital not to mess with them. Those religious systems within which the fear of divine punishment has been more prominent have consequently tended to be less tolerant and more zealous.

Some elements of religious devotion expanded widely, or only emerged, with the rise of large-scale and complex societies. As we have seen, religious systems have provided a map and compass for navigating one's way in a bewildering world and have offered an escape from and transcendence beyond its stresses, ills, and misfortunes. They have celebrated group togetherness and preached social fraternity, spreading into and merging with morality, another sphere of huge emotional mobilization now joined to and reinforcing that generated by religion.

Religion as a cultural system—the phrase was coined together with many acute insights by anthropologist Clifford Geertz[31]—needs some further elaboration. The relative stability of cultural forms and people's conformity with them have long been noted. In processes known as socialization or social learning, the knowledge, know-how, norms, and other symbolic forms peculiar to a culture and largely shaped by its environmental challenges are imparted to its members at a young age, when brain structure is most elastic. Once internalized, cultural patterns are hard to replace and changes usually take place with difficulty, most notably in response to internal and external challenges. Recent studies in evolutionary and cognitive psychology suggest that our evolved capacity for learning from and teaching each other, no less than individual discovery and invention, is the great secret of our success.[32] The adoption of conceptual frames and grids put together by the collective efforts of others is the ingenious shortcut to knowledge that our species has carried far beyond anything known among other animals. The human world of ideas is a product of a division of intellectual labor over extended periods, whose fruits are socially shared and cumulative.

Furthermore, the same studies have demonstrated how deeply adaptive the routine procedures and customs so transmitted in traditional societies were to the challenges of their particular environments in vital activities such as the making of shelters, clothes, hunting and fishing implements, and food processing. They were useful without the participants often being aware of the exact reasons behind the elaborate sequence of actions and meticulous design minutiae embedded in these routines by the wisdom of the ages.[33] This is not to suggest that all social practices and customs were originally adaptive, as some anthropologists of an earlier generation insisted;[34] certainly not that all of them remained adaptive under radically changed conditions. Many traditional practices and taboos persist stubbornly as a relic of bygone circumstances, and some of them probably never had any adaptive basis. The point, however, is that social learning, with its huge benefits, has predisposed us toward a large measure of conformity to socially transmitted customs and practices, saving us the need to rethink and recreate each of them individually, an obvious impossibility. Note our remarkable conformity in the acquisition of our native language, whose tiniest nuances of expression and pronunciation non-native speakers find almost impossible to acquire after passing a certain age. Such meticulous conformity has applied with particular force to religious rituals and beliefs.

Moreover, some cultural practices are regarded by the culture group's members as central to group identity, far more significant than, say, cake recipes. In the hunter-gatherer tribe of our "evolutionary state of nature", shared culture and close kinship ties went together, and their integrity in the face of foreign threats was critical to individual and group survival. The evolved human propensity to rally around them has endured in large-scale historical societies.[35] Since any deviation from religious beliefs, customs, and rituals has additionally carried the threat of a cosmic backlash, sometimes in the form of divine punishment, religious symbols and practices have tended to figure most prominently at the very core of social identity. Institutionalized religions, with professional clergy, permanent places of worship, and codified protocols of creed and ritual—all of them typically buttressed by state authority—tended to make adherence to and conformity with the shared religious identity yet more entrenched during historical times. A special relationship with a patron god was common among historical peoples and polities. The Jews are famous for their self-perception as God's "chosen people", but with only a little weaker emphasis similar views were widespread even with respect to the national churches of universal religions.[36]

Rulers took special interest in religious matters, sometimes because of religious devotion per se, but more typically because religion, being the dominant popular ideology in premodern societies, was inseparable from politics. State authority everywhere relied on the legitimacy of divine grace, rulers were proclaimed sacred and occasionally divine, and religious unity, often through state-induced syncretism of local deities and cults, cemented political unity. While religious plurality that posed no threat to the state was tolerated, religious dissension presented a grave threat to the unity of the realm. With the exclusivist monotheistic religions in particular, questions of religious identity became a major cause of political unrest. Throughout Christendom and the lands of Islam, such questions regularly necessitated political intervention and, often, religious leveling by force. In religiously pluralistic and more tolerant political systems, the new monotheistic creeds were occasionally regarded as highly subversive precisely for their exclusivist and intolerant traits. Famously, Christians were thrown to the lions in religiously tolerant Imperial Rome, and thousands were executed in Tokugawa Japan around 1600, when foreign and religiously exclusivist Christianity was banned as a threat to the country's cultural integrity, internal peace, and political unity. To be sure, church and state have often been in conflict, and religions have occasionally been transformed or replaced either due to a foreign takeover or as a result of a voluntary change of creed. That said, religions have been among the most enduring of cultural forms.

Religious faiths are a collective phenomenon. Just as with languages, there are thousands of religious faiths in the world today, and there have been innumerably more that no longer exist. However, as with languages, the symbols and practices of religion are shared by a group and are imparted to, and communicated between, its members. Religions are highly contagious, especially within the group. Even when the practices of religion might be very individualistic, even solitary, as with hermits, they are still characterized by adherence to a shared creed and codes of behavior. As with all cultural forms, conformity to socially inherited shared beliefs and practices are deeply grounded in the human innate aptitude for transmitting and preserving valuable knowledge. This conformity is all the stronger in the case of religious symbols and norms, for the reasons explained.

Thus, Dawkins is largely correct in his sometimes criticized claim that young age socialization within the family and confessional community is the reason for the endurance of what he regards as religion's absurd beliefs and practices. We know that the large majority of people follow the religious (and secular) creeds of their parents and of the social circles within which they grew up. Indeed, it is always somewhat amusing to witness people explain why their native religion just happens to be the true one, when it is quite obvious why it is theirs. At the same time, Dawkins's explanation may underplay the innate element of the religious phenomena and attraction in general, as opposed to the adherence to a particular confessional creed. Furthermore, attention should be given to the fact that people do change their creeds—sometimes radically—individually or en masse. We shall get back to this shortly.

Conformity to cultural forms, all the stronger in things religious, breeds the uncompromising, zealous, and even militant devotion to beliefs and practices—taboos, rules about the "impure" and other points of creed and dogma—that might appear entirely senseless and arbitrary to outside observers but mean the world for the community of believers. Hindus and Muslims sometimes kill each other over whether it is pigs or cows that must not be eaten or allowed to be slaughtered. And the medieval Christian world was famously divided over one word, in Latin, regarding the nature of the Trinity. Examples are of course innumerable, and eighteenth-century satirist Jonathan Swift ridiculed all religious zealotry over seemingly absurd bones of contention by concocting an example that was not associated with any known faith and was therefore free from deep emotional identification by any party. In his *Gulliver's Travels* (1726), Swift describes the religious dispute between the peoples of the Island of the Lilliputians and their Blefuscu neighbors, thinly veiled representations of Protestant Britain and Catholic France. The dispute concerns the question from what end eggs should be broken before eating them, from the larger or smaller end. Bloody civil wars in Lilliput Island and wars with the Blefuscu Empire were caused by this doctrinal dispute. In Swift's fable, those who are devoted to breaking their eggs from the forbidden end are banned from holding political office and from publishing their views, and sometimes they become martyrs.[37]

Theology and Folk Beliefs

Institutionalized religions plus literacy—the rise of "religions of the book" or of books—have seen some divergences opening between elite and folk perceptions of religion, between theology and popular beliefs, which would run through and for the most part be successfully accommodated within the great historical religions.

Folk beliefs have centered on the existence of occult forces and superior agencies, on their occasional effect on the world, and on the attempt to neutralize, appease, and negotiate with them. Sacred or holy sites, objects, instruments of worship, and some people have been held to be endowed with special magical properties that inspired deep awe and needed to be handled with great care. Narrative epic myths surround all these beliefs. Ever since the Axial Age, there has been an increasing tendency to regard the "supernatural" forces as the guardians of justice and morality, as well as a source of transcendence, consolation, and salvation, in this or the next life. In the monotheistic religions, elite, theological conceptions were generally in agreement with these popular beliefs. By comparison, as already noted, in East Asia, deities, magic, and miracles were much more prominent in the folk beliefs and practices surrounding the great spiritual systems than they were in these systems' tenets and written scripts. Either way, theology had its particular preoccupations and concerns, largely extending beyond the scope and interests of the masses of believers.

Theology weaved together religious myths, symbols, and rituals into comprehensive, literarily compelling and emotionally evocative narratives, connecting the cosmos, deities, and humanity. However, as it grew in tandem with the emergence and spread of the written medium, which vastly boosted "slow thought"—the systematic formulation, development, and codification of ideas—theology became equally preoccupied with internal coherence and consistent chains of argument. Scholars have long traced the changes in thought patterns that took place with the transition from oral to literate societies. In the former, there were very strict limitations to the amount of information that people could store in their minds. Therefore, epics, fables, verses, and proverbs were the main, intrinsically memorable vehicles of grand narratives and religious content. While much of these survived into literate cultures, sustained abstract reasoning in prose was increasingly gaining weight.[38] Theology was progressively directed to answer the big questions, meet rising standards of validity and plausibility, and defend against doubts and criticisms, actual and potential. All these were increasingly in demand among the educated and intellectual circles. Theology thus developed in parallel with philosophy, another field that was emerging with the new literate culture. Indeed, theology and philosophy often merged. The main, frequently cited, distinction between them was that philosophy was supposedly not anchored to uncompromising presuppositions—to dogma—about the divine order, was allegedly free-thinking and methodologically skeptical. Famously, though, religious systems have differed widely in the level of their adherence to and enforcement of dogma, as well as in the significance they attributed to concepts versus practices.

Responding to changing sociohistorical conditions and intellectual challenges, theology varied from conservative to revolutionary. In the latter form, it has occasionally broken through the crust of older religions, cosmologies, and metaphysics, either transforming or entirely replacing them with new creeds. Note when such radical transformations take place. Religions can withstand, accommodate, and even be empowered by tremendous shocks to the foundations of the faith. The early followers of Jesus, for example, had to come to grips with the devastating reality that their messiah had been executed like a common criminal, in the most gruesome, excruciating, and humiliating of deaths. Still, they were able to adjust their theological outlook in no time. Research has shown how sects that acted on a prophecy that the end of the world was coming on a certain day and time quickly found explanations for the fact that the prophecy failed to materialize.[39] As with the paradigms of science, outlooks do not change by a refutation of this or that claim within them, because alternative explanations for the failed element may leave what is regarded as a generally sound outlook intact. Rather, outlooks are revolutionized and replaced when the challenges to them become overwhelming, when they cease to meet the conceptual prerequisites of those who hold them, and when more satisfying alternatives emerge.

This chapter is not a comparative history of religions, but here are a few notable examples. We have already cited Xenophanes' dissatisfaction with the immorality of the ancient gods, which, with the rise of Greek philosophy from the sixth century BCE onward, began to be viewed as unbefitting of divinity. This supposed fault was amended or at least adjusted by all the spiritual movements of the Axial Age, in both Western and Eastern Eurasia, as often as not independently of one another. Additionally, Xenophanes viewed the anthropomorphism of the gods, their portrayal in human terms (as well as the projection of them in animal forms or as human-animal hybrids in archaic societies where some animals were still regarded with awe), as intrinsically suspect. Such portrayals, and, hence, perhaps also the gods themselves, looked too much like a figment of the human imagination. As Xenophanes wrote: "mortals suppose that gods are born, wear their own clothes and have a voice and body." "Ethiopians say that their gods are snub-nosed and black; Thracians that theirs are blue-eyed and red-haired." "But if horses or oxen or lions had hands or could draw with their hands and accomplish such works as men, horses would draw the figures of the gods as similar to horses, and the oxen as similar to oxen, and they would make the bodies of the sort which each of them had."[40]

Such problems of plausibility have given rise to notions of a figureless, abstract, and, indeed, single, cosmic God emerging here and there in ancient civilizations, most seminally within early Judaism and among Greek philosophers. Eastern spiritual doctrines, as they tended to allocate little space to deities, were left surrounded by a plurality of colorful gods, demons, and spirits at their popular folk level. However, with the monotheistic religions, too, it proved close to impossible to eliminate anthropomorphic traits and agencies at the level of mass folk belief, as well as in theology itself: in Him, with angels as His helpers and heavenly court entourage, and, indeed, as concerns divine family members of God. Protestantism's iconoclastic break with Roman Catholicism, for example, was partly motivated by a quest to purge the latter from what the reformers criticized as lingering idolatry. As mentioned, recent cognitive studies of the religious phenomena have emphasized how deeply imbedded the archetype of "supernatural" personal agencies in our psyche is.

Furthermore, strict monotheism and the view of God as omnipotent and omniscient, matching the idea and ideal of the perfect, brought in its train a whole new host of intellectual problems for theologians. Aristotle (and Plato before him) reasoned that a perfect God must be motionless, as any change in Him, or generated by Him, would mean that He was lacking in something and less than prefect. This concept created a huge problem for Aristotle's Muslim, Christian, and Jewish "rationalistic" theological disciples during the Middle Ages, because it called into question the two functions most closely associated with God: a creator of the world and supervisor over its workings, not least in the administration of justice (to say nothing of the performance of miracles). The practice of offerings was rendered absurd by the rationalistic view of God, as indeed were all subtler forms of negotiating and pleading with Him. Rationalistic theologians now tended to interpret rituals as intended to purify people rather than directed at God. Adding to the problems, the concept of God that Plato and Aristotle bequeathed could be judged as pretty much redundant, as it was identified and identical with the eternal forms of the cosmos and little else, a pantheistic tautology or semantics. As the rationalistic theologians' views often clashed with folk perceptions of God or the gods as personal agencies, they sometimes deliberately obscured their message, which was indeed regarded by many others as being one step from heresy.

Even more problematic for the concept of an omnipotent and omniscient single God has been the presence of "evil" and the suffering of the innocent in the world. We have already mentioned this in the previous chapter. It has not been clear why God did not create a world that was all good. The common theological answer—that He has given people the right to choose—has been fraught with problems. It begs the question what the point of this, some would say sadistic, game is, especially as there is little escaping from the conclusion that ultimately He calls all the shots and is in command of all the odds. Predestination, as a solution to the conundrum, the belief that God preordains some people to salvation and other to eternal damnation, might seem to make the game even more senseless, and cruel. Indeed, the problem concerns not only people but all living creatures, which are not supposed to be given the choice to be moral. A. J. Mattill, a clergyman turned evolutionist, writes as follows:

> How could a loving God have planned a cruel system in which sensitive living creatures must either eat other sensitive living creatures or be eaten themselves, thereby causing untold suffering among these creatures? Would a benevolent God have created animals to devour others when he could have designed them all as vegetarians? What kind of deity would have designed the beaks which rip sensitive flesh? What God would intend every leaf, blade of grass, and drop of water to be a battle ground in which living organisms pursue, capture, kill, and eat one another? What God would design creatures to prey upon one another and, at the same time, instill into such creatures a capacity for intense pain and suffering?[41]

The all-pervasive, often horrendous suffering of the innocent in a world created by a benevolent God and in which He administers justice has scarcely had any good explanation, except, as a last line of defense, that His ways are mysterious, beyond the comprehension of people's limited powers of reason.

This latter argument has often been deployed by both the masses of folk believers and by those theologians who could not be bothered with the rationalists' concerns. Some rationalistic theologians attempted the argument, most famously associated with late seventeenth- and early eighteenth-century philosopher and mathematician Gottfried Wilhelm Leibniz, that God was constrained by the laws of physics and logic from creating a world that was all good. However, such a proposition conflicted with the notion of His omnipotent perfection. Even before evolutionary theory suggested a viable alternative to the argument from design for the existence of God, the skeptical Hume pointed to the existence of evil in the world as one of the weaknesses of that argument in his *Dialogues Concerning Natural Religion* (1779), a book he was careful to have published only posthumously. Attributing the following counterargument to Epicurus, Hume wrote (part 10): "Is he willing to prevent evil, but not able? then is he impotent. Is he able, but not willing? then is he malevolent. Is he both able and willing? whence then is evil?"

As Hume has noted in another of his books on the subject, *The Natural History of Religion* (1757), polytheistic religions may have provided more satisfactory solutions to some of the above problems. Manicheanism has assumed a cosmic struggle between opposing deities of good and evil. (The devil has variably performed a similar role less satisfactorily—both ontologically and morally—in monotheistic systems.) In gnostic systems, whose ideas have here and there penetrated the monotheistic religions themselves, people have been called upon to actively take sides and enlist in the cosmic struggle to purge the world of evil by doing good.

Subtle theological questions and problems scarcely preoccupied the masses of believers, with their devotional energies, without which there is no religious phenomenon, only philosophical ethics and metaphysics, or cosmology. This, however, is not to say that doubts regarding both the existence of the gods and the efficacy of the rituals intended to appease them have not been widespread among educated and lay people alike. On the contrary, such doubts have famously been inseparable from religious faith. Indeed, side by side with claimed rationalistic proofs for the existence of God, theology has turned the leap of faith in the face of doubts about the Unknown into a supreme test of religious devoutness. All in all, religious people have lived with various degrees of a split personality about faith, many of them adopting the view of "better safe than sorry" regarding religious commands and rituals. Even the most devout, although taking comfort in the belief that their departed dear ones went to heaven for eternity and were released from the pains and sufferings of their short stay in this world, still deeply mourned rather than rejoiced in this change.

Finally, it could and has been argued that the religious phenomena have basically been symbolic and metaphorical projections of genuine human ontological and ethical concerns, and that it is mainly from this perspective that their inner significance and value should be judged. Indeed, with the coming of modernity, both the religious ontological assumptions, or picture of the world, *and*, less noted, religious moral codes have been profoundly challenged. This applies most notably to the monotheistic religions, less so to the spiritual systems of the East.

The Challenges of Modernity: Cosmological and Ethical

The clash between science and religion has dominated the discourse on religion over the past few centuries. It has taken place mainly in the West for two main reasons: it is there that the rise of modern science, with its immense achievements, has taken place; and, on the other hand, it was in the West, and in Islam, that the prevailing monotheistic religions committed themselves to a particular cosmology, sacred historical narratives, and concept of God as a creator and ruler of the world, all at the theological-doctrinal level. Most of these theological elements could not withstand scrutiny in the face of the new qualitative and quantitative standards of evidence and the resulting notions of plausibility. For these reasons, the clash between science and religion in the West has been the starkest.

There have been innumerable accounts of this clash, and its outlines are all too familiar.[42] The tension between free-thinking, methodologically skeptical philosophy and customary religion is famously epitomized by Socrates' execution by the Athenians. But this event was quite exceptional in classical antiquity. By contrast, from the rise of Christianity to the early modern period, philosophy in Europe was subsumed within and subordinate to theology. During the early modern period, the church reacted with hostility toward, and carried out a fierce rear-guard war against, the Scientific Revolution, which was removing Earth, and by extension man, from the center of the universe. Furthermore, the emerging view of a cosmos governed by exact natural laws was inhospitable to the concept of miracles and to divine intervention and revelation in general. It limited God to the increasingly abstract role of the original "watchmaker" designer and creator. The people of the Enlightenment, in turn, preached freedom of thought and inquiry, rejected dogma, sacred authority, and received tradition, and recognized only empirical evidence and the judgment of reason as the criteria for genuine knowledge. As more rigorous methods of testing hypotheses and measuring cause and effect were being introduced, compared with more intuitive reckoning, the credibility of miracles eroded. This in turn undermined the great religions' foundation stories, which were increasingly viewed as myths. Deepening historical research from the eighteenth and nineteenth centuries on, including a critical scrutiny of the Scriptures, has accelerated this trend. Furthermore, the vast expansion of the age of the earth and the universe since Charles Lyell and Darwin has subverted the accepted religious chronology of the cosmos and the creation stories, while for the first time offering a natural mechanism for explaining life's design complexity. In Max Weber's phrase, a "disenchantment" of the world was taking place, as it progressively lost its magical and mythical aura.

Problems of plausibility and acceptability have also plagued aspects of the traditional monotheistic religions' moral teachings, a process that has drawn much less attention than religion's clash with science. Religious morality has increasingly fallen behind the changes in perception and sensibilities with respect to what should be regarded as fair, just, and "enlightened", especially among the more educated, fast expanding circles. The biblical prophet Jeremiah (12:1) long ago complained about the apparent lack of providential justice in the world. As other aspects of the traditional religious worldview weakened, this observation has become more compelling in people's minds. Indeed, in view of the horrendous atrocities and all-pervasive suffering and hardship in the historical and more recent record, the verdict of Maya Ulanovskaya, the mother of my friend Alexander Yakobson, has a strong claim to be included in the ten most important theological arguments ever: "His only possible defense is that He does not exist".

Most Axial Age religions responded to the problem pointed to by Jeremiah by invoking reward and punishment in the afterlife. Yet, not only do traditional graphic portrayals of heaven and hell in some religious systems, or of the reincarnation and transmigration of the soul in other, appear archaically crude; they are also in many ways at odds with modern moral notions and sensibilities. Both eternal hell for the wicked, that is, torture without parole or rehabilitation, and a transfiguration into a dog or a pig in the afterlife, seem to make divine justice inferior to current human standards of morality, and even to our worldly penal code, far from perfect that it is. The same applies to the still widely shared fear of divine retribution in this life—for example, in the form of a lightning bolt from the sky, or death of a dear one—as a punishment for blasphemy or sin.

Similarly, the exclusion from heaven of those who by circumstance happen not to be born into the right religion appears arbitrary and suspiciously contrived. Old and most powerful religious doctrines, such as that of the Original Sin which supposedly haunts humanity since its deportation from Eden, seem both entirely mythical and hugely unjust by modern standards of plausibility and morality. The powerful notion of a divine-human person experiencing the agonies of crucifixion to redeem humanity from the Original Sin and pave the way for its salvation appears by the same standards as at once morally incomprehensible from all sides and mythically monstrous. Attitudes to all forms of non-heterosexual identities and behaviors is another, recent example of the gulf opening between modern moral views and sensibilities and traditional religious precepts.

Thus, as with the Greeks of the Classical and Hellenistic era, the traditional mythical picture of the world and of the divine has been increasingly regarded as implausible and unacceptable by the educated, who, as a result, have adopted an increasingly secular worldview. The trend has been much stronger and broader during modern times than in antiquity, because of both the much greater challenge posed by modern science and the far wider dissemination of the new knowledge and outlook through the massively more extensive educational systems and other channels of communication offered by modern society. Secularization has been a "paradigm shift", as sweeping as the Axial Age, and it has been similarly caused by a radical transformation of both our understanding of the cosmos and of our normative sensibilities.

While I believe this brief historical and intellectual outline is generally representative, to gain a more complete picture we now need to cross to the other side and view the modern religious phenomena from within. For just as our outlook on the world in general, so modern religious perspectives, and perspectives on the religious phenomena, have not remained static either. They too have responded to the revolution in how we view the world since the advent of modernity, as well as to the changes in our moral notions.

Religion's Endurance and Adaptation

The clash between Christianity and science in their shared home in the West has had a powerful cultural and public resonance. The Catholic Church in particular, finding its traditional percepts threatened from the sixteenth and seventeenth century on, reacted violently when and where it could. Its trial of Galileo Galilei for advocating the heliocentric view of the world committed the Catholic Church to an erroneous cosmology and set it against experimental science. The Church remained sullen toward science and everything that surrounded it until well into the twentieth century. On the whole, Protestantism was far more open to the Scientific Revolution and largely accommodated its views of the cosmos and God accordingly. Many Protestants were content with leaving Him mainly with His role as the creator and original "watchmaker" designer and guarantor of the moral order. However, the Darwinian Revolution has generated a far stronger resistance, because it has established a picture of life and complexity that has undermined God's main remaining cosmic attribute. Perhaps the most significant backlash has taken place in the United States, from the "Monkey Trial" (1925) on. The "fundamentalist" groups within the Evangelical movement, undergoing a powerful revival in recent decades, have stepped up their struggle against evolutionary theory. They espouse a staunchly traditionalist view of religion, whereby the creation and historical narratives of the Scriptures are held to be true factual accounts of actual events.

As is well known, the United States is an exception within the developed world in having such a stark public and political conflict between religion and science alive and kicking. The fundamentalist campaign has sparked a fierce counteroffensive by the so-called New Atheists, such as Richard Dawkins, Christopher Hitchens, Daniel Dennett, and Sam Harris, who have set out to defend science, most notably evolutionary theory, from attempts to censor it in the educational system or bracket it as one competing theory, side by side with creationism. In the process, the New Atheists have pointed out how shaky and untenable many of the fundamentalists' claims in the scientific domain are. They have also insisted on the moral failings of, and positive damage done to individuals and communities by, traditional religious teachings and practices. Moreover, they tend to regard religion as an affront to human intelligence and dignity, and exhibit a scarcely veiled scorn as to how obstinately stupid people can be.[43]

The New Atheists signify a growing legitimization of the designation "atheism" in the American public sphere, where until recently it used to have an extremely negative resonance and was synonymous with "godless" immorality. I am an atheist myself, and share in the defense of science as the key to truth and cornerstone of the tremendous achievements of modern civilization. I, too, am often variably amused and incensed by many religious beliefs and practices. At the same time, I differ from the New Atheists on various grounds. In the first place, some of them are distinguished evolutionists who explain religion, plausibly, as a built-in "bug" in or "virus" on our sophisticated biological and cultural software. However, if religion is indeed so deeply grounded, it may be a bit futile to attempt to mock it out of existence or to convince the masses of believers by a frontal assault that what they hold dear is a bundle of silly superstitions. There appears to be some contradiction here. Threats to the freedom of science should surely be opposed, and there is great value to articulating a clear intellectual platform for this struggle. That said, I am perhaps more sanguine than some in assessing the fundamentalist threat to scientific advance in the United States. (And yes, I am aware of much-cited examples to the opposite, but overall still do not believe, maybe wrongly, that they are going to change the broader picture.) Of course, religion has become a major element in the broader ideological and political divide in the United States, which makes it all the more contentious.[44]

Finally, some of the New Atheists declare that while mainly fighting the virulent attack on science, they leave aside—though they are not indifferent to—what they regard as the less- or non-harmful expressions of religion. As a result, they direct their fire almost exclusively at the more traditionalistic manifestations of religion, and rightly so, given their self-assigned task. However, precisely for this reason, they largely overlook the diversity of the modern religious experience, thereby limiting our understanding of the religious phenomena in general.

Indeed, religious responses to the sweeping challenge that modernity has presented to both the traditional religious picture of the world and traditional religious morality has ranged across a wide spectrum. There is the "funda-mentalist" naive and/or defiant adherence to the so-called literal truth of the Scriptures. Next, at a higher level of sophistication, there is the view that there should be no quarrel between religion and modern scientific knowledge. One such line of argument follows the older theological claim that the traditional narratives and moral message of religion were adapted by divinity to humanity's level of knowledge and understanding at the time. The Jewish rabbinic sages had widely adopted this view by the medieval period: דיברה תורה כלשון בני אדם ("The Torah speaks in the language of people"). Medieval Christian theologians expressed a similar view: *Scriptura humane loquitur* and the doctrine of "di-vine accommodation". In this view, there is no more point in attacking religion as fictitious on account of its patently erroneous cosmologies than there is in rejecting science for the long string of its past false or primitive theories. Not only the picture of the world but also the divine message is progressively re-vealed to humankind in its journey toward truth and morality. Researchers of re-ligion have widely noted the trend within the historical world religions to adopt more benign moral norms during the centuries and millennia, and this process continues, with regressions and exceptions, of course.

Another religious response to the challenge of modern science and outlook has been the removal of religion from ontological-cosmological claims and, more emphatically than before, also from the test of human reason. The seventeenth-century mathematician, scientist, and Catholic thinker Blaise Pascal expressed the view that religion is a matter of the heart, not of reason. In the wake of the Enlightenment, in the first half of the nineteenth century, theologian Søren Kierkegaard similarly revived the medieval doctrine according to which the hallmark of faith in a perfect God is the willingness to embrace the Absurd, the seeming improbabilities of the religious message, in a "leap of faith". As he saw it, all speculations about God by inherently limited human reason, whether they come from a secular perspective or from a religious one, in defense, are pitiful child's play that can never measure up to His infinite wisdom and goodness.

A withdrawal from claims about the cosmos and deity has also characterized the so-called modernists in religion. Advancing further along paths charted by "rationalistic" medieval theologians, modernists regard the religious narratives as symbolic and metaphorical expressions of profound inner moral truths, as a guide, offered in the popular language of narrative and myth, for finding a virtuous way in the world. Some rationalists and modernists have overtly or covertly regarded the concept of God as little more than a symbolic artifact that people need as something to rely on, cosmologically and ethically.[45] (For a comparison from the opposite side, think about the cults of so-called Satan worshippers. They pin their celebration of antisocial behavior and rebellion against accepted morality—often also involving wild and violent sex—on this symbolic figure.)

In the churches of some north European countries, the modernist view has become sufficiently common to warrant fictitious dialogues such as the following in the episode "The Bishop's Gambit" in the immortal British television satire *Yes, Prime Minister* (1986):

- The Church wants to maintain the balance [within itself].
- What balance?
- Between those who believe in God and those who don't.
- Is there anyone in the Church who doesn't?
- Oh, yes. Most of the bishops. . . .
- What's a modernist in the Church of England?
- Ah, well, the word "modernist" is code for non-believer.
- You mean an atheist?
- No, no. An atheist couldn't continue to draw his stipend, so when they stop believing in God they call themselves modernists. . . .
- Does he [the candidate for bishop] believe in Heaven and Hell?
- Of course not.
- The virgin birth? The resurrection?
- No, nothing like that. . . .
- The Church is run by theologians.
- So?
- Well, theology is a device for enabling agnostics to stay within the Church.

And with respect to the "traditionalist" candidate:

- What's wrong with him?
- Well, I have heard say that he's an extremist.
- You mean he believes in God?

For modernists, the concept of God has variably changed its substance and semantics. Distancing themselves from the "literal truth" of the Scriptures, many of them tend to refrain from ascribing any attribute to the Unknown. This would classify them as being somewhere on the "agnostic" range in current parlance. However, modernists typically eschew this label and seek to use a language that would be as respectful as possible of both the traditional interpretation of the religious historical and cultural tradition within which they operate and the more traditionalist elements within their religious communities. Moreover, God is probably more than a pure metaphor for the majority of modernists, figuring somewhere between an agency and the ultimate rationale of the cosmic and moral order. Sixteenth-century Protestant reformist John Calvin pointed to the natural, universal *sensus divinitatis* that people possess as yet another proof of His existence. Whereas he held that there was only one true and legitimate expression of the sense of God, modernists are inclined to the view, formulated by the post-Enlightenment German theologian Friedrich Schleiermacher, that all religions are various cultural-historical manifestations of a single, deeper sentiment and approximations of a profound truth.[46] In turn, this implies much greater religious toleration. In that most religious modern society, the United States, some 90 percent of the people today are reluctant to assign a unique status to any religion as "true", and they believe that good persons of other faiths can also go to heaven.[47]

Thus, there is a two-level discourse in the modernist religious currents with respect to both traditional beliefs and God. This is due partly to the built-in tension between tradition and modern concepts, and partly to a genuine ambiguity about how God and His role should be conceived. Some critics regard this two-level discourse as a hypocritical double talk, or an evasion of the issue. Dawkins's antagonists from the religious side respond to his probing by mocking the view that they believe in God as a bearded old man sitting in the sky. Dawkins, in turn, holds that they refuse to stand behind the familiar tenets of religion and, perhaps even more important, that they cannot escape the meaninglessness of what they actually do believe in.[48] However, precisely those who maintain that the religious phenomena are projections of the human mind and are most plausibly understood in naturalistic and historical-cultural terms should exhibit greater sensitivity to the plurality of forms, constant fluctuations, and intrinsically unresolved tensions that mark these phenomena.

Critics of religion who come from a scientific or philosophical background typically regard religion as a fundamentally cognitive outlook and, hence, as a cognitive mistake. Certainly, historical religions incorporated strong factual propositions about the cosmos and deities, and many of their followers still do, sometimes promoting them militantly. A great deal of this outlook can now be demonstrated to be deeply implausible. And yet, the religious phenomena are very far from being reducible to, or perhaps even from being primarily about, a cognitive outlook. Evolutionary theory in fact suggests why intellectual concepts and the pursuit of truth are typically not people's first priority. For one, as we have seen, the affirmation of group identity and solidarity has always been a central element of the religious phenomena. Hence the heated defense of traditional narratives that we have been witnessing across the monotheistic religions. It is both a function of these narratives' deep, "warm", emotive force within their particular religious-cultural traditions and of a rallying-around-the-flag effect in response to what is perceived by the religious community members as grave threats to their identity and coherence.

Identification with the community of faith as a bulwark against an alien world has been a major feature of all the spiritual movements that emerged in the large-scale societies of the Axial Age. The same promise of a supra-egoistic solidarity remains one of the most enticing attractions of religious communities. Furthermore, such communities offer an antidote to the pervasive feeling of social loneliness widely reported by people as an existential condition of modern mass society. The special role of religion in the modern United States has drawn much scholarly attention, and can be largely explained along these lines. In an immigrant country with weaker kin-culture bonds of solidarity on a national scale, people have tended to rely more on their communities of descent, which have often been marked by a shared denomination and whose congregations have doubled as centers of communal gatherings.[49] Furthermore, the more the economic-social system has been geared toward a "faceless" market competition, the greater the sense of social "alienation". Marx was far from being entirely wrong, of course.

Moreover, in all modern societies, as well as in traditional ones affected by the pressures of modernization, religions took the form of spiritual opposition to the dominance of materialistic, individualistic and hedonistic values. This has been an old stance, central to both religious creeds and secular philosophies from antiquity onward. Both have rejected the excessive pursuit of such values as intrinsically frustrating and self-defeating. The same critique has resurfaced with renewed vigor in response to the traits of the modern, secular and affluent world. However, while this perspective on life and virtue has had a variety of secular expressions, on the left as well as on the right, it has been intrinsic to practically *all* the major religious creeds.

Here again we have the quest for a "spiritual" transcendence of the mundane— a rise above Sisyphean desires and disappointments, stifling routines and social conflicts—a quest that people continue to express, in some ways with even greater force, in our societies of plenty. The pursuit of ecstatic elation widely takes forms such as narcotic consumption, ecstatic dancing, and singing and promiscuous sex—"sex, drugs, and rock and roll". However, these forms of ecstatic trance often end with a feeling of emptiness and turn out to conflict with the quest for transcendence. Indeed, while in some ways traditional religious attitudes to sexuality have fallen hopelessly behind modern realities, most notably with respect to female (and non-heterosexual) sexuality, the religious message of sexual restraint as part and parcel of virtue has remained a source of attraction. The creation and consumption of art are celebrated as another, benign, form of spiritual elation and transcendence. But religious faith, gathering, and ritual have a much broader popular appeal than art.

Some would argue that religion is a more popular kind of addiction; whether it is a benign or malign one depends on its particular expressions, as well as on one's point of view. Side by side with criticisms of religious doctrines' harmful effects on people—of oppression, suppression, intimidation, and other forms of emotional abuse—there is a substantial body of psychological and medical data suggesting that "religion is good for you", as religious people reportedly have a stronger sense of meaning, communal support, harmony with the world, and optimism.[50] True, the monotheistic religions in particular have often been associated with aggressive and murderous militancy. However, my studies of war suggest that religious motives in past history tended to be more of a "superstructure" over more mundane causes of warfare, in what used to be a very bellicose world of conquest and pillage regardless of religion.[51] Furthermore, religion's role in charity work for the poor and weak and in preaching peace and brotherly love was always at least as prominent, and it tends to supersede religious militancy in modernized societies. One study has found that "religious attendance relates to generosity worldwide. Religious and the secular [are] more charitable if they attend services."[52] Indeed, some of the established churches have adopted attitudes that have earned them the label "religious socialism". On the other hand, religious people in the United States have been found to be more prone to racist attitudes and to bigotry toward outgroup people, though these attitudes have been on the decline among them, too, over recent decades, in line with changing social attitudes.[53]

People continue to express a strong need for a comprehensive framework that would impose order on and provide meaning to what they experience as a chaotic and anomic reality. Many yearn for guidance as to how to work in the world and achieve virtue, and are willing, even eager, to submit to regimes and codes of belief and behavior that offer such guidance. As noted earlier, religious belief should not be viewed solely or even primarily in cognitive terms, and as a cognitive mistake. I have found this strikingly expressed by Linor Abargil, the Israeli beauty queen who won the Miss World beauty pageant in 1998. She became even more famous when she openly revealed how she had been raped, and launched a public campaign against sexual violence. Later in life, Abargil embraced Orthodox Judaism. This is what I read in an interview with her in an Israeli newspaper: "Even if one day it is proven to me that everything was rubbish and that there is no heaven and no personal providence, I would still say that it was worthwhile living this life in modesty, observe the Shabbat, cover my head and maintain the purity of the family." Interviewer: "Why was this worthwhile?" Abargil: "Because I had no life before accepting this way of life. I was in hell."[54]

There is extensive interest and adoption in the West of Eastern spiritual systems, most notably the spiritual strands of Hinduism and Buddhism, as well as of a great variety of so-called New Age cults and beliefs. They have had the advantage of being less encumbered by dogmatic and coercive cosmological baggage, as well as being more attuned to modern liberal sensibilities, as they are tolerant and aim at individual salvation through enlightenment regarding the proper attitude to life, society, and the cosmos. They can still be classified within the family of (religious) faiths or creeds, rather than ethical and practical philosophy, because of their mass popular appeal. This appeal involves a variety of folk cosmologies, folk physics, folk anatomy, and folk medicine; evocative mythical narratives; and occult and mysterious powers (e.g., karma, energies). All these are understood either more metaphorically or more literally, with practices variably interpreted as rituals and/or spiritual-meditative exercises. A variety of magical devices (charms and other protective or enabling objects), healing practices, and future-telling techniques (astrology, reading in playing cards, tea leaves, coffee grounds, hand palms, and numerous others) are widely resorted to. Given the state of our knowledge and the best empirical evidence, most of these can now be judged to be superstitions, while very few await further research. This, however, does not mean that they do not often help people through a "placebo effect". As often, though, they get people to waste time and money on useless or positively harmful illusions.

The main emphases in many of these contemporary trends have been on the moral and communal dimensions of religion, spiritual transcendence, and a behavioral guidance toward virtue. Religion is conceived or felt by many—more or less consciously or explicitly—as the most effective, tradition-grounded, framework for achieving all these as a social reality. The relationship with deities and occult forces, while barely disappearing, has been variably weakened, abstracted, and otherwise redefined, or relegated to the level of folk beliefs. There is some shedding off, and withdrawal from, the cosmological aspects of religion as archaic and immaterial.[55] Some scholars insist that the belief in personalized agencies is so strongly embedded in us that it constitutes the bedrock of religion and is unlikely to cease to do so. Maybe. Perhaps the answer to this question is not a clear-cut yes or no, and we might see such beliefs remaining in a much weaker forms, or witness the growth of spiritual systems that lie on the verge of our historically framed conception of "religion". Time will tell.

Religious-Atheistic Exchanges

Like Weber, I am "religiously unmusical" entirely—as far as sharing in religious beliefs and sentiments, old or new, is concerned—while, at the same time, being very curious intellectually toward, and capable of emphatic understanding of, the religious experience and attraction. I assume very few religious people of the more traditional brands would appreciate my understanding, which is indeed not a "defense" of (or an attack on) religion but an intellectual exploration of major human phenomena. So here are some further arguments and counterarguments in the religious-atheistic exchange.

One religious argument is that science and religion are two separate and unconnected domains: the one deals with facts, the other with beliefs. However, as we saw in the previous chapter, the word "belief" is confusedly used to describe both views about facts in the world and choices of values people uphold. To the extent that religion is conceived purely as a system of values and norms—probably still a view shared by only a small minority—there is indeed no clash between religion and our scientifically informed knowledge of the world. However, for most religious people, religion does incorporate at least some views about agencies and the cosmological order.

A variation on the previous argument is that while religion indeed involves factual propositions, they are of the kind that lies beyond empirical observation and verification, or the domain of science. Traditionally, these are known as "metaphysical" propositions, speculations about the essence of being that is not merely unknown but unknowable, which is not to say that it is not there and perhaps highly significant. Metaphysics comes in both secular and religious forms. Some critics have argued that religious metaphysical beliefs are not only dogmatic but are also especially conducive to the most fanciful ideas about imagined beings. Why not believe in a flying teapot circling the sun, asked renowned philosopher Bertrand Russell (surprisingly, at least to this author, an acute psychologist and sociologist of religion); or in a flying spaghetti monster, in the version popularized by Dawkins.[56] Indeed, it is difficult to deny that religions incorporate what would seem to be some very bizarre untestable propositions as part and parcel of their systems of belief and historical traditions, which have come to be seen as even more bizarre within our current understanding of the world. Furthermore, the untestable beliefs of competing religious systems—which are often accorded the status of dogma—awkwardly conflict with each other. As the sixteenth-century political philosopher Jean Bodin has put it, the diversity of conflicting religious propositions constitutes their own refutation—"all are refuted by all".[57]

Still, as we have already noted, there is a growing religious view that historical religious propositions of all stripes were and are in fact echoes—sometimes archaic, fanciful, or bizarre—of fundamental truths about the deeper *logos* of the cosmos. According to this view, if we set aside what used to be regarded as being within the range of supernatural plausibility in past, archaic, worldviews but is no longer regarded as plausible within our current understanding of the world, a purified core of beliefs about this mysterious deeper *logos* remains. Moreover, it is suggested that the widely and deeply shared human notion of a superior Being is a strong indication that such a Being is there. The alternative explanation, of course, has always been to regard this notion as a pure projection of the human mind, accounted for by the natural mechanisms and cultural processes mentioned.

We leave the question of beings that are assumed to exist beyond experience for a moment to touch on another question. It is widely argued that atheism is itself a belief comparable to religion—that it is actually a kind of quasi-religious faith dogmatically held by its believers. Why would a belief in God/s be different from a belief in the absence of God/s? Are these not just different metaphysical assumptions? Agnosticism, a profession of intrinsic, non-committing ignorance and reasoned skepticism regarding the validity of all metaphysical claims about deities, is held to be the only coherent non-believing position. At the dawn of Greek philosophy, Protagoras phrased the agnostic position as follows: "Concerning the gods I cannot know either that they exist or that they do not exist, or what form they might have, for there is much to prevent one's knowing: the obscurity of the subject and the shortness of man's life."[58] A standard response to the argument that atheism is itself a religious-like dogma is that there is a profound difference between the religious belief in claims for which there is no testable evidence and the atheistic rejection of such claims. As Russell has put it: you cannot prove a negative.

True, despite all the remarkable achievements of science, the world remains a deep mystery, full with questions we have no clue how to approach, let alone answer, and possibly will never be able to answer. We have mentioned the mind-body problem as one of these questions, and, indeed, the living experience of consciousness is an enigma that defies explanation within our current understanding of matter. However, recall that for millennia there was no conceivable answer to the question of on what the earth stands. People satisfied their intellectual urge to understand what prevented the earth from falling by resorting to all sorts of infinite regressions, such as that the earth was supported on the shoulders of the giant Atlas, or standing on the back of elephants that stood on a giant turtle. It took Newton and later Einstein to reconfigure the question itself by changing our understanding of gravitation—of the deep structure of the cosmos—thereby explaining why the earth was not falling. As we have seen, evolutionary theory has similarly recast many old problems, such as the explanation of organic design and the existence of suffering and of "evil". The mind-matter problem may one day be resolved by a no less momentous change in our understanding of the world that would reconfigure both matter and consciousness. All the same, a view of (human) consciousness as a spark of the divine was and remains quite common.[59]

There are many other deep mysteries within our current understanding of the world, such as that of the origin of the cosmos and the mathematical symmetries of its elementary building blocks. The religious position regards this vast realm of the mysterious as the space for belief in the divine. Agnostics, for their part, take intrinsic doubt a step further, avoiding any speculations about what is unknown and possibly unknowable. However, the claim of mystery is not, in and of itself, an open check and exemption from our standard criterion of validity— that of plausibility.[60]

As we have seen earlier in Chapter 1, all our knowledge is conditional and depends on everything else we hold to be true. There is no way to definitively refute *any* proposition, including that the earth is flat or that Elvis is alive, without an agreement on prior assumptions, standards of verification, and criteria of plausibility. Any religious claim, even those which seem to us to be the most fanciful and absurd, cannot be definitively refuted either. Of course, the test of logical and empirical plausibility itself can be dismissed as inherently tenuous and illusionary, as the historical transformation of ideas may demonstrate. However, if the significance and relevance of this standard is not entirely dismissed, then any meaning ascribed to the divine may be examined in its light. An experimental cognitive psychologist of the religious phenomena, Justin Barrett, is a scientist who is at the same time a believing Christian. He insists, correctly, that our "agency detection device", even if hypersensitive (HADD)cannot by itself either prove or disprove the existence of God. At the same time, he holds that our innate, universal natural propensity for detecting agencies should give the benefit of the doubt to the existence of such agencies. He does not, however, explain why we should prefer the notion of god(s) to, say, fairies, dwarves, nymphs or unicorns. Additionally, Barrett advocates reliance on the instinctive, "folk" category of divine agents, the *sensus divinitatis*, rather than on formal theological doctrines, which he feels may be losing ground.[61] However, theology has been there largely because of the deeply sensed need to iron out what appeared to be inconsistencies and improbabilities in folk beliefs. And the question of the plausibility of these beliefs given everything else we seem to know becomes even more pertinent with our scientifically informed picture of the world.

We shall only briefly reiterate some of the problems relating to the attributes of the divine. The existence of the world and God's role as a creator only regress the problem one step, as it raises the question of what or who created the creator. Furthermore, the gradual and haphazard evolution of life sits very awkwardly with an omniscient and omnipotent creator, while being remarkably accounted for by the evolutionary rationale. Despite attempts to the contrary, the two accounts seem to be incompatible.[62] Alternatively, maybe the divine is not omnipotent and omniscient. This would still leave the problem of regression in creation, but would supposedly account for His experimentation with life's forms. An imperfect God would supposedly also make the problems of pervasive suffering of the innocent in the world and of divine justice more intelligible, as He might be helpless, indifferent, or a sadist. Whether this sits comfortably with the image and supposed functions of God is a different matter. Even more significant, the alternative explanation that accounts for suffering and "evil" in the evolutionary terms of blind natural processes, devoid of any meaning, would seem to be a more plausible account of the harsh realities we observe around us, and of so much else. Finally, some argue that given our limited faculties, we cannot ascribe any attributes to the divine. But then again, in this case, what does the concept of the divine mean at all, what are its supposed function(s), other than being a pantheistic tautology or semantics. What does the statement I believe in God, or in some superior force, mean within such a framework? What actual content does it have? One might be thrown back on the French scientist Pierre-Simon Laplace's famous alleged reply to Napoleon's query about the role of God in his system: "I had no need of that hypothesis."

Conclusion: Religion as Ideology

Premodern ideologies were overwhelmingly religious. Like all ideologies, they combined factual claims about the world with prescribed codes of proper behavior in it. They tied together a cognitive map and manual for action into a cognitively economical packed form, meeting the innate human need for understanding, meaning, and guidance that would help navigate a complex reality. First and foremost, the religious phenomena were built around pervasive beliefs in occult forces and hidden agencies, which had to be dealt and negotiated with. From our current perspective, the search for forces beyond the perceived phenomena is most plausibly interpreted as an expression of the human investigative faculties; the beliefs in hidden agencies as oversensitivity and hyper-activation of our agent-detecting cognitive mechanisms; and ritual and magic for coping with occult forces and hidden agencies as techniques on par with more "practical" ones. All these are evolutionarily understood as expressions and byproducts of natural human propensities. Only in hindsight and given improved methods of empirical investigations and higher standards of verification can they be defined as "superstitions". The same applies to archaic cosmologies and interpretative myths. Moreover, the religious phenomena have been tightly linked with archetypical images and narrative forms that are highly evocative and deeply grooved into our collective psyche. As noted earlier, Freud's fanciful speculations on the sources of religion—mythical in content and form as can be—offer an ironic demonstration of this point.

Later on, religion expanded into and merged with morality, another sphere of intense human emotional commitment. Furthermore, religion is a deeply collective phenomenon, because of the innate human conformity to socially inherited ideas and practices—the secret, no less than invention, of our species' unique accumulated and cumulative knowledge and capabilities; and because of religion's close connection to group identity and survival, and the strong sense of belonging it confers on community members. People are born into their communities of outlook, identity, and early life socialization, which does not preclude dynamic transformation, sometimes even paradigm shifts, in response to changing circumstances.

Hence the familiar syndrome of cognitive and emotional "closure" widely studied by psychologists. To the members of the religious group, the specifics of the religious system—cosmological beliefs, miraculous and sacred narratives, minutiae of ritual, detailed codes of proper behavior, other points of principle or dogma—constitute intimate and cherished elements of a comprehensive cognitive outlook, normative regime, and cultural identity. They are as vivid to insiders as they may appear strange and alien to outsiders. Swift has captured this remarkable dichotomy in his fictional bloody theological dispute concerning the side from which eggs should be cracked open. Indeed, other, let alone rival, religious faiths and collectives have regularly been parodied, denigrated, and colored with all the negative attributes of Otherness which are deeply rooted in human groupishness—have been widely perceived as evil and morally corrupt. For most of their histories, the monotheistic religions eradicated the respect for other faiths that had prevailed and still prevails in more pluralistic, polytheistic cultures. Many of their believers still do. As all elements of the religious faith were, and are, perceived as representing deep truths about both the world and human conduct, on the strict adherence to which so much hinges, devotion and often zealotry are only to be expected.

Even when sanctified cosmologies and sacred narratives have been losing credibility and increasingly viewed as mythical, as occurred in Swift's time, adherence to them, although challenged and often reformulated, has remained strong within the communities of believers. Denial is the most common reaction to what is widely known as "cognitive dissonance", an emotional discomfort caused by a suggestion of contradiction in one's views of or attitudes toward the world. Additionally, adherence to the traditionalist mythical narratives of the religious system is attributable to their warm emotional resonance, evocative archetypes, and other human cognitive and proclivities or biases. In terms of their concreteness and fundamentally human scale, they speak in a language that is more natural to us than the abstractions, rigor, and detachment of science.

Thus, the data waved by atheists and sullenly dismissed by religious people indeed shows that religiousness (especially of the traditionalist brands) decreases with higher levels of education, as people are exposed to knowledge and perspectives that render traditionalist narratives highly implausible.[63] However, at the same time, it would also seem that the religious phenomena—in traditionalist, modernist or "New Age" forms—have sufficiently deep roots in the human psyche, in our cognitive mechanisms and emotional needs, to render Nietzsche's famous proclamation of the Death of God somewhat exaggerated or premature. The religious phenomena are apparently not going to be entirely laughed out of the social arena. Like many others, I hold that fundamentalist attempts to refute and restrict science should be staunchly opposed. That aside, many people feel, for a variety of reasons, that religion, in this or that form, is good for them, a claim that finds some support in the data. Similarly, religion's claimed stand on the side of virtue cannot be dismissed either—depending of course on one's point of view—even if it may be counterbalanced in many cases by bigotry, emotional abuse, and narrow-minded superstition. Religion's contribution to civic virtue was a common theme among thinkers of the early modern period. It was observed by Alexis de Tocqueville as one of the cornerstones of American democracy and is still well documented in the United States.[64]

This does not mean that religion is historically and culturally immutable or that its presence and power are a given quantity. Individuals and societies can be more or less religious, or not religious at all, with modernity in particular marking a real and deep turning point in this regard.[65] The prevalence of religion has shrunk, and its power has weakened in modernized societies. Furthermore, established religions have been readjusting their positions, some streaks within them shedding off archaic cosmologies, withdrawing from discredited metaphysical claims and revising their moral codes. Of course, at the same time fundamentalists have dug their heels in. Simultaneously, there has been a surge of new spiritual creeds, possessing even less commitment to ontological claims, to the extent that they may be considered practical philosophies or therapeutic methods, rather than religions. The point, however, is that the religious phenomena in their diverse historical-cultural manifestations have reflected deep proclivities in our cognitive and emotional makeup. And the effects of such proclivities have not disappeared in secular contexts either.

The Enlightenment and its legacy have secularized the discourse on both the world and morality in the developed parts of the world. Although many participants in this discourse have professed some sort of religious beliefs and sentiments, divine intervention and miraculous occurrences have ceased to be accepted currency. The new ideologies that have emerged in the wake of the Enlightenment and have vied among themselves on the question of how modern, industrial society should be shaped have all been ostensibly secular, at least in this sense. And yet it has been widely noted that in some crucial respects, and in various degrees, they can be described as secular religions or religion substitutes. All of them have combined factual claims about the social world with views as to what its proper conduct should be and instructions for how to get there. They have all been collective creeds that have grouped people around them. This has been so because their model of the world, at once highly simplified and quite sophisticated—as this is how our mind works—has been communicated among their devotees, who could not possibly devise it each for himself from scratch; because there is reassurance, increased confidence, and a sense of belonging in numbers; because the shared worldview becomes inseparable from people's identity; and because ideologies center on a number of major responses to basic human concerns and sensibilities, as applied to the specifics of historical-cultural settings, with significant variations among individuals, of course, partly rooted in character traits and partly shaped by social settings.

This does not at all mean that religion has disappeared from the ideological sphere during the last centuries. Obviously, it has continued to play a role in various modern ideological contexts, including, from the late twentieth century on, the public-political re-emergence of a significant religious element in some strands of modern American conservatism, as well as a powerful Islamist back-lash whose shockwaves reverberate globally. All the same, religious ideologies have moved to the sidelines in modern societies and ideological discourse, while the phenomenon of Islamic radicalism is distinctively rooted in what are fundamentally still largely premodern societies by the standards of socioeconomic modernization. Indeed, it represent a defensive, sometimes defensive-aggressive, response to the encroachments of modernity on traditional premodern cultures. Even when paralleling in time, societies do not necessarily inhabit the same timeframe in their relative position on the process of socioeconomic modernization, with the huge consequences that such differences entail, least of all ideological.

Secular ideologies have taken over from the religious ones the human quest for meaning and, to some ways, salvation. In various degrees, their members are united by an enthusiasm for a creed that promises to transcend and resolve the world's problems, tensions, and frustrations. Connection to the world's *logos*, to the universal, and, in some cases, to fate itself are widely and deeply felt. The central interpretive narratives of the ideological creed—often standing on a shaky factual basis, while at the same time being highly evocative and endowed with immense powers of mobilization—become sanctified myths. Core values and norms are treated as sacred. Challenging them appears almost blasphemous.

Toleration of other ideological creeds is often very low, and there is a strong tendency to attribute evil intentions, bad faith, and all other character flaws to their adherents. Conversion from one creed to another sometimes also takes place, typically involving a no lesser commitment to the new creed.

This is not to say that all ideological factual claims are invalid, equally misleading, or equally mythical—far from it; nor that the differences of value between ideologies do not matter. On the contrary, ideologies deal with questions of how the world should be organized that are of the highest importance to people's lives. What we seek to point out is how enclosed within themselves ideological creeds and communities are, with their adherents largely incapable of interpreting the world through anything but the creed's internal view. This is a pretty trivial idea. Intellectuals in particular are well aware of all this: the prevalence of ideological bias in the understanding of reality, the allure of grand narratives, and the need for methodical skepticism and for emotional detachment in research. Still, in different compartments of their minds, it appears that many—all too many—of them simply cannot help it.

The Major Contenders of Modernity

Liberalism, Socialism, Fascism

Three major ideologies, each consisting of a variety of sub-currents and admixtures, vied in the socio-political arena during the nineteenth and twentieth centuries: capitalist parliamentarian liberalism, eventually embracing democracy; socialism and communism of different varieties, some of which were democratic and some not; and a wide range of mostly authoritarian, often popular, creeds—traditionalist, revolutionary, or both—with fascism as their most radical and most impactful variety. In a deep sense, these ideologies' respective visions were not accidental. They comprised three basic alternative programs for coping with the unprecedented challenges and dazzling opportunities generated by the greatest transformation humanity has undergone ever since its transition to agriculture and statehood—the emergence of modern industrial society.

The transformation of modernity involved the decline of the traditional rural community and its replacement by urban mass society; the rise of integrated industrial economies that relied on exchange on a national and global scale; and exponentially, potentially unlimited, growing wealth—a sharp break from the premodern reality of precarious existence on the verge of hunger. Inseparably, especially during its early phases, the massive transformation and upheavals of modernization also brought about pervasive feelings of social dislocation and alienation; shabby living in cramped, squalid, and unhealthy urban slums; harsh labor conditions in regimentalized factories; and a deep sense of wrongness and injustice concerning the unequal distribution of the new massive wealth, which endured even after standards of living throughout society rose dramatically during the later stages of industrialization. Much else has been involved in the modern transformation, of course. Indeed, in addition to the above three opposing visions of the future, there were also full-blown reactionary ideological responses to modernity. Clinging to forms of preindustrial society and to premodern sources of legitimation, they were typically embraced by the old rulers

Ideological Fixation. Azar Gat, Oxford University Press. © Oxford University Press 2022.
DOI: 10.1093/oso/9780197646700.003.0004

and social elites, engaged in what they often recognized to be a rearguard action against a deluge of change.

By the 1950s and 1960s—with fascism having been destroyed in World War II, communism mellowing after Stalin, and the capitalist liberal democracies creating extensive welfare systems—some theorists, observing a narrowing of the ideological rifts, declared the End of Ideology.[1] At the close of the twentieth century, following the demise of communism, a similar End of History was proclaimed, this time with the alleged complete and final triumph of liberal ideology over its old rivals.[2] In both cases, however, the news of the death of ideology has proved to be as premature as the Death of God. Ideological currents and disputes—some old, some new—have re-emerged with characteristic intensity and ferocity. Thus, religion has resurfaced—most notably in the lands of Islam, in societies that have not yet successfully embarked on the road to modernization—in an often violent reaction against the encroachments of modernity and its threat to traditional values. Additionally, there is a powerful reassertion of non-liberal and non-democratic creeds in those modernizing and modernized societies that have always stood apart from the Western liberal tradition. These include, most significantly, China and some other societies of East and Southeast Asia, Russia, and some countries of Eastern Europe. Furthermore, and most intriguingly, the liberal consensus itself has fractured, with bitter ideological disputes flaring up between the currents and creeds that have branched out of it. It is as if a law of conservation of ideological fervor exists.

In this chapter, we examine the three "classical" ideologies of the nineteenth and twentieth centuries. Many studies have been written on these and other modern ideologies, and it is not our purpose here to offer yet another.[3] While some detail is necessary, we explore the chief historical ideologies above all to shed further light on ideology as a template of human cognition and social discourse and, indeed, to further investigate the phenomenon of ideological fixation. These, too, are familiar subjects in the scholarly literature. From its earliest appearance, the concept of ideology has had conflicting connotations—both positive and negative. First coined during the French Revolution, the term "ideologues" was given a derogatory meaning by Napoleon in reference to the "purist" critics of his dictatorial rule among the philosophers. They opposed the abolition of the Republic established by the French Revolution, a regime he and others at the time judged defunct. In the English language as well, the term "ideologue" carries the meaning of a zealous advocate of a rigid creed, closed to the complexities and constraints of reality. Marx influentially defined ideology as a self-interested, biased, and distorted interpretation of reality, appearing to its proponents and adherents as the objective truth but actually determined by and justifying their privileged standing in the socioeconomic order.[4] Ideology is "false consciousness", in the term coined by Marx's lifelong friend and collaborator Friedrich Engels.[5] It supposedly contrasted with Marx's own truly objective, unmasked understanding of social realities. Some twentieth-century Marxist activists and theorists, such as Antonio Gramsci and Louis Althusser, regretfully concluded that the ruling bourgeoisie had succeeded in propagating its ideological outlook—its motivated false picture of reality—throughout society by means of its hegemony over social organs such as the education system and the media. Those who profited from the existing order were thus able to convince not only themselves but also the exploited masses that this order was natural, advantageous and irreplaceable.[6] Partly to combat this, Marxists from Lenin onward began to celebrate their own mobilizing creed as "communist ideology", diverging from Marx's meaning of ideology as intrinsically false.

The followers of other social and political creeds have similarly and proudly declared their adherence to their particular ideology as signifying both conceptual clarity and moral commitment. On the other hand, the notion that ideology functions for its followers as a secular religion or religion substitute has been widely noted.[7] Moreover, during the twentieth century, the attempts to zealously realize ideological creeds often ended in massive failures and resulted in horrendous loss of life and human suffering. As a result, criticisms of and cautions against the ideological mode of thinking have been repeatedly voiced. And yet, none of this seems to have significantly reduced ideological commitment and dampen party fervor, or rein in the acrimony and venom of the disputes. Supposedly secular ideologies have proved to be as resistant to doubts and misgivings as the traditional religions themselves. Indeed, scholars, starting with Karl Mannheim and continuing increasingly today, have largely put aside the treatment of ideology as either positive or negative. Instead, they have "normalized" ideology by focusing on its ubiquitous and universal nature as a necessarily simplified interpretative map put together for the practical imperative of charting people's way in a complex world. They have emphasized the irreducibly context-related and value-laden nature of ideological outlooks and, hence, of ideological disputes between conflicting, intrinsically partial perspectives and interests. Furthermore, they have pointed out that ideologies incorporate not only false ideas about the world but also many valid ones.[8]

I explore both aspects of ideology. On the one hand, I marvel at and wish to shed more light on the phenomenon of ideology as a basic form of human cognition, emotional mobilization, and social interaction that, moreover, deals with questions of paramount importance for human life. On the other hand, I wish to increase awareness of ideology's intrinsic cognitive flaws and biases, so as to help mitigate them. To be sure, it is part of my argument that secular ideologies are deeply resistant to such an effort almost as much as religious ideologies are.

Still, they—we—are not entirely immune to such efforts, and, in any case, the venture is worthwhile, even if only for the purpose of intellectual clarification.

To remove a possible misunderstanding, the cognitive "problem" this book addresses is not ideology per se. Everybody—yes, including me—has their value preferences, often passionately held, together with some notions as to how these preferences should be realized in the world: alias ideology. Furthermore, different sets of values may conflict with one another, and sometimes there is no overarching normative criterion outside these values themselves that can bridge or decide between them. What I mean by ideological fixation is different. It refers to the ways in which devotion to value preferences may distort understanding of reality, the assessment of past events and future potentialities. True, cognitive biases in interpreting the world may serve the causes people pursue, as single-minded and sometimes narrow-minded convictions are often conducive to galvanizing support and pushing through intellectual and social agendas in the public sphere. This is very much the name of the game in social bargaining. However, strong biases in the understanding of reality can also undermine a cause and lead people astray, away from their desired objectives. Such biases are even more of an obstacle if one is after pure knowledge, unassociated with any particular social creed or normative aims. As argued in our chapter on truth and contrary to pervasive "postmodernist" rhetoric, while all knowledge is intrinsically partial, not all of it is equally biased, equally true, or true at all.

Liberalism: First and Last in the Arena?

Of the "big three" modern ideologies—liberalism, socialism, and fascism—liberalism was the first to emerge. It developed from the late seventeenth century onward, hand in hand with the rise of commercial capitalism even before industrialization. Its formative phase, in the wake of the English Glorious Revolution of 1688, was about limiting royal power, defending against its arbitrary use and giving more say to the rising classes of capitalist entrepreneurs represented in Parliament. It was in this context that the fundamental liberal rights to life and property and the primacy of the legislature based on the principle of representation and the consent of the governed were formulated, most notably in John Locke's *The Second Treatise of Civil Government* (1689). Freedom of expression and association gradually grew from the reality of increasing political competition during the eighteenth century. Greater religious toleration, also advocated by Locke, was to follow. Liberalism became the ideology most closely associated with the Enlightenment and its core belief in free thinking, released from all religious dogma and political censorship, and capable of bringing about a major improvement in the human condition through the application of reasoned inquiry, scientific discovery, and social and political reform.

As Britain rose to the rank of being the richest nation on earth in the age of expanding commercial capitalism during the eighteenth century, economic liberalism based on market entrepreneurship became increasingly prominent within liberalism. Theoretically codified in Adam Smith's *The Wealth of Nations* (1776), it stood for the limitation of government in the economy as well. State involvement was to be kept to a bare minimum, both domestically and internationally, confined to the provision of security and the enforcement of the rules of the game. The freedom of individuals from outside constraints became the cornerstone of liberalism. There were, however, both compatibilities and strong tensions between this principle and that other central liberal postulate: the equality of all individuals. Already posited by Locke as the two pillars of liberalism, freedom and equality were celebrated by both the American and French revolutions. Locke and eighteenth-century liberals found reasons why equality should not mean universal suffrage and, even more, equality of wealth.[9] Their critics from the left would regard this reasoning as both contrived and unjust.

This story is familiar enough. In addition to its opposition to unlimited royal power, liberalism was originally developed to advance the rights of economically and socially rising commoners against aristocratic privilege. Its proponents, from Locke on, turned the Protestant emphasis on the equality of all individuals before God into a legal and political principle. They were progressively able to establish equality before the law. However, as their victory over the old elites was becoming a reality, they increasingly faced a greater challenge coming from the opposite direction, from below. Both individual freedom and equality implied equal political rights to all people, above all the right to vote. Yet only a minuscule part of the population, a few percent, held voting rights in eighteenth-century parliamentary Britain, with the overwhelming majority of the population remaining politically disenfranchised.

The problem was that democracy had a terrible reputation in the eighteenth century, and not without reason. The classical authorities such as Plato and Aristotle blamed democratic Athens' defeat in its great clash with Sparta on the excesses and hubris of the Athenian demos, easily swayed by irresponsible demagogues. Furthermore, majority rule, or, less charitably, rule by the "mob", conflicted with and threatened liberalism as much as it flowed from it. Can the masses—illiterate, ignorant, destitute, desperately struggling to avoid hunger—be relied upon to make informed decisions? No less important, will they respect the liberal rights to life and property, to say nothing of free speech and toleration? Will they not be tempted to rise against the propertied classes and distribute their wealth among them? As contemporaries reasoned, this would not improve the masses' lot, given their vast numbers, while ruining the prospects of overall economic advance and growth. Finally, will the masses not be swayed by the promises of popular leaders into scraping not only liberal rights but also democracy itself, paving the way for a tyrant?

All these were valid questions, irrespective of the self-interest and privileges of the propertied classes. These questions were made all the more relevant by the failure of democracy during the French Revolution. Having enacted universal male suffrage in 1793, the Jacobins embraced terror and drowned the Revolution's liberal phase in blood—all in the name of the people's will. Suffrage was again limited by the Constitution of 1795. The French Republic was ultimately taken over by Napoleon. Formally reintroducing universal male suffrage, he enjoyed massive popular support for his dictatorial rule, but also the support of the bourgeoisie who were reassured by the promise of security and order. Indeed, Bonapartism became a generic term, re-emerging in nineteenth-century Europe as well as in today's developing world. In France, for example, attempts at democracy repeatedly failed. The Second Republic of 1848 succumbed to Louis Napoleon (a nephew), who was first elected its president and later made himself Emperor Napoleon III. His name was sufficient to win unrivaled mass popularity, and his regime drew legitimacy from plebiscites under universal male suffrage, while also allaying the propertied classes' fears of a violent social revolution. It was not until after 1871 that the Third Republic, based on universal male suffrage, was established. Indeed, until well into the latter part of the nineteenth century, voting rights were limited by criteria of property and education in all the European countries that possessed genuine electoral political systems. In Britain, where the suffrage was gradually expanded during the nineteenth century, the majority of the men were given the vote only with the Third Reform Act of 1884, and universal suffrage had to wait until after World War I. Similar developments took place in the Low Countries and in Scandinavia.

The failure of democracy to win the day even in Europe's liberal-parliamentary countries prior to the late nineteenth century is too sweeping to be attributable to unfortunate accidents. Nor should it be blamed solely on the ill-will of and obstructionism by the propertied classes, finally overcome by social pressure and the triumph of right. Certainly, rulers and social elites throughout history were unwilling to enfranchise the often-subjugated masses. But there were other, deeper reasons why democracy was so hard to establish under premodern conditions. It is scarcely noted that before modern times, democracy *never* and *nowhere* existed in a large country, beyond the city-state or canton scale with their direct democracies. Government by representatives solved some, but not all, of the problems of large territorial scale, and it too necessitated a developed level of bureaucratic and logistical infrastructure. The dispersal of the peasants—around 90 percent of the population in premodern societies—across the countryside prevented them from pulling their weight together. In Marx's

striking phrase, they were "like potatoes in a sack".[10] This widely dispersed population, thinly scattered in small, self-contained households and isolated rural
settlements, was unable to cooperate effectively. Nor could it bridge over the
problems of premodern communications—indeed, the absence thereof—and
receive any information about the political questions at hand. It was virtually
impossible for them to overcome the conditions that Marx, in "The Communist
Manifesto" (1848), described no less strikingly, in reference to premodern
societies, as "the idiocy of rural life".

Certainly, the first country-size democracy ever, the United States, was established a little earlier than those in Europe, in the late eighteenth century,
with practically universal white male suffrage and other democratic reforms
enacted at the state and federal levels in the 1820s. However, the founders of
the United States were deeply worried about the people; named its new regime
a republic, as in ancient Rome; and, as in Rome, adopted a whole range of constitutional precautions to filter and cushion against the popular will. Moreover,
the American experiment depended on crucial preconditions. Newspapers and
pamphlets, rolling out of printing presses, were widespread and continuously
connected people to the political issues and debates. Literacy levels were very
high by premodern and early modern standards, apparently encompassing the
majority of the population.[11] Relatively well-to-do (white) freeholder farmers,
rather than subjugated peasants, were the norm in the new country. This was
partly because of its background as an immigrant haven, free from the rigid social constraints of Europe, and partly because of the continent's plentiful free
land (if the natives are not counted).[12] Last but not least, much of the business
of government was carried out at the local and state levels. Thus, democracy on a
large, country-size scale was not simply a good idea finally recognized and readily
implemented, as it is sometimes perceived. It rested on certain preconditions
created only with modernity.

Some of these preconditions, such as spreading literacy and mass newspapers,
increasingly materialized mostly in the countries of northern Europe from the
beginning of the nineteenth century on. But the most decisive push toward democratization was given by the process of industrialization and attendant urbanization. The masses were now increasingly concentrated in the country's centers
and were able to make their presence felt, sometimes violently. Political communication also vastly intensified because mass popular newspapers proliferated.
Indeed, the new industrial state societies had the means and infrastructure necessary for creating universal education systems, "to educate our masters", as one
representative of the deeply concerned old elites in Britain memorably put it.
Moreover, with their exodus to the cities, the masses became invested in the new
industrial economy. And over time, contrary to Marx's prediction, their stake in it
only increased, as rising affluence gradually elevated them to middle-class status

and made them part of the "bourgeois dream". As Aristotle noted millennia ago, a stable polity is based on the predominance of the middle class.[13]

Democracy tended to lag behind industrialization for an additional reason: it threatened industrialization's prospects of success. The preconditions for industrialization in Britain, the world's first industrial nation, were largely created in the early modern period by the uprooting of the peasants, the vast majority of the population, from the countryside and turning them into an urban proletariat. They would never have consented to this process had they had the vote, as their hardship was immense and the enormous long-term benefits to their children and children's children lay far in the future and were anything but obvious. Similar problems still plague economic modernization in today's developing societies. The world's fastest economic modernizers in the post-1945 era were the East Asian "tigers": South Korean, Taiwan, and Singapore. All of them were ruled by authoritarian or semi-authoritarian regimes during the first decades of their independence, regimes that ruthlessly pursued economic modernization. More recently, much the same applied to authoritarian-capitalist China's much faster growth in comparison with democratic India during the first decades of their embrace of the market and economic take-off, when the majority of their populations was still rural (in India it still is). Poor democracies have been very rare and unstable—India is the most notable exception—for very deep reasons. One hastens to clarify that the great majority of authoritarian regimes were economic failures rather than economic modernizers.

This discussion of the historical socioeconomic preconditions necessary for the growth and success of democracy, while not entirely unfamiliar, is nonetheless alien and often unwelcome to adherents of the liberal creed. It tends to create a strong dissonance between their normative principles and interpretation of the world, on the one hand, and potentially inconvenient observed realities, on the other. In today's West, liberal democracy is perceived as a timeless ideal, unconditioned by extraneous circumstances and just waiting to be recognized and adopted by all right-minded people. The liberal democratic countries' own long journey notwithstanding, there is an implicit assumption that the rest of the world should profit from our experience and wisdom, skip all intermediate phases, and leap right to the end. Certainly, such idealistic conviction and energies, intrinsic to the ideological mindset, often help to advance liberal aims, as pressures by the United States and the West have played a crucial role in the democratization of large parts of the world. At the same time, they can as often backfire and/or prove disastrous for the intended recipients. As we saw in the chapter on morality and contrary to our gut feeling, good intentions, "doing the right thing", do not guarantee the right results or desired consequences, sometimes effecting the opposite.

The "Arab Spring" of 2011, which quickly collapsed into the "Arab Upheaval", is a recent case in point. Initial enthusiasm and support for it in the West have been replaced with deep disappointment and bewilderment as democracy has failed to take root and murderous civil wars, bloody anarchy, Islamist regimes, military dictatorships, and old-style monarchies alternate throughout the Arab world. It cannot even be argued by way of an explanation, as it was after the American occupation of Iraq, that democracy cannot be imposed by force. In the first place, democracy was conspicuously and most successfully so imposed, in the wake of World War II, on Germany and Japan, where modern socioeconomic infrastructure had already been in place; and, second, because the Arab Upheaval was self-inflicted, even if in Libya, for example, the toppling of Gaddafi (which so far has resulted in a bloody mayhem) was actively aided by military intervention by the European Union.

The Arab world's sorry state before and after its recent upheavals has deep social and cultural roots, and change may be slow to arrive. Our point, however, is the deep dissonance that these realities create in the liberal consciousness. Thus, the American administration found itself on the horns of a dilemma, choking over the question of whether the United States should endorse the Islamic Brotherhood's government in Egypt. Democratically elected, it was thoroughly anti-liberal and dubiously committed to the continuation of democracy. This was a combination that the West has forgotten for close to a century (and which may also appear today in some countries of Eastern Europe). Conversely, the United States has found it difficult to support the military dictatorship reestablished in Egypt, even though the only viable alternative would appear to be Islamist. Indeed, this would seem to be the case throughout much of the Middle East. Saudi Arabia has in many ways a deeply reactionary (albeit currently a modernizing) social and political regime. But is a liberal democratic alternative feasible there at present or in the foreseeable future? Has the regime of Khomeini and the Ayatollahs in Iran been a better option from the liberal point of view than the Shah's modernizing one, with all its flaws? Indeed, were the Bolsheviks and the untold horrors they inflicted a superior alternative to the reactionary and reprehensible tsarist regime, under which Russia was nonetheless beginning to experience industrialization and social change?[14]

Such questions have always called for careful assessments, hard choices, and awkward normative compromises regarding security, alliance politics, and, moreover, the advancement of a liberal world order. Let me be clear: there is every normative and practical reason for the liberal countries to pursue a liberal world order as their ultimate aim and to advance it wherever possible. But no simple rule of an unflinching liberal democratic crusade—directed at both friend and foe—of the sort preached by some American pundits has ever worked or can be rationalized in terms of the desired objective.

This book is not about concrete policy recommendations in complex real-world situations. Rather, what it seeks to highlight is the predominance of abstract normative principles in the ideological mode of thinking. In case of a clash with reality, normative notions are more emotive, more deeply grooved in our psyche, because of their significance in social bargaining, which largely revolves around the justification of social arrangements. Furthermore, thought by principle is our ingenious shortcut for coping with the world's complexity. Again, adherence to the normative compass is in various ways crucial for advancing a cause. At the same time, it is often a source of deep cognitive dissonances in the interpretation of reality and in the struggle to implement a normative vision.

This observation is not new. In the case of liberalism, it goes back to the late eighteenth century, when that doctrine won its first crowning victories, in Britain and the United States, but also encountered its first major setback, in the French Revolution and its aftermath. The British politician, reformist, and theorist Edmund Burke famously anticipated the French Revolution's worst excesses and ultimate failure in his *Reflections on the Revolution in France* (1790). We shall not repeat here the various themes of his often-cited critique, but only focus on that point which is most relevant to our subject. Burke, a staunch liberal, was followed by many, often anti-liberal and reactionary, critics of the mindset of the Enlightenment, whose message spread like fire across continental Europe in the wake of the French Revolution. They all charged that there was a wide and all-too-often unbridgeable gap between abstract principles of justice and abstract programs of socio-political reconstruction—worthy, just, and necessary as they may appear to their originators—on the one hand and, on the other, the actual conditions, social forms, and historical-cultural traditions prevailing in the societies in which these principles and programs were to be realized, indeed, often imposed. There was no point in thinking about any political question on the basis of principle alone, without first becoming fully acquainted with the concrete circumstances involved. In continental Europe of the time, a major advance in the understanding of history, known as historicism, matured. Reacting against timeless normative and theoretical abstractions, its proponents highlighted the fundamental interdependence between, and concrete nature and particular historical evolution of, all the features of human societies—material and normative.

Some liberals came to recognize and adjust to this profound insight, most notably the leading liberal thinker of the nineteenth century, John Stuart Mill. He experienced a painful break with the views of his mentors, the liberal philosophers and social reformers Jeremy Bentham and James Mill (his father), on precisely these grounds. He concluded that their programs, developed as if deductively from first normative principles, were all too often divorced from the realities, complexities, and sentiments of the societies in which they were to be implemented: "I ceased to consider representative democracy as an absolute principle, and regarded it as a question of time, place, and circumstance."[15]

Make no mistake: Mill remained a staunch liberal, democrat, and reformer, passionately committed to the advancement of liberal rights, liberal government, and the market economy, free of government interference, as far and as wide as possible given the conditions at hand. What this meant was obviously a matter of judgment. So Mill, for example, championed the granting of the vote to women, and feminism in general, in a period when this was still quite a distant reality. At the same time, while supporting the principle of granting voting rights to all people, he also insisted on some criteria for the vote: basic education (which he thought the state should enforce universally, regulate, and subsidize for the poor, but not hold a monopoly on its provision); and the possession of some property (tax payment).[16] This was when universal male suffrage was moving closer on the horizon—but, indeed, finally materialized only after universal, state-sponsored elementary education had been instituted.

Mill is less popular among liberals today. This is partly because his views on some such matters, whether or not considered in reference to the conditions of his times, are regarded, often rightly, as outdated given the conditions of later times, which, moreover, were to spark changes in the liberal doctrine itself. But Mill's flagging popularity is also partly due to the more circumstantial and therefore more moderate view he held—despite his deep liberal convictions— with respect to the application of the liberal doctrine. Consider Mill's two pronouncements that would sound so familiar in the current American political debate. In one of his chief works, he memorably called the Conservatives in Britain the "stupidest party", for what he regarded as its mindless obstructionism of any necessary reform.[17] But in another of his major works, he argued as a matter of course that "A party of order or stability, and a party of progress or reform, are both necessary elements of a healthy state of political life. . . . Each of these modes of thinking derives its utility from the deficiencies of the other; but it is in a great measure the opposition of the other that keeps each within the limits of reason and sanity."[18] Such a view is often at odds with the more radical streak within liberalism, more inspired by abstract principles and moral zest. In his classic *The Heavenly City of the Eighteenth-Century Philosophers* (1932), historian of ideas Carl Becker has gone back and highlighted this duality in the thinkers of the Enlightenment's appeal to calm and reasoned discussion—free from heated, clouding "passions"—and their own passionate and often messianic vision. From the Enlightenment on, many liberals have perceived the unceasing forward march of freedom in almost metaphysical terms, a view that historians of ideas have labeled "The Whig Interpretation of History".[19]

To be sure, rather than in a dichotomous manner, one should think of the tensions between abstract principles and moral commitment, on the one hand,

and reality checks, on the other, as existing in various mixtures and degrees in people's minds. Different people are predisposed to view questions in the public sphere from a perspective closer to one or the other pole on this continuum. Furthermore, as already noted, such tensions are intrinsic in ideological conflicts, in which moral energies are essential for success. Most important, far from being predominantly an abstract doctrine divorced from reality, liberalism has always been very closely intertwined with the most fundamental social, economic, and political developments of modernity. Hence also the tremendous success of the liberal platform over the last centuries. While not preordained by "History", the forward march of freedom, and so much else in an expanding liberal sphere is nonetheless a conspicuous, deeply grounded empirical reality. Over time, liberalism has led to the abolition of slavery, has instituted the rule of law, has made (a sometimes strained) peace with democracy, has increased government accountability to the public, and has continuously advanced the frontiers of social toleration, while, on its economic side, it has been responsible for the creation of unprecedented and unmatched levels of affluence. Indeed, in hindsight, liberalism has been extraordinarily successful, by far the most successful of the modern ideologies, bringing with it, as Mill suggested, huge rewards to the societies that embraced it.[20]

However, by the time liberals were coming to terms with democracy, or political equality, they were increasingly faced with the challenge of economic inequality, for the two liberal tenets of individual freedom and equality both partook of and conflicted with one another. Economic inequality threatened individual freedom and hindered the development of the masses of individuals held back by their low starting point in life. Liberals had always stressed reward for enterprise and skill as the motivating forces behind economic prosperity and as the justification for an often massively unequal accumulation of wealth. However, they found it harder to justify hereditary, idle wealth, except as an unavoidable price to be paid for the otherwise hugely successful principle of private property. Most important perhaps, leaving the masses of the poor behind to their fate not only hindered these people's prospects of realizing their potential and pursuing happiness; it also, in various ways, threatened the interests of the more well-off—indeed, the common good—because of the significance of this multitude of individuals as fellow citizens, producers, and consumers. This is the consideration that Alexis de Tocqueville called "enlightened self-interest" in his classic *Democracy in America* (1835; 1840).

Liberal individualism had already been widely charged with fostering universal egotism and with lacking both sociability and social compassion as natural human sentiments. With respect to the economic aspect of this criticism, liberals responded that personal accountability and individual initiative were not only moral virtues but, together with the "hidden hand" of the market, had also proved to be the best engines of growing wealth and prosperity, from which everybody ultimately profited. Moreover, suspecting that these qualities were not enough to counter the selfish misuse of freedom, liberal thinkers had traditionally assumed and promoted civic virtues, such as benevolence, social responsibility, duty, and dedication to the common good.[21] Still, with the rise of industrial mass society, many liberals came to the view that all these were insufficient—from a *liberal* perspective—for the reasons mentioned above. Moreover, by the late nineteenth century it was becoming clear that if liberals would not take up the cause of social reform, socialists would.

From the late nineteenth century on, many liberals have come to believe that state involvement is necessary for providing the basics needed for the flourishing of the individual—the masses of individuals—most notably by providing education and some security against hunger and illness. These liberals have amended the main liberal principle of the freedom of the individual from external constrains to mean the cultivation of individuals' "autonomy", their right to prosper and realize their potential, unhindered by the constraints of their arbitrary starting point in life and much else. In the philosophical parlance, this is known as a change of emphasis from "negative liberty", freedom from, to "positive liberty", freedom to.[22] Furthermore, more developed capitalist economies seemed to call for state checks on the huge power of the new magnates of industry and trade, whose monopolistic or semi-monopolistic position threatened both economic competition and the socio-political process. Some modern managerial guidance of the economy from above, lest it become chaotic, was also viewed as the order of the day. Indeed, the old and troubling problem of recurring economic crises in the capitalist system, the cycles of boom and bust, resurfaced with the utmost severity with the onset of the Great Depression in 1929. Here too, many liberals arrived at the view that some state involvement is necessary to counter these ruinous cycles and save capitalism by protecting it from its more problematic aspects.

Thus, in the late nineteenth and early twentieth centuries, liberalism reached a fork in the road. One current—which came to be known as progressives, social liberals, left-liberals, or welfare liberals—would become increasingly identified with state involvement in society and the economy: to level the ground, advance opportunity to those at the bottom, offer a social safety net against misfortune, and correct market failures. In this, they would be drawn closer to the more moderate and democratic among socialists, together converging on the so-called Welfare State. An opposing current kept its allegiance to the classical liberal principle of minimal state intervention for any purpose—social or economic—rejecting the normative basis and denying the efficacy of such intervention. Throughout the West during the twentieth century, these right-liberals, or libertarians, increasingly joined hands with conservatives, whose doctrine also gradually transformed.

Previously, conservatives defended the old social, economic, and political forms inherited from premodern agrarian society (and, in the United States, slavery and, later, racial segregation, which many leading progressives also supported). They emphasized tradition, custom, social hierarchy, and authority, and they tended to be nostalgic toward a romanticized past. They were suspicious of both the capitalist economy and the individualistic set of values associated with it. In their updated version, from the twentieth century on, conservatives have continued to stress family, community, country, law and order, and other traditional virtues and institutions (in the United States in particular also religion). They kept their skeptical approach toward "abstract reason" and abstract principles as applied to practical politics, as well as toward radical attempts to reshape human nature and society at large. On these grounds, they eventually formed an alliance, and in some places merged, with the right-liberals, sharing their opposition to ambitious state sponsored projects of social engineering. After a hiatus during the middle of the twentieth century, this modern neo-liberal-conservative synthesis has emerged as a powerful social and political force.

Both progressivism and conservatism are relative terms, which, especially regarding conservatism, tends to confuse those (sometimes unsympathetic) scholars who seek to define its "essence". Thus, both movements have undergone a far-reaching change from the nineteenth century to the present in terms of what they have been progressing from or toward, or conserving. Progressives have inherited from liberalism the belief in social reform and expanding social toleration, especially toward groups or individuals who were oppressed, marginalized, or discriminated against. They have diverged from classical liberalism in assigning a much greater role to the state in achieving these and other objectives and in becoming less sure about the unlimited exercise of the market principle. More recently, they have become less certain even about the unlimited exercise of free speech, when regarded as being offensive to the dignity of those perceived as underprivileged. On the other side, modern conservativism, in contrast to its old namesake, has taken from liberalism its belief in the principle of self-help, the primacy of the market and minimal state intervention in society and the economy. At the same time, its adherents have partly upheld and partly adjusted the conservative social code in the face of changing social mores. As we shall see later in this book, the ideological disputes between the two currents that have flowed out of the liberal democratic synthesis have, over time, become almost as bitter and emotionally charged as liberal democracy's earlier struggles with socialism and fascism, the two ideologies to which we now turn.

Socialism: The Next Stage in History?

Ideological views and social movements—religious or secular—that decried vast socioeconomic inequality and the oppressive and exploitative power of the rich and mighty have been a recurring theme in world history. Some of them preached the abolition of private property. However, socialism became a major force only in the wake of the Industrial Revolution in the nineteenth century. It grew with the emergence of urban mass society and with the stark tensions that developed between exponentially growing wealth and the poverty and hardship of the industrial working class or proletariat in the factories and mines. In the industrialized countries, this class had become the largest segment of the population by around 1900.

Socialism centered on a set of closely related ideas: collective ownership of the means of production (or even of all property), which would guarantee an equal distribution of the fruits of production, abolish class differences and antagonism, and achieve greater sociability and fraternity. Socialism promoted central planning, as opposed to free market competition, for supposedly being less wasteful and not prone to periodic economic crises. There were various emphases within this socialist menu in different places and times, particularly with respect to the levels of collectivization and socioeconomic equality to be pursued and to whether it was more on production or distribution that the drive for equality was to be focused. Additionally, perhaps the most significant divergence within socialism, certainly from the point of view of our subject, was between Marxist and non-Marxist socialist currents, movements, and parties. Early nineteenth-century visions of socialism, which Marx would label "utopian", relied on the supposed attractiveness and justness of these visions to gain support, including that of the propertied classes. Major non-Marxist socialist movements later on relied on electoral systems that had become democratic to win majorities and victories for their cause. Marxism, for its part, having crystallized before universal suffrage, continued to identify with revolution and the "dictatorship of the proletariat" as the means to achieve and hold on to power. Its main difference from other nineteenth-century revolutionary socialist creeds—and perhaps the main source of its attraction and strength—lay in the fact that the Marxist supremely addictive millenarian vision of salvation was anchored in an astoundingly sophisticated, thoroughly secular, conception of society, the economy, and history.

Marx took historicism to a new level and deeply changed our understanding of the world, irrespective of whether one is a "Marxist" (I am not) or how successful his predictions and overall vision of the future turned out to be (not very). His insights make him one of the fathers of sociology, and they have deeply influenced historical scholarship. The following is my construction of where his huge contributions and enduring legacy lie. This construction is knowingly "filtered" of Marx's many shorthand formulations and catchphrases—often deliberately one-sided, polemical, and intended for effect. For while always a deeply serious thinker, Marx was primarily interested in the impact of his works on real life, in their translation into "praxis", fashioning himself above all as an intellectual midwife of a sweeping economic, social, and political revolution.

Historical writing before Marx mainly focused on political events and the actions of leaders, while social and economic theory tended to revolve around abstract ideas and principles. By contrast, Marx brought to light and vastly heightened awareness of the deep, underlying structures of, and close connection between, economic modes of production, social relations, political power distribution, political and judicial institutions and norms, and view of the world or "ideology". He called attention to the interconnected processes of transformation in these elements that account for the transitions between major historical eras. He turned the spotlight on the full scope and broad spectrum of society, beyond the well-documented rulers and social elites: the large social estates, classes, and groups hitherto hidden from sight, and the perennial conflicts of interests and struggles among them, open or suppressed. Indeed, he highlighted the way people's views, norms, and actions are decisively shaped by their socio-economic position and, hence, by their interests: "It is not the consciousness of men that determines their existence, but their social existence that determines their consciousness";[23] or, in a more colloquial American: "where you stand depends on where you sit." In this, he countered both the naive, idealistic view of human motivation and the interpretation of ideas as if springing abstractly from one another or out of thin air. Much of the above is removed from our immediate experience and requires a wide-angle historical perspective from the heights. Since people lack such a perspective, they tend to perceive the social patterns they are familiar with as given or "nature-like", in Marx's phrase, rather than as dynamic and ever-changing creations of humanity's own past history. Hence also people's tendency to theorize existing social forms and norms into timeless abstractions, concepts, and principles—"ideologize" them.

Some would argue, not without reason, that this presentation of Marx's ideas has been filtered of much of what is most typically Marxian. Marxists might think that it strips away his most significant doctrines, while critics would argue that it is too lenient on him. However, as noted above, I opt for a broader view of the context and intentions of Marx's various propositions. Thus, his "materialism" was an epoch-making reaction against the dominant "idealistic" streak within historicism, most notably associated with Hegel. Like other "Young Hegelian" critics, Marx stressed that real people in concrete circumstances, rather than mystifications like the "world spirit", were the stuff of history. More important, he rightly emphasized that humans were fundamentally geared for survival, for extracting their livelihood from a harsh natural world in competition and cooperation with other people, rather than for lofty abstract thought. Certainly, human ideas shape material reality no less than the other way around. Marx was well aware that purposeful human invention, the work of ideas on the material world, which in turn created the conditions for further invention, was the engine of our species' remarkable development. Still, Marxists, from Engels onward, grappled with and were often confounded by the supposed primacy of the material over ideas, of the "economic base" over the political and normative "superstructure".[24] Similarly, Marx fully recognized that individual action, especially by leaders and other influential persons (like Marx himself), can have a great effect. What he rejected was the naive "voluntarist" view of human action, which regarded everything as a function of the human will and overlooked the massive array of "objective" or "objectified" conditions that fundamentally constrained people's choices in any particular epoch and society. Indeed, Marx's formulation of the interaction between agency and historical conditions has not been superseded: "Men make their own history, but they do not make it as they please . . . but under circumstances existing already, given and transmitted from the past."[25]

In much the same way, history "is the history of class struggle", the famous line from Marx and Engels's agitating pamphlet "The Communist Manifesto", which was intended to stir the masses during the Revolutions of 1848, and later. It highlighted what Marx saw as the major historical process and mission of the time. However, he could have told the same story also from the perspective of any of the other elements that have participated in the upward spiral of historical transformation, such as technological innovation. Similarly, Marx's "dialectic" explained history, in all its aspects, as a dynamic process of transformation, much looser than the quasi-metaphysical matrix underlying reality that dialectic had been for Hegel and, indeed, would be for Marx's own disciples. Marx's admiring devotees, struggling to fully comprehend the master's gigantic intellectual work, recited his famous lines like sacred tenets of belief and pounded them into a doctrine and dogma. This was often so much at odds with Marx's agile, original, and critical mind to elicit his famous reaction, albeit made in a different context: "Je ne suis pas marxiste", "I am not a Marxist."

This is not to belittle Marx's own dogmatic and ruthless streak and his major errors. We shall shortly return to these errors, as well as to the long-term relationship between Marx's ideas and Marxism. But first, we look closer at the reasons for the tremendous attractiveness of Marx's doctrine, most notably for intellectuals. During a period of epoch-making change, Marx framed socialism as the next step in the unfolding march of history. He admirably traced—historicized—the rise, expansion, and triumph of capitalism as a soci-oeconomic and political process gradually taking place from the early modern period on. Capitalism, as presented by Marx, was a chain in the historical trans-formation of humanity, a seminal and highly successful regime that ultimately brought about industrialization and a dramatic break away from the low, sub-sistence levels of production and wealth that had been the lot of humankind throughout history. Marx's analysis of capitalism's revolutionary dynamics, the socioeconomic relations it shaped, and its impact on human existence, has been pathbreaking and remains an indispensable starting point for any historical and sociological analysis of capitalism. This is so even if Marx's main concept in this regard, the human "alienation" of his early writings, has been greatly ameliorated since capitalism's initial phases and has turned out to be that much sweeter than he anticipated. Moreover, as critics have pointed out, alienation was much more a "universal" of the human condition than Marx allowed, and its predicted im-minent abolition was utopian.

Liberalism, historicized like capitalism, was to be understood according to Marx as the normative platform of the new capitalist regime's dominant class, the bourgeoisie—its biased, interest-based "ideology"—rather than as a theory of universal justice. Classical liberal political economy, from Adam Smith on, was seen by Marx as the admirably keen and fruitful theoretical codification of the capitalist system and modus operandi, rather than comprising the universal principles of either the economy or economics as such. While this historization of the principles of capitalism was deeply insightful, it would be responsible for the belief among socialists that phenomena such as supply and demand or incentives were nothing but transient historical and ideological constructs that could be transcended and overruled. Finally, projecting historicism into the fu-ture, Marx insisted that the capitalist system's ultimate dynamics—its simulta-neous production of both potentially unlimited wealth and great poverty—was an intrinsic contradiction that would lead to capitalism's collapse and transfor-mation into the next and final socioeconomic historical regime: socialism.

The secret of Marxism's huge attraction lay in its combination of a number of mutually reinforcing elements: its highly sophisticated, "scientific", interpre-tation of history in general and of the structure and dynamics of capitalism (the meaning of the German *Wissenschaft* is famously much looser than the English science); the sense of eschatological inevitability it conferred on socialism as the dialectical-historical heir of industrial capitalism's huge capacity for wealth creation and correction of its glaring socioeconomic ills; and, indeed, the deep feeling, which Marxists shared with other socialists, that the massive inequality created by capitalism and the poverty and miserable living and labor conditions of the workers—which have been such a distinctive aspect of capitalism's early phases, then and now (in developing countries)—were insufferably unjust and immoral, as well as being hugely inefficient. For its adherents, Marxism was the irresistible wave of the future, underpinned by both history and justice—a secular theory of ultimate salvation.

The problem is that theory does not stop things from happening, nor is great historical sophistication a guarantee for an ability to predict the future. For one, Marx was famously wrong about his main prediction: that the continued evolution of capitalism was destined to destroy all the middle strata of society and drive everybody, except for the capitalistic magnates, into the ranks of the proletariat, thereby sowing the seeds of capitalism's own demise. By around 1900, so-called revisionists within the Marxist movement and parties, most notably Eduard Bernstein, had already discerned that this was not happening.[26] While small businesses that could not compete were often destroyed, new niches for small and middle-size businesses were continuously opening up, in a process that economist Joseph Schumpeter would describe as capitalism's "creative destruction". Furthermore, new well-paid technical professions and professionals, necessary for the advanced industrial economy, were being created and greatly expanding in number. Moreover, the workers experienced a steady improvement in their wages and labor conditions, achieved by a combination of overall rising prosperity, trade union action, and increasingly democratic electoral systems. Bernstein also noted that, given the great complexity of developed capitalist economies, it was futile to imagine that they could be run by the government rather than by a substantial private sector. Indeed, he reasoned that for all their conflicts of interest, workers and employers have a shared interest in a thriving economy. Revisionists became convinced that the way forward was through continued socioeconomic reform by democratic means, rather than by violent revolution and the dictatorship of the proletariat. In this, they moved closer to non-Marxist, democratic, socialist movements, while increasingly parting ways with revolutionary Marxism.

It was, however, at that junction that the Bolshevik Revolution of 1917 in Russia proved so decisive. Against Marx's expectations, it occurred in a backward country in terms of industrial development and other features of modernization; and the next major success of revolutionary Marxism took place in a similarly backward China, in 1949. These momentous events, as well as the world crisis brought about by the two world wars and the Great Depression, gave a new lease of life to Marxist parties in the West, now separated from the social democratic variants. Furthermore, the materialization of the dictatorship of the proletariat—totalitarian state communism—proved to be the final step in the hardening of Marxism into a rigid dogma. The ingredients for this development had long existed: in the grandeur, all-knowing exclusivism, mobilizing revolutionary imperative, necessary ruthlessness and messianic promise of salvation of Marx's vision. To these there was added the Leninist-Bolshevik central idea regarding the historical duty of the revolutionary elite to lead the masses toward the desired goal that only it perceived clearly, irrespective of the people's petty wishes and by whatever means. Together, all these were responsible for the remarkable paradox of Marxism, deeply ironic in its cognitive aspect and deeply tragic in practice.

We begin with the cognitive aspect. The Marxist avowedly secular and rationalistic ideology assumed all the features of a religious cult and church, and a most fanatic and intolerant one at that. Marxists practically rejected the possibility, intrinsic to any rationalistic theory, that the theory may be incomplete and open to new evidence, revisions, and possible refutation. Bernstein was early to make this point even before the Bolshevik takeover. Instead, Marxist ideology transformed into a dogma, whose principles and prescriptions were offered for general consumption in the form of "catechism". With unintended irony, this was how *The Short Course on the History of the All-Union Communist Party (Bolsheviks)* (1938), compiled under Stalin, was unofficially known. Any deviation from the tenets of the faith, from its sacred Scriptures, or from the bosom of its church was branded as heresy. Open debate, originally the norm in the Party's institutions, would be violently suppressed everywhere. It was replaced by cult worship of a dictatorial leader, whose wisdom, like that of the Pope, was regarded as infallible. Inquisition-like police agencies were responsible for discovering and uprooting any heresy—real or invented—and, moreover, for saving souls and purging the community from evil through public show-trials involving confession, repent, redemption, and execution.

In the Soviet Union of the 1930s and 1940s, followed by Communist China in the 1950s and 1960s, hundreds of thousands and millions were killed by the state, including, in the Soviet Union, the Party's own cadre of leaders and activists. Millions and tens of millions died of hunger in the effort to enforce collectivization. Tens of millions were imprisoned in forced labor camps or exiled. Nonetheless, as long as many believed, both inside and outside of the communist countries, that what was at stake was the toppling of a thoroughly oppressive, unjust, and defunct capitalist system and the ushering in of a bright new era of equality and justice, they came to terms in various ways with all the above. They denied that it was happening, as information was in any case heavily censured, fabricated, and uncertain. They held that any major historical revolution of such magnitude was never a pretty sight and that it necessarily entailed great upheavals, sacrifices, and suffering as "growing pains". In the famous words of Nikolai Yezhov, head of the NKVD, who carried out Stalin's Great Purges of the Party's most loyal (and ultimately became their victim): "When you chop wood, chips fly". They emphasized the new regimes' positive achievements in previously backward countries: the provision of universal education and basic medical services, as well as, in the case of the Soviet Union of the 1930s, massive industrialization and, allegedly, full employment (an acute problem in the capitalist countries during the Great Depression). And they highlighted the communist stand against fascism. The socialist vision's allure and mystique, the mythology surrounding it, and the tremendous romantic devotion it invoked were as powerful and addictive as can be on the ideological spectrum.

Intellectuals were among those most conspicuously captivated, as were many of the young and educated who did not remain indifferent to the Marxist gospel of social justice and fraternity. It took time even for those who observed the Soviet Union from close to confront some very awkward realities. Phrasing these realities in the terms of Marxist theory, the conflicts were exceedingly difficult to digest. Marx's projected emancipating socialist "Kingdom of Freedom"—freedom not only from coercion but from any sort of necessity—turned out to be totalitarian and among the most violently oppressive regimes ever. Social "alienation", rather than dissipating, as Marx anticipated, was acute and all-pervasive.

Some previously communist or sympathetic intellectuals in the West became aware that there was a problem with the communist path to paradise by the late 1930s, following the Stalinist era's violent collectivization, mass famine, show trials and execution of the Party's leadership, and news of the Gulags. Arthur Koestler's *Darkness at Noon* (1940) and George Orwell's *Animal Farm* (1945) and *Nineteen Eighty-Four* (1949) were resounding literary expressions of disillusionment. Others joined by the late 1940s, despite lingering admiration and gratitude for the Soviet Union's heroism, huge sacrifices and decisive contribution to the defeat of Nazism (which helped to erase the devastating impression of the Molotov-Ribbentrop Soviet-Nazi Pact of 1939). *The God That Failed* (1949) was a collection of essays by leading, previously communist, intellectuals, with the God of the title speaking volumes about the status of the communist secular religion in the eyes of its believers. Milovan Djilas's inside view, exposing *The New Class* (1957) of privileged party functionaries and bureaucrats in the communist countries, was another blow. All the same, the allure of the Marxist salvationist message of emancipation remained enormous. Sartre was the most famous intellectual convert to the creed in the late 1940s and 1950s. His opposite number on the French liberal right, Raymond Aron, shrewdly paraphrased Marx's characterization of religion as "the opium of the masses", describing Marxism as a secular religion and branding it *The Opium of the Intellectuals* (1955).

Still, no level of shrewdness in itself is ever sufficient to bring down a major ideology—religious, secular or something in between. Much more is needed. Nikita Khrushchev's secret speech in the Twentieth Congress of the Communist Party of the Soviet Union (1956), in which he denounced "Stalin's crimes", was a devastating blow, undermining the regime's claim of infallibility. The bloody Soviet suppression of the Hungarian anti-communist revolution (1956) was another major blow and was accepted with dismay by many communists. Prague

1968 would be even more shocking, especially in the West. To be sure, it could always be maintained that, like Robespierre for the French Revolution, Stalin, and subsequent major embarrassments, were merely unfortunate historical accidents, not indicative of the correctness of the ideology. What mattered much more for the fortunes of communism and of the communist idea was, appropriately, deeper developments taking place on each of the opposing sides: in both the communist and the capitalist liberal democratic camps. Consciousness was indeed determined by existence, as realities were slowly undermining the massive walls of denial, selective blindness, and cognitive dissonance surrounding what was increasingly becoming, with profound irony, the Marxist "false consciousness".

In the Soviet Union, the massive industrialization of the 1930s and the reconstruction after World War II were followed by endemic and ever-clearer economic stagnation. As all the attempts to revive the economy failed, the regime's intrinsic problems became increasingly evident. Partly, as Aristotle had seen at the dawn of history and as Hume had argued before Adam Smith turned this into the cornerstone of modern economics: in the absence of incentives of gain, people showed little motivation to work and create wealth, and they did not much care about the common property.[27] All-pervasive ideological indoctrination proved insufficient to overcome denied yet deep natural human proclivities. Although massive coercion was applied to bring about the Kingdom of Freedom, to force people to be free, it yielded ever diminishing returns. The more up-to-date parts of the problem, as relating to the modern economy, were most acutely formulated by economist Friedrich Hayek's *The Road to Serfdom* (1944). As he foresaw, the "command economy" lacked the wisdom of the market: the signals that the vast number of consumers in a highly complex modern economy give, and to which the producers respond, as to what the former actually want. The results were low levels of production, poor quality, and a low variety of the merchandise, as well as endemic shortages coupled with the overproduction of unnecessary goods. Unrealistic production quotas imposed by the authorities spawned an all-pervasive culture of deceit, faulty products, and silent evasion at ground level. Thus, while the regimentalized economy was able to generate massive industrialization in the 1930s, albeit at a terrifying human cost, it failed to cope with the requirements of a more advanced economy.

By the 1960s and 1970s, not least among the leaderships in the communist countries themselves, there was an increasing loss of faith in the formerly tremendously captivating and firing vision of a successful communist society overtaking the capitalist countries. The murderous repression of the Stalinist era all but disappeared in the Soviet Union (although in China, Mao unleashed the violent Cultural Revolution, to say nothing of the horrors of Pol Pot's Cambodia or of North Korea). However, social alienation and cynicism were spreading in proportion to the falling hopes. They engulfed much of the top echelons of the Party and the managerial apparatus, who increasingly despaired of the prospects of fixing the system. By the late 1970s in China and mid-1980s in the Soviet Union, the leadership in both countries, independent of each other, voluntarily set about to radically transform the system, which ultimately led to its dismantling.

These developments were not unaffected by those that took place on the capitalist side. In the West, there was the post–World War II boom that ushered in the historically unprecedented "affluent society" of prosperity and comfort. In East Asia, in addition to Japan, the spectacular modernization and meteoric economic growth of some of the formerly poorest countries in the world, such as South Korea and Taiwan, as well as of Singapore, contrasted sharply with the poor performance of Communist China. The Chinese leadership could not fail to notice this by the late 1970s. One of the main tenets of socialism, that the planned economy would be much less wasteful and more efficient than market competition, was increasingly losing credibility with experience. Furthermore, the view that capitalism could never bring affluence to the masses was belied by growing prosperity and the rise of the welfare state. Moreover, liberalism, considered the sham-enlightened face of exploitative capitalism, generated a massive increase in social toleration and acceptance in the liberal democracies during the post–World War II era, with a special takeoff point in the 1960s. As important, imperialism was conventionally interpreted, from Lenin onward, as the inevitable extension of capitalism in its final, monopolistic stage. We shall see about this claim in the following chapter. But, in any case, imperialism was now rolled back. The Western empires, regarded by many as both a major moral offense and the cause of wars, were dismantled. Finally, the greatest blemish on the face of American democracy—racial segregation and discrimination—were outlawed and fought against. The contrast with the oppressed and alienated communist societies became ever more glaring.

Echoes of this accentuating dissonance could be heard in the emerging dissident talk of "socialism with a human face" within the Soviet Bloc from the 1960s on. Such voices and the attempts at this direction were suppressed by robust force up until the total collapse of the Soviet totalitarian system in the 1980s and early 1990s. All the same, despite the great dissonance between its promise and its realities, Marxist devotees found it exceedingly difficult to shake off the ideology's immense emotive spell and give up on its millenarian gospel of justice and salvation. Indeed, Marxism's strength as a secular religion or religion substitute probably fed directly on the religious energies released and redirected with the process of secularization and the "Death of God". Hence the willingness among its followers to embrace the most incredible beliefs, accept "darkness at noon" as a fact, which is reminiscent of the celebration of the absurd as the mark of the true believer in the religious doctrines of old. The same holds for the devotees' ability to explain why the messiah had failed to come at the designated times of his prophesized return. Note the painful process of quasi-religious dis-illusionment of those who, in time, came to disavow the "God that failed". With the profoundest of ironies, Marxism as a political doctrine became the "false consciousness" *par excellence*. As the enthusiasm for the Soviet model waned, the idealistic and dissenting energies of intellectuals and the young embraced other cult figures and myths of salvation and purification: Mao, Fidel, Che, and even Pol Pot.

In addition to the emotive appeal of its eschatological promise, there was the tremendous attraction of Marxism as a cognitive framework for the inter-pretation of history and reality. With a largely justified reputation, Marxism functioned as a modern-day theology in the sense that it offered the best of minds a doctrine of very high level of intellectual sophistication with which to grapple, work, and identify. Indeed, the paradox of Marxism lay not only in the fantastic gap that separated its theory and its practice; it was also evident in the gulf that opened up between the doctrine's tremendous intellectual sophisti-cation and the complete blindness to the mounting evidence exhibited by its devotees, many of them individuals of the highest intellectual caliber.

Achieving a dominance of sorts in intellectual and academic circles between the 1950s and 1970s, particularly in Europe (and the "Third World"), Marxism has faded away as a mass ideology with the paradigmatic crisis and meltdown that followed the collapse of communism. In the study of history and social theory as well, the main insights of Marxism have been largely absorbed, while its more dogmatic aspects have been mostly transcended. All the same, Marxism retains an unusual presence among intellectuals and academics, most notably its critique of capitalism. As an ideology, Marxism has survived among a dwindling number of loyal faithful, who seem to come in two main forms: diehard dogmatists; and people who, in an apparent contrast to the supposed Marxist approach, are far more affected in crystallizing their ideological outlook by ab-stract ideals than by the evidence of historical experience.

At about the same time that communism experienced bankruptcy, suspicions had been growing that democratic socialism was also afflicted with some of the same problems that plagued its communist counterpart—albeit to a far lesser degree and with none of its brutality. A sweeping surge of so-called conserva-tive neo-liberalism followed. While neo-liberalism has set out to correct serious problems revealed in the welfare state model, its ascendency has again brought to the fore problems and question marks long associated with capitalism. As a result, a great divide has opened up within the liberal democratic camp. We shall return to examine this ideological divide later in the book. But first we turn to the third major ideological contender of the twentieth century: fascism.

Fascism: A Third Way to Modernity?

Fascism took its name from Mussolini's party and regime in post–World War I Italy. But it quickly became a generic term for a characteristic mood, array of ideological convictions, and broad family of political movements, parties, and regimes active during the first decades of the twentieth century. The differences between them were sometimes very significant, but so were also the similarities. Nazism was the most distinctive family member in terms of its historical impact, while imperial Japan's nationalistic and militaristic regime during the 1930s was a more distant cousin. There were French, British, and other fascist variants in industrial Europe. And there were the authoritarian-conservative regimes and right-wing radical movements in the predominantly agrarian countries of Eastern Europe, the Iberian Peninsula, and Latin America, which adopted many features of the fascist political culture during the 1930s. In view of the great diversity of "fascism" and the question of to whom the term should be applied, scholars have attempted to put together a "fascist minimum". But a looser concept based on "family resemblance" may be more fruitful, with family members and relatives hovering at various distances from the fascist historical "core". In the same spirit, fascism "per se" may be viewed as historically confined to the particular conditions of the early twentieth century. Some later ideological creeds and political regimes may partly share sentiments and concerns with the fascism of old, whether they exhibit a close affinity with it or not.

Fascism emerged as a cultural mood from around 1900, on the heels of industrialization, urbanization, and the growth of mass society. With its proponents arriving from both the left and the right, it was championed as a "third way" to modernity, an alternative to—a transcendence of—both capitalist liberal democracy and socialism. It enjoyed a strong appeal among intellectuals and was taken up by enterprising leaders who transformed it into the ideological basis of political movements that galvanized the masses. Those who partook in the fascist mood rebelled against bourgeois culture, with its petty conventions and "philistine" tastes, "decadent" materialism, commercialism, atomistic and alienating individualism, liberal-humanitarian values, and "weak", "sickly", "over-sensitiveness". They rejected the political and class antagonism intrinsic to the capitalist democratic system. They dreaded what they saw as the further advance of plebeianism and mediocrity and the trivialization of life expected with growing democratization. While resenting the old elites and the establishment, they found socialist leveling equally repellent. Calling for a spiritual and idealistic revival and for a re-enchantment of life afflicted by over-rationalism, they exalted dynamism, action, vitality, and vigor. They sought to overcome the divisiveness of both parliamentarianism and socialism by the celebration of a communal creed that would mobilize the masses around unifying national traditions, myths, and ideals.

Varieties of fascism thus blended various degrees of preindustrial nostalgia and agrarian mythology with the most vivid modernist and futuristic visions. Whereas the Nazi variant has been dubbed "reactionary modernism", other fascist brands, most notably the Italian original, were avowedly forward-looking, regarding themselves as the truly modernist order for a modern society. Fascists held that government should be firmly kept in the hands of a worthy meritocratic elite, and the most prominent fascist varieties gave a central place to the figure of a strong supreme leader. In this way, fascism could encompass the masses without being dominated by them—create a popular and cohesive national community without being democratic. The national community, embodied in the state, overrode all else. An incorporated economy, syndicating employers and workers, would bridge over the antagonisms of the capitalist labor market; inject capitalism with the stability it lacked; be overseen toward greater efficiency by an expert state administration responsible for forward planning; limit plutocratic exploitative power; and both give justice to and restrain the workers.[28]

Fascism became a major political force and was catapulted into power in a number of leading countries with the upheavals, instability, and economic crises brought about by World War I, the Bolshevik Revolution, and the Great Depression. It introduced a new, carnival style of political activity (also shared by communist countries and movements), involving the masses in emotionally arousing marches, parades, rallies, and ceremonies, carefully choreographed and supported by the most up-to-date technologies of radio and film.[29] Like the congregations of old, these perpetual mass public displays and rituals embraced both participants and onlookers in an uplifting spirit of togetherness and celebrated a deep sense of belonging to the national community. Stirring, hypnotic speeches evoked mass psychosis bordering on hysteria, of the type affected by charismatic preachers and later associated with pop and rock stars. Mass indoctrination by means of catchy slogans hammered in the tenets of the ideological creed, warned and incited against enemies within and without, and elevated the power of the will to conquer all.

In Italy, especially in retrospect, all these often resembled a somewhat comic operetta, and the fascist regime itself would appear increasingly clownish. In Germany (and Japan), the image projected was more intimidating and sinister. Contrary to the Nietzschean ideal of greatness which inspired proto-fascist, fascist, and sympathetic intellectuals—and to their deep disappointment—the leadership, functionaries, and rank and file of the fascist movements and regimes were made up in large part by social misfits, thugs, and other lowly creatures, who mixed fanatical ideological devotion with opportunistic nihilism.

As disappointing, the same and other intellectuals found the regime's cultural tastes and policies equally philistine and vulgar. However, what brought fascism to an abrupt and ignoble end were the horrific, monumental orgies of killing and destruction that some regimes of the fascist genre perpetrated and, ultimately, brought upon their own peoples. Again, fascist Italy was a lightweight in all this. Nazism, with its unique racialist fanaticism, stands out in the scale and scope of its program of conquest, enslavement, and genocide. Japan's militaristic regime can be counted as second only to the supreme heights of brutality and killing reached by Nazi Germany. By the end of World War II, all these countries lay in ruins, leaving their peoples with very little appetite for repeating this experiment. But, indeed, to what degree was this historical outcome intrinsic to fascism and foretold, and how transient was this ideology?

Certainly, fascism was inclined toward chauvinistic nationalism, and violence and repression were central to both its theory and practice. In countries like Italy, Germany, and Japan, which felt themselves deprived in the international arena, fascism was also characterized by a strongly revisionist foreign policy and aggressive militarism. These constituted an important part of the fascist appeal and helped movements of the fascist genre into power. However, although fascism was by nature antagonistic and in some ways war-prone in its foreign relations, it may not have been necessarily as horrifically aggressive and murderous as its association with the Nazi chapter in history suggests. In satisfied, status quo, Britain of the 1930s, for example, Oswald Mosley's British Union of Fascists, amplifying the isolationist sentiment in the country, declared itself the "party of peace" and eschewed foreign commitments and entanglement in great power wars. Much the same applied to "pacifistic" movements of the fascist genre in France of the 1930s and, of course, to the Vichy regime. Fascism was regarded above all as being about domestic affairs also in smaller countries, like Belgium and/or less developed ones, such as those of Eastern Europe, the Iberian Peninsula, and Latin America. Many of them were all quite cautious about getting involved in foreign adventures, and some, in Eastern Europe, were swept into World War II under pressure from Nazi Germany and because of revisionist temptations brought to life by Hitler's momentous victories.

Still, was the defeat and demise of fascism preordained, rooted in its very nature? Furthermore, was fascism just a phase, limited to the particular conditions of the early twentieth century and unlikely to re-emerge? We shall address the second question first. It can plausibly be argued that the fascist spell was strong in early industrializing and relatively poor societies, whose people still deeply felt the dislocation and alienation that the unsettling transition from traditional rural to modern urban existence entailed. The fascist spell was supposedly thereafter dissipated with the massively rising levels of affluence and comfort the world has seen since then. GDP per capita in today's developed countries is ten to twenty times higher than a century ago, during the classical fascist era. There remain pervasive expressions of existential boredom and complaints about a lack of meaning, stifling routine, rampant materialism and consumerism, absence of a communal spirit, and the banality and vulgarity of the media and entertainment industry. All the same, people in the affluent parts of the world are anything but willing to sacrifice their comfortable lifestyle and liberties, let alone enlist in military adventures.

A time of trouble, most notably that which has come in the wake of the Great Recession, from 2007–2008 on, followed by the immigrants crisis, has shaken liberal democratic societies. It has given rise to so-called populism and nativism and saw the massive growth of ultra-right parties and movements in Europe. "Populism" in the United States and Western Europe, despite occasional derogatory comparisons in the public discourse, does not come even close to "fascism", the authoritarian and totalitarian ideology, movements, and parties that came to power during the earlier time of crisis in the 1920s and 1930s. At the same time, some of the ultra-right/alt-right parties and movements in Western Europe have a fascist ancestry. Within the more radical parliamentary and extra-parliamentary elements of some of them, there is also covert and overt flirtation with fascist and even Nazi themes. The ultra-right is certainly challenging the post-1945 political order, outlook, and consensus. Most notably, this applies to issues relating to immigration, national identity, and multiculturalism, in which the ultra-right is instrumental in effecting a change across the political spectrum. How significant the ultra-right is going to become beyond this, how likely it is to win power or establish "fascism" in the economically most developed parts of the world, is a matter of assessment. In my humble one, this is not very likely.

If so, what about developing countries, which are still behind the cutting edge of modernization and affluence and whose conditions are more akin to those of the classical fascist period? In today's world, a number of cases raise this question. One of them is Putin's Russia, deeply resentful after the loss of an empire and the disappointments and crises of Russia's liberal phase during the 1990s. The regime in Russia has not only become increasingly authoritarian and nationalistic, but to some degree has also revived Russia's imperial ambitions and has adopted a more militant stance. Moreover, it is increasingly cultivating the traditional, centuries-old Russian disdain for Western liberalism—regarded as degenerate, immoral, and hypocritical—turning this into a semi-official state ideology. As an antithesis to liberalism, the regime is celebrating the equally deeply rooted notions of a Russian-Slavic great soul, idealistic spirituality, and love of country. Corporatism in the economy, a central element of "classical" fascism, has since fallen out of fashion. But state intervention to regulate the economy in the national interest and prevent labor disputes is alive in today's Russia. Indeed, in reality, what this means is a kleptocracy by a cynical, opportunistic, and corrupt elite, a common enough feature in the fascism of old. The Russian economy, wholly reliant on the exports of raw materials, is a complete failure. How likely is this regime to survive and/or be carried to greater extremes, and at what price, is anybody's guess.

China is a more intriguing, and challenging, case. Ruled by a party that is only nominally communist, it has embraced the market economy with great success. While still a fifth to a sixth as rich as the developed countries in per capita terms, China is fast becoming an economic and military superpower. In recent years and contrary to earlier expectations in the West, the stronger China becomes, a more authoritarian a form its regime assumes and the tighter its surveillance and control of society becomes. It employs the most up-to-date information technologies for that purpose in what may become a new brand of totalitarianism. Simultaneously, the stronger China becomes, the more assertive and even aggressive its foreign policy. Furthermore, the regime is increasingly stressing China's ideological difference from and antagonism toward the liberal West, highlighting Chinese traditional values, such as respect for order, hierarchy, and social harmony. It is actively fueling nationalist sentiments. Bureaucratic rule by the Party's functionaries is often stifling and corrupt. However, the deep crisis of the liberal democracies ever since the outbreak of the Great Recession in 2007–2008 has badly tarnished the democracies' previously unrivaled reputation for success and prosperity, bringing to mind the disastrous consequences of the earlier crisis of the democracies in the 1930s. Against this background, the rulers, elites, and many of the people of China have had their view confirmed that a meritocratic state elite—modern-day mandarins—is better equipped to run the country and manage the economy rationally than is the dysfunctional democratic system.[30]

That said, China's regime is going to face daunting challenges that will test its durability, including an increasingly more affluent, educated, and opinionated public, inevitable economic crises, and a rapidly aging population. I wrote about the return of the authoritarian capitalist great powers before the crisis of the democracies began, when capitalist liberal democracy was still almost universally regarded as the unchallenged model for the future.[31] Even before Xi Jinping became leader of China, had the laws limiting the term of his office abolished and made control and oppression by the regime much stricter, I speculated that a more totalitarian turn might be one potential avenue for China. Whether the regime in China survives into the future as China continues to develop, what directions it will take and how much of the fascist features of old it might adopt remains to be seen.

Finally, one could mention some contemporary developments in countries of Eastern Europe, most notably, at the moment of writing, Viktor Orbán's Hungary. Eastern Europe's legacy of chauvinistic nationalism, anti-liberal authoritarianism and fascism during the 1920s and 1930s (except in Czechoslovakia) was viewed as a thing of the past following the collapse of communism and the great enthusiasm for the incorporation of the countries of this region into the European Union. However, since then, the dimming luster of the Western liberal model, the pressures of mass Muslim immigration and other developments have seen the rise of what Orbán has called "illiberal democracy", whose democratic character is in effect continuously rolled back and limited.

It should be emphasized that quite a few themes and concerns amplified by fascism continue to reverberate in other contexts and within other ideological creeds without these necessarily making them fascist. We have already mentioned pervasive expressions of existential boredom in today's affluent liberal democracies and distress and criticism concerning a lack of meaning, excessive materialism, absence of a communal spirit, and the triviality and vulgarity of the media and mass entertainment. After World War II, this criticism came mainly from the left and was most famously associated with the neo-Marxist Frankfurt School, which was in vogue in the youth culture of the 1960s.[32] Many fascists also dabbled in mysticism, occultism, and "New Age" rites. These are still with us, together with a widespread yearning for a more spiritual and idealistic life experience. For their part, political philosophies such as "republicanism" and "communitarianism" posit democratic antidotes to the alleged atomistic individualism of modern society. Liberal nationalism (as well as illiberal varieties) promotes the value of national communities with their unique cultures and sense of belonging and solidarity, in contrast to out-and-out cosmopolitan views that recognize only the individual or humanity as a whole as legitimate categories of identification. Populism, defined as mistrust of and rebellion against the established, sometimes ossified or self-serving, elites and conventional politics, and occasionally reaching the helm, holds a significant place in the annals of the democracies. In some cases it has been a catalyst for reform—think, for example, of Jacksonian democratizing populism in the history of the United States. In other cases, populism might lead democracies astray, away from effective, rational solutions to the challenges they face, if not from liberal democracy itself. Finally, its cult of nature makes fascism a precursor of modern environmentalism, which does not of course make the latter—or any of the above-mentioned sentiments and movements—synonymous with fascism in any way.

The "End of History"?—Who Won and Why?

As the twentieth century drew to a close, it appeared that only one of the three major ideologies that had vied among themselves on the shaping of modern, industrial mass society remained standing. Against this background, the triumph of capitalist liberal democracy was widely regarded as the verdict of History.[33] Democracy was supposed to possess intrinsic selective advantages, which conferred an air of inevitability on the past as well as on the future. However, as I have argued at some length well before the "crisis of democracy" and can only briefly summarize here, while capitalist democracy may still inherit the earth, this is far from being a foregone conclusion, proved by past experience or the lessons of history.[34] Famously, history is written by the victors. There is a strong tendency to read history backward and view the final outcome—which may be strongly affected by contingent factors—as predetermined and, indeed, as a vindication of the victors' path. There are two main, interrelated, perspectives on the question of why the liberal democracies won during the twentieth century: that of great power politics and that of internal development.

We begin with the former—great power conflict and war. I argue that there were very different reasons for the defeat of the communists, as opposed to that of the capitalist non-democratic challengers, including those of the fascist genre. The communist great powers, the Soviet Union and China (in its genuinely communist phase), even though they were larger and therefore had the potential to be more powerful than the capitalist democracies, ultimately lost because they proved to be economically inefficient. It was their *system* that failed, as their own leaders ultimately came to recognize. On the other hand, the capitalist non-democratic great powers were not defeated because of inefficiency. Technologically and economically, Germany was as advanced as its rivals in both world wars, and Japan exhibited the fastest growth rate of any country between 1913 and 1939. Their problem was that they happened to be too small. Both Germany and Japan were middle-size countries with a limited resource and manpower base. Unable to contend with the giants, most notably the continent-size United States (in World War II, in alliance with the continent-size Soviet Union), they were crushed under the weight of the coalitions assembled against them. The reason for their fall was therefore largely contingent. Throughout the twentieth century, the United States' power consistently surpassed that of the next two strongest states combined, and this decisively tilted the global balance of power in favor of the democracies. If any factor gave the liberal democracies their edge, it was above all the actual existence and continental size of the United States rather than any inherent advantage of liberal democracy.

Put differently, if it were not for the existence of the United States, the liberal democracies would most likely have *lost* the great struggles of the twentieth century. For a start, Britain and France would probably have lost to Germany in either of the two world wars. This is a sobering thought, making the world created by the twentieth century's conflicts appear much more contingent—and tenuous—than unilinear theories of development and the view of history as Progress would have us believe. In a very real sense, we might have had a very different—and non-democratic—twentieth century, a very different world today, and a very different story to tell in the form of grand theories of development. If it were not for the "US factor", the judgment of later generations on liberal democracy would probably have echoed the negative verdict on democracy's performance issued by the Greeks in the fourth century BCE, in the wake of Sparta's defeat of Athens in the Peloponnesian War, a verdict reiterated by political philosophers down to the eighteenth century. We are inclined to rationalize backward, but the lessons of history are a tricky thing.

We now turn to the argument of domestic development. It is widely held that after crossing a certain threshold in terms of development—wealth per capita, education, urbanization, and so forth—societies tend to democratize. This has been the case during the latter part of the twentieth century in East and Southeast Asia, southern Europe, and Latin America.[35] But again, I suggest that this notion is an abstraction from a very particular set of circumstances that prevailed after 1945, with the result that the sample is skewed. This is so because all the post-1945 cases of development leading to democratization involved small countries, which after the defeat of the capitalist nondemocratic great powers—Germany and Japan—could only choose between the communist and capitalist-democratic camps. If they chose the latter, they were exposed to powerful pressures from the hegemonic liberal democratic center, pressures that contributed significantly to their eventual democratization.

The question that arises then is whether a modernized giant China (and, less crucially, Russia) might set its own course, based on its own historical traditions, retain an authoritarian-capitalist-nationalistic regime, and globally revive an ideological alternative to liberal democracy. Indeed, this is probably the greatest political question of the twenty-first century. As already mentioned, I raised this question and examined some of the arguments and counterarguments that it involves when commentators still espoused the End of History.[36] All in all, I do not presume to know the future and only suggest that the outcome is far from being preordained as the post–Cold War mindset would have had it.

Might the most discredited ideological challenger and loser of the industrial era, fascism, stage a comeback—ironically, on the ruins of communism, the modern ideology regarded by many at the time as the inevitable next stage of history, extending the implementation of equality from the merely legal and political to the economic and social? Capitalist-étatist authoritarian and semi-totalitarian regimes might proliferate as the communist totalitarian brand is clearing the scene. One is reluctant to apply the label fascism to either the China or Russia of today. While both promote an increasingly vehement anti-liberal creed, both lack the fanatical mobilization of the masses in a perpetual political carnival that characterized the signature fascist regimes of old (and that we still witness, for example, in today's communist North Korea). They also lack their radical revolutionary edge. Over time, the absence of these two elements might breed cynicism or, alternatively, protect them from messianic disillusionment. In contrast to the autarkic leaning of historical fascism, China in particular is deeply integrated into the world economy, at least for now. Indeed, while Russia's crony capitalist regime is more appropriately described as kleptocracy, the economic regime in China is best characterized as a state-party-nationalistic-ruled market, intended both to protect the Party's undisputed dominance and project loyalty to the goal of greater social equality. This, too, is a combination both somewhat reminiscent of the pretense of the fascist regimes of old with their anti-plutocratic ideology and rhetoric *and* expressing an erstwhile, revived commitment of China's nominally communist ruling party. In summary, the range of authoritarian-capitalist-nationalistic regimes is broader than the historical fascist varieties. All the same, and provided that the regimes of China and Russia survive higher levels of economic and social development, ideological diversity in the developed parts of the world might return, with a global ideological rivalry outliving the supposed "End of History".

Conclusion

The three major ideologies of the industrial era each responded to fundamental, deep-seated, but often conflicting human yearnings, motivations, and concerns as they received expression under modern conditions. Liberalism and liberal democracy rode on people's desire for freedom from external constraints, a sense of equality, and belief in the primacy and advantages of self-interest. Socialism was predicated on the deep quest for equality, arising from human sociability but ever in tension with people's natural inequality and competitive self-interest. Fascism celebrated the sense of communal togetherness and cohesive unity within the tribal-national group and against outsiders; it expressed a shared human desire for emotional elation and feeling of transcendence, as well as the propensities to lead and be led. The particular ideological propositions and political, social, and economic regimes and institutions advanced to fulfill these diverse human aspirations have undergone the grinding test of historical experience. Some of them have stood the test better than others in terms of their practical feasibility, rewards, and drawbacks, with obvious consequences in terms of people's perceptions, expectations, and preferences. In the process, people have changed or adjusted their ideological convictions, even if the basic human sensibilities that gave rise to them endure and questions regarding their possible implementation in reality in one way or another remain open.

The test of reality should warn us against hindsight and wisdom after the event in judging ideologies. There is a process of practical trial and error that is indispensable for clarifying what ideological assumptions and solutions actually produce the desired results. We had better treat with some skepticism the often-heard claim that there were people at the time who correctly foresaw the outcomes. While not disregarding their wisdom and foresight, what we might have here, at least partly, is a retrospective selection bias. Many people said many things at the time, and some of them were likely to have turned out to be more prescient in their assessments and predictions simply by virtue of the diversity in the marketplace of ideas. The term "utopia", for example, is often applied to the communist vision of the future and is intended to underscore this vision's supposed idealistic disconnect from reality. But it is only in the light of historical experience that we can venture some judgment on how realistic this vision has proved to be. Indeed, the liberal program of the Enlightenment could be regarded as no less fantastic, or utopian, had it not proven so remarkably successful in implementation.

A distinction should also be made between ordinary mistakes and those caused by ideological biases and fixations. Mistakes are inevitable in any cognitive process of learning, and all the more so in assessing complex future potentialities. Furthermore, any conceptual framework can withstand a great deal of counter-evidence and survive problems, contradictions, and refutations, without being thereby wholly dispelled. It is only when the weight of the evidence becomes overwhelming, societal conditions change radically, and more successful alternatives move to the fore, that people become prone to a paradigm shift. That said, and as we have seen with respect to historical religions, the phenomenon of ideological fixation is very distinctive and strong.

With ideology comprising an amalgam of values and a map of how to implement them in reality, people are spread along a continuum with respect to the weight they ascribe to each of these elements. Some people are inclined to be more ideal-oriented, while others more reality-directed. Many students of ideology have referred to this tension, pointing out the "ahistorical", "utopian" approach's frequent conflict with reality. Max Weber has written about the balance that needs to be struck between the ethics of conviction and the ethics of responsibility, which more or less parallel the distinction between ethics of good intentions and ethics of consequences.[37] As we have seen, both are basic perspectives that our mind employs to assess normative situations, with the former taking psychological precedence, presumably because evolutionarily it proved more crucial in social bargaining. All the same, normative convictions have always had to be weighed against and adjusted to the realities of the world, or be crushed by experience, for ideology is highly resistant, and often impervious, to evidence.

Rather than as a weakness, the revolutionary syndicalist (and proto-fascist) thinker Georges Sorel, author of the influential *Reflections on Violence* (1908), viewed this as a positive source of strength: "People who are living in this world of myths are secure from all refutation; something which has led many to assert that socialism is a kind of religion. For a long time people have been struck by the fact that religious convictions are unaffected by criticism. . . . Renan was very surprised to discover that socialists were beyond discouragement: 'After each abortive experience they begin again; the solution has not been found, we will find it. The idea that no solution exists never occurs to them, and there lies their strength.'"[38]

All this applies to all ideologies—albeit not in equal degree—and there are additional dimensions to their appeal. What keeps people within the ideological frame is largely a sense of belonging to a community and congregation of identity and shared belief. In the words of one sociologist, the benefits of utopian ideology "depend only on participation, not on success."[39] As noted earlier, conformity combines deep-seated social, normative, and cognitive aspects.[40] The social aspect of identity and belonging is reinforced by communal rites and ceremonial gatherings. We have seen that in some cases they can take the form of an intense and perpetual political carnival intended to inculcate solidarity, common values, and shared narratives. In the Nazi case, for example, evocative themes and symbols of pagan worship were widely integrated. But, with obvious differences, there is of course an extensive array of civil sacred myths, ceremonies, and rituals in liberal countries as well.[41]

The cognitive aspect of ideology is rooted in the fact that knowledge and frameworks of interpretation are collective and cumulative human constructs. People inherit, internalize, and become reliant on these interpretive scripts in the process of socialization, as they cannot possibly devise them each for him or herself. Systems of values and norms are equally communal and socialized into. They are buttressed by the most powerful feelings of rightness and wrongness, easily translated into moral indignation and rage. Together, these cognitive and normative scripts determine the boundaries of what is regarded as reasonable and acceptable in the social discourse and what should be fought against as evil, heretical, or blasphemous. Hence, again, the all too familiar characteristics of ideological "closure". As the ideological conceptual framework and manual for action are intended to guide human collective behavior in relation to normative issues that people regard as most crucial for the proper functioning of the world, they typically feel most strongly about them. Therefore, the factual claims of ideology tend to be upheld with far greater emotional investment, and greater zeal, than those aroused by ordinary assertions of facts. Furthermore, because of the unique, overriding significance of shared collective life in human evolution, normative issues tend to take precedent over factual questions in our psyche. For this reason, the factual in ideology tends to be subordinate to the normative when tensions, or "cognitive dissonances", emerge between them. There is a strong resistance to recognize and accept factual claims that appear to be at odds with the ideological creed, to a degree that often makes such a creed almost immune to the test or reality. Potentially valid claims from other perspectives— and other ideological creeds—simply do not register. As ideological disputes are largely a matter of social bargaining, any cognitive "concession" to the other side might weaken one's position. Only rarely can a massive, "tectonic", shift in the factual picture of the world—what we judge to be real or possible—lead to a transformation of people's normative array.

Each ideology possesses its own particular mythologies, sacred histories, icons, and iconic figures: prophets, heroes, saints, and martyrs with their epics and memorable tales, as well as villains and scarecrows. As Sorel has argued, it is the great myths that get hold of people's minds that drive history, no less so than the material forces emphasized by Marxism. Just consider the historical impact of that poor carpenter's son from Nazareth, who, contrary to Stalin's famous quip with respect to the Pope, had no divisions except for a tiny group of equally in- significant followers. Indeed, Stalin, his regime and his divisions are long gone, while the Pope, the Church, and their legions of believers are still around.

Certainly, rather than belonging to two opposite poles, visionary programs and concrete social power relations are tied together in many ways. Nor should the mythologies surrounding ideologies detract from the seriousness of their visions and of the conflicts between them, as these competing visions touch on questions of the utmost significance for people's lives (and deaths), well-being, prosperity, and happiness. The struggle among liberalism, socialism, and fascism over the last centuries is the most eloquent testimony to this. The mythologies of the historical religions may appear entirely fictitious to us, and bloody conflicts concerning, say, the nature of the Trinity may nowadays seem absurd, although both were not so regarded at the time, given the prevailing cosmologies and ge- neral picture of the world. Either way, the historical religions have also functioned as systems of virtue, addressing central questions and advancing manuals for proper human conduct in a complex social world, in life. From our modern per- spective, the assumptions and worldviews underlying the secular ideologies of the nineteenth and twentieth centuries have been far more grounded in reality, even if their assumptions and answers have often ultimately proved less so. The clash of these ideologies demonstrates that no system of government and orga- nization of society can endure without deep legitimation, quite often generating tremendous emotional and cognitive mobilization, no less intense than that which animates the religions of old. Similarly, a loss of faith and conversions of creeds may assume avalanche proportions during deep paradigmatic crises and shifts. The religion-like features of the secular ideologies as widely held com- munal creeds—into which people are socialized and which they may deeply internalize and devoutly uphold—are integral to ideology, the cognitive and emotional template through which people deal with social questions of great significance.

The conceptual line between "socialization" and "indoctrination" is a fine one, of course. Many would insist that the practice of indoctrination applies as much to the liberal ideology and societies as it does to the authoritarian-totalitarian ideologies. The neo-Marxists of the New Left in the 1950s and 1960s claimed that it applied more.[42] There is, however, a very marked conceptual—and practical—difference between liberalism and the authoritarian-totalitarian ideologies in terms of their pluralism, toleration of diverse opinions, and ruthlessness of suppression of divergent views. That said, a tension within liberalism between toleration as a constitutive element of the creed and commitment not only to oppose intolerance, but also to advance liberal values, norms, and institutions against those of other creeds, is as old as the Enlightenment. This commitment has always involved a measure of intolerance and sometimes also dogmatic and messianic zeal. The classical, moderate nineteenth-century British liberal brand supposedly relied on rational, "common sense" arguments to convince and convert, without being less committed and passionate on that account. It has largely given way to more zealous and sometimes fanciful varieties, as liberalism has split, remixed, and been further energized within a larger number of ideological currents from the twentieth century on.

PART III

CURRENT DEBATES
AND FIXATIONS IN THE
DEMOCRACIES

This part addresses some major ideological premises and fixations that have dominated the public and political discourse in the economically most developed countries of the world (currently, say, above $20,000 GDP per capita from non-oil resources) since 1945. Presently, all these countries are liberal democracies. The great majority are Western in terms of their cultural heritage, while a few are largely "Westernized", in the sense that during the process of their modernization they adopted a great deal of the political institutions and normative codes originating in the West.

By this I do not imply that the ideological views and debates that have taken center stage in the developed world are the only ones that matter in today's world. Far from it. As noted in the previous chapter, it remains to be seen whether the right-wing authoritarian/semi-totalitarian regimes that have resurfaced in some of the world's major developing countries will survive as these countries achieve higher levels of economic development. This may be the most crucial political question of the twenty-first century, suggesting a strong potential for a global ideological conflict not seen since the demise of communist totalitarianism. In addition, militant fundamentalist currents within Islam have been engaging in a stark, sometimes violent, conflict with Western liberalism. Notably, though, this harkening back to the seventeenth century's Wars of Religion springs from societies that are among the world's least developed and most resistant to socioeconomic modernization, and whose GDP per capita (from non-oil sources) is only around one tenth of the minimum threshold cited above for the developed countries. Although salient in today's world, militant radical Islam is basically a premodern response to the challenge of the modern world, and it may be expected to transform and lose much of its sting when socioeconomic modernization finally takes off in the societies concerned. This does not mean that religion will cease to play a role in the ideological landscape of the developed world. However, when it does play a role there, religion, being a historically evolving phenomenon, generally takes its place within the framework of democratic and even liberal norms, institutions, and practices. By and large, this has also applied to so-called religious fundamentalism in the United States.

The reason we now turn to discuss ideological views and debates that have figured most prominently in the world's most developed societies is these societies' dominant, hegemonic, position and the huge gravitational force they exert throughout the world: past, present, and, most likely, in the future. Liberal democracy has been more or less their consensual ideological and political framework since 1945. As we have seen, it encompasses the two major ideological creeds that branched out of classical liberalism, both of which embraced democracy by around 1900: right-wing, minimal government liberalism, which has joined hands with modern conservatism; and left-wing, welfare-state liberalism, which has come closer together with modernized social democracy. In addition, there has been a host of ideological newcomers to the liberal democratic scene. Some of them can be described as later-day offshoots from the liberal stem. Others have taken stances in stark opposition to the liberal democratic consensus. They have become influential dissenting voices in the public and political discourse within the liberal democracies and have been partly absorbed into mainstream liberalism. Such dissenting creeds and/or offshoots have included, among others, the New Left, and feminist-gender, anti-racist, and environmentalist ideologies and movements.

In some ways, this part has been the most challenging to write, as it deals with ideological rifts that are very much alive and kicking. Many people deeply identify with, are wholly immersed in, and define themselves by the ideological outlooks in question, whose tenets often function for them as articles of faith, both cognitively and emotionally. Moreover, the premises and fixations suggested here have been buttressed by massive arrays of prestigious, authoritative, and seemingly highly sophisticated intellectual work. Much of it has gained canonical status and has been inculcated in people's minds by years of training in educational systems. Having been socialized into them, people hold such premises to be self-evident. Living ideologies seem to the people that hold them as "transparent", simply as the natural way of the world, rather than as colored spectacles or a particular perspective. Challenges to the canons of the creed tend to be perceived as flying in the face of reason, sacrilegious and malevolent, often outrageous. Indeed, people derive their sense of ideological identity, affiliation, and confidence from the large groups of like-minded people who typically constitute their social circles. Moreover, their ideological outlook is famously associated with their socioeconomic interests. Thus, unlike past ideological misconceptions and fixations about reality, which people are willing to recognize much more easily, they are almost incapable of accepting them with respect to their present-day outlook— the cognitive, normative, and emotional guidebook that constitutes their secular religion. For this reason, it is in relation to the present that the topic of this book is most pointedly demonstrated and tested.

Once more, it should be clarified that what we are addressing is not the value element of ideologies, whose differences in this regard are often fundamentally irreducible and irreconcilable. Nor do we dispute the paramount practical significance of the questions that ideologies deal with for people's lives. However, the realization of any value preference or social objective depends on a reliable roadmap for navigating the world, which in turn requires a roughly valid interpretation of reality. And it is here that ideological closure is so evident. Again, ideological zeal strengthens one's hand in social bargaining, the forcing through of ideological platforms in the teeth of opposition. At the same time, if it is the cause of serious distortions in people's picture of reality, it might lead them astray off the road to their objectives. Furthermore, excessive zeal and fixation might backfire by galvanizing resistance on the other side, thereby forestalling the attainment of the desired aims.

The scope of current ideological creeds, debates, and fixations in the democracies is daunting. The ideological clash in the United States in particular between progressives and conservatives has flared up with surprising and escalating ferocity from the 1980s onward. The arguments and counterarguments in the public debates have elucidated many of the issues while, predictably, having often had little impact on the respective positions of the opposing sides. It is not the intention here to add yet another review of a vast ideological landscape, nor to rehash the all too familiar arguments from the American culture war. Everything about them has already been said and written. Instead, we propose to dig into a select number of fundamental positions and premises that have underlain the dominant liberal discourse and that of its often dialectical offshoots and rivals. Taking their place within a comprehensive ideological framework of great cognitive, emotional, and normative power, the positions and premises selected have greatly distorted reality, while their impact on the intellectual and public discourse has been immense.

The West's Guilt toward the "Rest"

This chapter discusses views and attitudes concerning the all-important process of modernization, in its relation to the West—historically the spearhead of this process—and to the West's interaction with other parts of the world, the "Rest", past and present. This relationship has been a major subject of debate and soul-searching within the liberal democracies. In earlier studies, I have done some extensive scholarly work on quite a few of the issues we shall discuss. Thus, much of the challenge here is to distill my findings and arguments into a few pages.

Modernity: Enlightened or Sinister?

Classical liberalism, from Locke onward, held a core belief in humanity's ability to advance toward more beneficial forms of socio-political organization and life. By the time of the Enlightenment, the traditional view in all premodern societies of a mythical virtuous past and the superior ways of the forefathers had been replaced by the new concept of Progress: from savagery to "higher" and more benign forms of civilization. The nineteenth century experienced the Industrial Revolution, involving the explosion of productive powers and wealth, generated by relentless, potentially unlimited, technological advances. Correspondingly it saw the establishment of the rule of law and of peaceful, orderly political procedures in the developed countries, particularly the liberal ones. The view took hold that humanity was progressing from the harsh living conditions of the past into an increasingly plentiful, secure, and just life. This view was shared both by liberals, like Mill, who argued that it validated the liberal socio-political and economic project, and by Marx, who regarded liberalism and capitalism as crucial scaffoldings to be dismantled on the upward dialectical assent to socialism.

There were other voices, of course, not only among reactionary enemies of the Enlightenment but also on its peripheries. Rousseau was a landmark in this regard. He famously deplored the oppressiveness of civilization's socioeconomic

Ideological Fixation. Azar Gat, Oxford University Press. © Oxford University Press 2022.
DOI: 10.1093/oso/9780197646700.003.0005

and political power relations, contrasting them with the state of nature, before agriculture and statehood, in which he speculated that people had lived in elementary harmony and peace in nature's bosom. Subsequently, the romantics celebrated a return to nature and the yearning for a lost, supposedly more organic communal life of the past. These sentiments blossomed during the twentieth century. The complexity of modern industrial, urban, and bureaucratic society—Max Weber's invisible "iron cage" in which people were locked and felt themselves as cogs in a machine—sparked a longing for a simpler way of life. At the same time, traditional norms and social conventions, inter alia those governing sexual behavior, were losing their grip, at least among the intellectual elite. Margaret Mead's best-selling book *Coming of Age in Samoa* (1928) was a seminal expression of neo-Rousseauism, a celebration of the harmony and absence of frustration and inhibitions, sexual and other, supposedly characteristic of aboriginal societies living close to nature.

By the 1960s, Rousseauism had reached its zenith in the liberal democracies, in conjunction with a sweeping critique of modern civilization. Several strands came together in this critique. Highly influential were former Marxists, disillusioned with communist totalitarianism while retaining a critical stance toward liberal-capitalist society and its hegemonic ideology. Being an ideology, they argued, liberal capitalism was projected as the most natural, beneficial, rational, and justified socioeconomic and political order, while its profound wrongs were whitewashed. Some of these critics equated capitalist society with modern civilization writ large. Capturing the intellectual headlines at the time, Frankfurt School thinkers combined their social critique, rooted in Marxism, with that other most celebrated and highly influential intellectual creed of the twentieth century, Freud's. Central to his teaching was the claim that civilization's whole edifice, and its achievements, were made possible only at the price of an out-and-out repression of man's most elementary drives.

Having experienced the devastating trauma of Nazism, the members of the Frankfurt School set themselves the task of explaining the abysmal record of the first half of the twentieth century, which also included the two world wars and the Great Depression. They can therefore be excused for their pessimistic reading of this record, which traced the whole course of modern civilization, in which Nazism was presented as having been merely the most extreme manifestation, to the "rationalistic" legacy of the Enlightenment. This was the thesis advanced in Max Horkheimer and Theodor Adorno's *Dialectic of Enlightenment* (1947): the Enlightenment's "dialectic" legacy was capitalist society's "instrumentalist"—brutal or more subtle—oppression of people's individuality and humanity. By the 1960s, the Frankfurt School enjoyed great vogue among intellectuals.

This and other critical views of modern civilization were somewhat paradoxically tied up with the emergence of affluent society after 1945, when for the first time in history the masses in developed societies were released from the specter of hunger and began to be flooded with a tremendous variety of consumer goods. Nowadays, many social critics regard the affluent-welfare state of the post-1945 era as a golden age of economic prosperity cum equality, marred only by profound race and gender discrimination. But at the time, it was presented by members of the Frankfurt School—Herbert Marcuse was the most influential here—as a new stage in capitalist oppression, anesthetizing the masses with puny bribes, empty consumerism, brainwashing commercials and banal entertainment, a deluge of "artificial needs", a new form of "bread and circuses".[1] The "company man", tied to the big corporations' work regime and social ethics—which many now associate with the era of well-paid jobs and job security—was castigated as the new face of capitalist alienation.

Here was another "dialectic"—probably more genuine than Horkheimer and Adorno's—an outgrowth of a revolution of rising expectations in the new, unprecedented affluent society. Young people of earlier generations had few options. Basically, they could either work or starve. It was only in the context of the new affluent-welfare society that the counterculture of the 1950s and 1960s could flourish, most decisively shaping the outlook and social mores of the young, far beyond the actual number of emblematic "hippies". The masses of university students in the 1960s were themselves a wholly new phenomenon, as university education had previously been the preserve of only a small privileged minority. The Sexual Revolution, the far-reaching liberalization of sexual mores in the 1960s, widely associated with the birth control pill, was similarly closely connected to the general conditions of the new affluent-welfare society (more on that in the following chapter). As sociologist Ronald Inglehart has documented, it was affluence that both has made possible and has prompted the new set of values in economically developed societies around the world, centering on self-fulfillment, rather than survival as in pre-industrial and early industrial societies.[2] The more successful the new affluent society has been in alleviating want and advancing liberties, the greater the criticism leveled at it, in what one observer has dubbed the "culture of complaint".[3]

Postmodernism has reinforced and largely taken over from the Frankfurt School in terms of its hold over the intellectual scene. It came into its own in the wake of the 1968 Paris students' demonstrations. And it was to become hegemonic in American universities, intellectually and ideologically transformed by the cultural revolution of the 1960s, in which the campuses played a prominent role. Foucault, the most influential of the postmodernists, argued that social oppression, the product of power relations, was the rule in all societies. It was disguised everywhere by matching ideologies that dictated social norms and shaped the intellectual categories of thought prevailing at the time. As we have seen, there was enough truth in this message to leave a deep and striking impression on the humanities and social sciences. Although most of the postmodernist themes were hardly original, postmodernism heightened the awareness of the historicity of norms and ideas and of the all-pervasive connections between power relations, categories of thought, and ideological justifications. It radicalized notions regarding the partial and elusive nature of truth, which can be viewed from an infinite number of perspectives. And it deepened the suspicion that the dominant perspectives were those which served the interests of the powerful. Not least, postmodernism resonated with a generational revolt against traditional values, norms, and conventions, the celebration of unfettered freedom, and a marked loss of faith in the establishment and state authorities.

The more provocative, frivolous, and dubious aspects of Foucault's epistemological and social message were swept aside in the general hype and, indeed, probably contributed to his popularity. The postmodernist super-skeptical and self-contradicting notion of truth has already been discussed in our first chapter. Foucault's implicit or explicit social message, enthusiastically embraced by many, was that oppression merely changed its forms, that there was no real fundamental difference in this regard between so-called liberal democracy with its sham freedoms and any other socioeconomic and political regime, past or present.

It has been widely noted that the young participants in the cultural revolution of the 1960s were those who would fill the ranks of university professors in the decades to come, bringing with them its intellectual proclivities and ideological messages. Welfare liberalism had already attained hegemony in the post-1945 era, dominating socioeconomic policy and occupying the intellectual high ground throughout the developed world. The 1960s marked a new upturn. Their legacy included, in addition to the Sexual Revolution and many other things, a revolutionary change of attitude, legislation, and policy on race and, eventually, on gender; heightened emphasis on individual and group rights; and an overall increase in social tolerance. It also involved attitudes and perceptions critical of and sometimes hostile toward the liberal-capitalist state entering progressive liberalism from the post-communist New Left and charging it with radical energies. These influences have left a deep mark, particularly on intellectuals and, consequently, on both the academic and public discourse.

Certainly, there have been many things for people to be unsatisfied with in the new affluent societies. Far improved conditions constitute a new baseline against which people measure their lives, point to old and new wrongs, and demand yet more improvements. Economic inequalities and their social effects have remained a major issue, and, indeed, have greatly intensified from around 1980 onward. Many people find their jobs or the balance between work and leisure in their lives unsatisfactory. Many feel—having the extra time and leisure to feel—existential boredom. Some deplore materialistic values, all-pervasive consumerism, and banal entertainment and seek a greater "spiritual"-idealistic content to life. Some are unhappy with what they view as rampant individualism and egotistic hedonism, and mourn the loosening of family and community ties and a loss of greater proximity to nature in the new urban mass society. Along with enormous gains, modernity has also brought some losses. While many denigrate old-time social conformism, many, sometimes the same people—from both the left and the right—look back with regret on the decline in social cohesion and social trust.[4] There is nostalgia for the small-scale, intimate—though often boring and suffocating—towns and countryside communities of the past. The hectic pace of modern urban life breeds a yearning for a lost, more relaxed existence. This sentiment has been captured by the slogan "Stop the World–I Want to Get Off". Although people in developed modern societies have much greater control over all aspects of their lives, many feel captive in a system they have no control over. They feel locked in Weber's "iron cage", which has grown globally and over which even states have been experiencing diminishing control. Erosion of confidence in and growing disillusionment with government have also, in part, been a natural outcome of rising levels of education and a loss of naivety and deference. Race and gender have remained potent issues.

Without minimizing any of the above, it may be added that we are biologically programmed to be largely unsatisfied, in order to hold our own or make gains in the trials of life and the constant bickering of social bargaining. For similar reasons, we are programmed to experience a certain level of anxiety, with individual differences, of course. And the aches and stresses of life, at some level, are difficult to escape. Furthermore, the massive arrays of choices and opportunities presented by modern society may themselves raise levels of anxiety, as too many options are often psychologically unsettling. *Escape from Freedom*, the title of Erich Fromm's 1941 book, has in this sense been supported by more recent psychological research.

People tend to voice their grievances and seek corrections and improvements to the existing order, and their complaints are often bitter and vocal. There is nothing necessarily "wrong" about this. Indeed, this is pretty much in line with how social bargaining over resources and status—and the ideological discourse on justice and the way of the world—works. However, in the process, we might be overindulgent, exaggerate present-day ills, and be overly nostalgic about the past. This has resulted in a number of very powerful, ideologically grounded, myths and misconceptions that achieved intellectual, public, and, indeed, cultural hegemony, at least for a while. In many cases, they have sparked powerful countermovements.

A Lost Eden?

From Rousseau on, the critique of civilization's real and imagined ills has often been associated with a posited contrast with a lost harmony and authenticity of feeling and behavior supposedly prevailing in aboriginal societies, before civilization. We have already mentioned Margaret Mead's sensational *Coming of Age in Samoa* (1928) and its great resonance with the American intellectual and artistic elites. As Freud had already broken the taboo on the discussion and significance of sexuality, they found the norms and conventions of "bourgeois" society narrow-minded, oppressive, and stifling. However, the spirit of Mead's depiction of native societies did not enter mainstream anthropology until the 1960s. Very little has changed in the evidence, overwhelmingly derived from ethnographic reports and anthropological research of pre-agricultural and pre-state societies that survived until recent times or still survive in some isolated corners of the world. But the interpretation took a decisive turn, in conformity with the sweeping ascendance of Rousseauism.

In earlier scholarly works, I have written extensively on the nature of pre-state and pre-agricultural societies. The following is a condensed summary, and the interested reader is advised to follow the referenced literature. Studies have indeed confirmed some of the virtues that Rousseauism attributed to hunger-gatherer life, and have lent support to the view that the human transition to agriculture resulted in a significant deterioration in some crucial respects. Hunter-gatherers were not subject to the back-breaking toil that was to become the norm among many agricultural societies. Additionally, hunter-gatherers enjoyed a more healthful diet than later agriculturalists, who became reliant on a smaller variety of staple foods, most notably grains and therefore carbohydrates. Hunter-gatherers were healthier and lived longer also because they were far less susceptible to the epidemic diseases that would come with dense sedentary life in the company of farm animals and surrounded by human and animal excrement. That said, half-serious catchphrases such as "the original affluent society" took things much too far, as hunter-gatherers' life often involved periods of great ecological stress and a struggle against starvation and the elements. Very few people from modern affluent societies would trade their comfortable and secure life and much extended longevity for the harsh conditions of aboriginal life idealized in the 1960s. Finally, it is also true that in the absence of accumulated property, hunter-gatherer societies tended to be more egalitarian than later historical societies. Yet they were far from being as egalitarian as imagined in the 1960s. Power differences, largely rooted in clan size, were marked and social competition was very significant.

Indeed, the picture of aboriginal life projected in the 1960s, featuring peaceful existence, free from the inhibitions and frustrations of modern life, was a figment of the Rousseauan imagination. It was vastly exaggerated and in some respects plain wrong. Hunter-gatherers and horticulturalists enjoyed far stronger kin ties and kin support than those prevailing in modern societies. But competition and conflict within the community, most notably—surprise, surprise—over women and sex, was endemic. The more powerful and socially astute men were often polygamous, which left younger and less successful males in the group without female partners. The most significant Rousseauan deviation from reality has concerned violence and violent killing. Homicide rates among hunter-gatherers, mostly associated with rivalry over women, were sky-high, far higher than in any modern society. The abduction of women and fierce competition over sources of livelihood, particularly hunting territories, were also the root causes of endemic warfare that took place between hunger-gatherer tribes.

Anthropologists during the first part of the twentieth century were fully aware of the massive evidence for widespread violence and ferocious warfare among hunter-gatherers around the world.[5] The same applied to pre-state agriculturalists. Indeed, by remarking briefly that "war and cannibalism are long since passed" in Samoa, Mead herself revealed that she was actually aware that things had been very different, and far more violent, before the arrival of Europeans.[6] However, from the late 1950s on, new tunes were heard. One of the leading pioneers of the new trend, anthropologist Richard Lee, propagated the view of the Kalahari hunter-gatherers as a "Harmless Society", which conformed to his Marxist concept of "primitive communism". However, after the initial spate of enthusiasm for the peaceful children of the earth, Lee himself discovered that before the imposition of state authority, these people had more than four times the 1990 US homicide rate, which was itself by far the highest in the developed world (though it has since halved).[7] Similarly, the Inuit of mid-Arctic Canada were celebrated as peaceful in titles such as *Never in Anger*. However, it was later revealed that in the not-so-distant past their violent mortality had been ten times higher than the 1990 US rate.[8]

Remarkably, none of these findings stopped anthropology's embrace of Rousseauism, which more or less grew to dominate the discipline by the 1970s. Older views and new evidence have been pushed to the sides, sometimes treated with hostility.[9] Fortunately, given the vast discrepancy between the new hegemonic view and the evidence, a reaction has finally taken form. Step by step, Rousseauan anthropologists, still dominant, have had to give up their claims regarding the peacefulness of hunter-gatherer life. Indeed, the ethnographic data from around the globe indicate that violent mortality rates among the men in hunter-gatherer societies was probably as high as 25 percent, on average—around 15 percent of the overall population—with all the rest of the men covered with scars. These rates were far higher than those experienced by historical states, with only the most severe state wars coming close.[10]

The agricultural societies of the paradise islands of Polynesia have fascinated Western imagination ever since the Europeans arrived there in the eighteenth century, shortly after Rousseau's work was published. The mutinous sailors of the *Bounty*, the painter Paul Gaugin, and actor Marlon Brando, who all established homes on Polynesian islands, have added to the mystique. Nonetheless, research has shown that social stratification and bloody wars were endemic on the islands of Polynesia, large and small.[11] True, sexual norms were far more relaxed in Polynesia than those prevailing in the West until the Sexual Revolution—a major element of Western fascination. All the same, it has been revealed that Mead failed to notice that her Samoan girl informers were pulling her leg, responding to her eager probing by feeding her with stories of unfettered free love.[12]

As we shall see, the story of anthropology is indicative of much that has happened in the social sciences and humanities. Rather than being merely simple mistakes, which can be expected as scholars try to resolve complex empirical questions, these major deviations from reality have largely been ideologically rooted, the product of ideological proclivity and preconceptions. They fed on the overall cultural sweep toward a Rousseauan celebration of nature—in reality, as the poet Alfred Lord Tennyson had put it, "red in tooth and claw". In turn, Rousseauan anthropology greatly reinforced popular Rousseauism, endowing it with the weight of scholarly authority. It is difficult for outsiders to grasp the measure of the resistance to the challenges to the orthodoxy manifested by scholars who have invested a lifetime in misguided notions and claims. Much the same applies to the generations of students whose socialization into the discipline involved the adoption and assimilation of its established cannons. Anthropologists have also shared the resistance in the social sciences and humanities to the ascendance of evolutionary theory as applied to humans, holding to the disciplinary precept that "everything is cultural". We shall see more about this in the following chapters. Those within the discipline who have not shared the orthodoxy have often avoided expressing their views. In a casual conference conversation, I once told an anthropologist whose views in this regard pushed him to the opposition that anthropology was 90 percent delusional. To which he responded with a sad smile: "why only 90 percent?" At another conference, an anthropology graduate student asked me if I couldn't find anything good to say about the discipline. To which I replied that, on the contrary, all of the source material that eventually was serving to refute the claims that hunter-gatherers were peaceful and demonstrate that they experienced far higher violent mortality rates than state societies had come from anthropology.

It is in the nature of hegemony that those who come under its sway and abide by it in their research as a matter of course do not necessarily have to be ideologically motivated; most of them are probably not, and there have been genuine, stubborn empirical and methodological conundrums obscuring the issues and making them difficult to resolve. For others, however, Rousseauism often functions not merely as a scholarly position, but as an ideological creed.[13] Nowadays, this creed is commonly adopted by those who work to protect the rights, cultural inheritance, and well-being of aboriginal populations still scattered here and there in remote areas of the world. This, however, may be a very worthy cause even if these populations are not presented as virtuous and innocent creatures living in a lost paradise.[14] Moreover, during much of the twentieth century (as with Rousseau himself), Rousseauism served as a statement about modern society, an expression of attitude toward its supposed ills. This was the cultural mood, the *Zeitgeist*, which climaxed in the 1960s, when modern civilization, and especially capitalist society, including its democratic-welfare forms, was charged not only with being the cause of human alienation but also with being intrinsically associated with war, imperialism, racism, slavery, and genocide.

Does Capitalism Beget Imperialism and War?

The view that capitalism was the driving force behind imperialism and war was developed by Lenin as an explanation for World War I. Given the catastrophes of the world wars, and with the struggles for decolonization leading to the dismantling of the large British and French empires in particular after 1945, this view gained currency among intellectuals, in the universities and with the public.

However, the original view about the relationship between capitalism, imperialism, and war had been quite the opposite. In his *The Wealth of Nations* (1776), Adam Smith argued that peaceful production and free trade were the real sources of wealth. He regarded colonial possessions, and particularly protectionist tariffs surrounding them to keep foreign competitors out—the monopolistic system known as mercantilism—as political obstructions to and distortions of the efficient operation of the markets and market competition. Shortly after, in his *Perpetual Peace* (1795), Immanuel Kant suggested that liberal constitutionalism, growing trade, and international institutions were increasingly wsorking against war. The nineteenth century, between 1815 and 1914, the period of the Industrial Revolution and exploding trade, indeed turned out to be the most peaceful period in European history until then. Wars among industrializing countries declined in frequency to about a third of what they had been in the previous centuries, an unprecedented change. However, in the wake of World War I and with the coming of World War II, the promise of peace was shattered and widely regarded as one of those nineteenth-century delusions of Progress.

Again, I have written extensively on this subject, and the following is only a précis.[15] The record shows that there has been a steep decline in the occurrence of war over the past two centuries, most notably in the developed world. However, this trend was broken by a huge, Himalaya size, "exception"—the two world wars. So what is the right answer: Was capitalism an engine of peace? Or was it the cause of imperialism and war? Smith and Lenin agreed on one thing: monopolistic capitalism, protectionist "mercantilism", increased the prospects of war. However, whereas Smith maintained that free trade between the nations was the key to both prosperity and peace, Lenin argued in his *Imperialism, the Highest Stage of Capitalism* (1917) that capitalism's intrinsic trajectory was toward monopolism, as big business put pressure on the political system to protect their eroding margins of profit against competition. Historical experience has shown that, both at home and abroad, there is indeed a tension in capitalism between competitive free trade on the market principle and monopolistic tendencies. Yet Lenin was, unsurprisingly, dogmatic about the final outcome of this tension.

Before discussing trade, attention should first be directed at an often overlooked point. The proliferation of trade was itself a function of a much deeper development generated by capitalism: the Industrial Revolution. And the cardinal effect of industrialization was the breaking of the trap of deprivation that had plagued premodern societies. According to the British demographer and economist Thomas Malthus, writing just before this dramatic change (1798), the dismal fate of humanity was to live precariously close to subsistence levels, as slowly growing productivity was offset by more children and more mouths to feed. However, from around 1800 onward, contra Malthus, industrialization has brought about an exponential rise in wealth. Wealth per capita increased some thirty- to fiftyfold in the countries that have successfully gone through the Revolution. This massive change has meant that wealth no longer constitutes a fundamentally finite quantity and a zero-sum game, when the only question is how it is divided. The economic pie has been continuously growing, with growth coming predominantly from economic investment at home, from which war has tended to become a wasteful distraction.

Modernity: Escape from Malthus

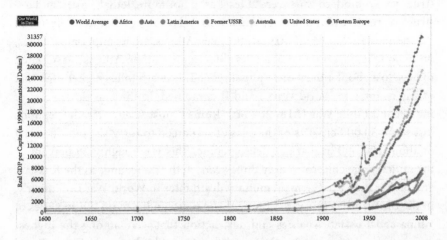

Growth in real GDP per capita (PPP) before and after industrialization
Note the exponential rise in wealth since the beginning of industrialization, but also the still huge gap between the developed and developing countries. However, growth in (large parts of) Asia, and, less dynamically, Latin America, has taken off, while Africa has yet to demonstrate that it has embarked on the road to modernization.

Trade has been a corollary of industrialization and has further reinforced its pacifying effects. Trade has ballooned to entirely new dimensions, and greater freedom of trade has become all the more attractive in the industrial age, because the overwhelming share of fast-growing and diversifying production has now been intended for sale in the marketplace. This was a radical change from pre-industrial societies, in which production was predominantly consumed by the family producers themselves. Thus, having become increasingly interconnected by specialization, scale, and exchange, economies are no longer overwhelmingly autarkic. For this reason, devastation abroad potentially depresses the entire economic system and is detrimental to a country's own well-being. This is what Mill discerned in the abstract as early as the 1840s, and John Maynard Keynes's *The Economic Consequences of the Peace* (1919) was to emphasize in its criticism of the harsh reparations imposed on Germany after World War I. As he argued, if the German economy was crippled, the global economic system would find it very difficult to recover.[16]

Some common misconceptions need to be set aside. It is not true that wars never paid, as people in contemporary affluent societies have become accustomed to believe. In premodern times, war and empire were actually the major avenue to wealth. Nor is it true that modern wars have become

more costly in terms of life and treasure, or that they have become more destructive. Premodern wars were at least as, if not more, lethal, costly, and destructive, relative to the size of populations and resources. For example, in the
Peloponnesian War (431–403 BC) between Athens and its imperial satellites,
on the one hand, and Sparta and its allies, on the other, Athens is estimated
to have lost about a third of its population. This death toll is higher than that
of any country in World Wars I and II combined. In the first three years of
the Second Punic War (218–202 BC), Rome's most severe war, the republic
lost some 50,000 citizens of the ages of seventeen to forty-six, out of a total
of about 200,000 in that age demographic. This was roughly 25 percent of
the military-age cohorts in only three years, in the same range as the Russian,
and higher than the German, military death rates in World War II. Similarly,
in the thirteenth century, the Mongol conquests inflicted on the societies of
China and Russia casualties and destruction that were among the highest
ever suffered during historical times. A final example, during the Thirty Years'
War (1618–1648), population loss in Germany is estimated at between a fifth
and a third—again, either way, higher than the German death toll in World
Wars I and II combined.[17]

Thus, rather than war becoming more costly, it is actually *peace that has been
growing more profitable*, with the exploding yield of competitive economic cooperation in the wake of the Industrial Revolution making military conflict
appear that much more counterproductive and less attractive. Economic modernization, with capitalism as its main and most effective engine, is what has
driven the trend. Democracies, fighting among themselves ferociously in classical antiquity, completely ceased to fight each other in the new realities. But
non-democracies also participated in the decline of war in the industrial age.
Compared to their record during the eighteenth century, Austria and Prussia,
for example, fought about a third to a quarter as much during the century
after 1815.

In the middle of the nineteenth century, Britain, the first industrial nation and the world's economic hegemon, abolished all tariffs and adopted
free trade. In compliance with liberal economic precepts, it no longer
wanted to acquire new colonies, as in the past. Its policy of choice—in Latin
America, China, and the Ottoman realm—was what scholars have termed
"informal imperialism" or "imperialism of free trade". Rather than extend direct rule over foreign lands and shoulder the expenses, responsibilities, and
commitments involved, Britain only intervened, sometimes by force, to open
them, and make sure they were kept open, to trade, investment, and other
economic activities.[18] The United States, taking over from Britain, was associated with—often criticized for—this policy during the twentieth century.
Notably though, the imperialism of free trade differed from the older tributary

imperialism (elements of which obviously lingered on) in that its underlying rationale was not extraction, but mutually beneficial commerce. This supposedly generates growing wealth and the whole range of attendant benefits—in principle, to everybody's advantage. Informal liberal imperialism constituted a radical departure from the past to the degree that the industrial take-off itself constituted a radical departure.

To be sure, the process was anything but saintly. The Opium War (1839–1842), which forced China to open to British export of that drug, is the most infamous of many examples. Still, in the final analysis, connecting others to the new, industrial world economy—whether voluntarily, through pressure, or even through force—was their only road to sustained growth and away from the material deprivation, stagnation, zero-sum competition, and high mortality of the premodern world. Again, to avoid a misunderstanding, the driving motives of this process were far from being altruistic. Still, economic liberalism has always rested on the idea that the activity of self-serving agents working to advance their own economic interests through the market turns out to produce the greatest prosperity.

For all that, by the last decades of the nineteenth century, things were changing. During their period of industrial take-off, the United States, Germany, France, Russia, and Japan all adopted strong protectionist policies. The logic behind this was that nascent industries in these newly industrializing countries needed the protection of tariff barriers in their home markets against the products of more established industrial economies (Britain's), at least until they developed sufficiently to be able to compete successfully. The unforeseen return of empire-building from the 1880s onward was the corollary of national economic protectionism. It was and remains puzzling, because according to a maxim well recognized at the time, "imperialism does not pay". In a telling confirmation of this, it was the British treasury that stood out in its objection to colonial expansion. Indeed, the New Imperialism centered on Africa, the least developed of continents, which accounted for only 1–2 percent of the world's trade.

Contrary to the famous thesis promoted by the British economist and publicist J. M. Hobson and adopted by Lenin, investment in Africa was not only negligible but also yielded the lowest returns.[19] By far the lion's share of the world's wealth was derived from home-based production and from trade within and among the developed countries, as it continues to be. The point is illustrated by the fact that Britain and France—the leaders in the new colonial race and possessors of by far the largest empires—were the two powers that sharply declined in their relative share of the world's wealth and power between 1870 and 1914. At the same time, the two powers whose relative share increased spectacularly during that same period were the United States and Germany, whose participation in the colonial grab was much more limited.

So if imperialism did not pay, why did it return with such a vengeance? This question preoccupied thinkers at the time and has continued to do so ever since. Obviously, many factors contributed to the New Imperialism, including strategic considerations of security; great improvements in armaments, medicine, and transportation, which made the penetration of Africa that much easier;[20] local initiatives by colonial officials and businessmen; a desire to bring Christianity and civilization to the natives; and, last but not least, the massive popular appeal of and prestige associated with colonial acquisitions and empire. However, the main driving force of the resurgence of imperialism lay elsewhere.[21] Because tariff barriers among the industrial countries had already been rising, fear grew in the system that the emergent global economy might become closed rather than open, since the world was being carved into large imperial blocs that would be barred to economic access from others. If this was the direction of the future, then each power felt the pressure to seize as much territory that was up for grabs as they could, while they could.[22] It was this "prisoner's dilemma" situation that drove the powers to press their claims in Africa. Although colonies in Africa were close to being worthless at the time, they might become profitable in the more distant future, after they would have been developed by the imperial country as part of a larger empire or commonwealth. A runaway snowballing process ensued.

Free trade has the effect of disassociating economic access from the confines of political borders and sovereignty. It is not necessary to politically possess a territory in order to profit from it. Furthermore, the size of a nation makes little difference in an open international economy. The citizens of little Luxemburg are as rich as, if not richer than, the citizens of the United States per capita. By contrast, size becomes the key to economic success in a closed, neo-mercantilist international economy, because small counties cannot possibly produce everything by themselves. Moreover, in a partitioned global economy, economic power increases national strength, while national strength defends and increases economic power. It again becomes necessary to politically own a territory in order to profit from it.

Thus, the British-dominated free trade system was being eroded by the reality and prospect of protectionism, which was a self-reinforcing process and self-fulfilling prophecy. Here was the main driving force behind the rising tensions and repeated crises among the powers in the late nineteenth and early twentieth centuries, which eventually erupted into World War I. The slide toward national economic protectionism accelerated further after the outbreak of the Great Depression in 1929. All the major countries responded to the crisis by raising their tariffs, a disastrous development, economically and, even more so, politically. In 1932, even Britain abandoned free trade and adopted the protectionist policy of "Imperial Preference". By far the most ominous consequences concerned Germany and Japan. For Adolf Hitler, the creation of an economically self-sufficient German Reich whose *Lebensraum* would bestride continental Europe was inseparable from his racist plans and vision of a perpetual global struggle. Much of this also held true for Japan. As it lacked raw materials and was heavily dependent on trade, the erection of protectionist barriers by the other great powers in the early 1930s hit Japan hard. It is therefore unsurprising that Japan regarded the establishment of its own economically self-sufficient empire, or "Greater East Asia Co-Prosperity Sphere", as essential to its survival. Correspondingly, Japan's liberal parliamentary regime of the 1920s gave way to militarism and authoritarianism.

After 1945, the United States was the driving force behind the far-reaching institutionalization of free trade around the world. The West European colonial empires, most notably the British and French, were dismantled. In the process, affluence levels rose dramatically throughout the system, with unprecedented political results. The probability of war between affluent democracies has declined to a vanishing point, where they no longer even fear each other or see the need to prepare for the *possibility* of a militarized dispute among them. Thus, the Netherlands and Belgium no longer fear in the slightest a German (or French) invasion, a historically unprecedented situation. Similarly, Canada is not at all concerned about the prospect of conquest by the United States, though people find it difficult to explain why exactly this is so. In East Asia, the most developed countries, such as Japan, South Korea, and Taiwan, do not fear war among themselves or with any of the other developed countries, though they are deeply apprehensive of being attacked by less developed neighbors, such as China or North Korea.

The same applies to civil wars, which have all but disappeared in the developed parts of the world. War's geopolitical center of gravity has shifted radically. The modernized, economically developed parts of the world have become a "zone of peace". War is now confined to the less developed parts of the globe, the world's "zone of war" in Africa, the Middle East, parts of Asia, and around Russia, where countries that have lagged behind in modernization and its pacifying spin-off effects occasionally still fight among themselves, as well as with developed countries, while also being prone to civil wars. Russia, a failed modernizer whose GDP per capita is around $10,000, derived mainly from energy and mineral resources, has invaded Ukraine as this book is being prepared for the press. Having failed to join the process of economic growth and mutual prosperity during its post-Soviet period, it continues to gamble on imperial military intimidation and coercion, as in the past.

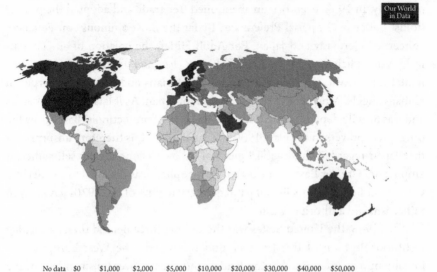

No data $0 $1,000 $2,000 $5,000 $10,000 $20,000 $30,000 $40,000 $50,000

World map of GDP per capita, 2020 (constant international dollars)
Wealthy, developed regions, marked by the darkest shades, are the most peaceful (oil and gas producers are a partial exception), while the poorer, less developed regions, marked by the lighter shades, have afar greater occurrence and potential for both interstate and civil wars.

Many doubt the picture presented here, citing and often criticizing the many wars in which the United States has been involved over the past decades. However, it is precisely in its role as the world's policeman, securing a liberal order based on mutual economic growth, trade, and peace against its enemies, that the United States has been embroiled in war. As General and former US Secretary of State Colin Powell has put it: "One of the fondest expressions around is that we can't be the world's policeman. But guess who gets called when somebody needs a cop." Indeed, note the panic in the democracies at the suggestion that the United States under President Trump might withdraw from that role.

This is not the place to address the many questions that the reader may have about the decline of war. No, everything is not all right. Above all, there looms the question of China's future trajectory—and its effect on world peace—as China emerges from low to intermediate and then, expectedly, higher levels of wealth. Additionally, the prospect of unconventional terrorism, using weapons of mass destruction, casts a long shadow. I wrote about all this at length, already when the consensus still was that China would smoothly integrate into the liberal world order, and before the coronavirus pandemic became an ominous sign for the disturbing potential of biological terrorism.[23] But, indeed, all the above is my own interpretation of history, and there are enduring debates in the scholarly community on the various questions involved. It can therefore be asked why a scholarly discussion of fascinating yet complex and controversial developments regarding war should figure in a book on ideological fixation.

After all, most of the debate among scholars concerns legitimate differences of opinion. And among the public at large, suspicion of good news is only natural. Still, much of the resistance to the claim of a close connection between capitalism, modernization, affluence, and peace derives from a lingering, deep-seated legacy of earlier ideologies. I recently was interviewed for a program on the decline of war produced by a prestigious American television network. During a break in the interview, the director of the documentary told me with a whiff of real wonderment that he had found that people were genuinely *offended* by the argument that war was declining. This is even truer of the claim that the process has been by far stronger in the developed parts of the world—those mostly affected by liberalism, capitalism, and modernization. Moreover, many people feel this claim to be yet more offensive, because it reflects on the still sad state of the world's undeveloped societies.

Decolonization and Its Ideological Legacy

The struggle, occasionally armed, against Western colonialism was a major political and ideological theme in the decades following World War II. Significant sectors of Western public opinion, most notably within the democratic imperial powers themselves, threw their support behind the colonial peoples' struggle for independence, based on the right to self-rule and self-determination. The passions stirred by the debate ran high, and for very good reasons. These were cardinal issues at the time. Furthermore, as decolonization was overwhelmingly associated with Western dominance, the democracies were perceived as being particularly implicated in imperialism, and their conduct was presented as especially pernicious. The intellectual-cultural legacy of decolonization remains a powerful element in the Western psyche. In the process, some fundamental truths about imperialism have been greatly obscured.

The first thing to note is that the dismantling of imperialism was a direct, most specific, and, indeed, unique outgrowth of Western liberalism. This applied both to liberalism's economic and normative aspects. Decolonization was in many ways a novelty in world history in which bloody imperial conquest and ruthless suppression were the rule, pursued by anybody powerful enough to do so. Thus, in all of the Western imperial domains of the early twentieth century—in Africa, India, and Southeast Asia—empires and the quest for empire had been the norm throughout history. Furthermore, the right of the victor

and conqueror had always been a major legitimizing principle. Resistance to empire by subject and subjugated peoples hoping they had a chance to break free
(and often seeking to establish their own empire and subjugate others) had been
as common. However, modern resistance in the colonies, upholding universal
moral principles of equality, self-determination, and self-rule, was a novelty and
a cultural borrowing from the liberal book. The liberal countries' own principles
were adopted by the colonial elites and proved to be the most effective weapon
of decolonization.

To be sure, both Britain and France were reluctant to withdraw from their
empires, and often tried to forcibly suppress the people and movements
struggling for independence. The French in particular fought vicious counterinsurgency wars in Indochina and, even more so, in Algeria. All the same, both
Britain and France eventually retreated everywhere, in the majority of cases
without a fight, because of a number of mutually reinforcing reasons. Firstly,
although the glory and prestige of empire were still very high, both internationally and at home, its economic value—contrary to popular perceptions—
was almost negligible under modern conditions, as already explained. Indeed,
sustaining the empire became a heavy economic burden. Note the spectacular
surge of the Japanese economy after 1945, and that of the French economy after
the departure from Indochina and Algeria. Britain's relatively poor economic
performance after decolonization and until the 1980s was due to domestic
reasons. Secondly, rule over other peoples against their will had been losing its
legitimacy, as it ran counter to liberal democratic norms. This meant that the tide
was turning against empire in this domain as well. Indeed, thirdly, liberal norms
also meant that the democracies had been losing the traditional, cheapest, and
most effective weapon of imperial rule throughout history: ruthless suppression, culminating in the threat and execution of wholesale massacre and even
genocide.[24]

I am quite sure that many people will find these propositions, particularly
the last one, surprising, disturbing, or even outrageous. They run counter to so
much that people have been used to hearing. So let's take this step by step. The
struggles for decolonization were taking place against Western democracies,
which turned all the attention at them, causing an optical distortion of sorts.
Sherlock Holmes called this "the curious case of the dog that didn't bark". We
only notice the dogs that bark. In a more professional jargon, there is a serious
selection bias here. Thus, although authoritarian and totalitarian great powers
in the twentieth century also possessed empires, none of them was broken up
by wars of national liberation, which had practically no chance of success in
their cases. The empires of both Imperial and Nazi Germany, as well as that of
Imperial Japan, were eliminated by the victors in the two world wars. The Soviet
empire, both inside the Soviet Union itself and in Eastern Europe, fell apart and

its many peoples broke loose only after the Soviet totalitarian system had been dismantled. So long as the totalitarian system was in place, everybody within these empires knew all too well what fate awaited those that would dare to revolt.

Skeptics might argue that the Soviet Union failed to subdue Afghanistan (1979–1988) despite the Soviets' brutal tactics. However, Afghanistan—vast, desolate, and sparsely populated—historically the ideal guerrilla country, was the *exception*, the *outlier*, in the Soviet vast imperial system. Chechnya is a more telling example: under Stalin, the Soviet Union experienced no scruples in deporting whole populations, including the Chechens, en masse from their homeland. By contrast, liberalizing Russia of the 1990s was forced to give in to Chechen insurgents, whereas Russia that has been turning in a more authoritarian direction under Putin proved tenacious in crushing this resistance by ruthless means. The order on the scale of brutality and effectiveness is unmistakable.

Gandhi, the Mahatma, became an iconic figure for advocating and successfully practicing the doctrine of nonviolent resistance against British rule in India. With the rise of Hitlerism and the outbreak of World War II, he advised the Jews to opt for mass disobedience against Nazi genocidal persecution. He later called on the peoples of Europe as well, including Britain, to embrace civil defiance against a German invasion, in preference over armed resistance, so as to "shame" Nazi Germany away from its prey. This fatuous universalization of his famed doctrine only highlighted the unique historical and political conditions within which it was able to work, and succeed: that is, solely when directed against a liberal democratic power. It was India's good fortune to have struggled for independence against liberal Britain. Had India been ruled by Imperial Japan, Nazi Germany, or the Soviet Union, Mr Gandhi, as he was referred to in British official pronouncements and newspaper reporting, would have disappeared after first raising his voice, and nobody would have known who he was.

None of this prevented the Soviet Union from claiming the lead in the struggle against imperialism after 1945. Nor did it prevent the Soviet claim from being accepted not only by the former colonial countries which drew support from the Communist Bloc in their struggle for independence, but also by the many Western intellectuals who regarded capitalism as the ultimate evil and the wellspring of imperialism. Of course, not all the Western intellectuals who opposed imperialism were as blind to Soviet imperialism and brutal oppression. Furthermore, it may be asked why the hideous totalitarian practices should affect, and be relevant to, the judgment of and opposition to Western imperialism. An often made claim is that we are not talking about others, but have the duty to correct ourselves first and foremost. There is a lot to be said for this attitude. Moreover, it is typical of an ideological discourse, which is not about producing fuller and more balanced historical pictures but, rather, about advancing deeply felt desired causes in the public arena. Notably, though, a fuller and more balanced picture is often the victim of the ideological discourse, especially as historians and social scientists enlist in or lead the effort to advance the ideological cause. Potentially yet more problematic: distortion by exaggeration or by omission might significantly affect our overall interpretation of the world and of our own society.

This has much relevance for the present. For example, while colonialism is a thing of the past, counterinsurgency wars in undeveloped parts of the world are very much around. Indeed, they have captured much of the attention with the decline of war among and within developed countries. The great paradox of counterinsurgency wars is that the mightiest of powers—the United States foremost among them—fail to win victories against otherwise weak opponents in some of the poorest societies on earth. In the scholarly literature, there have been a number of explanations, more or less contrived, for this paradox. But only my friend Gil Merom has pointed to the obvious explanation: the problem of winning counterinsurgency wars is predominantly the lot of liberal democracies, and it is encountered precisely because they are liberal democracies.[25] As already mentioned, all powers throughout history had no scruples about indiscriminate massacre, enslavement, and deportation of whole populations to root out insurgents nestled among them. The same applies to the conduct of present-day nondemocratic powers. By contrast, liberal democracies no longer regard such practices as legitimate, with the result that they find it exceedingly difficult to track down the insurgents within the civilian medium. Indeed, the insurgents fighting them exploit this self-restraint and move to take cover in dense urban environments, where they typically gain at least a partial immunity from attack.

Again, here is not the place to elaborate on this very topical subject. But think about one grisly example from today's headlines. The Russian intervention in the Syrian civil war from 2015 on secured victory for the Assad regime, which had been on the verge of defeat. The Russian force in Syria comprises just over thirty aircraft. By comparison, the United States has some ten times the number of aircraft in the Middle East, and the Israeli Air Force is also roughly ten times larger than the Russian contingent in Syria. Both the US and Israeli air forces are also several times more sophisticated technologically and tactically than the Russian air force. And yet neither the United States nor Israel has been able to achieve anything even remotely commensurable with the Russian victory in Syria in their own counterinsurgency campaigns. We all know why this is so, or we should know: because the Russians had no scruples about indiscriminately destroying the city of Aleppo, one of the insurgents' major strongholds, systematically felling the buildings on the heads of both the insurgents and civilian population. Thereafter, this example and the impending threat of further such actions were sufficient to bring about the surrender of the other rebel strongholds in Syria. Indeed, Putin's Russia had been as successful in suppressing the Chechen ferocious resistance (1999–2000), using similar methods and destroying large parts of the Chechnya's capital city, Grozny. For the same reasons, it should be quite obvious why a Uighur or Tibetan insurgency against China has very few prospects for success so long as China's regime remains what it is. To re-emphasize, the democracies' conduct in counterinsurgency wars has been far from being saintly. Civilians get killed and atrocities are sometimes committed, occurring either with the authorities turning a blind eye or on the troops' own initiative. War is brutal. Still, all these are a far cry from the conduct of totalitarian and authoritarian regimes under similar circumstances—with results to match.

One of the main obstacles to understanding these realities is that many people feel that the above explanation for the liberal democracies' failures in counterinsurgency wars, compared to nondemocratic powers, is so horrendous and morally upsetting that it cannot be allowed to be true. Obviously, however, there is no connection—logical or empirical—between these two propositions. Needless to say, the above is not a recommendation for the democracies to adopt the old ways of indiscriminate killing. Nor is it intended to provide a license for a relaxation of the efforts to maintain humanitarian standards of conduct as far as possible. It does, however, put things in the right perspective. The much-heard slogan in the West that the way to win counterinsurgency war is by "winning the hearts and minds" of the population has yielded poor results. In most cases, this goal is almost impossible to achieve in foreign countries whose populations usually identify more with their insurgent compatriots. In addition, it tends to be extremely expensive compared to the terrifyingly low costs of ruthless suppression. The US withdrawal from Afghanistan, after it spent more than a trillion dollars on occupation and huge hopeful and hopeless civil projects, is the last telltale demonstration of this sad reality.

Indeed, the real reasons for the liberal democracies' poor record of success in counterinsurgency wars are closely associated with what many people would regard as the democracies' most noble qualities. And yet, little of this is recognized in the political and ideological debate in the democracies themselves, or elsewhere. The democracies get little credit for their self-imposed restraint—none at all from their enemies, which are the main beneficiaries of their restraint, and scarcely any at home.

Since I wrote this chapter, and as the book is prepared for the press, Putin's invasion of Ukraine has reached its third month and so far has failed to reach its objectives. The reader may naturally ask how this failure impinges on the ideas presented here regarding the advantage that authoritarian and totalitarian countries have in counterinsurgency wars and Putin's earlier record of success in both Chechnya and Syria. Well, first, the war in Ukraine in not a counterinsurgency war but more a regular war in which the Ukrainians surprised everybody by the tenacity of their resistance, including that of their missile air defenses. Second, despite the widespread devastation inflicted by the Russians on Ukraine's cities, most notable Mariupol, they have been apparently much more restrained in treating Kiev and other highly symbolic centers of Ukrainian and Russian history in the way they had treated Grozny and Aleppo, that is, demolish them indiscriminately on the heads of both the civilian population and defenders.

Capitalism and the Presumed Exploitation of the Undeveloped Countries

Much of the domestic criticism in the West has been due to the lingering, combined legacy of Marxism, the New Left, and the struggle against colonialism in Western consciousness. The view that capitalism and the West are the root of all evil and that the less developed parts of the world are among their main victims has become entrenched in the democracies from the 1950s and 1960s on. Within this frame of reference, capitalist exploitation has been denounced, the West's wars have been viewed as exploitative interventions, and the economically undeveloped parts the world have been presented as the bearers of native innocence. All these propositions incorporate serious distortions of reality.

Capitalism has been deeply controversial ever since it became the dominant socioeconomic regime in the nineteenth century, and inevitably so. We have traced the debate over some of its supposed virtues and ills in the previous chapter. With the historical experience of two centuries behind us, the debate has narrowed considerably, or it should have. As competing systems for organizing modern society have failed to deliver on their promises and have lost their erstwhile tremendous cognitive and emotional appeals, the market principle is now more widely perceived as unchallenged as an engine of development, wealth creation, and prosperity. The current debate mostly revolves around the desired scope of action by states and by other authorities and institutions for regulating, correcting, and directing the markets, distributing their fruits, preventing market failures, and guarding against social and environmental ills. We shall see more about this later in this book. Concerning the economically less developed parts of the world, the charge of capitalist exploitation there has been widespread. In the 1960s and 1970s, socialist leanings in developing countries went hand in hand with what was known as "dependency theory". This was the view that capitalism and free trade worked to the advantage of the rich countries and left the world's periphery in a perpetually inferior and subordinate status. Joining the system was regarded as a continuation of colonialism, as "neo-colonialism".

Irrespective of its ideological underpinnings, "dependency theory" was a legitimate proposition at the time, whose test was empirical. It did not fare this test well. Singapore was the creation of Britain in the era of imperialism, and its leader after independence in the 1960s Lee Kuan Yew paid little attention to the alleged need to break away from "informal imperialism". He integrated Singapore into the global economy, making it one of the world's financial and manufacturing hubs, with the result that the former colony has become wealthier than its former imperial master. Singapore has thus been the great winner, successively, of both imperialism and informal, "neo-imperialism". Over time, other developing countries reversed course, embraced the markets, and opened up to the global economy. India, another former colony, went through this reversal from the early 1990s on, with spectacular economic results. Indeed, an old-new realization has grown, expressed in the half-whimsical, sweet-and-sour saying that the real problem is not the countries that capitalism exploits, but those which it does not care to exploit. While capitalism is still associated with labor and other abuses in developing societies, it is increasingly recognized that it has been lifting hundreds of millions out of abject poverty and into growing affluence throughout East, Southeast, and South Asia, as, indeed, it did in Europe, the West, and Japan earlier on.

The often heard view that capitalist prosperity rests, has always rested, on the exploitation of the poor, that it depends on and needs to perpetuate the poverty of others both at home and abroad, is greatly misleading. True, capitalism looks for employees with the lowest wages wherever they can be found. However, in doing so, it spreads the participation in the modern economy, and ultimately affluence, farther and wider. And rising affluence everywhere is the real engine of mutual prosperity, as there are more efficient producers and more consumers around with growing purchasing power. As noted, this was the process that took place in the West and Japan, and is now taking place in East, Southeast, and South Asia. Much attention is currently directed at the decline of older industries, loss of jobs, and much misery experienced in the developed countries, as such industries migrate to the parts of the world where labor costs are much lower. However, not only are these older industries replaced in the developed world by higher-value, high-tech ones in the capitalist dynamics of "creative destruction", while employment levels remain very high; viewed from the other direction, the movement of capital and industries to the less developed parts of the world is also the greatest global "socialist" project the world has been going through, perhaps ever. Capitalist-led modernization is expected to carry the newcomers to the process toward much higher levels of affluence, longevity, and comfort before long, which ultimately should benefit all the sides involved. By contrast, it is the societies that for social, political, and cultural reasons have so far failed to embark on the road to modernization and successfully embrace capitalist-led economic development—in Africa, the Middle East, and some parts of South-Central Asia—that have remained deeply poor and afflicted by all the miseries of premodern existence.

It is in these parts of the world that American-Western wars of intervention have taken place in the post–Cold War era. And the claim that in one way or another these have been wars of capitalist exploitation is still often voiced. However, the reality is that the United States and the West have little to no economic interest in the majority of the countries concerned and are, in fact, most anxious to avoid military involvement. Sometimes military intervention has taken place for humanitarian reasons, as has been the case with NATO's intervention in the former Yugoslavia and, occasionally, in various parts of Africa, where interventions have usually ended in failure. In other cases, military interventions have occurred in order to prevent attacks on the West, as in the "War on Terror". Economic interests have figured mostly in the Persian Gulf area, to protect that critical resource of the global economy: oil.

Critics have seen the oil motive as just the purest form of the Western effort to exploit, dominate, and suppress other peoples and cultures—of which the terrorist attacks have been the expected, or even justified, bitter harvest. Indeed, in the late nineteenth and early twentieth centuries, the British and French took possession of vast territories and ruled them as they pleased in the service of their interests, most significantly—in the British Middle East—the supply of oil (as well as the safety of the Suez Canal and the passage to India and the East). After 1945, it has been the United States that has intervened in the Middle East, often high-handedly, to secure the flow of oil, and, for a long time, to keep it cheap and keep the Soviet Union at bay. To this end, the United States buttressed the autocratic regime of the shah in Iran, the deeply religious and conservative autocracy in Saudi Arabia, and dynastic rule in the Gulf principalities. The United States also high-handedly intervened in Latin America and Southeast Asia, supporting dictators against left-wing, sometimes communist takeovers, and occasionally to protect the interests of American businesses. These examples of formal and informal imperialism have been denounced as cynical, inexcusable meddling in the affairs of other peoples and as a form of organized theft.

We ignore no part of the historical and contemporary record. However, with the experience accumulated ever since the countries of the Middle East won independence, disillusionment with the indigenous regimes has gradually set in and some reassessment has taken place. Celebrated in the postcolonial mindset as the champions of self-determination and progressive development, the new "republics" of the Middle East, almost invariably the product of military revolutions and led by young and charismatic officers, proved to be dictatorial, violently oppressive, corrupt, and complete economic failures. The luster of a "progressive" communist world that supported them has similarly dimmed, together with the onetime enormous romantic mystique of revolution, epitomized by "Mao", "Fidel", and "Che". The "Arab Spring" proved to be yet another bitter disappointment. Indeed, as already mentioned in the previous chapter, the main alternative to the current regimes in the Middle East—be they secular autocracies or traditional monarchies—is at present unlikely to be liberal democratic but, rather, far more oppressive religious fundamentalism. It has become commonplace to blame all of the Middle East's problems on the legacy of imperialism. But in reality they run far deeper, to social and cultural traits that predate colonialism and modernity and cast a long shadow over the future.

One of the main charges against imperialism concerns the artificial borders—those straight lines across Africa and the Middle East that the imperial powers drew with little regard for ethnic composition and the will of the native populations. The legacy of these borders is held responsible for the ethnic conflicts and wars that have taken place in these parts of the world. In reference to the Middle East, this criticism often goes hand in hand with an idealization of the Ottoman Empire, which had ruled the region until World War I and is credited with the virtues of multi-ethnicity and religious toleration. Ottoman imperial rule enjoyed great legitimation as Muslim, guardian of the faith, and leader of the faithful. At the same time, its ultima ratio was the threat of merciless suppression, and over time it was increasingly characterized by stifling corruption and overall stagnation, facts that are largely muted in the idealizing discourse. Moreover, because national identities were unable to crystallize in the Middle East during millennia of continuous imperial rule—ever since Assyrian times—local, tribal, and confessional foci of identity and loyalty dominated. It is naive to think that *any* drawing of borders would have prevented ethnic and sectarian strife, often violent, in this highly fragmented region. It is equally naive to hold that, if it were not for the Western imperial powers, the region could have retained the former unity it possessed under the Ottoman Empire without resorting to draconian means of violent tyrannical repression, of the kind that held together even smaller territorial units such as Assad's Syria and Saddam Hussein's Iraq.[26]

Sub-Saharan Africa, too, was a dense tribal and ethnic mosaic, and mostly pre-national, before the colonial era. In view of this reality, the fixing of any sovereign state borders could scarcely have prevented the often violent ethnic strife that has been the lot of sub-Saharan Africa both before and after colonial times.[27] Yes, divide-and-rule policies and violent suppression were practiced in both Africa and the Middle East by the imperial Western democracies during colonial times. However, the missing part of the story is that those times were also actually the most peaceful and most secure periods of these regions' history, compared to what took place both before and after the period of Western colonialism. In the prevailing discourse, the genocide in Rwanda (1994), for example, has often been conventionally blamed on Belgian colonial rule (German in Burundi). It has been alleged that the colonial powers practically created the ethnic distinctions between the Tutsi and Hutu, which reflected their prejudices and administrative needs. However, the precolonial history of the region reveals that the colonial authorities merely built on and formalized long existing ethno-social divisions and hierarchies. The Nilotic Tutsi pastoralists, originally invaders from the north, had maintained elite rule over the Bantu-speaking Hutu agriculturalists for centuries.[28]

In the postcolonial discourse, precolonial Africa has been portrayed as the scene of innocent bliss. But, in reality, as anywhere else in the premodern world, fighting among tribes and chiefdoms was all-pervasive in Africa, long before colonialism or the slave trade. Indeed, as we have seen and contrary to the Rousseauan imagination, tribal warfare was the most lethal form of warfare, predominantly because the small size of the tribal communities made them particularly exposed and vulnerable—men, women, and children. Moreover, when city-states, states, and empires emerged in parts of Africa—again some of them, as in Mali, Ghana, Songhai, Kongo, Uganda, and Ethiopia, before substantial contact with the West—they all carried out wars of looting, conquest, and enslavement. A particularly well documented example because it was observed by Europeans, yet before real contact with Europeans, is the creation of Shaka's Zulu Empire in southern Africa in the early nineteenth century. It involved large-scale conquest, ruthless subjugation, and hair-raising tales of cruelty.[29]

As the anti-colonial outlook and rhetoric became hegemonic in academia and among the public by the latter part of the twentieth century, some reaction, still on the margins, has been bound to emerge. For example, premodern India, like all parts of the premodern world, was the scene of endemic wars by successive local and foreign empires and states, ruthless subjugation, and all-pervasive social oppression. Marx, perfectly aware of all this, wrote as follows as early as 1853: "The question, therefore, is not whether the English had a right to conquer India, but whether we are to prefer India conquered by the Turk, by the Persian, by the Russian, to India conquered by the Briton."[30] He equally knew that indigenous Indian ruling dynasties and empires throughout history had been much more violent and oppressive than British rule. Overall, therefore, he had little doubt about the positive future results of British rule in India.

We do not have to trust a nineteenth-century "dead white male" like Marx on this. In 2005, after the heat of the struggle for independence had subsided, India's prime minister from the Congress Party, Dr. Manmohan Singh, drew the balance sheet afresh:

> Consider the fact that an important slogan of India's struggle for freedom was that "Self Government is more precious than Good Government".
> That, of course, is the essence of democracy. But the slogan suggests

that even at the height of our campaign for freedom from colonial rule, we did not entirely reject the British claim to good governance. We merely asserted our natural right to self-governance. Today, with the balance and perspective offered by the passage of time and the benefit of hindsight, it is possible for an Indian Prime Minister to assert that India's experience with Britain had its beneficial consequences too. Our notions of the rule of law, of a Constitutional government, of a free press, of a professional civil service, of modern universities and research laboratories have all been fashioned in the crucible where an age-old civilization of India met the dominant Empire of the day. These are all elements which we still value and cherish. Our judiciary, our legal system, our bureaucracy and our police are all great institutions, derived from British-Indian administration and they have served our country exceedingly well.[31]

Indeed, not only the miracle of Indian democracy, with its normative and institutional preconditions, but also India's unity itself, unity which India had never had, was the legacy of the British Raj. (The secession of Pakistan, also blamed on Britain in the postcolonial discourse, was actually a result of a deep ethno-religious cleavage that, as in Yugoslavia, could not be contained once authoritarian rule, British or indigenous, had gone.) Yes, of course, British interests came first. But British norms and sense of duty, as well as what Prime Minister Singh has termed "the elements of fair play that characterized so much of the ways of the British in India", have been too easily disparaged.

Rudyard Kipling's "The White Man's Burden" (1899), the mission to civilize the undeveloped parts of the world, has gained notoriety, both because of its racial undertones and as the notion that this patronizing mission could be carried out against the will of the local peoples has lost its legitimacy. However, in the nineteenth century, both Marx, highly critical of liberalism and capitalism, and Mill, their most notable advocate, had little doubt that Western pressure—direct and indirect—on other parts of the world was ultimately going to benefit the indigenous populations; that it was their only way, admittedly a long and difficult one, out of the miseries, tyrannical oppression, and social injustices of the premodern world.

This road is anything but easy, necessitating an often painful social and normative transformation, which many societies, past and present, have failed to undergo. In the nineteenth century, for example, the Ottoman Empire, Persia, and Egypt became mired in debt to Western banks and governments, as the loans they took produced only very limited socioeconomic development. Their case contrasted sharply with that of Japan's successful rapid modernization from 1868 on. The difficulties and pains of modernization bedevil many contemporary countries as well, with or without a colonial past. Yemen and Ethiopia did not fall under colonial rule (except, in Ethiopia, for a few years after the Italian occupation in 1936). Yet their abysmal record of civil wars, tyrannical rule, and economic backwardness (Ethiopian is finally showing signs of an economic takeoff, while being torn by ethnic civil war) provides comparative case studies for testing the widespread view that colonialism and its legacy were the source of the Third World's problems. Indeed, I once heard it be said by a Lebanese intellectual that the problem of his country and region was not colonialism, but, on the contrary, that the colonial powers did not stay long enough to leave a legacy comparable to British rule in India.

This does not mean that the developed countries should reassume imperialism in the form of a benevolent caretaking of the many failed and failing states in the non-developing parts of the world, as historian Niall Ferguson, for example, once suggested.[32] In truth, the developed countries do not want to assume that "burden"; its projected costs defy the imagination; and the chances of success in bringing about the desired transformation through foreign intervention are close to nil. There is a widespread sense that it is both futile and morally unacceptable by today's standards to try to get anything done without the consent and active participation of the indigenous peoples and elites or in disregard for the values, norms, and social practices they hold dear and with which only they are intimately familiar.

That said, it should be noted what these values, norms, and practices sometimes are. The Middle East, for example, is the region where today's enemies of the West and everything that it represents most committed to violent action thrive. Many see the rise of fundamentalist and militant Islam as a reaction against past and present Western political and cultural intrusions. But, indeed, it needs to be clarified against what exactly this reaction has taken place. It is above all a reaction by societies whose traditional norms have so far militated against successful socioeconomic modernization and whose values are threatened by and set them against the liberal principles of human rights, individual liberty, toleration, democracy, respect for minorities, equality to women and LGBTs, and so much else.

Intellectual Critics of the West, and the Mystique of the "Third World"

None of this has prevented major representatives of the radical left such as Noam Chomsky, the leader of the British Labour Party Jeremy Corbyn, and feminist professor Judith Butler from favorably referring to Islamist Iran, Hezbollah, and Hamas as part of the global front against the greater evil and greatest obstacle to human emancipation and equality: American capitalism and imperialism. This unlikely alliance between the radical left and Islamism has been only the most recent step in a long process. The following is a small selection of signature thinkers and ideas from among those that have both typified and defined the trend.

We again begin with Sartre, one of the celebrity pioneers of the post-1945 discourse. There is little doubt about the genuineness of his commitment to justice and human liberation. As we have seen, this famously led him to embrace communism and Soviet totalitarianism, whose promise of ultimate human salvation made him blind to or lenient toward all the evidence of supremely brutal Soviet oppression and mass atrocities. Furthermore, Sartre formulated what is probably the most distilled definition of the perspective and attitude that have underlain an entire approach to social questions. He proposed that to "look at man and society *in their truth*" means to do it "with the eyes of the least favored."[33] Leaving aside the validity of what Sartre offered as a cognitive criterion of truth, the question of how such a moral formula should be applied merits consideration. Sartre applied it in a way that postulated the proletariat at home, as well as the societies of the undeveloped parts of the world, as the victims of capitalist/Western oppression and exploitation, which ipso facto made them just. This was so irrespective of any other economic, social, and political realities, which, as with the Soviet case, Sartre either ignored or thought they paled in comparison to, or constituted a necessary and temporary evil in relation to, the greater cause of justice. Within this fundamental state of mind, the collectives of the oppressed were perceived as virtuous and could do no wrong. Like Marx, Sartre also regarded them as the living embodiment of objective truth.

Groundbreaking linguist Noam Chomsky has been a leading figure in the opposition to the American involvement in the Vietnam War and in denouncing US foreign policy in general. He has portrayed it as an instrument of exploitative American capitalist interests masquerading as an ideological struggle for democratic freedom and against communist despotism. Unlike Sartre, Chomsky has been far more circumspect in justifying violence even by the oppressed. In the spirit of the 1960s New Left, he was also critical of the Soviet Union, which he regarded as a tyrannical travesty of the socialist idea. However, in the same spirit of the 1960s, he was very positive about both communist North Vietnam and Mao's China, then in the throes of the Cultural Revolution. In China, he wrote, "one also finds many things that are really quite admirable".[34] (Decades later, he would retract this judgment with respect to Mao's China.) Moreover, in the late 1970s, Chomsky cast doubt on, and actively attempted to discredit and block, the news of the mass killings carried out by the communist Khmer Rouge regime in Cambodia (1975–1979). It is now estimated that between 1.6 and 1.9 million people, around a quarter of the country's population at the time, were killed. Chomsky claimed that what he was concerned with was the accuracy of the reports, the facts. However, he made it clear that what really worried him about the reports was the political implication that the United States' war against communist North Vietnam may actually have involved active, and perhaps morally justified, opposition to the spread of brutal and often murderous communist tyrannies. Additionally, he argued that whatever was taking place in Cambodia should be viewed as aftershocks of the war that the United States had waged in Indochina.[35]

Obviously, one can hold that the American war in Vietnam was a grave political-strategic mistake and/or morally wrong; be highly critical of capitalism, American capitalism, and American foreign policy in general; and argue, as Chomsky has, that one's duty is to criticize one's own country's wrongs first and foremost. This, however, should not in principle involve an effort to play down or whitewash inconvenient facts about the other side of the ideological-political divide in an attempt to make it more virtuous than ours or at least no less so. And yet this is precisely what can be expected in the partisan pleading of an ideological discourse, often, paradoxically, by those who vow to expose the truth as it actually is, stripped from the self-righteousness and deceit of ideological false consciousness. An anarchist socialist critic of American capitalism, Chomsky has sanctified the "indigenous" around the world. In doing so, he has turned a blind eye to what "indigenous" all too often meant in terms of human miseries, oppression, and horrors in traditional societies, as well as of their often ideologically borrowed efforts to modernize. Tenacious resistance to, and denial of the evidence for, mass killing and genocide have been only the most extreme manifestation of this tendency.

For most of his career, Foucault was singularly unimpressed by the cults of "Third-Worldism" and Mao, much to the surprise and irk of his friends. In a clear reference to Chomsky, he commented about an "example that is both most interesting and tragic for Western intellectuals—that of Vietnam and Cambodia. One felt that there was a people's struggle, a struggle that was just and right at its foundation, against vicious American imperialism. . . . But Cambodia, and to some extent Vietnam, present us with a face from which freedom, a classless society, a non-alienating society, were absent."[36] Overwhelmingly preoccupied with the Western tradition, Foucault took a firm stand on events outside the West only once. In late 1978 and early 1979, he traveled several times to Iran to cover the revolution against the shah for Italian and French newspapers. The revolutionaries were an assorted mix of Shia Islamists, communists, and liberals. But to the chagrin of his contemporaries on the French left, Foucault came out enthusiastically in support of the Islamic wing of the revolution.

The reasons for this have long been suggested. Foucault rejected the Western concept of universal reason (as well as of the advance of reason)—in part justifiably, as much of what is claimed to be universal in reason or morality is not; and in part, as we have seen, confusedly and causing much damage, as a plurality of valid narratives does not imply that all narratives are equally true or true at all. More particularly, Foucault was enthusiastic about the Islamic Revolution because he saw it as a wellspring of a new spirituality that he thought was lacking in the Western tradition of rationalism, be it liberal or socialist. He celebrated the masses' fearless rise against the shah's regime as an expression of an authentic, promethean embrace of dangerous life options in rebellion against suffocating conditions.

It should be noted that, based on his talks with Shia clerics, scholars, and politicians, Foucault believed that Shia Islam had the characteristics that made a government of freedom possible. As he wrote before the shah's fall: "One thing must be clear. By 'Islamic government,' nobody in Iran means a political regime in which the clerics would have a role of supervision or control."[37] For all his historical erudition, Foucault seems to have entirely forgotten the tendency of revolutions to go to extremes and devour their own children. Triumphantly returning to Iran, Ayatollah Khomeini got rid of the moderate government that had come to power after the shah had left the country, as well as of the subsequent moderate Islamic government. He plunged Iran into a reign of terror in which all enemies of the new regime—from the ranks of the old regime, communist revolutionaries, and opponents from within the Islamic movement itself alike—were persecuted, tortured, and killed. Appalled critics from the French left reminded Foucault that the new Islamic Republic was a huge setback for women's liberation, to say nothing of the persecution of homosexuals. In the spirit of his own writings, they called on him to confess his errors. Dismissing these criticisms at first, Foucault very quickly fell silent. The episode proved a major embarrassment for the rest of his life.

Chomsky, although an iconic figure in many ways, has always been on the more radical margins of the intellectual-cultural scene in the United States. Foucault's Iranian episode was accepted with dismay by friends and contemporaries of otherwise similar ideological stripes. By contrast, few have matched Edward Said and his book *Orientalism* (1978) in their sweeping influence on their subject, on the entire field of cultural studies, and on the overall academic and public discourse on the relationship between the West and other cultures of the world. A professor of English and comparative literature at Columbia University and US citizen of Palestinian descent, he both helped shape and typified an era.

Naming Foucault as one of his main sources of inspiration and Chomsky as a kindred spirit, Said argued that the "Orient" has been an artifact of discourse, defined by the West as its exotic other, historical rival, and colonial subject. The "Orient" has been either romanticized as exotic or portrayed in negative terms as weak, corrupt, cruel, and primitive. Part of Said's argument is obviously true, even if his presentation of it is wholly one-sided. He documented the long tradition of Western negative stereotyping, bias, and bigotry toward the civilizations on their eastern frontier, focusing particularly on the civilization of Islam from the Middle Ages to the present. Notably, though, in his rich historical tapestry, Said conspicuously passed silently over major examples of favorable references to, and sympathetic attitudes toward, the Orient—examples with which he was undoubtedly familiar—from the "Father of History" Herodotus onward. Furthermore, Said failed to mention that the image of the West in the lands of Islam—in both its Christian and modern-liberal guises—has tended to be as negative and hostile. Christendom and the West have typically been posited by Islam as the religious and, later, cultural archrival Other. For long periods of history, they were also the target of large-scale conquest by Islam. As late as the sixteenth and seventeenth centuries, the Ottomans' heavy military pressure on Europe twice carried them as far as the gates of Vienna.

Since the picture has been reversed and the West has won dominance in this relationship over the last two centuries, it is perhaps of greater importance to expose and correct stereotypic and bigoted attitudes in the West toward the Orient. An examination of history by Western scholars has emphasized that during medieval times the civilizations of Islam were more prosperous, more enlightened, and, in some ways, more tolerant than the lands of Christendom. From a humanitarian perspective, the West's often gruesome record during the early modern period might also be regarded as scarcely superior to the gruesome conduct of the West's archenemy, the Ottoman Empire. These historical cognitions are important. However, in order to complete the historical picture, it should be asked what has happened since the eighteenth century in both the West and the Orient, which is of course the period with which Said is mainly concerned.

Like any other general concept, the "Orient" and the "West" are indeed intellectual constructs, as Said fashionably argued. Yet, properly used—giving due attention to diversity, detail, and nuance—this does not make these concepts invalid, lacking correspondence to reality and less cognitively indispensable. We shall shortly revisit this crucial point. Indeed, while "deconstructing" the Western concept of the Orient, Said, despite his claims to the opposite, freely construes the concept of the West. More ironic still, he was *right* to have done so, as the West indeed has historically tended to exhibit a family of characteristics broadly associated with it. Furthermore, the same applies to the concept of the Orient, including its Islamic form. Said is right to reject stereotyped and bigoted views of the Orient, to call for awareness of historical and local diversity, and to stress shades and nuances; but does Said really mean, does he try to persuade us, that a phenomenon such as Islamic civilization has no grounding in reality at all? Do the people who themselves belong to this civilization hold such a view? Clearly not.

Said himself followed his introductory presentation of his thesis with "a number of reasonable qualifications. In the first place," he wrote, "it would be wrong to conclude that the Orient was essentially an idea, or a creation with no *corresponding reality*. . . . There were and are cultures and nations whose location is in the East, and their lives, histories, and customs have a *brute reality* obviously greater than . . . anything that could be said about them in the West. About that *fact* this study of Orientalism has very little to contribute, except to *acknowledge it tacitly*. But the phenomenon of Orientalism as I study it here deals principally, not with a *correspondence* between Orientalism and Orient, but with the internal consistency of Orientalism and its ideas about the Orient . . . *despite or beyond any correspondence, or lack thereof, with a 'real' Orient.*"[38] Indeed, after this opening, brief, "reasonable qualification" or disclaimer, Said never returned to how the "real" Orient should be understood in *his* interpretation, even though this is surely crucial for the task of showing where the Western tradition of Orientalism has gone wrong.

For example, for various geopolitical conditions that we have no space to discuss here, the Greek city-states enjoyed levels of political plurality and freedom that contrasted sharply with the empires of the East. The same applied to the latter-day European state system, where, from medieval times on, monarchic power tended to be more constrained by the power of the aristocracy and of representative assemblies, with considerable variations across time and space, of course. Hence the concept of "Oriental despotism" that Western thinkers and authors, from classical to modern times, elucidated. This does not mean that the "Orient" and the "East" have an unchanging "essence". It does mean, however, that there are deep, historically grounded, cultural and sociopolitical traits that need to be recognized and considered when assessing both past and present conditions and prospects.

There is obviously a considerable diversity of conditions and conflicting trends in today's Arab Middle East. Said cited with indignation traits that contemporary texts in the West, some of them quite crude, attribute to the societies of the region. The cited traits include social conformity; the cultural predominance of shame and honor; the prevalence of murder to wipe out shame (including "family honor", as applied to women's sexual behavior) and in the form of "blood revenge"; and clan- and tribal-based norms of rivalry, suspicion, and distrust.[39] No, these traits do not apply to *every* Arab person, everywhere, under all circumstances, without exceptions and qualifications. But does Said seriously claim that the failure of the entire region to undergo socioeconomic modernization has nothing to do with shared cultural, social, and political traits, many of which associated with the prevailing civilization of Islam in the form it has taken? As the great scholar of the Islamic world and Said's *bête noir* Bernard Lewis pointed out, this failure has largely been shaped by the fact that the Islamic world has not experienced transformations akin to the Renaissance, the Reformation, and the Enlightenment, which paved the way for modernity in the West, and that the Arab world has remained adversely indifferent to the Scientific Revolution from the seventeenth century onward.[40] Is all this only a meaningless "construct" or, more sinisterly, an expression of cultural and racial bigotry and prejudice?

As Said wrote: "it has been estimated that around 60,000 books dealing with the Near Orient were written between 1800 and 1950; there is no remotely comparable figure for Oriental books about the West."[41] He intended this as a demonstration of the West's alleged obsession with the Orient. However, he seemed to entirely overlook the point that the West has been a wellspring of a huge amount of books on *all* subjects, that there was nothing special about the number of books dedicated to the Orient. Moreover, it never occurred to Said to ask why there has not been even a remotely comparable number of books published in the Orient on the West, or, indeed, on any other subject. *The Arab Human Development Report*, a series of publications sponsored by the United Nations Development Programme and authored by a group of Arab scholars (2002–2009), painstakingly details the deep-seated problems that have hindered the modernization of Arab societies. As the report points out, the entire production of books in the Arab world is smaller than that published in Spain alone.

Similarly, Said wrote as follows about what he described as the Arab and Islamic world's subservience to Western perspectives (he does not eschew these generalized concepts in this instance, indeed, throughout): "The Arab and Islamic world remains a second-order power in terms of the production of culture, knowledge, and scholarship. . . . For example, there is no major journal of Arab studies published in the Arab world today, just as there is no Arab educational institution capable of challenging places like Oxford, Harvard, or UCLA in the study of the Arab world, *much less in any non-Oriental subject matter*."[42] In pursuing his point, Said seemed to be entirely oblivious to the damning—and, alas, accurate—assessment of the realities of the Arab and Islamic world in terms of scientific and educational advance he inadvertently disclosed. No "Orientalist" could have put it more clearly.

Said's interpretation of the "real" Middle East, "or the lack thereof" of such an interpretation by him, does not help the people of the Arab and Islamic world to engage the process of reckoning and reform that they need to undergo if they want to find a way out of their current sorry conditions. Let it be clear: I am not arguing that they "have to" undergo reform and modernization. Yet it must be recognized that their failure to do so explains why South Korea, for example, which was one of the poorest countries in the world in 1950, poorer than Egypt, is now some ten times wealthier than Egypt in per capita terms. Indeed, this failure has made the societies of the Arab Middle East the victims of poverty, dictatorship, violence, and despair. One of the founders of "postcolonial studies", Said did not help these societies break free from their tendency to attribute all their misfortunes to outside forces. Indeed, he himself can be regarded as a victim of this tendency, which he influentially combined with the Western tradition of self-criticism and the new spirit of political correctness, both of which he rode, and reinforced, so effectively.

In his afterword to the 1995 edition of *Orientalism*, following the book's spectacular international success, Said rejected what he described as readers' misrepresentations of his arguments. He contended that he "was painstakingly careful about not 'defending' or even discussing the Orient and Islam. Yet", he wrote, "*Orientalism* has in fact been read and written about in the Arab world as a systematic defense of Islam and the Arabs, even though I say explicitly that I have no interest in, much less capacity for, showing what the true Orient or Islam really are."[43] Again, one wonders how Said's professed silence on the truth of what they really are is possible if this undefined true picture is not even suggested as a contrast to the "Orientalist" allegedly false or distorted picture of them. Nor does this complete silence serve to dissipate what a later great Arab scholar and severe critic of the state of the Arab world Fouad Ajami has called *The Dream Palace of the Arabs* (1999).

At this point it may come as no big surprise that research has discovered that Said—who famously defined his own vocation as and intellectual to "tell the truth against extremely difficult odds", "to speak the truth, as plainly, directly, and as honestly as possible"—falsified the circumstances of his childhood. He claimed that he grew up in Jerusalem, whereas in fact his family resided, and Said grew up and went to school, in Cairo.[44] Nonetheless, Said's legacy continues to set the tone of departments of Middle East and cultural studies throughout the West, most notably in the United States, and almost as powerfully in Britain. Said named Gramsci and his concept of ideological hegemony—which Said applied to the Orientalist discourse—as his second great source of influence, together with Foucault. Ironically, the multitude of Said's followers established a new hegemony in the Orientalist discourse, and the results of this discourse have been very damaging indeed. The momentous historical events that have taken place in the Arab and Muslim world since the publication of *Orientalism* in 1978 suggest that Said and his legacy are themselves in need of the "deconstruction" he offered the Orientalist discourse.

As Middle East expert Martin Kramer charged in his 2001 book *Ivory Towers on Sand: The Failure of Middle Eastern Studies in America*, the hegemonic discourse in the discipline was responsible for its complete failure to foresee and account for the sweeping rise of political Islamism and fanatical Jihadist terrorism throughout the Middle East and beyond. Furthermore, during the global wave of democratization in the 1990s, the followers of Said were busy explaining away why nothing similar was taking place in the Arab world. Conversely, they cheered the democratization promise of the "Arab Spring", only to fall silent when it failed. As the "Arab Spring" was generated by indigenous popular forces, its failure could no longer convincingly be blamed on the legacy of imperialism and the malevolent influence of outside forces. Indeed, a deepening recognition of the fundamental weaknesses of the Arab world has been silently growing, as its failure to modernize successfully contrasted sharply with the massive contemporaneous shifts taking place in East, Southeast, and South Asia.

Needless to repeat, the Arab world is not a monolith, and not all Arabs and Muslims are extremists, supporters of terrorism, or terrorists. At the same time, not all the broader trends that have been evident in that part of the world and account for its current condition have been figments of the "Orientalist" imagination and discourse. While Said and his many followers blamed Western scholars of the Middle East of cultural and ideological prejudice, theirs is a singular example of the strength and endurance of a Western-liberal cultural-ideological prejudice and fixation—specifically, the suppression of all genuine historical, cultural, and social differences in the name of equality, human dignity, and the fight against bigotry.

Capitalism, Liberalism and Slavery

One of the most severe charges against the democracies, figuring prominently in current ideological debates, concerns the role that the slave trade and slavery played in their history. Slavery was an almost universal feature of premodern agrarian societies. But it is true that it took a very distinctive form in premodern democracies and republics. The reason for this is quite curious. In most premodern state societies, stark social stratification meant that people of the lower estates were often subordinate to and subjugated by the nobility—legally, economically, and, therefore, in all aspects of their lives. In many societies, the peasants, who constituted the vast majority of the population, were required to provide part of their produce, services, and corvée labor to local masters. In order that they would not evade these duties, their mobility was sometimes curtailed and they were not allowed to leave their places of residence. They were reduced to the status of serfs, in feudal Europe as in many other traditional societies. Forms of so-called land bondage because of unpaid debts were also common. Slaves proper also existed in most of these societies and usually belonged to the lowest rank on the legal and social ladder. But coercive economic extraction was predominantly directed at a much larger population of variably subjugated peasantry. Thus, in many premodern societies, the category of free men was limited, graduated, and ambiguous.

By contrast, in ancient democracies and republics, such as Athens and Rome, the people had won the status of legally equal and free citizens. As a paradoxical result, slavery, which existed in all these societies, was more strictly defined and legalized as distinct from the status of free, and it became limited to people of foreign extraction, mostly prisoners of war. Thus, so-called chattel slavery, slaves as the full property of their owners, who could do with them as they pleased, barely different in this respect than farm animals or tools, became the standard form of slavery in the ancient democracies and republics.[45]

This distinction re-emerged in the early modern period. In the countries of Central and Eastern Europe the subjugation of the masses of peasantry as serfs continued. But in Western Europe, with Britain in the lead, an advancing capitalist economy generated a process whereby serfdom was giving way to wage labor. However, while the people in Britain and its colonies were gaining legal equality as free men, there was one huge exception. This was the plantation economy of sugar canes, tobacco, coffee, cocoa, and, later, cotton, thriving in Britain's (and France's) North American and Caribbean colonies, as well as in large parts of Spanish and Portuguese Latin America. They all relied on the mass importation of African slaves from across the Atlantic. Twelve to thirteen million Africans are estimated to have been enslaved by force in West Africa, and shipped chained in terrible cramped conditions across the ocean. Millions are estimated to have died before, during, and after the crossing. The captured Africans were thrown into foreign lands and forced to work as property of their owners, with no rights for them and their families, for centuries.

This monumental human ordeal and tragedy is very much alive in the historical and ideological discourse in the liberal West. This is most notably the case in the United States, where slavery and its legacy were and remain a major element of the American experience. In this context, any comparative perspective has little relevance. True, the slave trade and slavery were not unique to the West, either at the time or earlier in history. For the attention of the Afro-American "Nation of Islam", Arab slave traders were as active in East as well as in West Africa, across the Sahara, the Red Sea, and the Indian Ocean, as the Europeans were in West Africa, and for many more centuries. They transferred and sold millions of Africans into and across the lands of Islam. As one historian summarizes the admittedly very tenuous estimates of the Arab and Muslim human trafficking from Africa: "slave trades are in the range of 12 million individuals from 650 CE to the end of the sixteenth century, and another 4 million from the seventeenth through the nineteenth centuries."[46] Slavery had also been widespread in Africa itself. Moreover, it was local African chiefs, states and empires in both West and East Africa—the Oyo, Aro, Hausa, Fanta, Ijo, Dahomey, Kongo, and

Ethiopia—that were actually those that carried out the business of capturing and selling their neighbors to both the European and Arab slave traders in wars and raids.[47]

Nor was the experience of enslavement unique to Africans. During the very same centuries, millions of Christians were captured in the domains of Poland-Lithuania, in Ukraine, and the south of Russia by the Crimean Tartars, and throughout southeast Europe and in the Caucasus by the Ottomans. They were marched and shipped to be sold in the thriving slave markets of Istanbul and other Ottoman cities. In addition, more than a million Europeans are estimated to have been enslaved mostly in the Mediterranean but also on the shores of Western and even Northern Europe by the Muslim Barbary states of North Africa during the same period.[48] None of this distracts the attention of, and feelings of horror, shame, guilt, and responsibility felt by, people in the United States, Britain, and other liberal democracies of Western Europe with respect to the role of the slave trade and slavery in their own countries' history—and very understandably so.

Some aspects of the debate on the slave trade and slavery relate to the nature of capitalism, liberalism, and democracy. The discourse on these aspects often blends with the more general one on the defects, failings, and false pretenses of these ideologies and regimes—on the gap between their declared principles and self-image, on the one hand, and historical realities, on the other. For example, the slave trade and Britain's involvement in it, which captured most of the market from the Portuguese, Dutch, and French traders, was one of the sources of what Marx called, in one of his most penetrating chapters, "the original accumulation of capital" from the sixteenth to the eighteenth century.[49] Marx was right in arguing that the growth of capitalism, rather than occurring in a peaceful, idyllic way, as Adam Smith seemingly had it, involved massive violence, coercion, and human misery both at home and internationally. Thus, the slave trade and the plantation economy that rested on it helped create the preconditions for the formation of capitalism. They were part of the expansion of the European-centered Atlantic and world markets and of the increasing prominence of the commercial interests and commercial wealth that were the hallmark of this development. How vital the slave trade and slavery were in this development is a question about which recent scholarly opinion varies.[50] Later on, the Industrial Revolution, taking off in Britain from the 1780s onward and centering on the textile industry, led to the resurgence of slavery by hugely increasing the demand for cotton. The plantation economy of the American South, already in decline, was revitalized, and, indeed, experienced exponential growth. It supplied a large majority of the world's cotton to Britain's skyrocketing production. Slavery and the rise of industrial capitalism were closely interdependent.[51]

Ultimately, though, it was capitalism and what Marx saw as its political cor-ollary or handmaiden, political liberalism, that brought the slave trade and then slavery to an end, first in Britain and its empire, and later in the United States and throughout the world. Marx strove to demystify the connection between normative precepts and economic interests in a society, insisting that the latter pretty much determined the former. Indeed, the replacement of serfdom by wage labor during the rise of capitalism in early modern Britain and the institution-alization of personal freedom and equality before the law were interconnected in many ways. However, precisely for these reasons—because of the new, capi-talist, economic rationale mixed with the new, liberal, normative sensibilities—Britain barred slavery brought from colonies in the British Isles themselves in 1772; outlawed the slave trade in 1807; and actively moved to enforce this ban on others through the actions of the Royal Navy in the Atlantic and, later, world-wide. The prohibition of slavery in the British colonies had to wait until 1833, and in the French colonies (as opposed to continental France) until 1848.[52]

Close to 400,000 African slaves were brought to the British North American colonies that were to become the United States.[53] Although the international slave trade was banned first by the individual states of the United States and then by federal law during the first decades after independence, slavery itself survived in the United States long after its abolition in Britain and the other European countries. Indeed, slavery played a much more prominent role in American his-tory. It brought great wealth and political clout to the plantation economy of the southern colonies and, later, states. Moreover, historians have shown that the banking, shipping, and other industries in the rising capitalist economy of the North were deeply involved in the business of the South's plantation-slave economy during the first half of the nineteenth century. The total worth of the slaves in the United States in 1860 is estimated at close to a fifth of the national wealth. At the same time, the total wealth of the North was around three times larger than that, and it outstripped the total wealth of the South by about 3 to 2.[54] Moreover, it was largely derived from industrial production. Indeed, by the in-dustrial age, the process of capitalist industrialization was virtually unstoppable, and, in addition to the North's larger population, it ultimately gave the Union the military edge. It was this process, the falling behind of the slave economy in the face of both industrial capitalism and the ascendance of liberal sensibilities—the combination of economic and political liberalism—that eventually, after an ex-cruciating struggle culminating in a bloody civil war, brought about the abolition of slavery in the United States. Similarly, it was liberal and democratic norms and sensibilities that eventually brought an end to racial segregation and have ani-mated the fight against racial discrimination from the 1950s and 1960s on.

None of this should affect a national reckoning concerning the role played by slavery and its legacy in the American past and present. Nor, of course, does any of this detract from the enormity of the human tragedy of black slavery in America, in all its aspects. Moreover, the historical and ideological discussion and debate on slavery are an integral part of an ongoing struggle to reshape racial relations in the United States and improve the conditions of African Americans. At the same time, part of the current discourse is an offshoot of the more general critique of capitalism, liberalism, and democracy as phony and a sham. In this context, Thomas Jefferson, for example, has been portrayed as the supreme case of Enlightenment-liberal hypocrisy and of the duplicity of America's founding fathers. After all, he was both the person who authored the Declaration of Independence and a slave owner, who additionally fathered children with his slave woman Sally Hemings. Jefferson was indeed torn between his socioeconomic position as a Virginian estate owner and his Enlightenment views about the injustice of slavery. While his early attempts to legislate the abolition of slavery in Virginia failed, Virginia, on his initiative, became the first state to outlaw the international slave trade, in 1778. As president of the United States, Jefferson passed the federal law to the same effect in 1807.[55] During his presidency and after, he continued to agonize over the problem that he feared would split the Union. However, it was only the decreasing economic and political power of the plantations in the face of the rising capitalist-industrial economy that would resolve the issue with the victory of economic and political liberalism decades after Jefferson's death.

In August 2019, the *New York Times Magazine* launched its *1619 Project* (after the year the first African slave was brought to the North American colonies). The Project's stated aim was to highlight the central place of slavery in American history. A number of historians, while praising this cause, have disputed some of the Project's factual assertions, most notably the unfounded claim that the call for independence in the colonies was driven by fear of growing abolitionist voices in Britain. In the 1770s, abolitionism had not yet become a significant force in Britain, and the outlawing of the international slave trade in the American colonies turned states actually preceded the same act in Britain by decades (which even in 1806 did not ban slavery in Britain's colonies).[56] Still, the *New York Times'* response evaded full retraction. The cause and the mission were apparently too sacred to allow any withdrawal on fact.

From Marx onward, the concepts of liberalism, democracy, and capitalism of have been stripped from their saintly hallow in the official ideology and in the naive mind. Historians expose past realities and dispel popular myths. At the same time, they have often succumbed to lopsided historical assessments of, and ideological verdicts on, admittedly messy realities. Marx was unimpressed with the abolition of slavery and serfdom, as he regarded wage labor as merely a new, more sophisticated, capitalist, form of human exploitation. Indeed, during the early phases of industrialization, the masses lived in poverty and miserable conditions, which Marx thought were only going to get worse under capitalism. For this reason, he had no problem in arguing that capitalism was first propelled forward by, and then transcended and destroyed, the slave trade and slavery.[57] However, by now we know that economic and political liberalism, including the dominance of wage labor, have not only put an end to both slavery and serfdom, but also have brought about an enormous, unprecedented leap in people's well-being—economic and otherwise.

Moreover, it is all too easily forgotten in the prevailing discourse that it was colonial rule by the Western powers that abolished slavery in Africa itself. Slavery in Ethiopia, Africa's last independent country, was outlawed only after 1936, ironically by occupying fascist Italy. Similarly, it was British and French colonial rule that abolished slavery throughout the Arab Middle East. Indeed, it was in those Arab countries that remained outside colonial rule that slavery continued to exist until very late. In both Saudi Arabia and Yemen it was outlawed only in 1962, and in Oman in 1970.

Since slavery was pretty much a universal phenomenon in the premodern world, I am inclined to accept the verdict of one of its most brilliant early students: "Slavery was not born of racism: rather, racism was the consequence of slavery."[58] Either way, profound racism was inseparable from the experience of black slavery, and it continued to haunt the liberal democracies for a very long time. It still does. Moreover, not only slavery but also the colonial experience in general was closely associated with racist attitudes born out of a sense of European superiority and clear lead. This applied not only to the United States, the worst case with respect to the blacks, but to all the democracies, including France, the mother of the Revolutionary slogan *liberté, égalité, fraternité*, where quite a number of black American writers and artists took refuge in the first part of the twentieth century. As racism has been rolled back from the 1950s and 1960s on, Frantz Fanon, a black psychiatrist from the French colony of Martinique who also worked in Algeria, became a canonical figure in this struggle and in the new field known as postcolonial studies. His book *Black Skin, White Masks*, published in France in 1952, revealingly exposed the inside experience and deep sense of inferiority and stigma that characterized the relations between blacks and whites in both the colonies and metropolitan France. Fanon resigned his position in order to support the FLN's battle for the independence of Algeria. His later book *The Wretched of the Earth*, appearing in France in 1961 with an introduction by Sartre, focused on the struggle of the colonies for independence. In the spirit of the times, Fanon adopted Marxism and believed that the colonial struggle would generate a new humanity, not poisoned by Europe. In retrospect and in view of the sad record of most of these former colonies, including Algeria, not least in terms of human rights, it is clear how naive this message was, and, indeed, how the legacy of Europe has been sorely missing.

Were the Democracies Genocidal?

The liberal democracies' colonial record includes a particularly problematic element: the charge that in both the United States and Australia, democracies exterminated the native populations. The indigenous groups were displaced from their lands and experienced, respectively, an estimated 90 percent and 80 percent drop in numbers during the nineteenth and early twentieth centuries. This is the source of a profound sense of guilt in the two countries, reinforcing pervasive doubts about whether liberal democratic societies really behave better than others.[59]

To be sure, both the American Indians and Australian Aboriginals were victims of massive expropriation, and their violent resistance was suppressed by the more effective violence of governments and local white settlers. The land on which the natives lived was progressively taken from them, destroying their livelihood and way of life. The United States carried out a number of large-scale and deadly deportations, such as that of the Cherokee. Local militias, most notably in California, engaged in indiscriminate killings. Small-scale violence and killings were pervasive. Native women were occasionally taken away and raped by white men. The same applied to Australia, with the natives of Tasmania in particular suffering from all the above practices. In both the United States and Australia, the natives' lives, well-being, and culture were horribly damaged. Most of the white population saw the natives as a menace to be defeated and eliminated. The greatest presidents of democratic America—George Washington, Thomas Jefferson, Andrew Jackson, Abraham Lincoln, Theodore Roosevelt—prophesized the natives' ultimate doom, which they believed to be much deserved in light of Indians' acts of savage violence. All this is undeniably true. Hence people tend to assume the worst. Nonetheless, the demographic catastrophe that befell the US Indians and the Australian Aborigines was not caused by such means. The culprit was very different, and it struck indiscriminately, regardless of intent and regime type.

The source of the natives' demographic calamity in both the Americas and Australia was their lack of immunity to Old World diseases, including smallpox, measles, influenza, typhus, and tuberculosis. Most of these diseases had passed from domesticated livestock to humans during the Neolithic agricultural revolution and spread through the population of the Old World, which in time had developed resistance to them. The sudden joining of the Old and New Worlds spelled disaster for the natives of the latter, as the diseases migrated across the oceans with the European newcomers.[60] The current coronavirus pandemic is a (relatively mild) reminder of the decisive role that plagues played in human history.

But how can we determine precisely what part of the demise of these native populations was due to epidemic diseases and what part to human brutality? In history and the social sciences, where events cannot be replayed, the only means of answering such questions is through controlled comparisons. Let us begin with colonial Spanish America, which was of course neither democratic nor liberal. Although the Spanish conquistadores exhibited great ruthlessness during their conquests and brutally suppressed and abused the natives, they wanted them to live so that they could be exploited. They needed the natives to work for them in mines and on plantations—the common agricultural possession in Spanish America. Nonetheless, the natives of the Caribbean, where the Spanish first landed and established their rule, died of European diseases at such a fast rate that they were wiped out altogether. The Spaniards saw no alternative but to import African slaves, who despite great mortality rates during ocean crossings and horrible abuse over centuries thereafter, survived in great numbers in the Americas because of their natural resistance to Old World epidemic diseases.

Much the same applies to the rest of Spanish America, where European diseases were a major factor in the destruction of the Aztec and Inca empires, killing an estimated half of each population, including the emperors, at the time of conquest. To be sure, these native civilizations, most notably the Aztec, were among the most bloodthirsty in the gruesome annals of history, practicing among other things mass human sacrifices to the gods. Neither in their realms, nor anywhere else in pre-Columbian America, did there exist an aboriginal Eden of peace and bliss. This is yet another Rousseauan myth of great public appeal. Endemic warfare, very high levels of killings, and pervasive acts of cruelty were the rule throughout the Americas, as they were in native societies around the world. Still, it is not necessary to idealize aboriginal society to appreciate that post-Columbian America experienced a demographic catastrophe. Within a century after the conquest, the native population fell by about 90 percent and then slowly recovered in the following centuries, after the people gradually developed resistance to the new diseases. The natives of Amazonia, isolated until recently, have been much abused over the last generation by entrepreneurs and their workforces penetrating the rain forests to carry out large-scale projects of economic development. Above all, however, their lives are threatened by contact with outside diseases, whose deadly effects are today preventable by large-scale immunization.

We now return to North America. A dense agricultural-urban Native American civilization existed in the Mississippi River Valley, but a Spanish exploratory expedition led by Hernando de Soto observed in 1540 that its towns were deserted. This native civilization is believed to have succumbed to European diseases that spread from Mexico even before direct contact with the Europeans. When the English and French arrived at the same area in the following centuries, this civilization was already long gone. The same terrible process took place throughout North America, as contact and disease gradually spread across the continent. Sparse native populations, rather than falling victim to genocide, were afflicted each in turn by disease brought in by the settlers. Most native populations reached their lowest point some 100 years after contact. The natives of California suffered a disastrous decline, to an estimated half of their pre-contact population, under Spanish and Mexican rule and the mission and estate system. Their numbers continued to fall with the advent of American rule—again only minimally due to direct killings, cruel and indiscriminate as they were. For example, the natives of Pennsylvania and New Jersey were sheltered from harassment by the Quaker communities alongside which they lived. This did not, however, prevent their virtual elimination by disease. Well-known sporadic cases in which contaminated blankets and cloths were deliberately given to the natives to precipitate their demise were inconsequential to the general, practically unstoppable trend.

One last control case is that of colonial Africa. The atrocious treatment of black Africans in America did not cause the blacks to decline demographically—quite the opposite—because of their natural immunity to Old World diseases. Nor did colonial abuse in black Africa itself in the nineteenth and twentieth centuries have that effect, except for a few cases of direct genocide, such as those perpetrated by Imperial Germany—not a liberal democracy—to crush rebellions in German Southwest and East Africa (today's Namibia and Tanzania). The atrocious and murderous exploitation of the people of Congo, then the private property of King Leopold II of Belgium, is another exception. Although in much of the current discourse, the white man, the West, and the liberal democracies are treated as one, they are not the same thing. In North Africa, French occupation and settlement of Algeria after 1830 involved ferocious "pacification" of native resistance. Nevertheless, during the very same period in which the native North American population was plummeting, Algeria's population actually surged, from some 2.5 million in 1800 to about 6 million in 1920.

This is not to say that the natives of America and Australia were not treated harshly and often atrociously. The advance of dense agricultural settlement forced them from their land and disrupted their livelihoods, their way of life, and their culture. They experienced blatant discrimination and were subject to deadly deportations and killings. These purposeful acts contributed to their demographic catastrophe, but did not cause it, nor could they have. It is also true that liberal democracies' conduct in colonial settings were very different from those they practiced at home. Liberal democratic standards rose dramatically during the nineteenth and twentieth centuries, in large part due to liberal moral indignation. All the same, ideological preconceptions are often involved in the attribution of genocide to the democracies.

"False Consciousness", Hegemony, and Ideological Fixations

Almost everything suggested here stands in contrast to what has become pretty much the mainstream of research and teaching in Western academia and the tone of public discourse over the last decades. If the above is true, then we have witnessed a deluge of "false consciousness", mostly affecting the intellectual class and spreading through the most educated parts of society. Indeed, in keeping with the concept of ideological hegemony, this comprehensive outlook has swept aside everything before it. Its tenets appear as self-evident, undisputed truths, and they are passionately embraced and transmitted by intellectuals, the educational system, and the media. The agents and bearers of the hegemonic outlook most genuinely identify with these tenets; nearly everybody in their social circles does; and in consequence, one must add, opportunities in the marketplace of ideas, most prominently the academic one, flow in the same direction. From within this hegemonic perspective, any dissenting view appears absurd, heretical, and morally offensive.

All this teaches us a lot about the phenomena of ideology and ideological fixation. An ideological outlook takes shape at a time when its cognitive elements appear sound and compelling, and its normative imperatives pressing. Thus, some of the intellectual convictions and emotional proclivities that found expression in the West's post-1945 mindset seemed plausible, or were at least understandable, in the context of their time. Aside from the world wars and imperialism, capitalism was closely associated in many people's minds with the miseries of nineteenth-century industrialization, the lawlessness and rigged practices of the "Robber Barons" era, and the trauma of the Great Depression. Deep poverty was still widespread in Western societies, and in the United States it was closely intertwined with legally entrenched racial discrimination. Reformist or alternative socioeconomic systems stood at the zenith of their intellectual and public appeal. They extended all the way from the regulation of capitalism within the welfare state, to the mixed public and private ownership of the economy in social democracy, to the salvationist promise of communism. Capitalist greed was viewed as a major obstruction on the road to a future of prosperity and equality, both within and between countries. The United States, the West, capitalism, liberalism, and democracy were collapsed into one and castigated in this sweeping discourse as the source of all evil or at least as no better than others. In some minds they still are.

The breakaway from the patterns, values, and conventions of traditional, pre-industrial society has been viewed, from Marx on, as a loss of pristine harmony and, at one and the same time, as a Promethean liberation from the arbitrary,

narrow-minded, and oppressive chains of the past. Both views have been celebrated without a sense of contradiction in the post-1945/1960s era of prosperity and normative transformation, which inevitably adopted the attitude and
rhetoric of a generational, some would say adolescent, rebellion and criticism.
The captivating vision of human liberation from all constraints—economic,
social, political, and sexual—has gone hand in hand with the idealization of
premodern existence, whether aboriginal or in the undeveloped or developing
societies that became known as the Third World. Decolonization, the Vietnam
War, and the struggle against racial discrimination have further radicalized that
trend. Some—Marcuse and Fanon being famous examples—championed the
former colonial societies as the only hope of salvation for a world oppressed
by Western capitalism and injustices. At the same time, a loss of naivety regarding the intrinsic biases, self-justifications, and self-righteousness that people
and societies—including one's own—have with respect to their motives and
intentions has been boosted by the spread of higher education and growing intellectual sophistication.

All this reflects the two faces of the Enlightenment, its true "dialectic", as
opposed to that suggested by the Frankfurt School. The Enlightenment's chief
message was the primacy it gave to the freeing of human thought from all other
considerations and constraints that had taken priority over it in traditional
societies: social conformity, custom, prejudice, and biased self-justification. This
is the imperative of "dare to think!" (from the Latin *sapere aude!*) that Kant famously posited in his *What Is Enlightenment?* Among other things, the people of
the Enlightenment understood well that a search for the truth wherever reason
leads had to overcome the deep biases that both individuals and collectives have
in favor of themselves. And in meeting this challenge, the Enlightenment drew
on the legacy against significant parts of which many of its members rebelled: the
Judeo-Christian tradition—in this instance, its paramount emphasis on self-
criticism. Within that tradition, it is we, our sins and wrongs as individuals and
collectives, that ought to stand at the center of our attention and efforts, irrespective of what others do or do not do, as self-criticism and repentance are the only
road to self-correction and salvation.

The Enlightenment combined this moral message of self-criticism and self-
correction with its own emphasis on the unbiased intellectual search for the truth
as a necessary means for social and political self-improvement. Its legacy is largely
responsible for the centuries-long process of reforms and fabulous achievements
in terms of material well-being, freedoms, security, and human rights associated with modern affluent society. Moreover, the critical and even hypercritical
streaks within the post-1945/1960s discourse in the West have contributed a
great deal to this ongoing process. For example, concerning the issues discussed
in this chapter, they have fostered greater sensitivity toward and consideration

for the values of foreign peoples and their right of self-determination. And they have vastly increased the political and moral scrutiny of governments' foreign policies and actions. At the same time, the Western democracies' supposed vices have often been exaggerated in that discourse and rhetoric, their claimed virtues dismissed as shams, and their image largely blackened. Correspondingly, the supposed virtues of traditional, aboriginal, and Third World societies (as well as of the communist enemy) have been vastly exaggerated, their problems ignored or whitewashed and their image idealized. The foreign policy consequences of this trend may have been as negative as, and sometimes worse than, their positive effects. And yet one-sided exaggeration and distortion is in the nature of ideological discourses.

Let us examine some of the concepts that have played a major role in the dominant discourse within the democracies. We have already mentioned the charge of "essentialism", the attribution of uniform and fixed qualities to human groups, societies, and civilizations. Now, awareness and rejection of crude generalizations is an important step forward intellectually and a mark of the sophisticated mind. We become sensitive to significant nuances, shades, and differences in our picture of reality. Furthermore, with respect to human collectives, a rejection of crude generalizations has served as a crucial antidote to our strong propensity to view others through the lenses of stark stereotypes, which in turn involves and seemingly justifies prejudice and bigotry. It is this point in particular that has given the charge of "essentialism" such overwhelming power in the current intellectual and public discourse in the West.

And yet, in the process, the discourse has fallen into the opposite trap. We do not need to hold, as does Aristotle, that things that are grouped together under the same concept have an essence to appreciate the value of general concepts as the indispensable tools of our ability to make sense of reality. As we saw in the chapter on truth, both generalization and distinction are the way our mind works. We zoom out and in—generalize and make distinctions—depending on our cognitive need at a particular moment. We know that all trees or even all pines are not exactly the same. Yet they are sufficiently similar to validate the category, and we make distinctions within it when necessary. Much the same applies to general concepts of human-related categories, such as states, societies, capitalism, etc. We know that there are marked differences in the distribution and frequency of traits within and between human groups. After all, we talk, for example, about differences of values and norms, and so much else. Another example relating to this chapter, we distinguish between developed and developing societies on the basis of huge differences on a wide range of socioeconomic indicators. These are very real differences, with great significance for understanding the world and for people's lives. At the same time, it does not mean that all developed societies or developing societies are exactly the same;

nor that developed and developing societies are entirely or eternally different. Thus, there are good reasons why Said, despite his protestations to the contrary, regarded the "West", if not the "Orient", as a very meaningful category. He "over-essentialized" and crudely generalized the "West", yet still saw that this concept had a sufficient number of shared traits and continuities to make it meaningful and, indeed, indispensable. He was unable to recognize this even to himself, because this would have rendered his entire position with respect to the "Orient" incoherent.

Of course, what matters about "essentialism" and makes it such a dominant shibboleth in the current intellectual and public discourse is the concern, first, that people might attribute normative and socioeconomic traits and differences that are predominantly the product of historical and cultural developments to innate causes; second, that they tend to view often very real traits and differences as being also immutable, unchanging, and unchangeable; and, third, that people are prone to ascribe the traits in question to every individual and subgroup within the discussed category, thereby not only overlooking important differences but also stereotypically stigmatizing individuals and groups. All these, indeed, are very real cognitive and moral hazards that need to be guarded against. Yet the ideological zeal behind the charge of "essentialism" has far transgressed these important qualifications, and is the cause of no less significant failures. Many people rightly feel that the dominant discourse has severely curtailed the ability to call a spade a spade.

The charge of "essentialism" has coincided with, and has been reinforced by, a justified concern about racism. Brought to the fore by the horrendous Nazi doctrine and practice, it has gained prominence, from the 1950s and 1960s onward, with the struggle against the discrimination of the blacks in the United States. In the current discourse, the term "racism" has expanded in use to cover any negative or critical reference to other—not necessarily "racial"—ethnic, social, or cultural groups that might be understood as disparaging or derogatory. Such references have been viewed as particularly offensive when expressed by the more "privileged" groups toward the less privileged. Again, it is necessary to guard against stereotypical views and a bigoted characterization of alien cultural forms, pervasive even when there is no reason to regard such forms as non-benign. It is equally important to refrain from prejudging individuals and sub-groups on the basis of the alleged common traits of the group to which they supposedly "belong". At the same time, characterization of traits in other ethnic or cultural groups—as in ours—may be factually valid, on average of course, whatever the connotations of such a characterization, positive or negative, might be. It should be obvious that it is not in this sense necessarily racialist or inadmissible as such in the public discourse.

The conflict between real and meaningful differences, on the one hand, and the imperative or postulate of equality and non-bigotry, on the other, is classically demonstrated by the protests in the West against the dominance of "dead white males" in the academic curricula and intellectual discourse. The quest to broaden the intellectual horizons to other cultures and traditions is commendable. *Pace* Said, the cultural and philosophical heritage of the great civilizations of Asia in their periods of glory has long drawn attention and respect in the West. And the study of them has only intensified in recent decades, for very good reasons. A revision and rebalancing of the old Western-centered curriculum to reflect the new realities and new understandings of a more globalized world have been much called for. At the same time, this process has often gone too far, especially as it has tended to entail a radical criticism of Western civilization and a denigration of its spectacular achievements.[61] It is also understandable that ethnic and national groups should want to learn more about their own heritage. Hence the proliferation, for example, of African American studies, in societies that have become more openly diverse, most notably the United States, where slavery and its aftermath also constitute a major aspect of the country's history. Paradoxically, the call for greater openness to the cultural heritage of others has recently been countered by the opposite objection, by the same critics, to "cultural appropriation" of the cultural customs and practices of others by the dominant groups. Also, the quest to give special attention to a group's cultural heritage might be considered to apply to ethno-national majorities as well as to minorities. Finally, for reasons we shall discuss in Chapter 7, women have played a secondary role in the cultural, artistic, and intellectual history of traditional societies. Shedding light on their contribution is an aspect of their acceptance as equal to men in modern societies.

At the same time, it is typical of an ideological discourse that, in the name of all the above, it should reject all differences of quality, and make the fight against "hierarchies" its flag, out of concern for human equality and dignity. I shall leave aside the arts and the often made, quite relevant, counterargument of where the African Homer or, indeed, *Epic of Gilgamesh*, or the *Mahābhārata* and *Rāmāyaṇa* of the past are. As should be obvious from my chapter on morality, I regard arguments about questions in which quasi-objective and quasi-subjective values—whether moral or artistic—fuse, as largely futile. Furthermore, ever since the romantics, there has been in the West a great fascination with, and influence by, "primitive" art of whatever source. I shall also pass over philosophy and the question of where the Platos and Aristotles, or the Buddhas, Laozis, and Confuciuses, or the Ibn Khalduns of the less developed parts of the world are, to say nothing of the Western philosophers of modern times, from Descartes on. Since these parts of the world were mostly illiterate until recent times for reasons that will shortly be explained, nor is this absence surprising. With philosophy being a very abstract field of thought, measuring the "quality" of its great works cannot be tangibly quantified, though, again, this does not make the question any less relevant. By contrast, scientific and technological achievements are very tangible and measurable, and here, for historical reasons, the modern West has been groundbreaking, supreme, and, until recently, alone. As we have seen in the chapter on truth, claims that there is no such thing as progress in science, only changing discourse, most fashionable from the 1960s to the 1980s, cannot be seriously sustained and have ebbed with the peaking of the cultural hold of postmodernism. Indeed, now they are still being voiced mostly in the context of the ideological ethno-culture wars in the academic and public discourse.

Works such as Martin Bernal's fanciful *Black Athena: The Afroasiatic Roots of Classical Civilization* (3 vols., 1987, 1991, 2006) have created a stir only in the context of this ideological war. It had long been known that the civilizations of Bronze and Iron Age Greece were crucially influenced during their formative stages by their interaction with and cultural imports from the older civilizations of the ancient Near East. However, Bernal's claim that Greece was colonized by Egyptians and Phoenicians has no basis in reality and has been entirely rejected by the scholarly community. His claim that Egypt was "black" by virtue of its being "geographically" part of Africa, or by having an occasional ruling dynasty from Sudan, is demagogic. It blurs the crucial fact that "black", sub-Saharan, Africa was largely isolated by that huge geographical obstacle, the Sahara Desert, from the developments that were taking place in the ancient Near East, around the Mediterranean and throughout Eurasia. Because of geographical and ecological factors wonderfully laid out in Jared Diamond's best-seller *Guns, Germs, and Steel: The Fates of Human Societies* (1997), it was these parts of the world that spearheaded humanity's course toward more complex forms of social, economic, and political organization and that developed more sophisticated and potent technologies. There is nothing racist about the recognition of these historical developments, nor should it affect ethnic groups' struggle for equality and respect.

But, of course, this is not how ideological conflicts unfolding in the intellectual and public arenas work. Indeed, although the Enlightenment gave priority to the unconstrained pursuit of truth, and its heirs have been highly successful in this pursuit and in spreading the message, this has been an ideal that could never be fully realized. Nor perhaps should it. We do have other considerations, of vital importance to our individual and collective life, and we tend to balance the pursuit of truth with such other considerations. For example, you need to be a Kant to hold that telling a "white lie" in order not to hurt other people's feelings is morally wrong. The only question—a crucial one—is where the line should be drawn.

This is where other attitudes and sensitivities dominant in the ideological discourse in the West during recent decades come in. Thus, there is the great emphasis on the concept of human dignity. It has expanded our sensitivity to not hurting other people's feelings into an imperative of discourse, most prominently, almost exclusively, applied to groups perceived as unprivileged, weak, or marginalized. Notably, most of the people adhering to so-called political correctness probably view it neither as mere politeness, nor as a license to suppress or curtail the truth. Indeed, many of them tend to see this imperative as an expression and achievement of deeper and higher truths. Moreover, the emphasis on human dignity and "political correctness" also reflects a subtler notion that to help weaker groups out of their unfortunate condition there is no use, nor is it justified, to dwell on what might be their own role in explaining or perpetuating their current state. They need to be "empowered" by positive thinking.

The term "weakened" has replaced "weak" as part of this sweeping discourse. Of course, in many cases, the social groups in question have indeed been weakened by others. But just as often, this implicit or explicit charge does not exhaust or capture the reasons for their condition. Closely associated is the view that "weakened" groups' own stories of themselves should be given priority or even a monopoly: because it is their own "authentic" story; because their human dignity so requires; and because this is the most constructive way of bringing them to the fore as equal participants in the community—whether the domestic or international—in the service of justice and to their and everybody else's benefit. The charge of "cultural appropriation" and demands for exclusivity have been a recent extension of this trend.

This widespread "therapeutic" attitude is not without merit. At the same time, its hazards and pitfalls both as practical policy and in terms of the freedom of thought and expression are as obvious, or should have been. The current, growing atmosphere in American campuses, where anything that is proclaimed "offensive", particularly toward the category of "minorities", is vehemently condemned and censored, is a much discussed example. Again, libertarian objections notwithstanding, there are always social lines of demarcation as to what is regarded as legitimate and permissible speech in the public arena. The question is how far these lines are stretched. Orwell's *1984* and its "Thought Police" are an often mentioned allegory.

Conclusion

It can be objected that I have overly focused on and have vastly exaggerated the numbers and public impact of radicals of the left; that they have been in fact a small, if vocal, sect, active on the margins of mainstream public opinion; that the large majority of people hold the middle ground—the term the "silent majority" was adversarially coined in the wake of the 1960s to express precisely this point. All these objections are valid to some degree. And yet, although an intellectual avant-garde is small by definition, its cultural influence may be far broader and deeper. Its ideas are often viewed in wider circles as the more un-inhibited truth, and its moral precepts as the true, distilled voice of conscience. In addition, the representation of these ideas and normative outlook among intellectual and academics has been far higher than among the general public. In consequence, they have established a hegemony of sorts over the intellectual and public discourse from the late 1960s onward. In the process, radicalism of the left, although many of its sub-currents have framed themselves as a stark opposition to liberal doctrine and society, has significantly influenced mainstream left-liberalism. And even as the hegemony of the radical discourse has begun to be challenged from around 1980 on, its dominance remains supreme in large parts of academia and very influential in the public arena. It is for this reason that radicalism of the left plays such a prominent role in our discussion in this chapter of the West's post-1945/1960s ideological mood.

The majority of liberals in academia, the media, and among the public do not subscribe to the radical views in full or in its extremities—although this assessment may be losing some of its validity with the continued escalation of the ideological war in the United States. Especially since the demise of communism, enthusiasm for these views has subsided and appreciation of the virtues of democracy has increased. Still, the radicals' views are widely regarded as important contributions to and corrections of the democracies' historical and socio-political record, and as a moral compass. Furthermore, the radical view of the privileged West's attitude toward the Rest, both at home and abroad, captures a deep sense among liberals as to how, ideally, a desired domestic and international order should look like. Within this state of mind, people typically make allowances for the radical claims and fail to realize how deeply misleading, indeed often absurd and harmful for the cause of human emancipation, so many of them have been.

Remember that it is the factual rather than the normative aspects of ideology that are the subject of this book. Thus, while the radical left's agenda has generated opposition on both normative and factual grounds, it is only the latter that will concern us here. This chapter has mainly focused on the radical left's perceptions and criticisms of the liberal democratic societies of the West in relation to the Rest, be they the societies of the primordial or premodern past or those of the present undeveloped and developing countries. In their critical zeal, the radicals contributed greatly to the inculcation of norms such as greater toleration and inclusion, race and gender equality, the legitimization of LGBTs, and much else—all of which can be viewed as implicit in the classical liberal creed.

At the same time, many radical positions and claims about the world have been dubious. Radicals have implicitly and explicitly maintained that the legacy of the Enlightenment is poisoned, that liberal precepts are sham, and that the West has actually been just as oppressive as the Rest—indeed, far more so—that it carries a blame of unique historical proportions and significance that explains much if not most of the world's ills. In fact, the opposite is much closer to the truth.

That the radicals' view is still very influential is demonstrated, for example, by Steven Pinker's excellent recent book, *Enlightenment Now* (2018), which stirs against it. He has found it necessary to belabor, and admirably demonstrate, the rather obvious but widely contested point that the project of Enlightenment modernity has had a fabulous success by any number of measurable and highly significant indicators: affluence and comfort, health, longevity, peace and security, freedoms, social toleration, self-declared levels of satisfaction, and so much else. No, this does not mean that "everything is all right", that there is no room for corrections and improvements, some of them may be very significant, and that we no longer face major problems and challenges. But it does mean that the achievements of the modern West and of those that have followed its model are unprecedented and unmatched by a huge margin. The close connection between the Enlightenment and liberalism, almost synonymous concepts for centuries, has been severed with the infusion of the radical wing of left-liberalism with fundamentally anti-liberal currents. As Pinker writes: "The humanities have yet to recover from the disaster of postmodernism, with its defiant obscurantism, self-refuting relativism, and suffocating political correctness. Many of its luminaries—Nietzsche, Heidegger, Foucault, Lacan, Derrida, the Critical Theorists—are morose cultural pessimists who declare that modernity is odious, all statements are paradoxical, works of art are tools of oppression, liberal democracy is the same as fascism, and Western civilization is circling the drain."[62]

It is an ominous sign of the current offensive on free thought and free speech by radical progressives that 638 academics signed "an open letter by members of the linguistics community calling for the removal of Dr. Steven Pinker from both our list of distinguished academic fellows and our list of media experts."[63] His questioning of some of the radicals' sacred tenets on issues of the day has in their eyes rendered this fundamentally progressive thinker and champion of the Enlightenment's legacy of open discussion in the pursuit of truth a pariah who needs to be ostracized.

Bruce Gilley's article, "The Case for Colonialism", published in *Third World Quarterly* in 2017, offered a reassessment of the pros and cons of Western colonialism. Not all its scholarly arguments are beyond dispute; and its suggestion (also made by Niall Ferguson) that foreign caretaking by consent of the undeveloped countries by the former colonial powers to pull the former out of their sorry state is dubious above all on practical grounds. But the storm that broke out had much deeper roots. Gilley's article "generated two separate petitions signed by thousands of academics demanding that it be retracted, that TWQ apologize, and that the editor or editors responsible for its publication be dismissed. Fifteen members of the journal's thirty-four-member editorial board also resigned in protest . . . serious threats of violence against the editor led the journal to withdraw the article, both in print and online. Gilley was also personally and professionally attacked and received death threats. On the good side, many rallied to his defense, including Noam Chomsky, and many supported the general argument of the article."[64]

Indeed, I have little doubt that many readers will regard this chapter as ideologically grounded "excuses" and a whitewashing of the Western democracies' many past and present failings and crimes, an apologia masquerading as objective historical analysis, ironically authored by someone who presumes to write against ideological fixations. This would be very much in line with the prevailing ideological discourse. Ideological discourses tend to center on the expression of grievances, the corrections of perceived wrongs, and the pushing through of social platforms. People are naturally inclined to be far more attuned to the blame game of social bargaining than they are to the nuances and the balance of the facts, whether historical or contemporary. In his *Culture of Complaint* (1993), progressive Robert Hughes had made some points that are very similar to mine regarding the allegations of the West's unique oppressiveness, slavery, etc. However, although his book had considerable resonance at the time, the problems he described have only gotten worse since then. Ideological fixations, deeply rooted in a comprehensive cognitive, normative, and emotional worldview and surfing on the intellectual currents of the day, take precedence.

Old-style liberalism centered on two urges: for freedom and equality. Both a deep connection and tension have always existed between them. Diverging emphases on one or the other is a way to describe the split that has taken place between right-wing and left-wing liberalism. The radicals' discourse, driven by the urge for equality, centers on the notions of victimhood. In this context, every inequality—both within and between societies—is perceived as a result of wrongs and injustice done by the more privileged. The equally sanctified notion of human dignity forbids any suggestion that although many of the weak are indeed "weakened" by past occurrences by others, not all of them are; that the roots of some of their often grave problems lie to a larger or smaller degree with them. While "therapeutic" ideological perceptions can serve as a leverage for change—partly *do* serve as such—they might also backfire: not only might they be regarded as distortions of the truth and generate resistance; they might also, for example, discourage notions of responsibility and self-help among the less fortunate—virtues that are essential for their success. What we currently have and what fuels the American escalating culture war is a dual, parallel process: in some ways, the radicalization on the left of progressivism continues, partly feeding on its own internal dynamics, inter alia on questions of the West versus the Rest, both at home and abroad; at the same time, a conservative backlash has taken place and has itself radicalized in many ways. Hughes has shrewdly suggested that two types of PC now vie in the public arena: "political correctness" versus "patriotic correctness". Radicalization has in large part been a product of the ideological battle itself.

The following is a summary list of our propositions in this chapter concerning the Western democracies' record toward the Rest. Ever since the 1950s and 1960s, it has become commonplace that the modern West has been exceptionally and supremely bellicose, imperialistic, oppressive, and murderous. Even those who do not accept that the Rest, whether in the primordial tribal past or in premodern state societies, lived in innocent bliss, nonetheless tend to assume, explicitly or implicitly, that they were in any case less afflicted by all the above. However, all in all, the opposite is true. Tribal societies around the globe suffered far higher rates of violent mortality. Premodern state societies everywhere were the scene of endemic, highly lethal wars, imperial conquest, massacres, enslavement, brutal oppression by foreign and indigenous rulers, and an all-pervasive material deprivation. True, the West was the most successful in all the above during the early modern period, as it gained the advantages that made it more powerful than many others in the game. Yet it was soon to transform the rules of the game themselves. Furthermore, within the West, the emergent liberal democracies should not be conflated with the countries that were not. Indeed, the soul-searching and sense of guilt in the democracies is rooted precisely in the new norms that they themselves have established.

Thus, capitalist-driven modernization and democracy have together witnessed the practical disappearance of war, the threat of war, and the fear of war both between and within states throughout the developed-affluent world. The Rest are still afflicted by war, and the threat and fear of it, precisely because they have not gone through these major developments. Imperialism by the democracies in the late nineteenth and early twentieth centuries ran counter to the capitalist and liberal doctrines, was the cause of major great power wars, and involved high-handed treatment, with pronounced racial overtones, of indigenous populations. Notably, "imperialism does not pay", as they said at the time, and the grab for colonies gathered momentum only because of the mutual fear in the system that the emerging global economy might become partitioned and closed for trade. Moreover, although often violent and oppressive, imperialism by the democracies was the *least* violent and oppressive among both premodern and modern imperialisms, and was ultimately dismantled precisely for this reason and because of its clash with liberal norms. Indeed, in most cases, including

India, the democracies left without a fight. More recent military interventions by the democracies in the countries of the Rest have had a very poor record of success for the very same reasons. Finally, imperial rule by the democracies more often than not replaced rule by far more violent, oppressive, and corrupt indigenous imperial and local elites. In many places, it laid the foundations for modernization, including the establishment of modern administrative, judicial, and educational systems and the principle of equality before the law. Where it failed to do so, this was predominantly due to cultural, social, and political traits of the indigenous societies, which militated against such processes. As a result, these societies have fallen behind and have suffered all the ills of premodern existence. After writing this chapter and as I was finishing this book, Thomas Piketty's wide-ranging *Capital and Ideology* (2020) came out, repeating all the commonplace errors with respect to modern imperialism. You can find my criticism in a special note at the end of this chapter.

Again, none of this implies that the less developed societies *should* embrace modernization and what it brings. Normative preferences are not objective in the strict sense. Like Mill, my proposition is conditional: *if* they want the many blessings that modern civilization brings (and most of them do), then there are cultural and social transformations that they would need to undergo (which many of them fear, resent, or reject). Undeniably, political and military interventions by the United States and by other democracies often involved great misjudgments and resulted in appalling costs in terms of human life and suffering. The global Great Game over power and values is no game at all.

The rise of capitalism in the West was boosted by the massive Atlantic slave trade from Africa and by the institution of slavery in the plantation economy, with all their horrors. Ultimately, however, it was the combination of economic and normative liberalism that brought slavery (and serfdom) to an end, not only in the countries of the democratic West but, under Western pressure, throughout the world, where it had always been a common feature of premodern society. Finally, although the establishment and growth of both the United States and Australia involved the massive expropriation, sporadic killings, some deportations, and countless other abuses of the native populations, no genocide took place. As throughout the Americas, the natives fell victim to Old World diseases to which they had no natural immunity, causing a disastrous collapse in their numbers. Moreover, as the United States has been indispensable for the creation and survival of the modern liberal and affluent world order, with Australia being one of its strongholds, the expropriation of the native populations is one of these cases where the morality of virtue and good intentions and the calculus of consequences starkly collide, creating a very strong, unresolvable dissonance in people's minds. During the nineteenth century, it was widely held that the displacement of old, inefficient uses—and users—of territory and resources by vastly more productive modern techniques was justified. Yet we are no longer comfortable with such a simple assumption.

The drawbacks of capitalism are very significant by many people's standards and are the subject of never-ending and much necessary, indeed crucial, discussion and debate as to how and to what degree they should be dealt with. At the same time, the market principle has proved to be the unrivaled engine of prosperity, and capitalist exploitation, with or without quotation marks, the only proven means of spreading and sharing affluence among previously desperately poor populations throughout the world. As Winston Churchill had it: "Many forms of Government have been tried, and will be tried in this world of sin and woe. No one pretends that democracy is perfect or all-wise. Indeed it has been said that democracy is the worst form of Government except for all those other forms that have been tried from time to time." Presumably, Churchill would not have objected to the expansion of this dictum to cover capitalism in its various forms, including moderate social democratic forms.

Left-radical criticism of both liberal democracy and capitalism after 1945, gaining dominance and hegemony in academia and among intellectuals from the late 1960s on, has contributed to significant normative changes and social reforms in the democracies, some of them successful, some arguably less so. At the same time, it has created many misconceptions and has contributed to the erosion of self-confidence in the liberal democracies. It was a growing sense that the interpretation of reality by radicals of the left was distortive in many significant ways that has generated unease with, and ultimately a full-blown reaction against, some of its main tenets. The 1968 election of Richard Nixon to the presidency of the United States is famously interpreted as an emotional, normative, and cognitive revolt against the 1960s counterculture. It was around that time, the late 1960s and early 1970s, that a neoconservative intellectual opposition to the hegemonic outlook began to take form and win converts. Quite a few of its members had been renegade former radicals, "mugged by reality", as they described themselves.[65] Many of their misgivings concerned domestic socioeconomic issues. But relatedly, there was the growing unease that many people felt about the notion that everything about the West was really that bad. This was the mood most strikingly captured by political scientist, US ambassador to the UN and former Democrat Jeane Kirkpatrick. Her charge that "they always blame America first" became one of the chief slogans of the conservative backlash and the Reagan revolution.

The proponents of this countermovement have contended that in pursuing the Enlightenment's legacy of unbiased self-criticism, the radical left and, increasingly, left-liberalism have lost balance and were "bending over backwards". "Crazy" has been an often used word—indeed, on both sides—to describe the other. As another former US ambassador to the UN, the public servant,

Democratic intellectual and eminent senator Daniel Patrick Moynihan, who was among the earliest critics of many aspects of left-wing radicalism, has philosophically put it: "If you're outside a paradigm, people will think you're crazy. It is by that kind of pattern in the sciences, and what is wanly called social sciences, in which no argument ever gets settled in one generation. . . . And no one will say: 'Gosh, oh golly-gee, I got that wrong! My courses for the last 25 years have been wrong, but I have now changed my ways.'"[66]

A Note on Piketty's Analysis of Western Imperialist Exploitation

In his *Capital and Ideology* (chap. 7, p. 276), Piketty is aware that "The taxes paid in the colonies equaled government expenditure [in them] throughout the period 1830–1950". However, this fact, and the negligible overall sums involved, do not affect his thesis. As he continues: "but this obviously does not mean that there was no "colonial extraction"—that is, no profit to the colonizing power. The first to profit from colonization were the governors and civil servants of the colonies, whose remuneration came from taxes paid by the colonized populations. More generally, the colonizers, whether employed as civil servants or in the private sector (for example, in the agricultural sector in Algeria or on rubber plantations in Indochina), often enjoyed much higher status than they would have had in the metropole" (276).

All this is true and well recognized in the research, but again the actual sums involved were practically negligible in terms of the imperial powers' economies. Furthermore, Piketty entirely ignores the great benefits emanating from the establishment of modern administration and justice systems by the imperial powers in place of the thoroughly corrupt indigenous institutions (as acknowledged by India's prime minister Singh). While citing Edward Said with complete agreement, he fails to compare between all these countries before and after colonialism, and between them and countries that did not undergo colonization, such as China. Indeed, his treatment of the history of India and China plainly shows how profoundly unequal they, like all parts of the premodern world, had been before colonialism, and how deeply unequal they remain, like all developing countries, long after colonialism (chaps. 8 and 13). He blames the British for rigidifying India's old caste system, which they were in fact incapable of uprooting. As he writes (343), this system has not changed much (at least in the social domain) since India's independence either, by now almost a century old.

Most strikingly, Piketty must know that Africa, the main scene of the New Imperialism, comprised only 1-2 percent of the world's trade, and that the economic value of India was continuously shrinking from the late eighteenth century on, as the West was undergoing industrialization. This does not prevent him from developing an entirely novel argument. He cites the mountains of foreign assets accumulated first and foremost by the United Kingdom and, second, by France in the late nineteenth and early twentieth centuries, ascribing them to their colonial possessions (277–278, 284, 287). However, it should have been obvious that these huge assets could not be accounted for by the extremely poor colonial territories. Furthermore, it is pretty common knowledge that during the period in question Britain was the world's banker, whose greatest investment— among many other in the developed and developing economies of the world, from Europe to the Ottoman Empire to China to Latin America—was in the burgeoning economy of the United States. Indeed, as Piketty's own data show, this was the very same period the United States was continuously in the red. France, too, was a huge foreign investor, most notably in its ally, developing tsarist Russia.

Nature or Nurture?

Nations and Nationhood

The idea that humankind has little to speak of by way of its nature, that people's minds at the beginning of life are *tabula rasa*, a "blank slate", to be molded by culture and by other environmental factors, belongs to the very core of liberalism. It has a long pedigree, and its current presence and influence are all-pervasive. In the ways it has been developed and applied, this idea is responsible for major polemics, misguided notions, and resultant confusion in the intellectual and public arena, as it has touched on issues of cardinal significance for the way people view the social world. Flights of fancy in this regard by radicals and left-liberals have sparked a countermovement by right-liberals-conservatives, who have re-emphasized the notion of human nature. While this has been a very necessary correction, some of its expressions have missed the mark in the opposite direction. Thus, the question of nature versus nurture in human affairs is a major example of how a fundamentally factual question is filtered and refracted through the major ideological prisms of our time.

In his *An Essay Concerning Human Understanding* (1689), John Locke, the founding father of liberalism, maintained that all our knowledge originated from our experience of the world by way of our senses. This idea was further developed by later "empiricists", as the school is known. However, the empiricists' view regarding the source of human *knowledge* aside, none of them denied the role that our innate nature played in the human *psyche*. On the contrary, they all held that humankind had deep natural proclivities that played a cardinal role in shaping our attitudes, preferences, and behavior. Remember that Hume, for example, skeptical of all metaphysical abstractions, held that benevolence toward others and, hence, morality itself, was rooted in human nature. With the Enlightenment, the liberal conviction that the application of reason could significantly change social and political conditions and vastly improve the human condition—the idea of Progress—became widespread. It implied that while

Ideological Fixation. Azar Gat, Oxford University Press. © Oxford University Press 2022.
DOI: 10.1093/oso/9780197646700.003.0006

human nature was very much there, humans were not just its prisoners. Nurture, what kind of education humanity received and how society organized itself, was held to be as important as nature.

A more radical view arose during the nineteenth century with the advent of historicism and with the unprecedented transformation of society generated by the Industrial Revolution. Historicism shifted the emphasis decisively toward the cultural, social, and economic conditions that shaped human mores, values, and outlooks and accounted for their great diversity. The expansion of geographical and historical horizons that came with the European Age of Discovery and with the Enlightenment left a deep impression. There was an increasing awareness of cultural flux and a weakening of the belief in the supposed constancies of human nature. The Industrial Revolution, coming on the heels of this burgeoning change of perception, vastly boosted it. Given the massive transformation of socioeconomic forms, of human life, brought about by the Revolution, a view began to take root according to which the particular quality of humankind was that it had no meaningful nature, that it was self-creating and infinitely malleable by history and culture. This was the intellectual path that led from Herder to Hegel, to Marx and his followers. At the time, it was an important, extremely fruitful, intellectual advance. It marked a new recognition not only of the great diversity of human cultures but also of the newly revealed, seemingly infinite potential of human societies for future change, away from the familiar, millennia-old, and supposedly nature-like patterns of traditional society. The problem was that these important ideas were pushed too far. Great cultural diversity and a huge potential for social change were confused for unconstrained diversity and an entirely unbounded potential for change.

By the twentieth century, the view of humanity as all-culture or all-history, with no significant nature to speak of, had become the main doctrine of the social and cultural studies. Anthropology made this its first article of faith. In psychology, the empiricist tenet that all knowledge was acquired by experience of the world imprinted on the blank slate of the mind from infancy onward was expanded by the dominant behaviorist school. Its proponents held that all patterns of behavior were the result of social conditioning that could be manipulated almost at will. The first significant crack in this general outlook came with the Chomskyan revolution in linguistics. It suggested that the basic deep patterns of all human languages, as well as the potential for language acquisition itself, were innately grooved in the human mind. Furthermore, evidence of "human universals" in expressions, emotions, and basic patterns of social relations has been mounting, documented by anthropologists and psychologists in the most remote and isolated human groups across the globe.[1] The renewed application of evolutionary theory to the study of humans, taking place from the late 1970s on, has delivered a devastating blow to the prevailing doctrine that humans have no nature worthy of serious attention.

As we have seen, evolutionary psychology was received with dismay and dismissal in the humanities, social sciences, and cultural studies, as it ran counter to everything they had been taught to believe and were teaching for much of the twentieth century.[2] Although this resistance has been undermined over time—because of evolutionary theory's compelling logic and overwhelming evidence, gradually filtering in through generational change—resistance is still the dominant attitude in all these disciplines. The reasons run deeper than the mere challenge to old habits of thought. Richard Dawkins, the author of the most influential book of the neo-Darwinian revival, *The Selfish Gene* (1976), happens to be left-leaning in his political views. And he is only an example, demonstrating that there is no necessary connection here between scholarly views and political orientation. All the same, progressives during much of the twentieth century associated evolutionary theory and the concept of human nature with some of the gravest threats to the causes of human freedom and of human emancipation.

Given the history of the twentieth century, this concern is understandable. We have already mentioned Social Darwinism, the rightly discredited application of Darwin's doctrine to human affairs and social policy during the late nineteenth and early twentieth centuries. The Social Darwinists' misplaced attribution of all social differences to biological inheritance and their crude racism inevitably generated a backlash in the humanities and social sciences. The horrors of Nazism were the ultimate antidote against these views in all the developed countries after 1945. Moreover, there were intrinsic features within progressivism that strongly militated against the view that biology had much to do with human affairs. Liberalism is a doctrine of human freedom and equality, which have increasingly been projected as *unfettered* freedom and equality. Individual "autonomy" has become the key concept of liberalism. Therefore, the view that the individual's self-determination as an equal and self-creating agent could be constrained and in many ways be predetermined by our natural propensities— channeled through our genes and hormones—has been very difficult to digest for adherents of the creed. It has been regarded as an affront to human dignity and a threat to unconstrained human freedom and equality.

Basically, the philosophers of the eighteenth century yet again had it right and only lacked the evolutionary perspective to explain what they understood quite clearly: *both* nature and nurture count enormously, and they are interconnected and mutually affecting. Indeed, there is no other way to understand humankind. This means that we are capable of breathtaking transformations of every aspect of our individual condition and social relations, of our entire way of life; which, at the same time, does not imply that we cut loose of the deep natural propensities that form the basis of our system of motivation and emotional makeup.

Of course, who does not know that both nature and nurture count? This is commonplace in the current intellectual discourse. And yet, this simple notion is quickly forgotten when ideologically charged issues are on the table. We select two major themes in relation to which an ideological bias toward the "blank slate" and against human nature has dominated the academic discussion and public debate in the liberal democracies. In this chapter, we scrutinize the prevailing analysis of, and attitude toward, the phenomena of the nation and nationhood. In the following chapter, we proceed to examine the current approaches to all things relating to gender and sexual behavior. On both of these issues, the ideological fixations manifested have been integral to social transformations of historical proportions and significance. On both, they have also entailed some far-reaching and highly influential misperceptions of reality.

Does Nationalism Not Have Any Deep Roots in the Human Psyche?

As this book is being written, the world has been experiencing a nationalist resurgence. In both the United States and Europe, there is a powerful backlash against unrestricted immigration, most notably when integration in terms of culture, values, and identity appears problematic. In the United States, Donald Trump was elected president in 2016, waving the banner of "America first". The European Union—celebrated only a decade earlier as the paragon of a postnational future—has been experiencing Brexit; pressures to leave the EU and a rise of far-right anti-immigration parties in other member states; and separatist movements seeking independence from some EU member states. In a number of formerly communist Eastern European states of the EU, as well as in Putin's Russia and in China, anti-liberal nationalism is rampant. An ethnic and national resurgence is no less powerful across Asia and Africa.

The resurgence of nationalism comes as a surprise and shock to many, as the world has become increasingly interconnected and interdependent—economically, culturally, and with the revolutionary spread of digital communication networks. Cosmopolitism and the demise of the nation-state have been heralded and celebrated by many as the order of the future. This view has gone hand in hand with the teachings of the hegemonic "modernist" school in the study of the national phenomenon during much of the twentieth century. Modernists have claimed that the national phenomenon is recent, superficial, and contrived, that "nationalism does not have any very deep roots in the human psyche", as leading modernist theorist Ernest Gellner has put it.[3] For some modernists, nationalism is nothing more than a product of manipulation by often cynical state authorities. The modernists' teachings now dominate college education, where

Benedict Anderson's *Imagined Communities* (1983) tops students' reading lists, as Marx's "Communist Manifesto" did a generation earlier. Indeed, Marx himself, and his latter-day followers, famously failed to understand the power of national sentiments, which his version of *Homo economicus* and concept of class struggle could not accommodate. The communist vision of a universal workers' solidarity that transcended political borders came tumbling down with the outbreak of World War I. Furthermore, following the German invasion of the Soviet Union in World War II, Stalin substituted the call to the people to whom he referred as "brothers" to defend "Mother Russia" for the old communist appeal to the workers and the communist vision.

Nonetheless, in the context of the post-1945 climate of ideas and normative atmosphere, the tendency has grown within some strands of liberalism to question both the significance and legitimacy of the national phenomenon. Serious misconceptions regarding the actual operation of the world—past, present, and future—result. My book (with Alexander Yakobson), *Nations: The Long History and Deep Roots of Political Ethnicity and Nationalism* (2013), published just before the current nationalist resurgence, challenged the modernist claims. Although I cannot pretend to have predicted the sweeping nationalist resurgence that was about to break out, the book did spring from the conviction that the prevailing scholarly and public discourse on the national phenomenon had become deeply delusional, representing a severe case of "false consciousness".

Liberalism, Nationalism, and Humanity

The liberal attitude toward the national phenomenon has had many faces, and it has changed over time. British liberalism, from Locke onward, largely emerged in defense against the threat of foreign intervention by absolutist France and, earlier, Spain. Therefore, although predominantly preoccupied with the domestic order, British liberalism was infused with a very strong sense of Britishness and British patriotism that were taken for granted.[4] In continental Europe, following the French Revolution and during the nineteenth century, liberalism and nationalism were widely regarded by friend and foe alike as twins. For the leaders of national liberation movements, such as Giuseppe Mazzini and Thomas Masaryk, free government and national self-determination were the two inseparable aspects of the progressive agenda. As Mill wrote: "Free institutions are next to impossible in a country made up of different nationalities."[5] Indeed, given the vote and a free choice, the people of the different nationalities all too often choose to part ways. The people's will, once spoken, has been revealed to be unmistakably pro-national. In the wake of World War I, progressivist US president Woodrow Wilson posited popular sovereignty, liberal rights, and national self-determination, *together*, as the basis for a new—just, democratic, and secure—world order.

However, by the late nineteenth and early twentieth centuries, anti-liberal nationalistic doctrines and political movements had emerged, and chauvinistic and aggressive nationalism had widely demonstrated its horrendous potential. For this reason, in the wake of the two world wars and Nazism, liberal attitudes toward nationalism have taken a sharp negative turn. It is not a coincidence that nearly all the founding fathers of the modernist school that rejects the view that the national phenomenon has any deep roots—Hans Kohn, Karl Deutsch, Ernest Gellner, Eric Hobsbawm, Elie Kedourie—were immigrant refugees from the horrors of the 1930s and 1940s. Although liberal opinion has grown even more supportive of national self-determination in the case of the former colonial countries, mainstream national identities and sentiments in the developed liberal democracies themselves have been increasingly regarded with distaste. Not without reason, they have been suspected of being chauvinistic, detrimental to individual and minority rights, and an obstacle to growing cosmopolitanism. Only a few recent liberal theorists have had good things to say about the national category.[6] Iconic Democratic president John F. Kennedy's famous ringing call in his Inaugural Address (January 20, 1961): "And so, my fellow Americans: ask not what your country can do for you—ask what you can do for your country", sounds awkward to many contemporary liberal ears.

The reasons for the strong liberal ambivalence run deep. Liberalism centers on the individual, on the one hand, and on humanity, on the other. Thus, although liberals perceive group affiliations favorably if they are a product of free human association, they regard particularistic identities and affiliations that people are arbitrarily born into, most notably the national, as difficult to accommodate conceptually and justify morally. This is especially so because liberals view such affiliations as both imposing on the individual and conflicting with the general good of humanity. Ever since Kant (if not Plato), both the rational and the moral have been equated with the universal. Thus, the moral status of national affinities and loyalties has been viewed as deeply problematic, while their source has remained a mystery.

As the idea that human nature had *anything* to do with social realities was anathema to historians and social scientists during the twentieth century, scholars have lacked the theoretical tools to comprehend the deep roots of the ethnic and national phenomenon in naturally evolved human propensities. And that which we lack the means to comprehend we do not see even if it is staring us in the face. Repeatedly confounded by ferocious, "atavistic", irruptions of ethnic and national forces, theorists and commentators nonetheless dismiss them as the outcome of "manipulation" or as epiphenomenal expressions of some other factors, most notably economic. Although "tribalism" has often been invoked on such occasions, the relation of this phrase to the national phenomena has remained obscure. But, indeed, could the tremendous devotion people habitually have shown for their collective and country, the enormous emotional mobilization it has so often generated, sometimes to the point of a willingness to die for one's country, be merely the result of social conditioning and government manipulation? Could all this "not have any very deep roots in the human psyche", as Gellner has put it? Revealingly, in response to criticism, Gellner later confessed to be deeply moved by all expressions of his native Bohemian folk nationalism.[7]

It comes as some surprise that Pinker, who has subjected the doctrine of the blank slate to the most sweeping criticism in a brilliant book of this title, has recently expressed himself in a way that suggests that nationalism, which he consistently equates with its aggressive and populist forms, is nothing more than a manipulative and malevolent construct that is better left behind. He writes: "It's true that political salesmen can market a mythology and iconography that entice people into privileging a religion, ethnicity, or nation as their fundamental identity. With the right package of indoctrination and coercion, they can even turn them into cannon fodder. *That does not mean that nationalism is a human drive.* Nothing in human nature prevents a person from being a proud Frenchman, European, and citizen of the world, all at the same time."[8] I agree with the last sentence but disagree with the penultimate. Furthermore, they carry different meanings and do not quite cohere. Similarly, historian of the past and future and best-selling pundit Yuval Noah Harari, who occasionally has given the impression that the exceptional human cognitive capacity to create conceptual frameworks could produce practically any form, has preached a switch from national to global identity and orientation.

Neither Pinker nor Harari is a radical or extreme cosmopolitan who denies both legitimacy and value to national identities, sentiments, and borders. What they share is a strong emphasis on the huge advantages of globalization in enhancing both economic prosperity and peace, as well as an awareness of the great dangers of chauvinist nationalism. As should be clear from the previous chapter, I, too, am a strong supporter of the process of globalization, for the very same reasons, provided that it is not exploited by some countries, most notably to gain a military advantage in the service of an aggressive foreign policy. As Adam Smith himself, the prophet and champion of peaceful free trade, put it: in such cases free trade must be compromised, since "defence . . . is of much more importance than opulence".[9] Except for such critical circumstances, there are huge advantages to—indeed, in many fields, a pressing need for—international cooperation to cope with global challenges and prevent countries across the globe from falling into self-harming "prisoner's dilemmas". As the founding fathers of liberalism believed, national and international are not irreconcilable poles between which one must make a stark choice. They thought them to be complementary aspects of a liberal order. Furthermore, the realities that these concepts represent, as well as the relationship and balance between them, are changing and changeable, are, indeed, "construed" to a very large degree. The point is that they are not *merely* construed, as national sentiments of identity and solidarity have deep roots in human nature.

Kin-Culture Bonds of Identity and Solidarity

Modernists trace the beginning of nations to the French or Industrial Revolutions, from the late eighteenth century on, or, according to others, to the early modern period and the revolution of the printing press from around 1500 on. Their critics argue, as do I, that strong sentiments of shared identity and solidarity in their relation to politics—the close link between ethnicity or culture and political demarcations—although, like so much else, unquestionably revolutionized by modernity, very much existed in the premodern world.[10] This is not merely a semantic debate on what should be labeled "national". Rather, the debate is about historical realities: did people in premodern societies think and feel themselves part of a larger ethnic and culture community, far wider than their village and province, and did such self-perceptions and sentiments matter politically?

It is impossible here to deploy the mass of evidence presented in my book to show that they did—and, indeed, from the very beginning of statehood in ancient Egypt, Mesopotamia, China, Japan, and many other places, *millennia* ago. Ethno-cultural realities fundamentally shaped both the borders and internal political order of city-states, on the one hand, and multiethnic empires, on the other (in the latter an imperial people or ethnos was almost everywhere the empire's mainstay). Moreover, in many places ethno-cultural identity gave rise to a third category, what sociologists have called territorial or dynastic kingdoms—in reality, national monarchies, where ethnicity and statehood were intimately connected. Contrary to an all-too-common view, state-building in a preexisting ethnic space was an infinitely easier enterprise than welding a state together from different ethnicities and peoples. Most states were built upon a population of common ethnicity and depended on its sense of shared identity, affinity, and solidarity both in defending themselves against others and in conquering and ruling others in imperial projects.

That said, the debate between the modernists and their critics would seem to have little relevance to the question that concerns us here. This is so because even if one accepts the antiquity and political significance of premodern ethno-national affiliations, identities, and sentiments, they cannot be older than the earlier states themselves. These emerged only some 5,000 years ago at the earliest, whereas our species *Homo sapiens* goes back hundreds of thousands of years. Furthermore, in many places around the world, the national format has never taken root, and allegiance is reserved to the extended family, tribe, or confessional community. How, therefore, can nations and national sentiments of identity and solidarity have their roots in human nature if nations are a relatively recent historical development compared to the entire lifespan of our species, and are therefore in no sense "primordial"?

What I argue is that national sentiments are one historically shaped expression of a deeply rooted human propensity for affinity, solidarity, and mutual cooperation with their perceived kin-culture communities, a propensity that is evolutionarily engraved in human nature. For the overwhelming majority of our species' history, that community was the hunter-gatherer tribe of about "500". As we saw in Chapter 2, the tribe was a dense cluster of close kin and cross-cutting marriage ties, which explains why its members were evolutionarily predisposed to support each other against outsiders. Moreover, apart from biology, humans have culture, and are differentiated by their cultures. Since culture, particularly among hunter-gatherers, was local and thus strongly correlated with kinship, cultural identity became a strong predictor of kinship. Those around me in the tribal group who behaved, spoke, and looked like me were also most likely to be more related to me than outsiders. Even between relatively close ethnic groups, people are acutely attuned to the subtlest of differences in dialect, accent, dressing style, and behavior, and tend to give preference to those most akin to them. This is the key to what a perplexed Freud confusedly described as the "narcissism of minor differences" between close ethnicities.[11]

Culture sharing is crucial in another way too. Not only was it in itself a strong predictor of kin relatedness in aboriginal communities; it is also a highly significant tool of human social cooperation. Cooperation is dramatically more effective when cultural codes—above all language, but also customs, values, and other patterns of thought and behavior—are shared. Culture, cultural diversity, and, hence, the facility of shared culture cooperation are unique to humans and differentiate them from other social animals. Hence the innate human tendency to prefer those who belong to their kin-culture community over strangers.

This explains why, although competition and conflicts within the tribal group were rife, its members tended to unite against an external threat—what is known in state societies as "rallying around the flag". Similarly, although rivalry and warfare often took place between tribes that belonged to the same ethnos—that is, that spoke a similar language and held similar customs—such tribes habitually came together in inter-tribal alliances and confederations in response to a foreign challenge. These attachments, permeating social life and extending beyond family to tribe and ethnos, became integral to politics when states emerged.

Ethnicity has always been political and politicized, because people have always been heavily biased toward those whom they identify as their kin-culture community. Thus, the space of loyalty and benefit-sharing from the individual to humanity is curved rather than even—extending, as Aristotle saw, from family to wider kin-communal circles, real or perceived, and to their political expressions.

This does not mean that ethnicity and nationhood are given, unchanging quantities. Although ethnic and national identities are among the most durable and most potent of cultural forms, sometimes spanning centuries and even millennia, they are always in flux. Ethnicities and nations are complex, composite, multilayered, and multifaceted historically developed phenomena, to be sure. New ethnic and national identities emerge and merge, while others wither away, disappear, or are transformed beyond recognition. People and groups shake off one identity and adopt another, change their allegiance, and often share in a multiplicity of identities. Furthermore, rather than "blind instincts", sentiments of ethnic and national belonging are deep-seated but highly modulated predispositions whose particular expressions are largely a function of circumstances. Moreover, there are other, sometimes conflicting, considerations that feed into people's calculations. People regularly adopt foreign cultural forms, sometimes eagerly; they might also migrate from their native land (where conditions might be harsh) provided they consider these acts to be beneficial to them and believe that they can carry them out successfully. Notably, though, processes of shared identity formation tend to occur in their new and adopted homeland as well. Processes of cultural amalgamation bind together not only historical peoples and nations, but also modern immigrant ones.

But if so, are ethnic populations and nations kin groups? Given the complex historical processes of group amalgamation, identity formation, and transformation, scholars usually refer to a "myth" of common descent or kinship shared by ethno-national groups. In both scholarly and colloquial discourse, myth often implies falsehood. However, more discriminately it means a legendary communal story or tradition about great past events that may have a greater or lesser basis in reality. As it happens, genetic studies, exponentially growing in number and sophistication in recent years, reveal that most ethnic and national communities around the globe tend to be genetically related.[12] This is not that surprising because massive population movements were rare before the advent of modern means of transportation. The roots of most populations go back to the original settlement of their territories during the Agricultural Revolution and even earlier. Present-day populations tend to be descendants of these founder groups, and have mostly intermarried locally, among themselves, over millennia. Foreign migrations and conquests usually took the form of elite takeovers, with the majority of the population remaining unchanged.

Just as clearly, however, studies show that genetic continuums regularly flow into or are split between different—occasionally hostile—cultures, ethnicities, and nations. People are sometimes genetically more related to their neighbors across the border than to other people of the nation to which they belong and express allegiance. Contrary to superficial either/or reasoning, this does not mean that kinship is irrelevant. What matters is the *perception* of kinship (which, again, more often than not, has a genuine basis in reality), which peoples throughout history have been prone to project and act upon as a supreme bond. People everywhere have been strongly inclined to extend the images and idioms of kinship over those with whom they share cultural identity, territory, and political community. In some cases, the people of an ethnos might be aware that they originated from diverse groups and do not all share a common descent. However, the more ethnic and national collectives fuse culturally and integrate through marriages over generations and centuries, the more they feel themselves to be a kin community in which the various founder groups have been immersed.

Thus, while historical myths abound in the nationalistic discourse, modernist counter-myths have been created at a nearly equal rate. "Imagined communities" does not mean arbitrary invention, nor does invented tradition imply wholesale fabrication. The fashionable shibboleths that predominate in the social sciences obscure that social phenomena—including nationalism—tend to be *both* deeply rooted *and* constructed. There is nothing mutually exclusive here. The claim that nations and nationalism are modern ideological constructs invented by intellectuals and spread by means of state authority and the state's apparatuses is a misleading half-truth that is itself a modernist (or postmodernist) ideological construct originating with intellectuals and requiring deconstruction.

The Continued Potency of National Identities

While the decline and morally suspect status of national sentiments have been widely proclaimed, the crucial development of our times has actually been the *acceptance* throughout the developed world of national self-determination on the liberal principle that people are entitled to choose for themselves. At a time when national rights have been secured domestically and genuine foreign threats seemed to have practically disappeared, it is hardly surprising that national sentiments have been taken lightly or even viewed disparagingly in Western liberal democracies. As is said about good health, some things are noticed only when they are gone. National identity and sentiments in the West have become liberal, largely implicit, and predominantly defensive, rather than directed at conquering and subjugating others—transparent or "banal", as they have been called.[13] And yet they are anything but nonexistent. As liberal, prosperous, and peaceful countries like Canada (Quebec), Belgium (Flemings versus Walloons), the United Kingdom (Northern Ireland, Scotland, Brexit), and Spain (Catalonia, Basque Country) have discovered, and the challenges of immigrant integration has made all the more apparent, ethno-national divisions easily acquire supreme political salience.

An alleged contrast between civic nationalism, supposedly based solely on common citizenship and shared political institutions, and ethnic nationalism, based on descent and shared historical and cultural lineage, has been central to this debate. However, there have been very few nations, if any, whose existence has been divorced from ethnicity—that is, which did not share cultural and at least some kin affinities. In reality, civic nationalism too—indeed, civic nationalism in particular—generates assimilation into the national community, either as an explicit, "republican", requirement, as in France, or as a tacit assumption, as in the United States and Britain. Of course, the ultimate test of shared nationhood is the self-perception of the population in question— nineteenth-century theorist Ernest Renan's "daily plebiscite". However, in actuality people overwhelmingly *choose* to live together in a political community with their kin-culture likes, and exhibit a strongly preferential solidarity toward them. "Constitutional patriotism", in social thinker Jürgen Habermas's phrase,[14] is generally expressed, as he himself was not unaware, toward one's own patria, precisely because that particular patria happens to incorporate the above.

There is yet another semantic difficulty that needs to be cleared out of the way. In English in particular, the term "nationalism" has negative connotations. In hegemonic Britain during its time of glory, which took its national identity for granted, "nationalism" was something attributed to others. The same applies to the United States. Given this connotation, I opt here as often as possible for terms such as nationhood, nationality, national identity, and national sentiments, which carry less negative overtones. The term "patriotism", love and devotion to one's country, is used in the liberal discourse with greater ease. There have been efforts to distinguish it from nationalism by associating it exclusively with republican and civic virtues in free societies.[15] However, patriotism has been exhibited as strongly, often more so, by non-democratic and non-liberal societies. Moreover, the term patriotism itself is far from being unsuspected from a liberal perspective. As Dr. Johnson famously put it in eighteenth-century Britain: "Patriotism is the last refuge of the scoundrel." This attitude is still widely held, as patriotism is often associated with jingoism. Thus, for practical purposes, I ignore all such semantic peculiarities. We distinguish here between illiberal, chauvinist, and aggressive nationalism and liberal, non-aggressive varieties, and apply the same distinction to "patriotism". We now turn to see how this applies to immigrant countries, widely regarded as purely "civic".

Immigrant Countries: The United States as a Paradigmatic Case

Immigrant countries are clearly very different from the old nations of Europe, or China, Japan, and other old nations around the world, with their dominant, historical, ethnic core and much stronger kinship sentiments that bind the political community. For the sake of brevity, we shall focus on the United States as a major example, but much the same applies to other modern immigrant countries.

The American nation was created by immigrants. Immigration remains central to the nation's experience, ethos, and identity. It is widely believed that the United States is a quintessentially civic nation, because its people are multi-ethnic and supposedly united only by citizenship, allegiance to their adopted country, and adherence to its constitution. For this reason, the idea that nationhood has a kin-culture meaning rings strange to American ears; indeed, it goes against the national ideology and encounters instinctive resistance as both false and dangerous. In reality, however, the United States' national identity is infinitely thicker than its much-cited civic features. While sometimes retaining a distinct sense of their origin and cultural roots, especially during the first generations after immigration, the various immigrant communities take on a great deal more in terms of cultural baggage, replacing their language, most notably, and much more. They increasingly merge into a shared, amalgamated new American culture and identity, to which they also contribute. Typically, from the third generation onward, intermarriages among the immigrant ethnic groups rise steeply, as differences of culture and identity decrease and the common denominators become much stronger.

The rhetoric of multiculturalism and multiethnicity—justified and commendable as it may be in expressing new norms of respect for diverse group heritages in the public sphere—should not obscure the fundamental reality: there exists a very distinct American culture and identity, widely shared by the large majority of Americans and characterized by a common English language and all-pervasive folkways. These encompass mores, symbols, social practices, public knowledge, and a sense of common historical tradition; popular tastes, images, and heroes; music, sports, cuisine, public holidays, and social rituals. That this has been a fusion culture, drawing from many immigrant sources and traditions, is incontestable and is much celebrated as a wellspring of richness and creativity. The point, however, is that this fusion, ever-changing like any culture, is quintessentially American, widely shared by the American people and projected beyond the United States' borders as distinctively American. Indeed, the Americanism of American culture is deeply felt around the world, regarded either with approval or disapproval. Americans become very conscious of their cultural identity whenever they encounter the outside world. This common American culture far transcends the political civic culture that many theorists have posited, naively, as the exclusive binding element of the American nation.[16]

Certainly, throughout American history ethnic communities have often maintained ties with the old country and people. Some of them have also carried out lobbying activity in Washington for them.[17] Moreover, since the 1970s, a surge in the quest for roots in terms of origin and tradition has been very noticeable and much celebrated, even, indeed most typically, among people three generations or more in the United States. Still, the cultural identity of the so-called hyphenated Americans past the first generation or two after immigration is overwhelmingly American, with the search for origins and tradition playing a symbolically important but mostly secondary role.[18] American history and tradition become theirs at least as much as their consciousness of distinctive roots, in most cases much more so, with some strong variations, such as the experience of slavery for African Americans. Americans would say as a matter of course that they won the War of Independence, or World War II, even if their ancestors had not yet arrived in the United States when these historical events took place.

Were Presidents Theodore and Franklin Roosevelt or actor Humphrey Bogart "ethnically" Dutch because of their centuries-old ancestry on the male line? Indeed, there is no need to go that far back: was singer and actor Frank Sinatra, American-born to Italian immigrants and retaining some lifelong ties to the Italian community, including, reportedly, to the mafia, "ethnically" more Italian than American? And what about actress Jennifer Aniston of the popular television sitcom *Friends*, who is American-born to a father of Greek descent and to a mother of Scottish and Italian descent? The doctrine of a "melting pot" that dominated until the middle of the twentieth century has since acquired a bad name in the academic and public discourse as being oppressive and leveling. However, cleansed of its less tolerant aspects, it has very much remained the reality of immigrants' integration into American society.

Conventions of speech in the United States identify ethnicity with minorities, origins, and "shared blood". However, national, cultural, and even ethnic identity are not destiny. It has been suggested that immigrant ethnicities should not be labeled "minorities", because there is allegedly no majority ethnicity in the United States. People of British descent constitute only a small part of the American people, and even the broader category of European "whites" is quickly losing its majority status.[19] More plausibly, however, the majority identity in America is actually American, overarching and often ultimately replacing original ethnic identities.

Rates of intermarriage among the original ethnic communities are the most tangible and robust indicator of these processes. While intermarriages are still marginal in the first and second generations after immigration, they rise steeply thereafter. Interracial marriage between whites, Asians, Latinos, African Americans, and Native Americans, where differences in physical appearance variably remain after the cultural differences diminish, are nonetheless steadily rising in all categories. More than half of Native Americans marry outside their group, as do between one-third and one-half of American-born Asians and Latinos (marrying mostly whites).[20] Interreligious marriages also range around 50 percent. This is a huge change from the endogenous marriage patterns within Protestants, Catholics, and Jews still observable in the 1950s, which gave rise to the theory of three distinct melting pots.[21] Moreover, the focus on interracial and interreligious marriages is partly misleading. This is so because the barriers among the genuinely original ethnic communities, those by native country and people of origin—for example, among people of European descent—have been collapsing even more sweepingly through American acculturation and intermarriage.[22]

Thus, the more generations one's family has been in the United States, the more "fourth", "eighth", or "sixteenth" parts of descent from different countries and communities of origin one is likely to have and the more "ethnically" all-American one becomes. This has contributed to a growing sense of kinship among old-time Americans, which reinforces common culture and mutual so-cial cooperation in American national identity. As one study has put it: "These connections between assimilation and intermarriage may be said to describe how once distinct peoples become one stock, literally members of one family."[23] In a relatively young nation and with an ongoing immigration project, the shared-kin element is weaker than in other nations; yet it is very much there. To remove unnecessary quibbles, it does not at all matter whether or not one calls all-American identity "ethnic", especially as applied to old-time Americans. The point is that far more than civic allegiance to a constitution and political society, a common dense national culture, as well as increasing interracial and interethnic mixing, underlie the American sense of nationhood.[24]

It is not superfluous to stress that all the above implies neither homogeneity nor harmony, but a dynamic and highly variable process. Among other things, some ethnic groups and categories are less successfully incorporated into the American nation, as reflected in both social realities and perceptions, including self-perception.[25] For example, despite high levels of intermarriage, Native Americans remain somewhat outside American national identity and, indeed, have recognized rights as distinct "nations" in their reservations. Also, notwith-standing major strides in the past decades, the intermarriage rates and social integration of African Americans lags behind those of other groups. Moreover, since the 1960s, some African Americans have tended to define themselves as not only ethnically, but also nationally distinct. One dares predict that such trends will remain marginal to the more general process of integration into

American society and identity. In this respect, Barack Obama's election to the presidency of the United States was a historical landmark. With both Kenyan and Irish descent and a pronounced African American self-identification, his identity is surely, above all, American.

As in the United States, a shared culture and an expanding sense of kinship, from the core people to the newcomers, rather than civic allegiances alone, has always underpinned both Australian and New Zealander nationhood. By comparison, in Canada, marked by two major ethnic-cultural identities—English-speaking and French-speaking Québécois (and less significant politically, Inuit)—the prospect of a political partition of the country continues to loom.[26] Liberal philosopher of multiculturalism and Canadian citizen Will Kymlicka has made an important point in response to widely held misconceptions regarding a supposedly ethnic neutrality of the liberal state: all liberal states do in fact give preference to a particular ethnicity, their own, as reflected most notably in their standard language; all are engaged in nation-building.[27]

The Immigration Crisis as a Litmus Test

Mass immigration—legal and illegal—has become a cardinal political issue in both Europe and the United States and has accelerated the ideological polarization and radicalization of opinion and attitude between left and right. In the United States in particular, the immigration debate has further deepened the divide, growing alienation and hostility between progressives and conservatives.

Radicals and some progressives increasingly come to frame the world in post-national, cosmopolitan terms, where universal and individual rights should reign supreme. Some of them lean toward the view that any restrictions on immigration are unjustified and unjustifiable, as it is immoral to deny free access to a better life to people from the poorer and less fortunate parts of the world. Whereas until 2010 there was scarcely any difference between the attitudes of Republicans and Democrats toward immigration, during the last decade Republicans' attitudes have become very negative, while those of Democrats have become very favorable.[28] In this dynamics of mutual escalation—and mutual provocation—in the ideological conflict, some progressives increasingly tend to label any restrictive immigration legislation and policies as racist and fascist. In Europe, the humanitarian crisis of millions of people fleeing areas of war and famine and crossing perilous seas and borders strains moral sensibilities. On the other side of the ideological divide, immigration has become a central element in the conservatives-led backlash against what they regard as the abandonment of all the traditional notions of a core culture and common identity in a country, and their rebellion against what they view as the tyranny of political correctness. Throughout the liberal West, the right powerfully challenges the claim that it is illegitimate, in principle, for a country to impose restrictions on immigration. Both Canada and Australia, quintessentially liberal and multiethnic countries, have put in place very strict immigration regulations, and there is a hardening of immigration policies in the countries of Western Europe as well, with Denmark as perhaps the most conspicuous case. Sweden, another Scandinavian country, represents the opposite pole, adopting very liberal policies with respect to immigrants and refugees.

Different sensibilities and perspectives on universalism vs. national identity, as well as conflicting effects on the economy, crime, and terrorism, frame the debate. However, as Eric Kaufmann demonstrates in his important *Whiteshift: Populism, Immigration and the Future of White Majorities* (2019), relying on extensive evidence from polls, the major political divide in the West at present—inter alia accounting for both the Brexit vote and Trump's election—correlates with personal-cultural attitudes on immigration. It scarcely correlates with class, wealth, gender, or even education, as is often assumed.

I make no pretense to authoritatively pass judgment on the many practical policy issues entangled in the debate. All these issues involve complex questions of fact—both existing and projected (and thus conjunctional)—as well as no less intricate, and sometimes irreconcilable, value preferences. The most sensitive and contentious normative question is whether it is legitimate for a people and nation to seek to preserve their core culture. Since the liberalization of its immigration laws in the 1960s, the United States has experienced the greatest influx of immigrants in a century, proportionate to its population, let alone in absolute numbers. The debate about immigration and American cultural identity was catapulted to the headlines with the publication of Samuel Huntington's *Who Are We? The Challenges to America's National Identity* (2004), and his critics' counterarguments.[29] The question of immigration comes to the fore when the people of the ethno-cultural majority or core feel their identity is being threatened by large masses of newcomers. In Europe, misgivings have become even more acute with the mass influx of Muslim immigrants and refugees from the Middle East, whose integration into their adopted countries is slow and problematic and whose values are often illiberal.[30] Faced with the reality and prospect of a global exodus from the developing to the developed world, the salience of this question is inevitable. Ever since the 1960s, the preservation, protection, and, indeed, active promotion of the cultures of minority groups have been widely championed in the liberal democracies, as part of an effort to defend the rights of the weak against the crushing dominance of the majority. But are majority national cultures entitled to equivalent rights? Does multiculturalism, for all its blessings, have any limit? This question—long an anathema—has recently been placed back on the table.[31]

This is not to trivialize xenophobia, racism, and national bigotry—each of them a very real and ominous threat. On the other hand, those who, explicitly or implicitly, posit immigration as an acquired right must reckon with the prospect of a mass exodus from Asia, Africa, and Latin America to the affluent parts of the world. This implies a most radical notion of cosmopolitan egalitarianism, with everything it entails. Many of those who lean toward such a view might be partly influenced by the idea that the very concept of nationalism as a kin-culture communal identity is fake—nothing more than a manipulation by state authority, with no deep roots in human nature—as well as being illegitimate. To the extent that they do, it is an example of how (mis-)perceptions of fact—largely arising from ideological fixations—might affect and be affected by normative choices. However, if restrictions on immigration are not posited as fundamentally immoral and illegitimate, the question takes different proportions. Many, on both sides of the ideological divide, would agree that the United States, for example, has benefited enormously from immigration and a general openness to the world, and that it stands to benefit further. The question may then concern the pace of immigration, the numbers of immigrants involved, their qualifications, and the rate of their absorption in and integration into the adopted country—all interconnected. The pros and cons for the economy, law and order, and, indeed, humanitarian considerations are similarly weighed in.

Ethno-National Solidarity and the Welfare State

With the growth of the welfare state during the twentieth century, the question of for whom people are willing to pay has gradually replaced the traditional question of for whom they are willing to die as a test of collective affinity and solidarity. To be sure, social welfare policies and the redistribution of resources from the affluent to the poor are not entirely attributable to genuine solidarity and altruism. In large part, they are an expression of what people perceive as their enlightened self-interest, because helping to pull the poor of one's society out of their condition may be regarded as an investment to increase social wealth, lower crime, and so forth. Still, might differences among countries in the scale of their redistributive policies point to differences in social solidarity and to the causes of these differences? Some social critics have suggested that the growth of alien ethnic immigrant communities and the erosion in the sense and legitimacy of a homogeneous national community have resulted in a rolling back of the welfare state. Both the public and governments have become less willing to pay for ethnically alien poor, with whom they feel little solidarity because they barely view them as part of the national collective.[32]

This claim has been empirically substantiated by economists Alberto Alesina and Edward Glaeser. They systematically analyzed the data pertaining to the differences in wealth redistribution policies between the United States and the European countries. Government expenditure averages 30 percent of GDP in the United States, as opposed to a European average of around 45 percent. At the time of the research, expenditure on social programs totaled 14.6 percent of GDP in the United States, as opposed to a European average of 25.5 percent.[33] The authors recognized that these differences, which went back a long way historically, have had a variety of causes. They calculated that about half of the difference was attributable to differences in the political system between the United States and the European countries, and in the size of their populations. The other half they demonstrated to be rooted in the United States' ethnic and racial heterogeneity.[34] Throughout American history there has been little sense of solidarity with new immigrant communities, which have always constituted a large part of the poor population. Today, this attitude mostly applies to the Latino immigrant population. Predominantly, however, the sense of ethnic alienation has applied to the black population of the United States, which figures disproportionally among the poor. Among the various states of the United States, welfare policies appear to be less generous the larger the size of the black population.[35]

By contrast, Alesina and Glaeser highlight the relative ethnic homogeneity of the European countries as a major factor underlying their welfare policies. The once ethnically homogeneous and most socially redistributive Nordic countries head the list. The authors suggest that growing immigrant communities may change social policies in Europe as well. Finally, they show that by various indicators, including the Gini coefficient of income inequality, immigrant countries Canada, Australia, and New Zealand stand somewhere in between the United States and Europe.[36] Many variables and local idiosyncrasies combine in determining each country's redistributive policies.[37] All the same, the global data seem to be the most conclusive with respect to new immigrant communities negatively affecting redistributive policies.[38]

The difference between "us" and "others" is even more strikingly revealed in the data on foreign aid from rich to poor countries. In contrast to their lavish domestic programs, affluent countries' foreign aid amounted to no more than 1 percent of the GNI at most (Sweden), according to OECD data for 2008 and 2009. That of the United States, the greatest donor in absolute terms, amounted to 0.2 percent. To be sure, in foreign aid as well, utilitarian considerations play a significant role in addition to altruism. Foreign aid is often a tool for achieving political influence in the beneficiary countries. In addition, the gap between domestic and international aid spending is partly accounted for by people's self-interest in investing in their own poor rather than in those of faraway countries, even if the latter are much needier. All the same, the notion that altruism toward one's own people should take precedence is very deeply ingrained in people's mind. In a globalizing world of spreading cosmopolitan culture and individualistic capitalist gain, genuine feelings of national affinity and solidarity remain one of the main buttresses of the welfare state. One might regret this situation and preach undifferentiated universal compassion. Yet this is not how people's minds work. While they might be benevolent toward others, their families and then their people tend to come first.

Misconceptions of Nationality in US Foreign Policy

Common misconceptions in the United States regarding the nature of ethnicity and nationality sometimes spill over into American foreign policy and have been a contributing factor to some recent debacles and humanitarian disasters. The precept that nationhood equals citizenship is very far from being universally applicable. The notion that different ethnicities in a country should remain together and count as a nation even if they do not perceive themselves as such, or do not get along, is partly derived from the erroneous view that nationhood and ethnicity are *entirely* different concepts that should be kept apart. Contrary to American parlance—and best efforts—the Iraqi people, the people of Iraq, and the people *in* Iraq are not synonymous terms. The same applies to Syria.

To be sure, different ethnic communities in a country sometimes view themselves, and therefore are, one nation. However, in other cases, ethnic populations live in one state—voluntarily or involuntarily—without viewing themselves as part of a common nation. Sometimes, their national affinity lies with their kin across the border. In such cases, their citizenship status and national identity do not overlap. The alternatives to an existing nation-state are sometimes horrendous, as we saw in Yugoslavia and see now in the Middle East and, indeed, in so many other places, most notably today in Africa and parts of Asia. Still, creating a sense of common nationality where none exists is a far more difficult and uncertain undertaking than has been assumed as a matter of course since 1945. Indeed, keeping different ethno-national groups within the same state against their will may well prove more costly in human terms than the acceptance of national separatism. Whether in each particular case one chooses to support self-determination or the preservation of the territorial integrity of the existing state depends on one's assessment of the risks involved, and probably also on one's worldview.

There are opposite conceptual pitfalls, to be sure. Recently defending the national idea, conservative political theorist Yoram Hazony artificially presents nationalism and globalization as two opposites between which no compromise is possible. Insisting that globalization and imperialism are synonymous concepts, he argues that the dangers of doctrinaire interventionist internationalism are as great as those of chauvinistic nationalism. However, even if this were so, there is no need to embrace either of these options. In his zeal to defend national sovereignty, Hazony mentions the advantages and necessity of free cooperation among nation-states only once in his book, in the shortest of paragraphs and in the most trivial manner. In preaching the normative principle of sovereignty, he entirely ignores the very substantial record of successful liberal internationalism ever since the nineteenth century in creating the world of today. Inter alia, this record includes the forced democratization of Germany and Japan by the victors after 1945, and so much else. Nor, for example, does Hazony even mention the possibility of foreign intervention to stop genocide.[39]

Nature, Nurture, the International System, and War

Misconceptions of nature versus history with respect to the phenomenon of the nation and its relations to the international system extend to the form of the international system itself and the future of international conflict. Whether war is biologically rooted in human nature has been the cause of much confusion and a heated controversy.[40] Contrary to onetime fashionable notions, violence is not a primary drive that requires release, like hunger or sex.[41] The Swiss or Swedes, to use the cliché example, who have not fought for two centuries, show no special signs of deprivation on this account. But try to deny them food for more than a few hours, or sex, say, for more than a few days, and their response would be quite predictable. On the other hand, the fact that violence is not a primary drive does not mean that we are not hardwired for it. Margaret Mead's framing of the problem: "Warfare Is Only an Invention—Not a Biological Necessity" (1940) is the mother of all mistakes.[42] It expresses the widespread assumption that violence must be either a biological drive or entirely learned, whereas in reality, its potential is deeply ingrained in us as a means or tool, ever ready to be employed. People can *cooperate, compete peacefully, or use violence* to achieve their objectives, depending on what they believe will serve them best in any given circumstance.[43]

Cooperation, peaceful competition, and violent conflict are the three fundamental forms of social interaction (in addition to avoidance, or zero interaction). People have always had all three options to choose from, and they have always assessed the situation to decide which option, or combination thereof, seemed the most promising. Thus, the potential for *both* war and peace is embedded in us, is "in our genes". Although activated interchangeably and conjointly in response to the overall environmental and socio-cultural conditions, all three behavioral strategies are not purely learned cultural forms. This naive nature/nurture dichotomy overlooks the heavy and complex biological machinery that is necessary for the actualization of each of these behavioral strategies and responsible for the interplay between them. Clearly, the evolution-shaped strategies of human behavior are variably calibrated to particular conditions through social learning. However, the reason they are there, very close under our skin and readily activated, is that they were all very handy during our long evolutionary history.

A failure to grasp this point has led many astray. A well-known example is the Seville Statement on Violence, issued in 1986 by an international group of scientists and scholars under the auspices of UNESCO, the United Nations Educational, Scientific and Cultural Organization. Published during the heyday of Rousseauism and prompted by the best of intentions and an ideological humanitarian mission, the Statement rejected the theories that presented war as a primary drive rooted in human nature and irresistibly erupt.[44] Thus, the Statement correctly insisted that violence and war were not biologically inescapable: "There is nothing in our neurophysiology that compels us to react violently. . . . We conclude that biology does not condemn humanity to war." However, the Statement fell into the opposite fallacy, proclaiming that warfare "is a product of culture", and solemnly prescribing that "*IT IS SCIENTIFICALLY INCORRECT* [emphasis in the original] to say that war or any other violent behavior is genetically programmed into our human nature." The Statement carelessly concluded: "Violence is neither in our evolutionary legacy nor in our genes."

Conservatives, who have rightly reintroduced the concept of human nature, often err in the opposite direction. A recent example is neoconservative historian and commentator Robert Kagan's book *The Jungle Grows Back* (2018), in which he warns against the rising threats to the post-1945, American-created international system based on democracy, free trade, and peace. As is apparent from the previous chapters, I fully share this concern. Kagan, however, wrongly insists, as the running theme of his book, that the American-led order is particularly vulnerable because it "has been an act of defiance against both history and human nature."[45] He adds: "Liberal democracies have not been common in history. If they are not contrary to human nature, they are also not favored by it."[46]

Kagan's mistake is twofold, for he misconceives both human nature and history. Human nature is most significant in relation to our basic system of desires and motivations. By comparison, the means we adopt and the institutions we create for fulfilling them are largely depending on the circumstances and are much more flexible and varied. This is where Kagan's view of History fails him, indeed, is anti-historical and flat. As we saw, there are very deep reasons liberal democracies have come into being in the modern industrial world—not before—and have greatly proliferated during the nineteenth and twentieth centuries, with periodic regressions, of course. As mentioned in the previous chapter, all the economically developed countries in today's world are liberal democracies. They also do not fight each other or experience civil wars. This modern historical trajectory may not have been "inevitable", and its future is not "preordained"; but neither is it just the product of a heroic act of will by the United States (and economically and politically liberal Britain in the nineteenth century), steering against both Human Nature and History. The emergence of the liberal order is deeply rooted in modern historical developments which suggested that in the new, post-Malthusian world of rocketing mass production there were strong advantages to the cooperative and peacefully competitive strategies of human behavior over the violent one for attaining desired human aims. Certainly, there have also been other forces, ideologies, and regimes vying for dominance during the last two centuries, and they have clashed with the liberal political and economic project. This does not make the liberal project any less rooted in Human Nature, nor does it set it in conflict with History.

History—note that our species is the only one that has it—is a story of change: from people who were biologically like us and inhabited the savannas of Africa, through the agricultural revolution and the rise of states, to the Industrial Revolution and the emergence of the affluent societies many of us live in. While their effects have been staggering, none of these great historical-cultural transformations has proved unstable and prone to collapse because of allegedly going against human nature (not really) and earlier history. They have reshaped many of the ways we pursue our naturally evolved desires, and ultimately have made us much more successful in fulfilling many of them.

Pragmatic liberals from the late eighteenth and early nineteenth centuries onward have identified the pacifying effects of modern historical developments. Alongside them, the more idealistic strands of the creed have tended to espouse an unrealistic interpretation of human nature as the basis for both their interpretation of the human aboriginal past and sometimes fanciful visions of world peace. In reaction, conservatives have come out against the rosy portrayal of human nature, while also warning about the many lingering dangers and new challenges to the liberal international order and to peace. In the process, some of them, straying in the opposite direction to idealistic liberals, have anchored the persistence of war in human nature. However, both war and peace are deeply grounded in human nature. The ways they have manifested themselves in the international system and the balance between them have been shaped, reshaped, and reconfigured, sometimes radically, by our species' historical development.*

Conclusion: National Sentiments and Identities— Both Innate and Construed

Ethnic and national affinities have deep roots in the human psyche and have been among the most powerful forces in human history. They have had an emancipating effect and they are a major source of social solidarity, while also carrying a chauvinistic-aggressive aspect. To make the most of the former and contain the latter, a proper understanding of the phenomenon is crucial. Ethnic and national affinities are not merely a phase, a manipulative invention by cynical state authorities and elites, or an inexplicable and insufferable atavistic relic in a liberal, cosmopolitan, and universalistic age. While always subject to change, ethnic and national identities are not going away any more than are other deeply rooted and changing human associations and relations, such as the family. The news of their demise has been premature.

This does not mean that the nation and nationalism are eternal beings. Both have had far longer longevity than is recognized by some social science orthodoxies, and their future trajectories may prove to be far longer than cosmopolitanism enthusiasts predict. At the same time, in the ever-unfolding interaction between the biologically evolved human propensity for kin-culture solidarity and human historical transformation, neither the state nor the nation is, in principle, more than a particular and potentially transient reality. The future of the nation, the state, and the nation-state is a matter of assessment, as none of them is necessarily destined to retain its present form, or survive at all, with future historical transformation. They are no different in this respect than the tribe. I do not pretend to predict any of these future developments. Still, transformed as they might turn out to be and fluctuating in their manifestations and significance, kin-culture bonds of identity, affinity, and solidarity—which lie at the root of tribalism, ethnicity, and nationalism—are likely to remain a potent social and political force. They will continue to deeply affect people's choices and collective action as long as kin-culture communal heterogeneity itself remains. Furthermore, the various existing ethno-national identities are

---

* Students of international relations might be surprised that I do not refer here to the so-called realist school that preoccupies that discipline. I have expressed my views on this school's "theories" in my *The Causes of War*, chap. 5.

powerfully self-perpetuating, and as of now there is little indication that the difference among them is about to be eradicated anytime soon.

The efficacy of even the most strongly held ideological doctrines is limited, as their proponents are oblivious to, ignore, or try to suppress major elements of reality. The collapse of communism, an ideology enthusiastically embraced by many but which had to overcome some deeply ingrained human propensities, is a recent example. There may be good reasons—both moral and practical—for the abolishment of private property. They are at least as good as the reasons for the abolition of ethnic and national identities and sentiments, except that all of the above express deep human preferences toward one's own. So far, no social and political regime has been able to overcome these tensions to a degree that would enable the implementation of such purist ideological visions. Similarly, major spiritual ideologies throughout history, concerned by the excesses and pains of sexuality, endeavored to curb or suppress sexuality to the point of denial, with very limited success. Indeed, is sex a good or bad thing, given that it often involves endless frustration, broken hearts, and even rape? Surely, the answer must consider the fact that sexuality is one of the deepest and most cherished human propensities, and distinguish between its benign and malign forms.

All these preferences are subject to great historical variation and can be socially shaped and adjusted. But attempts to write them off out of the best of intentions go against people's natural inclinations, and may require tremendous coercion and cause far greater harm than the ills such attempts are intended to remedy. Moreover, they can be hugely counterproductive, as they are apt to generate a strong backlash, like that which we are experiencing today with respect to the question of national identity. Denying the deep roots and immense potency of ethnic and national sentiments, declaring them to be a recent invention, contrived manipulation, or an epiphenomenal expression of something else that can be eliminated once that something has been removed, are all ideological precepts that may resonate widely but are unlikely to meet with greater success.

Nature or Nurture?

Gender and Sexual Behavior

The revolution in the legal, socioeconomic, and sexual condition of women in modern societies during the twentieth century has been one of the most astounding developments of modernity. So far-reaching, transformative, and significant to human life—most notably the lives of women, but to men's lives as well—has this change been that a distinct ideology, feminism, has emerged to advance, construe, and moralize it. In a deep sense, this ideology has been an offshoot of the liberal and socialist creeds, with their (different) emphases on the twin goals of human freedom and equality, applied to women. In view of these diverse ideological roots, and as we often hear, there is no one feminist theory but a variety of strands. Some of them have been more radical and some less so in their assumptions and conclusions, with the more radical shades tinting the image of the entire movement in the eyes of many as sometimes being over-the-top or even "crazy". This is largely responsible for the apparent paradox that the majority of women polled do not declare themselves feminists. Indeed, our interest in feminism in the context of this book lies in the familiar dual role of ideology as, at one and the same time, an interpretation of reality and a platform for social and normative change. There is a close affinity, but also tension, between these two aspects. Moreover, since the theoretical edifice is subordinate to the social and normative cause—is existentially less important—the latter, and the emotional mobilization it arouses in the community of the committed, tends to take precedent.

Feminists have all too often been accused of lacking a sense of humor. But the opposite claim is that no sense of humor should be expected in the face of profound discrimination and blatant bigotry. The more substantive charge with respect to feminists is that it is nearly impossible to carry out a reasoned, dispassionate discussion of this or that factual element of their doctrine without stirring up a deep emotional response—often a stormy one. Emotional investment

Ideological Fixation. Azar Gat, Oxford University Press. © Oxford University Press 2022.
DOI: 10.1093/oso/9780197646700.003.0007

in the social cause trumps everything in the ideological discourse. Feminist claims are now zealously protected by "political correctness", and everyone knows how imprudent it is to step into this minefield in the public arena and largely also in academia.

The question of nature vs nurture has been central to this debate. Here too, the progressivist suspicion and rejection of the notion of human nature as thinly veiled bigotry and obstruction of human emancipation rose sharply during the twentieth century and went hand in hand with the scholarly dismissal of that notion. Moreover, the progressivist-feminist view has been strikingly borne out by the revolution in the condition of women during the last century, most notably from the 1960s on. This epoch-making transformation has created a reality that far transcends anything imagined as possible by most people only a few generations ago. It cast old-style conservative notions of the natural differences between, and consequent social roles of, men and women as hopelessly archaic and far-fetched. This, however, does not mean that natural differences between men and women do not exist, on average, and influence behavior and choices; nor does it mean that such differences do not interact with, and are reconfigured by, changing historical-cultural conditions; nor does it entail that they should impact the quest for legal and social equality and equal opportunity for women in all walks of life.

In preparing to write on this subject, I found that Pinker had written a lot of what I meant to say in his excellent *The Blank Slate* (chap. 18; we also share a most favorable normative attitude to the cause of women's equality). We have had such experiences in the past. Therefore, I quote liberally from him at some points, while expanding on a number of additional aspects relating to the subject. All in all, it is striking—but hardly surprising—how fairly well-known scholarly findings on the differences between the sexes have had so little impact on the ideological discourse and the fervor of the public debate.

Gender issues are not restricted to the male-female distinction and relationship. This "binary" categorization itself has been challenged at both the factual and normative levels with the sharply growing public discussion of and debate over LGBTs: lesbians, gays, bisexuals, and transgender.

Similar or Different? Are the Male-Female Differences Natural or Construed?

The natural differences between men and women have been taken for granted practically throughout the history of our species and in all known societies around the globe. Efforts by anthropologists during much of the twentieth century to call this reality into question failed, despite the great diversity of human cultures. Understandably, these anthropologists were motivated by a growing sense that many of the traditionally attributed differences between men and women, and the social roles built on them, were far from as clear-cut as they were commonly perceived. The erosion of these perceptions and roles with the massive social changes that have taken place during the last century have given rise to a growing suspicion, crystallized into a hard conviction with many, that, except for the obvious differences in sexual genitalia and women's exclusive role in childbirth, most, if not all, other differences were socially "constructed", or "engendered".[1] "Our society conditions boys and girls to this and that" used to be the mantra a few decades ago. It is still often heard, though with somewhat less conviction, as the experience gained with their children by new generations of parents dedicated to the equality of the sexes has weakened their belief that the differences between boys and girls were *entirely* constructed. The single line always quoted from Simone de Beauvoir's pioneering feminist book *The Second Sex* (1949) is: "One is not born, but rather becomes, woman."[2] This, however, was not at all the intention of this admirably erudite (for its time) book, which throughout stressed both the biological differences between men and women *and* changing historical conditions that redefine their relationship and social roles.

A very distinct divide, though one that has not been fully worked out, has always existed within the feminist movement and feminist theorizing. There have been those feminists who hold that, whatever the biological differences between men and women, women are entitled to equal rights and equal opportunity; moreover, that as part of this equality they should be able to reshape society, hitherto dominated by men, more in the direction of their own nature and own needs. On the other hand, there have been those feminists who regard practically all differences between men and women as artificial and socially constructed, and, moreover, as constructs of male oppression. So are women similar to men, or are women actually different from or even superior to men in some crucial respects? Do women, for example, tend to be emotionally more sensitive and caring, and men emotionally cold (a common feminist claim), or is this, on the contrary, only a crude stereotype that perpetuates women's inferior social role? Similar and equal or different but equal? It is quite common with many feminists—women and men—to hold both ends of this argument. And it is understandable why this ambiguity and ambivalence should persist even among those who are willing to acknowledge natural differences between the sexes. The suspicion that such an acknowledgment might perpetuate discriminatory attitudes and discriminating social practices is never far from the surface.

Here is how Israeli writer Amos Oz, in his greatest novel, the autobiographical *A Tale of Love and Darkness*, quotes his grandfather, a man of great Russian soul and lifelong admirer of women: "'Woman,' Grandpa said, 'nu, in some ways she is just like us. Exactly the same. But in some other ways,' he said, 'a woman is entirely different. Very very different. . . . But you know what? In which ways a woman is just like us and in which ways she is very very different—nu, on this,' he concluded . . . 'I am still working.' He was ninety-three, and he may well have continued to 'work' on the question to the end of his days. I am still working on it myself."

The key to answering the question that preoccupied Oz's grandpa, and Oz himself, is—how surprising—evolution by natural selection. Before elaborating on what this means, here is Pinker's summary of the psychological research on the cognitive and behavioral differences between the sexes, much of it done by women researchers:

men are not from Mars, nor are women from Venus. Men and women are from Africa, the cradle of our evolution, where they evolved together as a single species. . . . Their average levels of general intelligence are the same, according to the best psychometric estimates, and they use language and think about the physical and living world in the same general way. They feel the same basic emotions, and both enjoy sex, seek intelligent and kind marriage partners, get jealous, make sacrifices for their children, compete for status and mates, and sometimes commit aggression in pursuit of their interests.

But of course the minds of men and women are not identical, and recent reviews of sex differences have converged on some reliable differences. Sometimes the differences are large, with only slight overlap in the bell curves. . . . Men are far more likely to compete violently, sometimes lethally, with one another over stakes great and small. . . . With some other traits the differences are small on average but can be large at the extremes. . . . When two bell curves partly overlap, the farther out along the tail you go, the larger the discrepancies between the groups. For example, men on average are taller than women, and the discrepancy is greater for more extreme values. At a height of five foot ten, men outnumber women by a ratio of thirty to one; at a height of six feet, men outnumber women by a ratio of two thousand to one. Also . . . there are proportionally more males at the extremes. . . .

With still other traits, the average values for the two sexes differ by smaller amounts and in different directions for different traits. Though men, on average, are better at mentally rotating objects and maps, women are better at remembering landmarks and the positions of objects. Men are better throwers; women are more dexterous. Men are better at solving mathematical word problems, women at mathematical calculation. Women are more sensitive to sounds and smells, have better depth perception, match shapes faster, and are much better at reading facial expressions and body language. Women are better spellers, retrieve words more fluently, and have a better memory for verbal material. Women experience basic emotions more intensely, except perhaps anger. Women have more intimate social relationships, are more concerned about them, and feel more empathy toward their friends, though not toward strangers. . . . They maintain more eye contact, and smile and laugh far more often. . . . Women are more attentive to their infants' everyday cries (though both sexes respond equally to cries of extreme distress) and are more solicitous toward their children in general. Girls play more at parenting and trying on social roles, boys more at fighting, chasing, and manipulating objects. And men and women differ in their patterns of sexual jealousy, their mate preferences, and their incentives to philander.[3]

Where do these differences in average cognitive skills and behavioral propensities between men and women come from? The main biological difference between the sexes is women's exclusive role in carrying the fetus and childbirth. Under modern conditions, the social significance of this difference has shrunk dramatically. But it is wrong to believe, as many have impassionedly insisted, that this major biological trait has practically no relation, is simply irrelevant, to any other feature of body and mind. In actuality, natural selection largely "designed" our bodies and minds, as those of all other sexual species over geological times, around this crucial reproductive function.

Few would dispute that men and women differ, on average, in size and strength. Men are taller, weigh more, and have greater muscle and bone mass and less body fat relative to body weight (on average 15 percent body fat, as opposed to 27 percent for women). Their advantage is the greatest in upper body strength. While they are less flexible than women, only about 10 percent faster, and have 4:3 advantage in aerobic capacity, they are doubly as strong as women (except for the legs, where the ratio is again 4:3 in favor of the men).[4] Of course, many women run faster than many men, and a few are stronger than some men, but, as Pinker points out, the difference in the ends of the largely overlapping bell curves of men and women might be very substantial indeed. Hollywood's *G.I. Jane* notwithstanding, women are rarely likely to be strong enough for elite infantry and commando units; no more in fact than they are likely to compete successfully in any serious men's football league, let alone boxing or weightlifting. This is why, in fairness to women, men and women compete separately in all professional sports, which select for those at the very top in both sexes. Sport tournaments are social institutions, of course, which can be and have been changed at will, but the physical realities behind them are biologically rooted.

Why are men larger and stronger on average? In all mammalian and many other species, this so-called dimorphism between the sexes evolved because of the competition, often involving violence or the threat of it, between males over access to females. Additionally, in the human case, the need to care for exceptionally helpless babies and an exceptionally long period of childhood until maturity directed human evolution toward paternal participation, pair-bonding, and cooperation and division of labor between the sexes. While the men mainly hunted, women mainly foraged, nursed the babies, and cared for the children. Hence many of the different traits, great and small—physical, cognitive, and behavioral—with which we are all too familiar from our daily experience, and which we alternatingly find endearing or exacerbating, amusing, and bemusing.

The tendency to engage in physical violence is perhaps the most conspicuous behavioral difference between the sexes, cross-culturally. Among the !Kung Bushmen of the Kalahari Desert, all of the twenty-two killings registered in the period 1963–1969 were committed by men. Of thirty-four cases of bodily assault, all but one were committed by men.[5] In the United States, males comprise 83 percent of murderers, a similar share of those committing aggravated assault, 93 percent of drunken drivers, and about the same percentage of armed robbers. Even though murder rates diverge dramatically in different parts of the world and different periods of history, the woman/man divide remains roughly the same in favor of the men.[6] Indeed, the two parts of this record are extreme examples of both the great diversity and fluidity of historical conditions (in overall murder rates), on the one hand, and the remarkable endurance of natural propensities, on the other, in this case concerning the male/female divide.

As a comprehensive survey reveals: "Crime statistics from Australia, Botswana, Brazil, Canada, Denmark, England and Wales, Germany, Iceland, India, Kenya, Mexico, Nigeria, Scotland, Uganda, a dozen different locations in the United States, and Zaire, as well as from thirteenth- and fourteenth-century England and nineteenth-century America—from hunter-gatherer communities, tribal societies, and medieval and modern nation-states—all uncover the same fundamental pattern. In all these societies, with a single exception, the probability that the same-sex murder has been committed by a man, not a woman, ranges from 92 to 100 percent."[7] Cases of men's violence against and killing of women are exceedingly more common than the other way around. Given the biological differences in strength, it is clear why women are biologically less attuned in terms of their behavioral propensity to respond violently, except as a last resort, in a desperate defense of themselves and their children. Furthermore, in comparison to men's violent aggression, that of women tends to be non-physical, indirect, and anonymous.[8] As one feminist scholar has summarized the evidence: "just as some boys bully with fists and taunts, aggressive girls dominate through exclusion, cattiness, and lies."[9] Interestingly, studies have shown a strong tendency for women to vote for more dovish parties and candidates than men in national elections around the world.[10]

We are well familiar with the agents of these differences, which translate the genetic codes on the sex chromosomes X (female) and Y (male) in structuring our bodies, including our brains and, hence, our minds. These are the sex hormones, most notably estrogen, progesterone, and testosterone, which begin their work during the fetus's evolution in the womb. So-called tomboy behavior in girls correlates closely with higher levels of testosterone. On the other side, low testosterone levels in males result in unassertive and "feminine" behavior, while the highest levels of testosterone to which men are exposed during adolescence result in extra-aggressiveness.[11]

None of this amounts to "biological determinism". Biology is not destiny, and changes in social conditions and practices have a huge effect. At the same time, nor are biology and natural inclinations somehow irrelevant to behavioral trends of men and women. It should also be added that biological inclinations have no normative status, though they are not without an effect on the social expectations of both women and men. We begin with some history, to examine more closely the dynamics of the relations between men and women and the changes that have shaped, reshaped, and reconfigured these relations over the lifespan of our species.

A Short History of the Relations between the Sexes

An interpretation of history is central to every ideology, and this is also the case with feminist theorizing. Ideologically driven historical interpretations tend to take the form of abstract and highly moralizing constructs, for they are wholly harnessed to the advancement of the cause and are judged by their social utility. While they may include very substantial kernels of truth, they are also prone to deviate toward one-sided, often biased claims.

As Marx and Engels correctly noted in their 1846 manuscript "The German Ideology": "The first division of labor is that between men and women for child-breeding." In hunter-gatherer societies this was the division between "man the hunter" and "woman the gatherer" (and child-bearer), as the title of two landmark anthropological books put it. While the relations between the sexes were never symmetrical, they were more equal in hunter-gatherer societies, over more than 90 percent of our species' history. Men were more dominant in this relationship—on average, always on average—and not infrequently they were violent both toward women and toward other men in rivalry over women. Furthermore, a reality in which physical force was vital in fighting for family and tribe made men the natural leaders. At the same time, women always had their own ways of asserting their will, and they could draw either subtle or more overt support from their kin.

Although fanciful in many ways, Friedrich Engels's *The Origin of the Family, Private Property and the State* (1884), based on pioneering anthropologist Lewis Morgan's *Ancient Society* (1877), pointed to a crucial juncture in the relations between the sexes: the advent of private property and everything that followed this historical transformation. The institutionalization and accumulation of private property with the transition to agriculture and with the emergence of large-scale state societies created and progressively accentuated property-based class differences. Rights of property ownership for women differed considerably from society to society. In general, however, women were disfavored in this respect, often radically so. This made them that much more dependent on their husbands—and, before or in the absence of marriage, on their fathers and brothers—for their livelihood and that of their children than had been the case in hunter-gatherer societies. In tribal and, later, state assemblies, often dealing with war, in which only the men participated, the men represented the families while the women stayed at home with the children. Power relations between the sexes were thereby tilted greatly in favor of the men in agricultural and state societies, leaving the women in a much weakened and often helpless position.

Thus, as feminists have rightly stressed, "patriarchy", already the reality in hunter-gatherer societies, was much deepened by socially, legally, and politically construed institutions and norms during recorded history. At the same time, much of feminist theorizing is constructed as a moral tale of female oppression and male culpability, according to which women were forced into and marginalized in secondary and inferior roles by a kind of common male conspiracy. While this historical narrative is not without foundation, it is in some ways deeply unhistorical. The social roles of men and women in premodern societies were not an arbitrary imposition. Women and men, joined together in family units, cooperated in the struggle for survival in harsh natural and social conditions. Women typically gave birth to some half a dozen children (of which, on average, only about half survived into adulthood). This meant that women were either pregnant or nursing throughout most of their adult lives. While women mostly worked in and around the home, men were typically engaged in heavy duty agricultural work that often required great physical effort. In addition, an endemic lack of security made men's physical strength very much the arbiter in social conflict situations. Unquestionably, men exploited their physical and social advantages vis-à-vis women. But the more significant story, again, is the tremendous transformation of humanity's life conditions brought about by modernity; the far-reaching revolution this made possible—indeed, prompted—in women's social roles and in the relations between the sexes; and, at the same time, enduring natural differences between them.

Pinker nicely summarizes many of the changing conditions of life during modernity:

> technological and economic progress ... made it possible for couples to have sex and raise children without a pitiless division of labor in which a mother had to devote every waking moment to keeping the children alive. Clean water, sanitation, and modern medicine lowered infant mortality and reduced the desire for large broods of children. Baby bottles and pasteurized cow's milk, and then breast pumps and freezers, made it possible to feed babies without their mothers being chained to them around the clock. Mass production made it cheaper to buy things than to make them by hand, and plumbing, electricity, and appliances reduced the domestic workload even more. The increased value of brains over brawn in the economy, the extension of the human lifespan (with the prospect of decades of life after childrearing), and the affordability of extended education changed the values of women's options in life. Contraception, amniocentesis, ultrasound, and reproductive technologies made it possible for women to defer childbearing to the optimal points in their lives.[12]

A few more details and developments are worth mentioning. As part and parcel of the modernization process wherever it unfolded, fertility rates fell from 6–7 children per women toward fewer than 2. There have been growing security and decline of physical violence throughout the developed world (including most parts of the United States). Industrial societies inaugurated a sharper division between work and home, where the women stayed, than had been the case on the farm. Smaller families in less crowded dwellings also meant that the social engagement and excitement that prevailed among housewife neighbors in dense urban communities gave way to a more secluded existence. As pioneering feminist Betty Friedan showed in her landmark 1963 book *The Feminine Mystique*, post-1945 suburban life actually saw a regression in the status of women and in their ability to fulfill their potential and make use of their talents. By the 1960s in the United States in particular, the phrase "prisoners of the suburbs" captured many women's sense of loneliness, unfulfillment, and unhappiness, which drove not a few to depression. This condition contrasted sharply with the glowing 1950s image of the happy American family and smiling housewife. The two world wars, when women were called upon to take the place of men in the factories, were formative experiences. With the end of the wars, women were sent back home to make room for the returning men, a step that was generally accepted as natural and justified by both sexes. But the vast expansion of the service economy and the sharp decline of manual labor in farms and factories made women's incorporation in the labor market that much easier.

The transformation in the status and social roles of women in the developed world, starting with the granting of voting rights some 100 years ago, has been one of the greatest revolutions of modernity. In general, it has been an amazing success story. Women's participation in the labor market outside the household was on the rise throughout the developed world during the twentieth century, with a steep takeoff point registering during the 1960s. Since then, it has doubled to some 50–60 percent and more. It now constitutes about 80–90 percent of the men's participation rate in most countries of the developed world. The same trends have taken place in large parts of the developing world, with the Islamic countries in the Middle East and North Africa as the main exception (also India). An even greater revolution has occurred, overwhelmingly more so in the West, with the breakdown of professional barriers and women's entry into a wide variety of professions that used to be the exclusive preserve of men. The arduous struggle to make this possible had to overcome deep-seated social perceptions, norms, and expectations, mostly among men but also among women themselves. It entailed a far-reaching normative transformation, which again was most far-reaching in the West.[13] Hillary Clinton recalls that when she first appeared in court in Arkansas as a lawyer, judges looked at her as something as unusual as a talking dog. Even women bus drivers, let alone pilots, were viewed as a strange phenomenon. In line with the transformation in women's occupations, men's participation in domestic household chores and involvement with the children has increased dramatically. All this has made women economically more independent, and has changed nearly everything else in their lives, including a great deal of their relations with men. The overall significance of the realization and harnessing of the talents and abilities of half of humanity in the economy, science, and so much else cannot be exaggerated. (This does not prevent radical critics from castigating this development as one of capitalism's latest tricks to draw more labor force into the market.)

So is there any meaningful room left for the notion of biological differences between men and women as expressed in both the private and public domains? Two themes have attracted special attention: sexual behavior, and enduring gaps in occupational distribution and income between women and men.

The Tremendous Scope—and Boundaries—of the Sexual Revolution

The evolutionary rationale for explaining the differences in sexual behavior and attitudes between women and men is quite simple. Over geologic time, the outcome of sexual intercourse for women has been conception, childbirth, and childrearing (which is, evolutionarily speaking, the purpose of the whole exercise). Because there are only a few times women can conceive, women are generally attuned to look for the best male partner, so that he may impart his genes to the offspring. The best male partners in most departments of the animal kingdom are the strongest ones, and among social animals also those with other, social and leader qualities. Mating with such partners increases the chances of the offspring being endowed with these qualities themselves. In turn, this means that the offspring will likely be more successful in the following rounds of the mating game, with the result that their genes will be more widely represented in the following generations. Remember that this is the blind merry(marry)-go-round algorithm of evolution.

In humans, the mating game has additional dimensions. Childrearing among humans is exceptionally long and demanding because of the time it takes the large human brain to reach full size and, conjointly, to acquire necessary information by way of learning. This made paternal participation and investment in this process critical. For this reason, women also assess the prospective partner's expected loyalty and dedication to them and to the offspring, and his potential as a provider. Indeed, they often need to strike a balance—a compromise—between the partner's expected commitment and other qualities on the checklist of men's desirability. In the conditions of nature, sex for women involved a huge investment, and a great deal hinged on their ability to make the right choices. As a consequence, women's psychological proclivities are generally shaped in this direction.

By comparison, males' ability to fertilize females, thereby ensuring the representation of their own genes in the next generation, is theoretically huge. History's most astounding case has been revealed by a study of the Y chromosome in Central and Eastern Asia. It shows that some 8 percent of the population in the region (0.5 per cent of the world's population) carry the same Y chromosome, which can only mean that they are the descendants of a single man. The biochemical patterns indicate that this man lived in Mongolia about 1,000 years ago. It was not difficult to identify the only likely candidate, Genghis Khan, an identification confirmed by an examination of the Y chromosome of his known surviving descendants. This, of course, does not mean that Genghis Khan alone sired so many children from a huge number of women, an obvious impossibility even if he had ceased his military conquests altogether. The tremendous spread of his Y chromosome is due to the fact that his male descendants succeeded him at the head of ruling houses throughout Central and East Asia for centuries, all enjoying staggering sexual opportunities.[14]

Remember that in terms of people's emotional composition, their motivation is not so much more children per se but the desire for sex, Malthus's "passion", which functions in nature as a "proximate mechanism" for the attainment of that biological end. Thus, men tend to be more promiscuous, more inclined to sex with no strings attached, and more prone to polygamous relations, officially or unofficially. Polygamy and harems for the rich and the powerful used to be the norm in many premodern societies, reaching their apex with emperors, sultans, and kings. At the same time, men also are inclined to establish pair bonds, because of the interconnected needs of raising human children and the demands of their female partners. In entering pair bonds, men too are far more careful about making the best choices as regards the "quality" of their female partner. Furthermore, they tend to be even more jealous than women over their partner's fidelity, because infidelity means that the man might be "cuckolded", that is, invest all his resources in growing the children of another man.

Hence the different criteria of beauty, attractiveness, and general desirability of men and women. In terms of attractiveness, men look for physical traits that are reliable indicators of fertility in women, such as young age, "hourglass" body shape, health, and high estrogen levels as reflected in bodily features and odors. These are universally regarded as the elements of women's beauty. For more permanent pair-bonding, men also pay attention to the chances to get along with their prospective female partner, and to her potential contribution in terms of family and work skills. Women's notions of men's physical attractiveness—male beauty—are very different, for the reasons explained. Women tend to prefer men who are taller than average, strong, especially in the upper body—broad shoulders and chest (the former has become metaphorical)—agile, with high muscle and low fat body mass. Body symmetry, as a sign of good design and healthy development, is valued by both sexes. However, while physical attractiveness counts for a lot, women put greater emphasis than men on the non-physical qualities mentioned above, such as the man's social and worldly skills and success (self-confidence, ambition, charisma, astuteness, status); skills as a provider, potential or actual (wealth); dedication and loyalty to them (tested during courtship); and the man's ability to get along with them (kindness, humor).[15]

Trade-offs and compromises of all sorts between conflicting traits are the rule for both sexes. Love is nature's trick for keeping couples together long enough for the sustained joint effort of raising children. Broken hearts, frequent bickering, and built-in frustrations are the inevitable result of matching the often conflicting expectations of both sexes (and, of course, of two or more specific individuals) in what has been dubbed the "battle of the sexes". By and large, the evolution-shaped reproductive logic for being unfaithful to their partners is also different for men and women. For men, spreading their sperm around involves very few costs, if it remains undetected by their regular partner and sometimes also by society. By comparison, women's cheating is mostly documented to be motivated by either a quest for a supportive relationship—emotional, sexual, and/or economic—in case of an unsatisfying or failing relationship with their regular partner; and/or by the opportunity for a relationship with a man who is more attractive and successful than their regular partner.[16]

All this is a very rough, simplified abstract of a subject that has been extensively surveyed in the evolutionary literature on sexuality. You may remain skeptical and ask if all this is not actually the outcome of social conditioning and prejudices that stand behind both these findings and the studies themselves. So here are the results of the most recent, most up-to-date and most comprehensive study ever, carried out by some seventy-five researchers, in forty-five countries, half a century after the beginning of the sexual revolution and following the most far-reaching change of sexual mores: "Using a new 45-country sample (N = 14,399), we attempted to replicate classic studies and test both the evolutionary and biosocial role perspectives. Support for universal sex differences in preferences remains robust: Men, more than women, prefer attractive, young mates, and women, more than men, prefer older mates with financial prospects."[17]

This book's subject is not human sexuality but ideological fixation. People are intuitively very well aware of the basic realities described above and, moreover, tend to act on them in their lives. Additionally, a growing number of people nowadays, both men and women, have heard at least something about the evolutionary sources of the differences in sexual behavior between men and women. And yet the reaction of many of them to it tends to be mixed and often contradictory. Many are still unaccustomed to and feel uncomfortable about such a sublime and much idealized subject as love and the relations between the sexes—animated by the most intense human emotions—analyzed in naturalistic, non-personal, calculating, and supposedly deterministic terms. In addition, the "blank slate" tradition, with its premise of unconstrained cultural relativity, is still strongly embedded in the social sciences and "cultural studies"—on their teachers, graduates, and broader public impact. Moreover, these disciplines and public domains are deeply infused with a generally commendable moral mission to correct the world. Indeed, above everything else, there seems to be a concern about the supposed normative implications of all the above with respect to both men and women: a concern that men should be able to get away in terms of their sexual behavior with much that women fight against in the "battle of the sexes"; or that women's freedom of choice in their sexual behavior should be viewed as more limited than men's, be curtailed by engendered typecasting and stereotyping.

It is never redundant to repeat that all the recorded differences between the sexes express general trends and averages, and that there is much diversity in inclinations and behavioral traits among individuals within each of the sexes, as well as a great deal of overlap between them. It is similarly necessary to repeat that facts about the world, *in themselves*, do not prescribe norms, that, in and of itself, the *is* does not determine the *ought*. This does not mean that both men and women are not inclined to moralize sexual behaviors of both sexes, largely based on expected sexual propensities and gender roles. Indeed, here too, *both* biological traits and historical-cultural conditions and transformations weigh heavily. Neither of these two interacting elements should be ignored, dismissed, or underestimated.

Back to some broad-brush history. The differences in sexual attitudes between men and women are as old as our species—actually much older—with women being far more circumspect and choosier, for the reasons explained. Although the sexual norms of the Polynesian societies that fired the European imagination were far more relaxed than those prevailing in the West and in virtually all other state societies of the time, they were never as relaxed as Mead imagined them to be. Nor was there a symmetry in Polynesia between the sexual attitudes of men and women. All the familiar features of the "battle of the sexes" were always there.

That said, Engels was basically right in his (much overdrawn) claim, that the growth of private property and differences in wealth had an enormous effect on sexual norms. Considerations of property allocation between prospective couples and their respective families grew in weight in comparison to the forces of sexual attraction and romantic love. Let there be no mistake: in hunter-gatherer societies as well, the families of both sides were deeply involved in the arrangement of marriages. Particularly as women married very young, at puberty, the family adults on both sides, men and women, guided the process, and often carried out the exploration and made the decisions. This was done for the sake of the young ones but, not infrequently, also in pursuit of broader interests, as in marriage alliances or the exchange of brides between families (and sometimes between the patriarchs). Women-related quarrels and homicide of both men and women on these grounds by men were rife. Still, family involvement, mostly in women's sexual behavior and choices, deepened in propertied, class societies, for the following reasons: sexual relations and childbirth out of wedlock exposed the women and offspring to the danger of material deprivation that was very difficult to remedy, as the value of women with children in the marriage market plummeted; marriages were desired with equals or, ideally, with superiors in terms of property and social status; so the most was to be made of both the sexual attraction and social status of the woman to obtain suitable suitors and commit them to marriage. Within this context, control over women's sexuality by their families—often coercive, violent, and even homicidal—greatly increased. Norms aligned with these social realities. The virtue of women's "modesty" became central, much accentuating women's greater natural choosiness. The association of women's "modesty" with family "honor" and "shame" grew that much stronger.

Correspondingly, women were portrayed as almost devoid of "lowly" sexual drives, as the object of man's conquest, to which women supposedly surrendered and responded with a purity of devotion and love. As the twentieth-century Russian poet Anna Akhmatova—thrice married and sexually liberated—commented on Tolstoy's attitude to sexual relations in his novels (and real life): "In all his long life it never occurred to him that the woman is not merely a victim but an accomplice to the crime by 50%."[18] On the opposite pole from the idealized image of women, there was the stark image of "Lilith" and her many likes: demonic women of wild, insatiable, and calculating sexuality, depriving men of their powers with her magical forces of attraction and spelling doom. The more propertied the society, the more likely it was to hold the images and norms of women's sexual modesty, except for the aristocracy, whose sexual norms everywhere tended to be much more relaxed. The young among the rural poor were also somewhat less constrained in their sexual behavior, to say nothing of the "women of ill-repute" who had to sell their body to satisfy men's sexual appetites.

The movement for women's legal equality and freedom emerged in liberal Europe in the wake of the Enlightenment and the French Revolution. Beginning as little more than a curiosity, it gathered momentum during the nineteenth century. Through the suffragists' struggle, it led to the granting of voting rights to women in most countries of the West sometime after World War I. In this so-called first wave feminism, women also gained entry to institutions of higher education (at the time usually sexually segregated). The plea for the sexual liberation of women is more intriguing and more relevant to our current subject. In the proverbially "Victorian" nineteenth century, it came mostly from socialist circles (in France, of course)—particularly from Charles Fourier and the followers of Henri de Saint-Simon and, later, from Engels. They viewed sexual liberation for women as part of a more comprehensive project to free both sexes from the shackles of sexual deprivation and frustration. The "utopian" socialists preached free love, freed from sexual possessiveness and jealousies. So does sexual liberation for women mean freedom of choice? Or equal opportunity in sexual matters free from social stigmas? Or "free love" unencumbered by possessiveness and jealousies, equally applying to both men and women? Again, are the sexes similar and equal, or different but equal? These questions have continued to reverberate and perplex in both liberal and socialist circles ever since.

In mainstream socialist movements and parties, committed to the idea of women's equality, men continued to dominate in practice for most of the twentieth century. Enthusiasm for "free love" cooled in many of them, and while advocating equality between the sexes in this respect too, they tended to preach sexual restraint and sexual "purity" for both of them. Indeed, communist regimes were predisposed to interfere in and control the private lives of their citizens in matters pertaining to sexuality, marriage, and the family, a tendency pushed to literary extremes in Orwell's dystopia *1984*. On the other hand, controversial psychiatrist, disciple of Freud, and onetime Marxist Wilhelm Reich held that all neuroses were the result of bourgeois social structures that oppressed human sexuality. His writings, preaching human liberation through free love, became popular in the 1960s.

The sexual revolution of the 1960s was as profound and transformative as can be in terms of ideas, practices, and norms. And, as with ideologies, everything seemed so clear and simple to its followers and proponents. A distinct youth culture had already formed after 1945 and during the rock-and-roll years, as youth prospered with broader high school attendance, greater means, and more leisure time. In the 1960s, for the first time, women in large numbers went to college and/or sought employment in anonymous big cities. They were thus released from surveillance by parents and families, "gained privacy", and came in touch with large cohorts of their peers of the opposite sex. All this was unprecedented, as was also the introduction of the birth control pill, which finally alleviated women's ever-present fear of unwanted pregnancy. With increasing affluence and a more egalitarian social ethos, sensual and romantic considerations came to the fore in sexual attachments (at least within the same social circles). Past norms and practices appeared old-fashioned and outdated, narrow-mindedly bound to senseless social conventions and a major hindrance to human emancipation and happiness. The new feeling of sexual emancipation and freedom was exhilarating, and it seemed to have no bounds. The most iconic representation of this sweeping generational mood and its overwhelming public and artistic expressions was the Beatles' "All You Need Is Love" (1967). "Make Love Not War" was another signature slogan in American campus demonstrations of the time. Consider: how hard was the choice between being sent to Vietnam and going to college and having fun? Note that only a decade earlier, and in a very different sexual landscape, few protests had been registered among the draftees to the Korean War.

The scope and significance of women's sexual liberation has been dramatic. It has become widely accepted that women crave sexual relations, enjoy sex, and have the right to pursue sexual gratification as they please. It was only natural that people at the time should assume that there was no difference in sexual inclinations between men and women, and that all such differences were the legacy of oppressive social conventions and conditioning. Erica Jong's best-selling novel *Fear of Flying* (1973) symbolized the times. Written from a women's perspective, it sensationally introduced the term "zipless fuck" as an ideal form of sexual intercourse, which takes place between complete strangers for the sole purpose of sexual gratification. Undoubtedly, this is a widespread fantasy and not infrequently a desirable practice for women, as it is—almost universally and much less discriminately—for men. "One-night stands" and other forms of non-committal sexual relations have become common enough. However, the impression created was that there was no difference between male and female inclinations in this regard.

One consequence of this is that there has now been a new reason for women to find themselves sometimes engaging in sex that they do not feel they want. While this has always been an all-too-common reality in the relations between the sexes, there has been the added pressure since the 1960s that the woman was inhibited by outdated social conventions and not sexually liberated. Sexual liberation in the sense of free sex began to feel as greatly skewed in favor of the men. In the current era of online dating sites, women in particular often complain that men, faced with a huge variety of prospective dating partners and seemingly unlimited opportunities, are reluctant to commit to a relationship.

Such asymmetries in the relations between the sexes have given rise to a whole range of feminist arguments and ideological currents. Some radical feminists came very close to rejecting the whole female-male relationship as intrinsically oppressive for women. Andrea Dworkin would vehemently deny that she equated penetration with rape in her 1987 book *Intercourse*. But her critics have had cause to hold that her meaning was not very far from this. As Dworkin's book reads: "There is never a real privacy of the body that can coexist with intercourse: with being entered. . . . The thrusting is persistent invasion. She is opened up, split down the center. She is occupied-physically, internally, in her privacy. A human being has a body that is inviolate; and when it is violated, it is abused. . . . Violation is a synonym for intercourse. . . . There is no analogue anywhere among subordinated groups of people to this experience of being made for intercourse: for penetration, entry, occupation."[19]

The majority of women did not at all feel that way about male penetration—they felt the opposite—and the alternative, lesbian relationships, did not appeal to most of them. Furthermore, most women wished to see much of the old patterns of the relationship between the sexes preserved, albeit in a greatly revised and reformed format. Correspondingly, some of the most iconic pioneers of the feminist movement in the 1960s reacted in the 1980s against the radical turn in feminist ideology. As Betty Friedan argued in her 1981 book *The Second Stage*, bra-burning, anti-man, and anti-family feminism was the reason most women did not identify themselves with the movement. She came out against the radical voices that increasingly dominated the movement, quoting them that "all married women are prostitutes" and "only honest prostitutes are heroines"; "that women would never be free unless the family was abolished and foreswore motherhood and sexual intercourse with men." Friedan rejected as preposterous those "reducing any relation of men to women, and the military and economic depredations of the nation, to rape"; those "deciding that if they go home and sleep with their husbands, from now on they must be 'on top'; the belief that masturbation or sex with a woman was superior to any 'submission' to a man's penis."[20] As Friedan wrote: "*Reaction is dangerous in its denial of reality.* The underlying reality is no different for the bitterest feminists than for the most stridently fearful defenders of the family. None of us can depend throughout our new long lives on that old nuclear family to meet our needs for nurture, love and support, but all of us still have those needs. The answer is not to deny them, but to recognize that equality makes it possible, and necessary, for new kinds of family."[21]

While women wanted to have greater license to directly initiate a relationship, they still wanted men to court them. In most cases, they wanted their men to be dominant, but not domineering—respectful, considerate, and equal partners. They still wanted them to be "gentlemen" in the broad sense of this term. Most of them wanted the men to play the leading role in sex most of the time. In contrast to some manifestations of radical feminism, women still found that they wanted to be attractive to men and, indeed, do what they could to be pretty. At the same time, they did not want to be exclusively viewed as sexual objects in men's eyes, to be "objectified", in a relationship and even more so in other domains of life, such as the workplace. And they wanted the *differences* in sexual inclinations between women and men to be respected and acted upon. The allure of the radical feminist slogans, and the enthusiasm that greeted them in feminist conventions and mass rallies, is yet another testimony to the intoxicating power of ideology. At the same time, as Friedan warned, denials of realities might come crashing down onto the rocks of reality.

For example, a widely heard feminist claim is that the pressure on women to be beautiful and attractive to men is a product of male "patriarchy" and "capitalism", channeled through the beauty industry and the media.[22] But while some expressions of this pressure, especially in the United States, are grotesque, present impossibly unrealistic and frustrating standards, and constitute a health hazard, the beauty industry is only a product of the escalating race for success in the mating contest in affluent societies. Fundamentally, women are the drivers of this trend as much as they are its "victims". They naturally seek to excel in the mating contest that figures prominently at the very basis of our system of motivation. Men, too, do what they can to be attractive to women—according to the parameters women value most.

Ambivalence and confusing notions regarding the exact meaning of all this are inevitable in any theoretical discussion, let alone an ideological one. So, for example, the results of an illuminating experiment on the reactions of men and women to offers of the most casual sex have been received by both scholars and the public with mixed and sometimes antagonistic responses. The experiment was conducted at Florida State University in 1978 and 1982, when the doctrine that men and women were practically the same in sexual attitudes was at its height. The experiment went like this: Both male and female students of average attractiveness approached students of the opposite sex randomly on campus with identical questions. When they asked "Would you go out with me tonight?" men and women were equally receptive: 56 percent of the women and 50 percent of the men agreed to go out on a date. However, when they asked, "Would you come over to my apartment tonight?" or "Would you go to bed with me tonight?" the gender differences were striking. Whereas few women were willing to go to a man's apartment (6%) or to bed with him (0%), 69 percent of the men agreed to go the woman's apartment and 75 percent were willing to go to bed with her.[23] There are a number of YouTube replications of this experiment with pretty similar results, although the propositioned guys are often suspicious as to what the catch is.

The same point also caught people's awareness from an unexpected, tragicomic direction. With the coming of Jihadist Islamic suicide bombing, it became widely known that the men perpetrators were promised, and were largely motivated by the promise, that they would go straight to paradise, where according to the faith the prize of seventy-two virgins awaited each of them. As women in the West worked out what this meant, they could not help turning the formula around in their minds and respond with a bewildered giggle to the hypothetical promised prize of seventy-two male virgins for each woman. Something in the equation clearly did not work.

Rape

The claim that rape is not a sexual act but an act of violence intended to humiliate has become the widely accepted orthodoxy in both the scholarly and public discourse since the publication of Susan Brownmiller's *Against Our Will* (1975). Many people are deeply convinced by this claim, or at least piously uphold it. Any attempt to dispute it, especially by men, is regarded as scandalous. Pinker has already demolished this argument so effectively that only a short discussion here is necessary.[24]

In contrast to the false dichotomy between sex and violence, rape is actually an act of *violent forced sex*. While an element of intended humiliation by the man might be present (unintended humiliation is practically always caused), the main motivation for the men, almost invariably, is satisfaction of the perpetrator's sexual lust. In wars throughout history (and sadly in some parts of the globe still today), rape, like other forms of war booty, was regarded as one of the perks of wars that constituted part of men's motivation men to enlist. Individually, too, men resort to a variety of means to get sex, ranging from the consensual gentle wooing, to emotional pressure, to, sometimes, violence. Men also pay for sex, which makes the act consensual but not sexually desired by the female party to the transaction. Resort to prostitutes may be objected to and even outlawed on moral grounds as an offense to the women. But can it seriously be claimed that paid sexual intercourse is not a sexual act for the man involved but something belonging to an entirely different category—desired and carried out, say, in order to humiliate or violate? This is to grossly misunderstand the nature of male sexuality as shaped by the logic of evolution. Coerced sex, including rape, was all too often adaptive in terms of men's reproductive success. When Randy Thornhill and Craig Palmer explicated this logic in their *A Natural History of Rape* (2000), published by MIT Press, a storm broke out. It did not matter that the authors' normative attitude to the phenomenon of rape was unquestionable, and that they recommended a whole series of measures that society should adopt to fight it. The evolutionary logic does not mean that every man is a rapist or a potential one. At the same time, somber historical experience strongly suggests that women should better not be around in the open when the social and legal boundaries that protect them break down.

As Pinker concludes: "I believe that the rape-is-not-about-sex doctrine will go down in history as an example of extraordinary popular delusions and the madness of crowds. It is preposterous on the face of it, does not deserve its sanctity, is contradicted by a mass of evidence, and is getting in the way of the only morally relevant goal surrounding rape, the effort to stamp it out."[25] I assume Pinker's meaning also includes all too many in the crowds of intellectuals and scholars, who are a testimony to the immense power of conformity to ideological dogmas. Indeed, at present, the hold of this particular dogma shows no signs of abating.

There are additional aspects to the issue of rape. For example, ideological piety and the premise of equality has made it necessary to regard rape as a two-directional potential, a notion that is sometimes incorporated into the law. Never mind that it is technically impossible for a woman to rape a man, if this means conventional intercourse. In contrast to female sexuality, the man in question must be sexually aroused for the act to take place. Certainly, it is not impossible for this to happen, for example, under pressure from a female superior in the workplace and when the man still might not be interested in the relationship. Such pressure should be prohibited, of course, including by law. That said, women are much more likely to feel themselves sexually used, and not solely because of lingering social stigmas. Commonly enough, males' response to sexual advances that are typically regarded as harassment and violation if directed at females may be summarized by the attitude of "I should be so lucky".

Men all too often harass women sexually, sometimes to the point of rape. Powerful men sometimes take advantage of their position and use coercion and force. Thus, the "MeToo" movement that broke out in the United States in 2017 is a historical landmark in the fight against such phenomena. As with any ideological movement, there are some excesses and absurdities involved. These include the doctrine that a woman's testimony must always be accepted as true. While evidence suggests that in the large majority of cases it is, such a doctrine not only infringes on the right to due process but also increases the prospect of false accusations. There is also the very real danger of a summary judgment and punishment of the accused men by the media and social networks.

A letter to *Le Monde* (January 10, 2018) signed by 100 French women artists and intellectuals (celebrity actress and icon of female beauty Catherine Deneuve being the most famous of them) warned against all these dangers. But the letter is all the more remarkable for its ferocious objection to the lines of demarcation in the relations between the sexes that the MeToo movement is advancing. Not only does this remind us of the very marked differences in public sexual morality between France and the United States, most notably the French perception of flirtation and intimacy—including extramarital—as the taste of life, welcome and desirable in all of life's domains; it is also an expression of very real fault lines as to what feminism and women's liberation stand for.

Because of the sharpness of its message and tone, the *Le Monde* letter is worthwhile quoting at some length:

> Rape is a crime. But trying to pick up someone, however persistently or clumsily, is not—nor is gallantry an attack of machismo. The Harvey Weinstein scandal sparked a legitimate awakening about the sexual violence that women are subjected to, particularly in their professional lives, where some men abuse their power. This was necessary. But what was supposed to liberate voices has now been turned on its head. . . . Just like in the good old witch-hunt days, what we are once again witnessing here is puritanism in the name of a so-called greater good, claiming to promote the liberation and protection of women, only to enslave them to a status of eternal victim and reduce them to defenseless preys of male chauvinist demons.
>
> [Men's lives have been ruined] when their only crime was to touch a woman's knee, try to steal a kiss, talk about "intimate" things during a work meal, or send sexually charged messages to women who did not return their interest. This frenzy for sending the "pigs" to the slaughterhouse, far from helping women empower themselves, actually serves the interests of the enemies of sexual freedom, the religious extremists, the reactionaries and those who believe—in their righteousness and the Victorian moral outlook that goes with it. . . . Bordering on ridiculous, in Sweden a bill was presented that calls for explicit consent before any sexual relations! Next we'll have a smartphone app that adults who want to sleep together will have to use to check precisely which sex acts the other does or does not accept.

Philosopher Ruwen Ogien defended the freedom to offend as essential to artistic creation. In the same way, we defend a freedom to *bother* as indispensable to sexual freedom. Today we are educated enough to understand that sexual impulses are, by nature, offensive and primitive—but we are also able to tell the difference between an awkward attempt to pick someone up and what constitutes a sexual assault. Above all, we are aware that the human being is not a monolith: A woman can, in the same day, lead a professional team and enjoy being a man's sexual object, without being a "whore" or a vile accomplice of the patriarchy. She can make sure that her wages are equal to a man's but not feel forever traumatized by a man who rubs himself against her in the subway, even if that is regarded as an offense. She can even consider this act as the expression of a great sexual deprivation, or even as a non-event.

As women, we don't recognize ourselves in this feminism that, beyond the denunciation of abuses of power, takes the face of a hatred of men and sexuality. We believe that the freedom to say "no" to a sexual proposition cannot exist without the freedom to bother. And we consider that one must know how to respond to this freedom to bother in ways other than by closing ourselves off in the role of the prey. . . . Incidents that can affect a woman's body do not necessarily affect her dignity and must not, as difficult as they can be, necessarily make her a perpetual victim. Because we are not reducible to our bodies. Our inner freedom is inviolable. And this freedom that we cherish is not without risks and responsibilities.

I am not quite sure where exactly I stand between these two widely diverging cultural-normative attitudes—probably somewhere in the middle. My lines as to what constitutes harassment are stricter than those expressed in the *Le Monde* letter, and I regard sexual harassment as particularly vile. But, again, the important point for our discussion is the intrinsic and sometimes irreconcilable tensions that exist in both feminist interpretations of reality and normative imperatives between equality and difference, whose significance, one should add, pales in relation to the revolutionary, epoch-making, achievements of the women's movement aspect of modernity.

Nature, Nurture, and Sexual Norms

It is widely accepted that to argue that "men are from Mars, women are from Venus", in the title of John Gray's 1992 best-selling book and many others that followed,[26] is to vastly overstate the differences and underplay the similarities between the two sexes, both of which Oz's grandpa noticed and was intrigued by. Two opposing approaches fall short of reality. Concerning sexual behavior, the natural differences between men and women are on average quite significant, a function of their somewhat different positioning with respect to their joint venture. These differences are not just the product of social conventions and prejudices, whose actual source remains entirely mysterious if indeed they were simply arbitrary. On the other hand, sexual attitudes and roles are not immutable and wholly determined by biology. Changing social conditions over time and space have moved them here and there along a fairly broad spectrum. The changes brought about by modernity are as far-reaching as can be, more far-reaching than most people imagined possible only a few generations ago. The fluidity and elasticity of the relations between the sexes were certainly not imagined by Aristotle, who, observing the realities of premodern societies, famously determined (*Politics*, Bk I) that women were by nature subordinate to men. At the same time, socio-historical changes have not eradicated biologically rooted differences of attitude and behavior between men and women. Undoubtedly, a lot more change is in store, including, quite possibly, changes to our biology itself. For example, technological advances could make pregnancy a thing of the past and move the whole process to tubes in fetus-growing facilities. They can make sexual relations redundant in this process. Additionally, virtual relations and virtual sex of various "science fiction" forms seem to be around the corner. There is substantial evidence suggesting that the marked drop in sexual relations in Japan is a foretaste of trends now being registered in the West, as both sexes exhibit an increasing tendency to withdraw to the virtual world of social networks and focus on their professional careers. Only time will tell how such potential changes might interact with our deep emotional and behavioral proclivities.

Thus, although a huge change has occurred in social perceptions of sexual behavior, most notably that of women, are gender perceptions and expectations going to equalize entirely? Strong women who change many sexual partners often seem to have earned respect as "divas". But socially more marginal women who do so are more likely to be labeled as "sluts", whereas for men of all social ranks having many female sexual partners is more typically rated as a mark of success. Similarly, society is getting accustomed to women executives and women political leaders. But will gender perceptions and expectations regarding the personality and behavioral traits that women and men exhibit on the job become exactly the same?

When Golda Meir was prime minister of Israel, it used to be joked that she was the only man in her cabinet. This half-praise-half-joke is no longer considered legitimate on either count. Prime Ministers Indira Gandhi of India and Margaret Thatcher of the UK had similar reputations for great toughness. Chancellor

Angela Merkel of Germany is mild-mannered, but was reputed to be politically ruthless when necessary. In addition, her authority (as that of Meir) was grudgingly characterized by her critics as that of the nation's mommy, "Mutti", whereas early in her career she had been referred to as "the girl", "Mädchen", by her political mentor, Chancellor Helmut Kohl. Generally in the above cases, the women prime ministers' acknowledged toughness contributed to their political success. However, women widely and understandably complain that traits that would be regarded as natural for and expected of men politicians and executives give women a stigma of "bitch". Supposedly, there should be no sex-based difference in political or business decisions. But are gender expectations regarding subtle behavioral traits in leadership and managerial style going to fully disappear?

To approach this question from an opposite angle: there is a strong feminist claim that women in positions of leadership and management perform better than men, that there *is* a difference in the decisions they reach, and that this difference is actually in the women's favor. Supposedly, women are less motivated by ego and are less overconfident. There is some empirical evidence supporting this view. For example, it has long been documented that people tend to rate themselves as being above average, which cannot be the case overall. Psychologists have termed this phenomenon "illusory superiority". However, studies show that men are subject to this illusion significantly more than women, and are more confident about it.[27] The evolutionary explanation for this difference is that men's showoff paid off in terms of reproductive success, as women rank self-confidence in men high. (This does not necessarily imply poor judgment by women in this regard, as they might be assessing correctly that more confidence yields dividends for men in their relations with other men.) Interestingly, study after study have produced evidence that women are better long-term investors than men, for much the same reasons.[28] So, again, are women virtually the same and equal, or different (or superior) but equal? The range of social questions involved is wide, and the issues are complex and complicated. This is something feminist arguments often fail to acknowledge and, when faced by such complexities and conundrums, the result tends to be built-in ambivalences and confusion.

Here is another much-discussed issue. Is women's employment in prostitution an undue surrender to male domination that takes advantage of the plight of women who are all too often in desperate economic and social straits and are coerced by force by pimps and sex traffickers? Or, as some prostitutes contend, is it part of women's right to exercise their sexuality as they please without any stigma attached? This question has been even more controversial with respect to pornography and to women's participation in it. Is porn intrinsically demeaning to women who are called to satisfy men's fantasies, or is it, at least for some of the women participants, an act of free will and of female empowerment in a profession they choose and, as some of them insist, enjoy; a celebration of female sexuality that many women (albeit fewer than men) also like watching? The debate over porn created a rift in the feminist movement in the 1980s and 1990s.

To another issue: how are open sexual relations of couples or "polyamory" to be viewed from a feminist perspective? A standard reply is that this depends on the wishes and choices of the individuals involved, whether men or women. Clearly, some women wish to break away from the confines of monogamy and experience a multiplicity of relations and sexual adventures. However, what if the pressure for open relations and group sex comes mainly from the men, as evidence suggests?[29] Furthermore, on what basis should polygamy still be prohibited by law, especially if it is consensual, as, most famously, is the case with traditionalist Mormons? Or even if it is not agreed to by the legal wife, who is entitled to leave the marriage?

To be sure, there is nothing particularly unusual about the fact that reality is complex and that normative questions involve tensions, contradictions, and awkward choices. However, our specific concern is in how ideological premises prescribe and widely inculcate a skewed picture of reality. Relations between the sexes have never been simple, and they involve many imperfect choices, frustrations, and pains, for both men and women. But the sexual attitudes of men and women in the "battle-alliance of the sexes" is not quite the same, nor are the differences between them merely a social convention. Indeed, these differences are no more due to social conventions than are pair-bonding or the family, about whom we also have often been hearing that their time has passed. Changing conditions may add new pressures to old ones and otherwise greatly alter such human relations and institutions. And of course, people can make all sorts of choices in their lives. But this does not mean that natural human propensities cease to factor heavily in shaping people's actual choices.

Beyond "Binary" Sex

Gender issues go beyond the female-male split and heterosexual relations between the two sexes. Over the past several decades, there has been a growing recognition of the greater diversity and fluidity of sexual behaviors and identities, such as those coming under the acronym LGBT: lesbian, gay, bisexual, and transgender (and there are additional categories added). This recognition makes for a more nuanced and, hence, more realistic understanding of human sexuality. But the main engine of the change of perceptions has been normative. LGBT identities and sexual behaviors have become not merely tolerated in liberal societies, where they were not so long ago socially unacceptable and even punishable by law; they are now positively celebrated as a mark of human diversity and individual freedom. The stress on diversity and on the rejection of a "binary" division between two sexes sometimes appears almost to obscure the fact that the most common sexual behavior, by far, is heterosexual. According to the best surveys we have of various countries, the LGBT categories comprise only a few percent of the population each, some of them less than 1 percent. Not that this fact necessarily matters in this important venture. So much suffering and psychological agony for the people involved have been alleviated by the change of attitudes toward LGBTs. Rather than having to conceal their sexual inclinations, they now enjoy dignity and greatly decreasing social stigmas in liberal societies (while still threatened and persecuted in many non-liberal ones).

We do not yet know exactly what the cause of, say, homosexuality is, whether "nature" or "nurture". In my understanding, the trait is very unlikely to be hereditary, as genes for such a trait would be selected out as exceedingly non-adaptive; that is, homosexuals have been much less likely to produce offspring, who would carry the trait further. There are, however, other possible biological factors. They mostly relate to the condition of the egg, sperm, and fetus, also affected by "environmental" influences, including hormones produced by the mother in the womb. After birth, circumstances of social environment may also play a role in shaping sexual orientation under certain conditions, most notably, it would appear, during adolescence. The relative contribution of these (and possibly other) factors has yet to be determined. All the same, in the ideological debate that has accompanied the shift in attitudes over recent decades, the term "natural" has been widely deployed in different, both factual and normative, meanings by both sides.

Before the recent change of attitudes, homosexuality was castigated for being unnatural—whether going against God's design or Nature's—for childbearing has always been recognized as the functional logic of sex. In the framework of a God-infused morality, as especially projected by the monotheistic faiths, homosexuality was thus regarded as any other moral vice, arising from people's surrender to debased passions. The notion that homosexuals were misfortunates who deserved God's grace would be heard here and there in some religious circles later on. Even earlier, attitudes in liberal societies began to frame homosexuality as an "illness" rather than a crime. In the context of a secular-naturalistic worldview, all non-heterosexual sexual relationships and identities are rooted in mechanisms whose functioning diverges from their evolution-shaped design geared for reproduction; this is something that can occur in any design, whether man-made or created by the blind algorithm of natural selection. However, within this view of the world, the blind algorithm of natural selection means very little in normative terms. Moral criteria in liberal-secular societies have been increasingly and overwhelmingly inclined toward the goal of human well-being, as expressed in people's physical and psychological prosperity and happiness. The question asked tends to be what is natural to *them*.

The far-reaching change of attitudes toward LGBTs in liberal societies is yet another example of the interplay between deep-seated human emotional reactions and more elastic cultural-historical practices and norms. This goes way back. Homosexual relations were socially acceptable and indeed widespread and quite openly practiced—typically as an additional and secondary sexual outlet—in not a few cultures, most famously in classical Greece and premodern Japan. (It is necessary to add that the practice mostly referred to relations with "boys", a term that extended from boys to very young men.) How infinitely malleable are such norms? Consider these already classical experiments conducted by psychologist of morality Jonathan Haidt and colleagues. Haidt has suggested that we have strong innate moral predispositions that are differently activated and manifested in different societies and cultures. They are rooted not only in the principle of no direct harm but also in a feeling of disgust toward "impurity" and "uncleanliness" in things such as food and behavioral practices. These are naturally selected responses to that which could hamper people's survival during our long evolutionary past. Disgust toward incestual relations between close kin is one of these deep-seated emotional-moral reactions. Its evolution-based logic is the harm to the offspring caused by inbreeding. Note that inbreeding is avoided by various means not only among humans but in nature at large. Nowadays, as in the past, marriage between first-order relatives is prohibited by law, and incestual sexual relations are also a felony in many countries. The experiment carried out by Haidt and his colleagues asked students to express their views on the legitimacy of the following hypothetical case: grown-up brother and sister become sexual partners of their own free will. They use contraception, so there is no danger of a damage to offspring. The great majority of the student-subjects judged that such a relationship was immoral and should not be allowed. There was very little difference in this regard between conservatives and progressives.[30] Is this yet another moral attitude that is going to change with time, as no actual harm to anybody can be shown? Or will this moral precept and social taboo, rooted in a strong instinct of revulsion, persist?

Transgender people and groups charge that they are discriminated against not only by society at large—suffering from exclusion by both family and society, abuse, harassment and violence, job discrimination, and much else—but also by the other subgroups within the LGBT movement. Their case involves both factual and normative questions, and we begin with the former. Radical feminists have claimed that the differences between the sexes are entirely or almost entirely "constructed" by the process of socialization. By contrast, the homosexual and lesbian claim has typically been pretty much the opposite: that their sexual inclination is deep-seated and natural to them; indeed, that it is not a matter of choice—factually, before the normative question—and, therefore, that all attempts to "remedy" or "reform" them are futile. Now, the claims by the various groups that come under the transgender umbrella (including those who define themselves as bi-gender or tri-gender; a-gender, nongendered or gender-less; and gender-fluid) run both ways. Whereas gender-fluid, and sometimes bisexual, people argue that people's sexual identity is intrinsically flexible and fluid, transgender people argue that they have a deep nature that conflicts with their biological phenotype. In the same way that the LGBT movement dissolves into its constitutive elements on some questions, so does the transgender movement. In the way they are formulated, the above claims about the nature of human sexuality cannot all be generally valid. As statistics of people's self-definitions indicate, the vast majority define themselves as male or female and heterosexual, and their sexual orientation through life is quite stable. This does not contradict the fact that a few percent of both sexes are homosexual, and that this sexual orientation is deeply embedded in their nature. Nor does majority sexual orientation negate the fact that for a few percent of the population sexual orientation is more fluid, that this in deeply embedded in *their* nature; or, indeed, in the case of transgender people, that their natural physical phenotype as male or female does not accord with their naturally no less deeply embedded feeling of themselves as belonging to a different sex. None of these facts needs to be denied—or generalized—in the framework of an ideological discourse in order to establish or reject any social norm.

Normative questions are fundamentally not about facts but about how society views right and wrong and how it should organize itself accordingly. The LGBT demand for equality and dignity is practically irresistible as liberal doctrine unfolds and is increasingly woven into the fabric of liberal societies. There are many practical and normative questions of implementation involved, some easier and some harder or more confusing. Special bathrooms for transgender and the question of their gender placement in professional sport are among those that have hit the headlines. More important, there are questions such as the right for special medical care, above all relating to what is known as sex or gender reassignment surgery. And there are many other very significant questions. One of the most resonating issues has been that of gender pronouns, whether they should be gender non-binary or exist at all, not only in consideration of transgender people but also in relation to the male-female split. Neologisms such as "they" in the singular, as well as completely new forms such as "ze", "sie", "hir", "co", "ey", and "Mx", are increasingly used or experimented with. Any new linguistic form sounds strange at first—as was the withdrawal of Miss/Mrs, partly replaced by Ms., only a few decades ago. To what extent gender-neutral pronouns will become the norm has yet to be seen, but such a trend has already gained some traction.

Some Interim Comments

Critics might argue that feminist attitudes are much more aware than presented here of the natural differences between the sexes, as manifested, among other things, in sexual behavior; indeed, that the feminist main demand is to change the world, including male behavior and the relations between the sexes, in a way that would express women's particular needs much better and allow them equal opportunity to realize themselves in their own way. I agree that after the phase in which men and women were prescribed to be for all practical purposes the same, the latter voice has become increasingly prominent. There has been some swing of the pendulum, which is only to be expected in such cases, when the limits of the initial unfettered position are tested and reset. Hegel was probably the first to underscore this process. In the early nineteenth century, he noted the great liberating achievements of *his* "1960s", the eighteenth-century Enlightenment. The Enlightenment's precepts were pushed to the limit and then criticized and partly pushed back by a conservative backlash and the movement known as Romanticism. Hegel suggested that this dialectical process of "thesis" and "antithesis" tended to produce a higher "synthesis", which preserved the main achievements of both earlier movements in a more discriminate and refined form and constituted the basis for further debate and dialectical development.

So while I agree that feminism of (some) difference between the sexes is very much present in the public discourse, I argue that it is still mixed with the practically no-difference-at-all stance, with the two positions all too often expressed by the same people. It is almost inevitable that this should be the case in the kind of ideological campaign waged. Indeed, in view of the enormous changes that have taken place in social practices and norms relating to the status of women, it is rightly expected that we still have a long way to go, and it is only natural that the notion of no differences would persist. Even when differences in emotional proclivities between women and men are ambivalently recognized, including those relating to sexual behavior (or, for example, differences in medical conditions or longevity), the main battleground remains elsewhere. Most notably, there is the question of lingering gender differences in the distribution of occupations and income, and of their relation to possible differences in natural preferences and cognitive traits between men and women.

Are There Gender Differences in Occupational Preferences and Cognitive Skills?

Sexual preferences and behavior, while not dichotomous or "binary", of course, are a domain in which the divergence between women and men is among the most significant, more "hardwired", for the reasons explained. In many other spheres of life, differences between the sexes are small or barely exist, and their social manifestations are practically insignificant. In the great majority of occupations and workplaces in today's modern societies, the performance of men and women scarcely differs, and gender identities in hiring and firing play no significant role. For all that, there remains a great divergence in the distribution of occupations between the two sexes, which is also the main reason for the lingering differences in average income between them. This phenomenon is particularly glaring in the most egalitarian societies in the world, those of the Scandinavian countries, which exhibit the strongest ideological commitment to the equality of the sexes and have done the most in terms of education, legislation, and socioeconomic policy to realize that goal.

Here are the official data as to how the distribution of occupations between men and women in Sweden looks like today, after more than half a century of diligent efforts:

The 30 largest occupations, 2016
Number and sex distribution (%). Ranked by number of persons in each occupation.

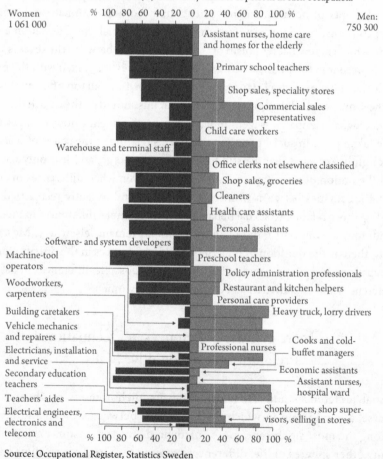

Source: Occupational Register, Statistics Sweden

Women and Men in Sweden 2018 Facts and figures Statistics Sweden 2018, 66; on the WWW.

And here are the resulting differences in income in Sweden between men and women:

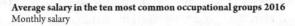

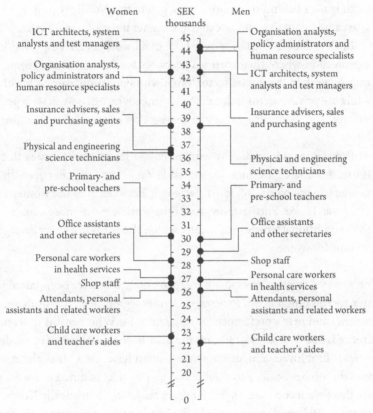

Average salary in the ten most common occupational groups 2016
Monthly salary

Source: Wage and salary structures, National Mediation Office, p. 75.

These data show that while men and women in Sweden are very close to earning equal pay for equal jobs (with small divergences in both directions), women are still far more inclined than men to choose jobs in the caring professions and in those that involve human interactions, whereas men are more inclined than women to choose professions that deal with things. The old stereotypes seem to be very much alive even in Scandinavia.

A survey in Denmark summarizes the data as follows:

Since the 1960s the Nordic countries have been renowned for their high level of gender equality as they have amongst the world's highest employment and education rates for women. At the same time the Nordic countries also have greater horizontal segregation by sex than the rest of the EU, that is, most women work in different occupations than most men. The gender segregation of labour is often seen as the main reason behind the gender wage gap in the Nordic region. It can also cause talent to go undetected and higher unemployment rates. . . .

In Denmark for instance over 60% of all workers are employed in a profession where their own sex accounts for 75% or more. Women mainly work in the public sector, often with education, care or health, while the private sector is dominated by men who often work with production and engineering. Gender segregation exists at all educational levels. . . .

Professions dominated by women have a lower average wage than those dominated by men which leads to a wage gap between the genders. In the Nordic region the wage gap between men and women in 2017 was 15.3%. Furthermore, part-time work is much more common in the traditional female professions, which also leads to a lower average income for women.

The survey suggests three possible explanations that have been raised in the research for this differences: "*Preference*: Gender segregation is partly maintained by women's and men's preference for different jobs. Whether this difference in preference is due to biology or socialisation has been the subject of much debate. *Stereotypes*: Employers and/or co-workers often have fixed ideas about which sex does the job best leading to discriminatory practices in hiring or a work place culture that favours one sex. *Different roles in the family*: Statistically Nordic men and women still have different roles in the family, where the woman has the role of primary caregiver and the man the role of primary earner."[31]

Some two decades ago, I wrote on the role of women in the military, as many jobs that did not require extreme physical force became common in modern warfare and were opening up to women, increasingly on the principle of equal opportunity. In the Netherlands from the late 1970s on, women were granted equal access to nearly all military jobs, and the authorities acted intensively to encourage them to exercise this freedom of opportunity. For all that, as the feminist authors of a study on the subject wrote with dismay: "The interest of women in the army seemed to diminish more than to increase. . . . The physical requirements remained a problem and so did the acceptance of women by their male colleagues. . . . The demands for combat jobs in the infantry, cavalry, artillery and the Royal Engineers are too high to be met by most women."[32] Female participation in the Dutch army remained in the low percentage points. (Today it stands at around 8 percent; in the United States, about 15 percent.) In Norway as well, another country with highly egalitarian legislation and policy, the picture is very similar, not least because of women's own lack of interest.[33] All this did not prevent—indeed, it probably prompted—"empowering" research titles on the subject of women in the military, such as "an unfinished revolution" and "no going back" (where, in some of the cases described, the women actually did go back).[34]

It may be that both men and women, even in the Nordic countries, are still far from being fully liberated, and that they ought to double and redouble their efforts. I am pretty sure that what we see in the most advanced countries in the world in terms of commitment to gender equality is by no means the last word and that we have more change in store. At the same time, it may also be that the divergence in job preferences between men and women is not merely the product of social stereotypes—perhaps explanations that invoke stereotypes are themselves too stereotypic—but is affected by deep-seated gender differences in natural inclinations. Quite obviously, a mixture of nature and nurture is involved. It fuses not only skills and opportunities, around which most of the debate revolves, but also the more neglected element of natural inclinations, which play a tremendous role—skills and opportunities being equal. Again, there is still considerable room for the advancement of state policies and social attitudes that would facilitate women's access to all professions and work against traditional habits and stigmas that might hinder women in general and any individual woman from pursuing the career of their liking. At the same time, we should be no less wary of pushing women into choosing professions and career paths that many of them might not really want—"force them to be free", as Rousseau urged in a different context. Indeed, we should be wary of investing a great deal of social capital in pursuit of an abstract and possibly illusive ideal of parity that extends beyond equal opportunity to the actual outcomes of free choices and preferences. A persisting gender gap in income might be the result of such realities—exasperating and ideologically unacceptable as it may be. We may see both an income gap and the ideological fury—both deep-seated—stubbornly persisting under foreseeable conditions.

A cardinal bone of contention is men's consistently recorded advantage in mathematics. This may suggest not merely different preferences, but differences in cognitive traits, all on average, of course. From the late 1960s to today, again over more than half a century, men's average score in the mathematical section of the Scholastic Aptitude Test (SAT) in the United States is consistently around 30 points higher than that of women. Among the best achievers, in the 600 to 700 range, men outnumber women roughly 2 to 1. This gap has persisted despite a massive change in social attitudes since the 1960s, the fact that slightly more high school girls than boys now take the test, and that the female students' overall average grades in high school and college are a little higher than those earned by boy students. The results appear to be even more tilted in favor of the men in the most extreme end of the excellence tail: "For example, in the Project Talent mathematics (total) scale, the sex ratio was 1.3 for scores in the top 10%, 1.5 in the top 5%, 2.1 in the top 3%, and 7.0 in the top 1% of the overall distribution. For several of the science and vocational aptitude tests, the sex ratio became infinite in the top 3% or 1% of the overall distribution because no females scored in this range."[35] These finds may largely account for the fact that among the winners of the Fields Medal, the highest honor in mathematical scholarly achievement, comparable to the Nobel Prize, there is only one women to date, out of some sixty medalists. Contra the hugely successful Netflix drama series *The Queen's Gambit* (2020), a similar vast imbalance exists at the very top level of professional chess, which is the reason why there are separate championships for women and men.

In the face of these data, the standard reaction is that stereotypes and skewed social expectations still persist and are responsible for the results—and who would deny that to some extent they do? The alternative explanation may be that men, on average, have a natural advantage in this cognitive domain, or that they are naturally more predisposed to dedicate their lives to it. (Might this has anything to do with the fact that the ratio of those diagnosed as autistic is 4 to 1 "in favor" of the men?) Yet such explanations would seem to be simply unacceptable to many. In 2005, Lawrence Summers, the president of Harvard University and former secretary of the treasury in the Clinton administration, pondered the scarcity of women in the science and engineering departments of top American universities. He offered a number of possible factors, which he believed were all present, including women's own preferences and social discrimination, but also "different availability of aptitude at the high end". The ensuing public outcry and a Harvard faculty vote of non-confidence forced him to resign.

Again, it is worth repeating that we are talking about averages, and that this does not mean that many women do not excel in mathematics and are entitled to every opportunity in the field. I am writing with a clear conscience, as I personally am an example of the fact that we are talking about averages. I have a fairly robust sense of numbers and quantities in the real world and a strong spatial orientation (in which tests consistently show that men tend to have an advantage, hypothesized to be related to their advantage in abstract mathematics). And yet my (natural) abilities in abstract mathematics, as well as my technical skills, are quite pathetic. (I also do at least half of the chores at home, since you ask.) The view that women are entitled to celebrate their special propensity to childbirth and motherhood has turned from being an anti-feminist argument in the past to a feminist one later on. Indeed, why are women's special traits and recorded advantages in some fields—such as their massively lower involvement in violent and other serious crime, superior reading abilities and memory for detail, overall better grades in school, and so on—accepted with delight by many, including me, whereas the data regarding mathematics, for example, encounters a sweeping rejection, hostility, and anger? The answer to this is pretty clear: the former is taken as a recognition of women's growing strengths in a world once entirely dominated by men, whereas the latter is suspected of being an intended or unintended obstacle impeding their progress, especially as it touches on some of the most lucrative and gainful occupations.

There has recently been a renewed pushback by a number of "neuroscience feminists", as they have been called, who apply brain scanning, a recently developed technique, to the study of sex differences in the brain. Finding that there is a great overlap between "male" and "female" features in the brain and cognitive traits, the "neuroscience feminists" have insisted that there is no such thing as a male brain and female brain. This conclusion is obviously true if by sexual distinctiveness in the brain we mean anything resembling the sharp difference in sexual genitalia. As we have seen, the great majority of scholarly studies on the subject fully recognize the general overlap between men and women in a whole range of cognitive and behavioral domains. Indeed, while the use of the brain scanning technique is a major scientific advance, its findings on the whole agree with those of more conventional cognitive tests. Remember that even classical traditional concepts such as *yin* and *yang* held male and female traits to be at once distinctive and flowing into each other. Where the claims of the so-called neuroscience feminists are misleading—where they create a wrong impression in both the titles of their works and overriding rhetoric—is in suggesting that the significant *average* differences in the *frequency* of cognitive and other traits in the brain between men and women, which they fully register, should not be labeled as sexual differences of the brain. This goes against any standard use of population statistics. My colleague at Tel Aviv, psychologist and pioneer brain scientist in the study of the sexes Daphna Joel, has coined the concept of a sexual brain "mosaic", adopted by her like-minded associates.[36] Mosaic, denoting variety and diversity, is a good word in the current liberal discourse. But in this case, it obscures the fact, recorded by the neuroscience feminists themselves, that the "blue" and "pink" "marbles" in the "mosaic" are differentially distributed between males and females, respectively, with each "color" found more on one side of the female-male continuum. As Joel herself writes: "it is possible to use one's brain architecture to predict whether this person is female or male with accuracy of ~80%."[37]

The "neuroscience feminists" vary among themselves in the extent of their reference to the innate differences between the sexes, which all of them concede and make sure to mention, often as an aside. At the same time, they hypothesize lingering sexual stereotypes for every recorded difference; systematically invoke ignorance, faulty methods, and past scientific errors to cast doubt over them; refer to the evolutionary rationale only cursorily and with supposedly sophisticated irony; and charge everybody except themselves with a political-ideological bias.[38] The most evasive of them, in my opinion, has had the good humor, and courage, to print what a woman critic wrote in a newspaper review about her book: "Pity the scientist. Locked up in labs, handling vials full of toxic liquids, surrounded by white mice and white coats—no wonder she sometimes loses her common sense."[39]

By contrast, the neuroscience feminist with the greatest intellectual balance, again in my opinion, has written as follows: "why does Hollywood keep regurgitating the same gender stereotypes about math and science? The answer: *because the stereotypes are accurate.*"[40] Thoroughly surveying the scholarly literature, she goes on to make the following important distinctions:

> boys and girls are different. But unlike the mostly subtle gaps in reading and math performance, their social and emotional differences are as clear as day. . . . Compared to most of the gaps we've considered up to now, emotional differences are more dramatic, and arguably the most important. More than verbal fluency or math SAT scores, sex differences in risk taking and nurturing account for the nagging chasms between the sexes in achievement and personal fulfillment—why men are better paid but have less-intimate friendships; why women make effective managers but are still banging the glass ceiling in many workplaces. Evolutionary psychologists have no trouble explaining such differences . . . sex differences in emotional and relational styles can more plausibly be linked to different selective pressures on male hunter/warriors and female gatherer/nurturers than most cognitive differences can. That's because differences in aggression, empathy, and competitiveness are more closely related to reproduction. . . . To the extent that evolution has programmed any male-female differences, it's done so through eons of mate selection, which has left its deepest mark on the way young men and women try to impress each other as worthy sexual partners. Still, as universal as some of the differences appear, none is as hard-wired as commonly portrayed. Like every other brain function we've considered, the social and emotional differences between boys and girls begin as tiny seeds planted by evolution and nourished by hormones but blossoming only under the hot sun of our highly gendered society.[41]

Concluding Comments—Gender and Ideology

Karl Ove Knausgård, the Norwegian author of the acclaimed series of autobiographical novels *My Struggle*, describes the following episode in the second installment, *A Man in Love*, from his experience in Sweden: "We went to the antenatal classes together, the room was packed and the audience sensitive to every word spoken from the rostrum; if there was anything remotely controversial from a biological point of view, a low sucking of breath ran through the rows, for this was taking place in a country where gender was a social construct, and for the body, outside what everyone agreed was common sense, there was no place. Instinct, came a voice from the rostrum. No, no, no! the angry women in the room whispered. How could you say such a thing!"

If you think this is a literary satirical exaggeration, consider this report in a major Israeli newspaper on a new order issued by the Israeli Armed Forces several years ago: "Any soldier was allowed to grow a beard, provided he (or she) informs their commander before hand."[42] I am pretty sure that it was the newspaper, rather than the military authorities, that chose this phrasing. Still, the fact that it was felt necessary is striking.

A whole variety of arcane and outlandish "theories" that claimed scientific status during the twentieth century have been celebrated in the humanities, social sciences, and cultural studies. Many of them are barely distinguishable from the mythologies of old, which, indeed, was how Freud was concerned Einstein might view his theory of a death drive, *Thanatos*, as the explanation for war.[43] Research in the "cultural studies" in particular has all too often taken the form of fanciful works of creative metaphors. Feminism has a very sound basis in reality, and its success as both an ideology and social movement is one of the most significant transformations of modernity. However, some varieties within it have been deeply influenced by dubious theories and claims that have dominated the intellectual discourse and academic arena. Against this background, evolutionary theory appeared as a somber party spoiler.

Here is how literary scholar, evolutionist, and author of a most brilliant book on the role of narratives in human cognition, Jonathan Gottschall, describes his first steps in academia in the 1990s. Unfortunately, this state of affairs is still very much applies today:

> tabula rasa theories had not lost their respectability in the humanities, and when I approached my epics professor with a plan for a seminar paper on male conflict in Homer from the perspective of evolutionary theory and research, he flatly forbade me to write it on the grounds of absurdity and irrelevance. Instead, he authorized me to write a paper based on . . . the perspective of Freud and Lacan, not Darwin. . . . For my professor, as for virtually all of the other graduate students and professors in the English department, psychoanalysis was considered respectable . . . despite the fact that psychology and other fields had long since rejected it. . . . Students and professors moved fluidly from

feminism to Marxism, to queer theory, to psychoanalysis, to continental textual theory, to structuralism, to poststructuralism, and to historicism [as well to many other approaches and disciplines]. . . . This tolerance reached its limits, however, when it came to evolutionary theories of human behavior and psychology, toward which students and professors evinced nothing but skepticism, hostility, and, most of all, fear.

Gottschall continues:

the "fact" that gender was an arbitrary social construct was announced by a classmate with typical casual confidence. . . . I noted that, actually, a confluence of different sources of evidence, deriving from an impressive array of disciplines, consistent with the expectations of evolutionary theory, and borne out in cross-cultural research, suggested that this constructivist orthodoxy was wrong—the dimorphic behavioral and psychological tendencies observed in populations of men and women were as much a product of biology as culture. A close female acquaintance seemed to speak for the whole seminar when she turned to me, shaking her head with a mixture of sadness, pity, and stubborn hope: "You can't really believe that, Jon, can you?"[44]

It is remarkable how successful we are in getting not to know what we know all too well. Or as Saul Bellow has put it (in reference to Sartre and the Soviet Union, but also, disarmingly, to himself): "A great deal of intelligence can be invested in ignorance when the need for illusion is deep."

The revolution in the status and social role of women in liberal societies has been one of the greatest changes of the last century. Its practical and normative significance cannot be exaggerated. It has also tested the distinction between nature and nurture to the limit. As argued here, both play a significant role, and the interplay between them can be very diverse indeed. The role of nature was greatly overestimated and that of social conditions hugely underestimated by previous generations for pretty obvious reasons, given the realities they were familiar with. The opposite has been true in much of the feminist rhetoric and theory, with respect to both the past and the present.

As Oz's grandpa commented, man and women are very similar in many ways and in many domains. They are significantly different, on average, on some other emotional, cognitive, and behavioral traits, and such differences are not entirely reducible to lingering social conventions, stereotypes, and prejudices, present as many of them may still be. Any suggestion that this is so provokes very strong emotions in the current liberal ideological discourse, with its postulate of equality. This is the nature of an ideological discourse, which is principally not about accuracy of explanation but about social change and getting things done. Hence the intrinsic and almost irreconcilable tension between the practically no-different-at-all and the different but equal stances in the feminist discourse, often expressed in the same breath.

My guess is that none of this will disappear any time soon. The hope expressed by Daphna Joel of a future of virtually genderless society, where the differences between the sexes would count no more than those between right-handed and left-handed persons has a scant prospect of materializing. To be sure, in many walks of life this is actually where we are or will soon arrive. Equal opportunity of choice is fast becoming the norm, and the dominant ideological expectation is that no individual should be hindered in her choices by her sex. However, in many other ways, the differences between the sexes are significant and the male-female distinction is central to many aspects of human life. The power of ideology over minds is immense, and it can move mountains. At the same time, experience teaches that there are limits to that power. This applies also to both the spectacular achievements and intrinsic ideological fixations of much of feminist theorizing and rhetoric, extending the liberal (and socialist) quest for equality, freedom, and human emancipation.

Can Anything Be Done?

Some Very Tentative Reflections on
Current Ideological Battlefields

This chapter is offered as an exercise. In contrast to most of the subjects discussed in this book, I claim no special knowledge and no special wisdom or foresight on any of the issues addressed here. The following tentative ruminations on some current ideologically charged debates are put forward in a quest to suggest how intellectual openness and an effort to avoid ideological fixations in the assessment of facts might look like, nothing more.

This may be the time for some proper disclosure about myself. I am an Israeli, which means that I live in a country that is steeped in politics and experiences deep ideological cleavages. Predominantly, they concern the conflict and prospects of peace with the Palestinians and the Arab world, as well as the future of the territories Israel occupied in the 1967 war. In Israeli political terms, I am a centrist. Although I have never voted for the right in my country's elections, I am not blind to the fact that not a few of the right's predictions and warnings regarding past events have materialized, and that its concerns with respect to future developments are not without foundation. Taking these concerns very seriously, I still assess that, on balance, the right's objectives and remedies with respect to the future of the territories, if materializing, pose a great danger to the country by threatening its character as both liberal democratic and a national home for the Jewish people. That aside, my discussion here revolves around more general debates and ideological bones of contention that preoccupy the liberal democracies, with special emphasis on the United States, where the ideological polarization is the most intense.

As noted in the Preface, this book was begun before the Trump presidency and before the terms "fake news" and "alternative facts" were coined. I am not going to write about Trump, because I have nothing particularly interesting to

Ideological Fixation. Azar Gat, Oxford University Press. © Oxford University Press 2022.
DOI: 10.1093/oso/9780197646700.003.0008

add to everything that has already been said about him and his presidency from all sides, and because the questions that intrigue me regarding the phenomenon of ideology and ideological fixation are more fundamental. Again, I stress that there is nothing exceptional about my opinions on current issues. In American political terms, I am an Independent; that is, had I been a US citizen, I could have voted either way, depending on the issues and personalities involved. On many issues my normative views are progressive. I am for the right of abortion during the early stage of pregnancy, out of the view that unwanted pregnancies are often the source of misery to both mother and child, as well as being a huge social problem; that there is no fixed point where fetuses become "fully human"; and that there is no real "slippery slope" here either. I am against the death penalty, primarily because of the risk of a mistake that cannot be corrected; many such fatal mistakes we know to have happened, and it is certain that such mistakes will persist. I am strictly against the unrestricted private ownership of guns, which greatly exacerbates the United States' very significant social problems, among them an exceptionally high homicide rate, unparalleled in the developed world. At the same time, I recognize very well that this is "a cultural thing" with many Americans—and hence that the chances of repealing or reinterpreting the Second Amendment are scant; that this is so even though the claim that the right to bear arms is still a safeguard against a threat of tyrannical rule in the United States strikes me (like the threat itself) as particularly preposterous. I am an atheist, a self-identification more associated with progressives than with conservatives (though in many respects I am a "non-hostile" atheist). By both calculation and normative inclination, I am a supporter of the welfare state—in what exact scope and form is a more complex question. And I regard universal healthcare in particular as an imperative in any affluent modern country.

On the other hand, I tend to accept, or at least take seriously, some major points of the conservative side. I pay close attention to the argument that there are intrinsic limitations to the tremendous growth of public spending that took place during the twentieth century: from less than 10 percent to 30–50 percent of GDP in all the developed countries. In addition, there is the effect of excessive taxation on economic growth, although there is also the opposite effect of underspending on economic performance. Furthermore, in the American case, one is forced to admit that much of the government's social spending, from the "Great Society" of the 1960s on, has failed to achieve anything remotely close to the hopes pinned on it. In some respects, government social programs have made things worse, because of the real "moral hazards" involved, such as "dependency culture" and the "poverty trap". While this does not mean that social spending should be eliminated or cut to the bone, it certainly should make one think. Among other things, there is no reason there should be a one-size-fits-all social policy for all countries: what is suitable for the Scandinavian countries, the model welfare states—with their specific cultural, civic, and demographic character—is not necessarily practical or desirable for the United States, or actually *desired* by its people as reflected by electoral majorities. Moreover, there are perhaps additional models and examples to be studied and experimented with concerning social policies except for these two supposed opposites. Switzerland, Japan, Australia, and New Zealand, for example—and not only the United States—are on the lower side in terms of government expenditure, and their practices and institutions might merit attention.[1]

In my view, the welfare state is here to stay, and for very good reasons. So again, the real question is the exact scope and form it should have. What are known as "entitlements" are exploding out of control in the United States with total disregard for rapidly aging demographics.[2] In effect, the older age groups practically live at the expense of their children. Conservatives are as irresponsible about this as are progressives, if not more so, as they have cut taxes without corresponding cuts in entitlements—which are popular with the voters—thereby steadily increasing the national debt. Against conservative doctrine, some conservatives have even rationalized this into a principle. Probably both some tax increases and a reining in of "entitlements" for the better-off majority of the population are necessary to close this gap and stabilize the American economy—and future.

The conservative critique has been sounder yet with respect to the so-called mixed economy that was the consensus—more in Europe than in the United States—from 1945 to 1980. This was the notion that it was best for the economy, companies, and businesses to be owned and run partly in private hands and partly by the state. This core doctrine of social democracy distinguished it from the other, liberal, branch of progressivism. Over time, state industries proved to be inefficient and particularly prone to strikes. One occasionally reads about the lost virtues of trade unions, whose membership and power have shrunk considerably over the last decades. But the authors of these writings scarcely mention that whereas in the private sector, the market in principle sets parameters for a possible compromise between employers and employees, the public sector lacks such a regulating mechanism. In consequence, this sector was notoriously ridden with strikes and obstructionist work practices, which contributed to its low efficiency, drove countries such as Britain to the ground, and plagued some other European countries as well.[3] The wave of privatization from the 1980s on emerged as a response to and reaction against this situation. And in the same way that conservatives had more or less acquiesced to the mixed economy consensus of the post-1945 period, privatization was to be embraced by social democratic parties and governments as well. The main distinction between social democrats and left-liberals has thus faded nearly into insignificance. The principal divide that remains in the ideological arena with respect to socioeconomic policies is that between progressives and conservatives, with their more or less expansive view of the welfare state and outlooks on a range of other normative-social issues.

The conservative-neo/right-liberal wave gathered momentum from around 1980 in response to the growing problems that had been besetting the left-liberal and social-democratic era. The rapid growth that had marked the post-1945 economic recovery—most notably in war-ravaged Western Europe and Japan—had pretty much exhausted itself and was giving way to stagflation. (The huge global boost of reconstruction is often ignored by those who compare post-1945 and post-1980 economic growth rates.) During the post-1945 period, top income tax rates in some countries climbed to around 90 percent. This included not only Sweden but also the United States and United Kingdom in some years, while in Germany and France, for example, it was around 60 percent. After 1980, the United States and United Kingdom have more than halved their top income tax rates, while the "average top tax rate in a group of twenty-five developed nations fell from 66 percent in 1979 to 50 percent a decade later." Indirect taxes on consumption have risen to make up (partly) for the shortfall.[4]

This about-turn in socioeconomic policy has brought new questions and concerns to the fore, mostly regarding the widening gaps in income and wealth, as well as about decreasing socioeconomic mobility and opportunity, especially in the United States. Expanding globalization, desirable in many ways, has reinforced this trend. It has created much larger markets, from which giant corporations and successful individuals can draw much greater revenues; has pressed down on blue collar jobs and wages in the developed countries, which have migrated to places of cheaper labor—thereby, it should be noted, reducing global inequality more than it increased inequality within countries; and it has much decreased governments' ability to levy taxes on capital, as capital might choose to flee elsewhere. As a result, the gaps in the distribution of income and overall wealth, lowest in the period between 1945 and 1980, have been greatly increasing, is some places recreating their levels during the early stages of capitalist industrialization. In the United States, the trend has been particularly sharp.

Wealth and Class: Coming to Grips with Some (Not Undisputed) Data

The reality, scope, and implications of this trend have all been the subject of bitter controversy between progressives and conservatives. Again, both facts and values are involved in the debate—and, in principle, the interpretation of the facts should not be affected by one's values. In Chapter 5, I criticized Thomas Piketty's analysis of late nineteenth- and early twentieth-century imperialism as deeply flawed. In addition, one may or may not agree with many of the conclusions of his work, and doubt the feasibility or the desirability of his policy prescriptions. At the same time, his special expertise, and greatest contribution, is in assembling the most comprehensive dataset to date on inequality, particularly during the last century and a half. According to this data, the upper decile's share of the total income in the United States has been steadily rising since 1980, to 45–50 percent, up from 35 percent in the period 1945–1980 and similar to its share in the 1920s and 1930s.

Source: Thomas Piketty, *Capitalism in the Twenty-First Century*, 291.

The gap in total wealth is wider still: "the upper decile own 60 percent of Europe's wealth and more than 70 percent in the United States. And the poorer half of the population are as poor today as they were in the past, with barely 5 percent of total wealth in 2010, just as in 1910." "the middle 40 percent ... owns 35 percent of total national wealth."[5]

Notably, official data suggest that although most of the new wealth has indeed been concentrated in the hands of the top percentiles, the claim that the majority of the population have seen their income stagnating or even declining in real terms is unfounded, especially after taxes and transfers are factored in. According to these data, the highest quintile of households in the United States has doubled its income in real, inflation-adjusted, terms since 1980, with the top percentile's income more than tripling. During the same period, the lowest quintile's income has increased by a third, but by 85 percent after taxes and transfers, not far behind the top quintile. The two middle quintiles—the middle class—saw their income grow substantially yet more modestly, increasing by a third, and nearly by half after transfers and taxes.[6]

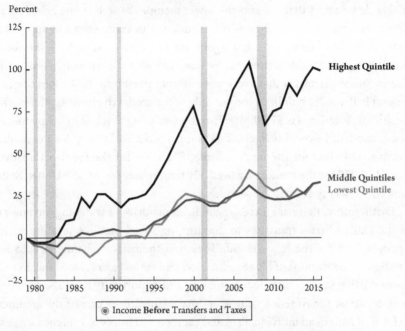

Cumulative Growth in Average Income, by Income Group, 1979 to 2016

Source: Congressional Budget Office, *The Distribution of Household Income*, 2016.

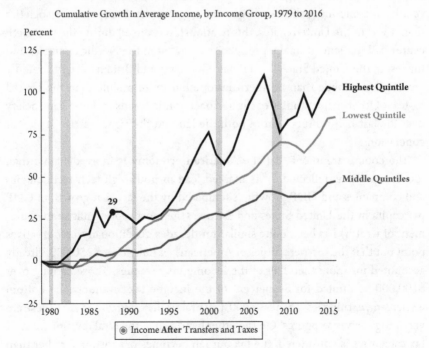

Cumulative Growth in Average Income, by Income Group, 1979 to 2016

Source: Congressional Budget Office, *The Distribution of Household Income*, 2016.

If so, the conservative argument that a prospering economy produces a trickle-down effect that benefits the lower incomes as well is not belied by reality to the extent some progressives maintain. This claim seems to apply even more to levels of employment, a significant factor to be sure. Still, the socioeconomic gaps in the United States have grown momentously. A study by Credit Suisse calculates that average wealth per person in the United States is around half a million dollars, second only to Switzerland. However, the *median* wealth for Americans is $79,000 per person (meaning that half of the people are above and half below this level). This compares with $230,000 for the median Belgian, $146,000 for the median Swiss, $125,000 for the median Canadian, and $122,000 for the median Japanese. By that measurement, the United States ranks only twenty-third in the world.[7]

Furthermore, there are increasing indications that the widening income gap in the United States translates to diminishing social mobility and decreasing opportunities for the less well-off. They find themselves channeled into less prestigious institutions of higher education and far less gainful jobs due to their lower starting point in life. Social mobility and opportunity have always been a central part of the American ethos, and have constituted part of the argument in favor of American individualism and capitalism. However, evidence suggests that social mobility is declining in the United States, perhaps to a lower level than in Europe. According to Piketty's data, whereas at the turn of the twentieth century income inequality was significantly greater in Europe's class societies than it was in the United States, this relationship reversed during the twentieth century: "Intergenerational reproduction is lowest in the Nordic countries and highest in the United States. . . . France, Germany, and Britain occupy a middle ground, less mobile than northern Europe but more mobile than the United States."[8] Other major studies of the socioeconomic trends in American society over the last half century—from both the left and the right—arrive at similar conclusions.[9]

The counterargument that the American economy is more dynamic than the European, as reflected in its marked lead in both high-tech technologies and companies and GDP growth, is tempered by the fact that growth in GDP per capita in the United States and Europe (the most representative measurement of wealth) has been quite similar for decades. Additionally, conservatives point out that the top percentiles of Americans, earning over $250,000, already accounted for more than half of the income tax revenues. Those earning over $100,000 accounted for 80 percent of the income tax revenues. The bottom 45 percent, earning less than $30,000, pay practically no income tax.[10] These are very progressive tax figures. On the other hand, when the total revenue from all tax categories is considered, the tax burden becomes proportional rather than progressive. According to the data, the top 1 percent of the population in terms of their income pays about a fifth of the nation's tax revenues, with practically the same proportion holds all the way down the income scale. The share for the lowest income groups in terms of their overall tax burden is proportionately only modestly lighter than that of the top 1 percent.[11]

As Warren Buffett, one of the world's wealthiest persons, has famously put it: he pays taxes at a lower rate than his secretary—mostly because corporations and capital gains are taxed at a much lower rate than wages.[12] Buffett is also known for his strong advocacy of higher inheritance taxes on the rich, to offset the formation of oligarchic families of wealth, a process much reinforced by the steep lowering of these taxes over the last decades. Whether the current taxation system in the United States, and its socioeconomic effects, is fair or desirable should be asked from a conservative no less than from as progressive perspective. The self-interest of the very rich seems to trump some major elements of conservative philosophy, which in principle balances the notions of self-reliance, small government, and respect for private property with the meritocratic ideal, opportunity, and disdain for idle wealth.

Some Questions to the Ideological Antagonists

Based on this tentative overview of the data, here are some questions for conservatives. Personally, I am unimpressed by arguments of pure principle, such as the libertarian claim that it is morally unjustified for states to tax, except for some well-defined purposes, or that it is illegitimate for them to redistribute wealth.[13] (I am equally unimpressed by abstract principles from the opposite side.) Like Mill, I am more interested in the actual effects in the world of institutions and policies, which may then be subject—are inevitably subjected—to normative preferences. So here are the questions: Is the trend, by which there is not only a widening income and wealth gap in the United States but also indications of decreasing social mobility and opportunity, sustainable economically, socially, and politically, let alone desirable from a conservative perspective? In a textbook demonstration of the phenomenon of ideology, studies suggest that the political views that people in the United States hold tend to correlate with their socioeconomic status—"where you stand depends on where you sit".[14] But even in terms of "enlightened self-interest" (assuming it has an effect on people's positions), can the most affluent isolate themselves indefinitely— as they have been doing quite successfully—from the growing gaps and rift in American society? Aristotle held that the middle class is the mainstay of a stable mixed regime or polity. Tocqueville believed that the United States' exceptional levels of education and landownership (property) in his time were central to the democratic spirit in America. This is surely also a modern conservative notion. In principle, conservatives need not be reminded by progressives that liberty and equality are not separate and wholly conflicting values, for the reason that without a significant measure of equality there is no true liberty.[15] Indeed, what might the growing gaps in the United States mean in, say, electoral terms? What, for example, is the significance of both the 2016 and 2020 US presidential election results from a conservative perspective? Are growing socioeconomic gaps not going to further escalate the cold civil war that is already raging in the United States? There is a strong tension within conservativism between mostly libertarian individualism and social conservative emphasis on the community (as there is sometimes tension in progressivism between championing the popular cause and contempt for the common people). How are these conflicting considerations to be accommodated effectively?

I am pretty sure that left-wing readers of the previous chapters have marked me as a supporter of capitalism—indeed, charge that I hold an undisclosed ideological position or bias in this regard. For many intellectuals—both inside and outside academia—economic "neoliberalism" has been the ultimate phrase of denunciation that requires no further discussion. Sticking to my guns, I maintain that the market principle has been proved by experience to be far more successful in generating affluence and prosperity—by most people's understanding of these terms—than any other tried system. At the same time, the blessings of capitalism are not unalloyed, and it would be a mistake to deny that it tends to be problematic in people's minds, sometimes very much so. Apart from many acute "practical" problems—past and present—described in earlier chapters and in this one, people tend to regard only so much inequality as acceptable and even justified, mostly if they judge the reasons for the inequality to be the product of true merit. Side by side with the conservative view of the "undeserving poor" who free-ride the system, there is the opposite view of the "undeserving rich" who exploit their position in the system to extract fabulous rents. This, indeed, is not just a progressive position but, in principle, also a modern conservative one, as free market doctrine opposes any distortion of efficient market operation by monopolies and rent-seekers. And yet the system appears "rigged" to many Americans, and in practice there does not seem to be any real effort by conservatives to remedy this situation. On the contrary, conservative politics appears to be captive of "big money".

Historically, capitalism has pretty much been rescued by the introduction of the welfare state and vindicated by its great successes and the failure of competing ideologies. However, if welfare capitalism fails to meet current problems and challenges, its success may be fragile and alternative programs may resurface— some of which are likely to be much worse and more dangerous than what they seek to replace. In his recent book, respected conservative columnist and public intellectual George Will chided people who are concerned about the widening gaps in income in the United States, writing, among many valid arguments, that envy is the "basest and ugliest" of the deadly sins.[16] However, quite apart from the actual problems that the current system now faces, conservatives, who profess to ground their view of the world in the deep traits of human nature, should find it hard to hold the stick from both ends. As we have seen, although not everything that has roots in human nature is inflexible and inescapable, there are limits to what can realistically be expected from restraining natural human propensities. Indeed, people value their relative status (in comparison to others) no less, often more, than their absolute status (how much they have, irrespective of what others have). The reason for this is that relative status—for example, in attractiveness (mating prospects) in all its elements—is the key to many of the things people desire most.[17] Preaching virtue to the poor apparently does not prevent the "deaths of despair", the rocketing rise in alcohol, drug use, and suicide mortality in the United States since 1990 (particularly evident among poor non-Hispanic Whites).[18] The United States is the only developed country where the life expectancy of the poor has been falling, even before the coronavirus pandemic.

None of this is to suggest that there are easy solutions to these dilemmas, given current domestic and global realities. The world is indeed a very complex thing, and many problems have no good "solutions". No wonder that the most acute students of the current trends in American society—both left- and right-leaning—are so much better on their diagnoses than on their prognoses, as they themselves are well aware or else are reminded by their critics.[19] Indeed, the difference between progressives and conservatives is often less about ideals than it is about the feasibility of implementing them. According to Robert Putnam's groundbreaking work: "More than two thirds of us . . . favor a more equal distribution than obtains today. [However] While large majorities favor pragmatic steps to limit inequality of condition, we are also philosophical conservatives, suspicious of the ability of government to redress inequality and convinced that responsibility for an individual's well-being rests chiefly with him or her. . . . we are less divided about the desirability of upward mobility without regard to family origins. About 95 percent of us endorse the principle that 'everyone in America should have equal opportunity to get ahead', a broad consensus that has hardly wavered since opinion surveys began more than a half century ago."[20]

How to balance these often conflicting preferences and realities has been the subject of intense debates and political struggles, and the issue is likely to continue to hold center stage in the public and political arena in the future. Capitalism and the application of the market principle, as well as political and social measures to cope with their less desirable effects, have undergone considerable development during modern times in response to changing conditions. There is no reason to think that they are not going to be transformed further and produce new political outcomes, policy measures, and tentative equilibria in response to yet new conditions and challenges as we progress into the twenty-first century. In his *Capital and Ideology* (2020), Piketty has recently laid out a most radical and far-reaching program for what he calls a new "participatory socialism". There are glaring gaps and fundamental weaknesses in his vision.[21] Nonetheless, I do not think anyone can rule out the possibility of a less polarized socioeconomic order. An open mind and a nonpartisan approach are essential for assessing future prospects.

For all that, it is typical of ideological battles that all sides dig in their heels and refuse to give way or accord any credit to ideas that come from the opposite camp that they deeply loathe and fear. Healthcare in the United States is one of these issues. Conservatives have many reasons to suspect growing costs and inefficiencies in a system of universal coverage involving the public sector. Moreover, experience has taught them to oppose anything smacking of messianic progressivism. In addition, many in the United States of course do not want to pay for the medical insurance of both the white and black underclasses, with whom they feel little solidarity. That said, and normative choices and even possible considerations of "enlightened self-interest" aside, it cannot really be denied that the American healthcare system is doubly more expensive than that of all other developed countries, while producing less healthcare than other systems. The reasons for this are all too familiar, and we shall not go into the many factors, intricacies, and complexities involved. The bottom line is that the American system is already swallowing up 17–18 percent of American GDP and continuing to grow, as opposed to 8–12 percent in all other developed countries. And this is despite the fact that the American population is younger than that of nearly all the developed countries—a decisive factor in determining healthcare costs. In addition, the fact that people who lose their jobs also automatically lose their medical insurance does not make sense. Conservative polemics pick, for example, on the long queues in the British public healthcare system. But, again, there are other state-regulated universal healthcare systems in the world—combining private and public elements—that are worth looking at: such as those in Switzerland, Germany, other European countries, Canada, Australia, New Zealand, Japan, Singapore, and South Korea. To be sure, it is exceedingly difficult to reform or revolutionize an already existing and deep-rooted system. But arguments of "American exceptionalism", which may very well apply in other contexts, sound particularly hollow in this regard. So far, conservatives have come up with few practical programs to fix the system, and their position appears to be predominantly obstructionist.

Socioeconomic questions are only part of the ideological divide. As we saw, there is also the view of the world that has migrated from the radical margins and taken root in mainstream progressivism. According to this view, "indigenous" societies represent natural virtue or intrinsic victimhood; and, inseparably, the West, liberal democracy, capitalism, and the United States—compressed into one—are the main culprits for their current condition, or at least bear great responsibility for it and are guilty of massive injustices and harm. Correspondingly, in contrast to the era of progressive presidents such as FDR, Truman, and Kennedy—and after Vietnam and the cultural turn of the 1960s—there is an all-too-common progressive tendency to forget that the world is a dangerous place that calls for well-measured vigilance; true, that without falling into the opposite trap of histrionics and precipitating self-reinforcing spirals of hostility. There is a tendency to turn a blind eye to or angrily deny that threats to world peace today come from the less developed countries, whereas the developed areas are invariably a zone of peace. Furthermore, there is a reluctance to admit that the less developed societies' only way out of their deep problems and misfortunes is by making the difficult and often painful social, political, and cultural adjustments that are necessary for successfully embarking on the road to modernization. As we have seen, by any comparative terms—indeed, very much according to the criteria and values of the critics themselves, adequately clarified and genuinely applied—the liberal democracies have the best record by far in human history. I share the deep conservative sense that the radical view of the world that has variably affected left-liberalism is greatly twisted and represents a far-reaching departure from reality.

This, of course, does not mean that the liberal democracies are flawless and beyond reproach, or that the efforts to fix their deficiencies should be relaxed. Nor does it mean that there is nothing that could be done to assist the "Rest", both at home and abroad, or that we should not double and redouble our efforts. However, beyond the normative question involved—to what extent people feel themselves obligated to do so—it needs to be recognized that our abilities in this regard are much more limited and less straightforward than many previously imagined, or still do. Progressive sentiments on all these are rooted in a strong and genuine moral impulse and tradition of self-criticism. Furthermore, progressive moral impulses, values, and policies have contributed to major social developments over the last decades—as earlier—which many would find most worthy. However, they have also been responsible for some deeply misguided attitudes and policies both at home and abroad, some of which have been reviewed in the previous chapters.

Similarly, the factual claim that national identities are contrived fictions is increasingly adopted by the left in the current ideological wars, going hand to hand with the normative claim that they are illegitimate and must not be allowed to play a role in domestic and global politics. The first claim is erroneous as far as deep-seated human sentiments of belonging, shared identity, and solidarity are concerned; and, once this is acknowledged, the normative position might also be tempered—if not in its value aspect, then perhaps in appreciation of the prospects of actually realizing it in the world. This, of course, still leaves much space for opposing views regarding consequences and effects related to hot questions such as immigration, as well as to different preferences concerning what is desired and desirable. In recent years, both sides have only radicalized their views on these matters—under pressure from new and pressing realities, but also because of the escalating dynamics of deep ideological hostility toward each other. In the United States, where well into the 2000s there used to be only small differences in attitudes toward immigration between Democrats and Republicans, a wide gap has since opened up, with by far the greatest shift occurring among Democrats.[22]

Extremely disturbing is the active and radicalizing intolerance in progressive circles toward the views of others, most alarmingly on American campuses and in flagships of progressivism such as the *New York Times*, formerly a champion of free speech and open discussion. As already noted, freedom of speech has always been limited to some degree in reality by social norms as to what is regarded beyond the pale. However, in recent decades, these boundaries have been pushed to cover, and curtail, ever-broader parts of the public debate and scholarly discussion proscribed as politically incorrect. On campuses, there is an increasingly militant suppression of speech and scholarly freedom—sometimes involving physical disruption—mostly carried out by student groups, but often joined by supportive, complicit, or cowed faculty and administration. One title in *Vox* has captured my eye: "I'm a liberal professor, and my liberal students terrify me." Subtitles in the article run as follows: "It's not just that students refuse to countenance uncomfortable ideas—they refuse to engage them, period"; "feelings become more important than issues"; "the real problem: a simplistic, unworkable, and ultimately stifling conception of social justice"; "now boat-rocking isn't just dangerous—it's suicidal."[23] Progressivism in the United States in particular— long associated, like liberal persuasions everywhere, with freedom of opinion and expression and a reasoned discussion in pursuit of knowledge and truth— has been increasingly turning into a zealous, intolerant, and sometimes fanatical sect.

Much has already been written about the causes of this turn in progressivism, most notably so-called identity politics, which has taken the liberal quest for human dignity and equality some extra miles. It has given rise to absurdities, such as the claim that only the weak or "weakened" group has the right to define its collective story, which must be considered the only valid and legitimate one. By identifying itself with such "narratives", much of the progressive discourse has acquired an obsessive and surreal character, has perpetuated a culture of victimhood, and has discouraged soul-searching, sense of responsibility, and efforts at self-help within these groups themselves. In the process, it has increasingly appeared as if the progressive left has distanced itself from, and is alien to, any concept of a collective national identity and shared culture.

Additionally, starting from the 1960s—and in sharp contrast to earlier times—the progressive center-left parties throughout the West have become the home of the most educated and more well-off (except for the very rich). In parallel, these parties have lost voting share among the (shrinking) working class, their traditional stronghold. Some observers in the United States have characterized the evolving progressive state of mind ever since the material-cum-cultural transformation of the 1960s as a new "bohemian-bourgeois (BoBo) synthesis".[24] As part of this change, the notion of "duties" seems to have lost ground, while that of "rights" has become dominant. A substantial part of blue collar voters, feeling both their interests and identity unprotected and threatened by the left's increasingly globalized and cosmopolitan attitudes, has switched its allegiance to conservative and so-called nativist/populist parties.[25] Hence the apparent paradox, especially in the United States, where large sections of the white working class vote Republican, the party of lower taxes on the rich. While their vote supposedly goes against their material "interests", it is more in line with their cultural predispositions on questions such as American identity, immigration, law and order, and much else.[26]

On the opposite side, my friend Peter Berkowitz has gently called on his fellow conservatives to give up their delusions that the remedy to the United States' social problems involves the undoing of both the welfare state and the Sexual Revolution.[27] After the initial great enthusiasm for both, and with experience, there has been some rebalancing, partly due to people's individual choices and partly by public policy changes. But both are here to stay.

The Battle over Race

As I was coming close to completing this book, the United States was engulfed by widespread and large-scale demonstrations, protests, rioting, and looting, ignited by the shocking scenes of the killing of a black man, George Floyd, by policemen. Interpretations of these events have stretched the nerves of both sides on the ideological-political divide to the very limit, as they have struck at the deepest core of their sensibilities, convictions, and identities.

For many progressives, African Americans are the holy of the holiest, as they are, indeed, the victims of what is regarded by the great majority of Americans as the most horrific and shameful aspect of American history: the institution of slavery, followed by racial segregation and discrimination, sanctioned by law well into the 1960s. Progressives in general and African Americans in particular charge that contemporary society and state institutions, most notably the police and justice system, are steeped in "institutional racism". They hold that it is largely responsible for the continued terrible condition of many black communities and, above all, accounts for their vast overrepresentation in the crime and prison statistics, as well as for the frequency of black men being killed by police. As a recent report summarizes the empirical evidence: "Black and Hispanic people are stopped more frequently, including traffic stops, and are more likely to be arrested. Once stopped, police are more likely to use force against, shoot and kill Black citizens. And then once in jail, Black defendants are more likely to be denied bail, which in turn makes conviction more likely. And when convicted, sentencing is also biased against Black defendants, with Black defendants more likely to be incarcerated."[28]

From the other side, while many conservatives concede that racism, stereotyping, and stigmatizing exist and need to be fought against, they argue that this is a very partial presentation of reality—a reality with which everyone is familiar but which polite society would not dare express in words or even think. They maintain that while the toxic legacy of centuries of slavery, racial segregation, and blatant discrimination is undeniable, the main problem by far of the black communities in the United States today—not in 1960, 1880, or 1860—is the terrible condition of these communities themselves, which is a danger to everyone around them, but most of all to themselves, as black lives matter. After all the biases of the police and justice system are filtered out, the reality remains that some half of the murder cases in the United States are carried out by blacks, of which more than 90 percent are perpetrated by blacks against blacks.[29] In view of this reality, fanfare gestures such as the pulling out the police from black neighborhoods inevitably ended, wherever such acts were attempted, in a sharp surge in black deaths. Objecting to the popular slogan among more radical progressives to "defund the police", the African American winner of the Democratic primaries for mayor of New York City (and eventual incumbent), Eric Adams, said in July 2021: "If Black lives really matter, it can't only be against police abuse. It has to be against the violence that's ripping apart our communities." Indeed, as a recent Gallup poll reveals, 81 percent of African Americans want the same or more police presence in their neighborhoods, not less.[30] As for the police conduct, in 2015, for example, 965 persons (practically all men) were shot by policemen—only 4 percent of these by white policemen shooting unarmed blacks. In large part, the policemen's easy use of their guns is due to the fact that they are scared for their lives when they enter black neighborhoods or hold up black men.

Thus, the recent mass looting and riots throughout the United States, primarily carried out by people from black communities, is an indication of the deep problem most citizens of the United States genuinely want to remedy, but which no one really knows how or even where to begin. The abysmal record of earlier attempts and the reasons why they have failed—foreshadowed by the "Moynihan Report" (1965)—weigh heavily on the present. Originally titled under different semantic-normative conventions "The Negro Family: The Case for National Action", the report was authored by sociologist (and later Democratic US senator) Daniel Patrick Moynihan. He was then serving as Assistant Secretary of Labor in the Johnson administration, and the report was commissioned to advance that administration's "War on Poverty". Rather unexpectedly, the report stressed the disintegration of the nuclear black family in ghetto culture. It warned that with the growing prevalence of children with no paternal presence, all efforts to help the black community by the state might fail. The Moynihan Report was vehemently criticized at the time as stigmatizing and for "blaming the victim". However, the percentage of African American children born to unmarried mothers has since tripled from some 25 percent to about 75 percent, with the majority of them growing up with no paternal presence in the household. The comparable rate among poor whites has climbed to more than 25 percent.[31]

Conservatives have stressed that this deeply disruptive state of affairs has been greatly reinforced by social security payments that have absolved both fathers and mothers from responsibility for the care of their children and have exacerbated the poverty trap. As prominent African American conservative scholar Thomas Sowell has put it in reference to the black population: "Rates of teenage pregnancy and venereal disease had been going down for years before the new 1960s attitudes toward sex spread. . . . These downward trends suddenly reversed and skyrocketed. The murder rate had also been going down, for decades, and in 1960 was just under half of what it had been in 1934. . . . The Black family, which had survived centuries of slavery and discrimination, began rapidly disintegrating in the liberal welfare state that subsidized unwed pregnancy and changed welfare from an emergency rescue to a way of life."[32] Still, the question remains what can possibly be done now to reverse the trend without pushing children deeper into poverty and social delinquency.

The race issue elicits very strong reactions on both sides of the ideological divide. Progressives are outraged by most of the above arguments, which they regard as blasphemous and dismiss as contemptable Fox News glee. They believe conservative views are fundamentally bigoted, heartless, and immoral, as well as being willfully obstructionist. They hold that whatever the genuine problems and difficulties involved, the main thing is to change public attitudes on race, and constructively get things going. From the other side, conservatives charge progressives with selective blindness to, and militant suppression of, entire, deep-rooted, and deeply problematic aspects of reality, and indeed, of an "assault on truth". Moreover, they argue that progressives continue to project messianic visions of radical reform that have repeatedly failed in the past for the very same reasons they are likely to fail in the future.

Conclusion

Progressives highlight the remarkable march of legal, political, and normative reforms that have transformed our world during the past two to three centuries. Conservatives opposed many of these reforms at the time, whereas they are now widely accepted as commonplace, including by conservatives. Progressives suggest that the same applies to current issues and controversies. From the other side, conservatives point to major progressive visions and projects of the past—advanced by left-liberals and social democrats and achieving hegemony at the time as the inevitable dictates of reason and morality—yet proven by experience to be failures. They further claim that some past changes to which conservatives objected at the time were indeed premature, as conditions were not ripe for them then. And they add that some reforms—such as the growth of the welfare state—have reached their limit and cannot continue to expand indefinitely.

From both sides, these are valid points, and their respective weight is a matter of judgment—as well as of normative preferences. I have already cited John Stuart Mill: "A party of order or stability, and a party of progress or reform, are both necessary elements of a healthy state of political life. . . . Each of these modes of thinking derives its utility from the deficiencies of the other; but it is in a great measure the opposition of the other that keeps each within the limits of reason and sanity."[33] Hopefully, in the long run and in some dialectical way, this will prove true of the United States as well. However, in the short run, the two political-ideological sides to the American culture wars not only push each other to extremes, but also literally drive each other crazy, with each of the sides deeply convinced that the other has indeed gone crazy. They may both be right. Even the non-wearing of protective masks during the coronavirus pandemic has become politicized and an ideological emblem for some conservatives (not to mention vaccination, which has turned the tide on the disease, but about which side-effect concerns could perhaps be described as more rational and legitimate, at least initially, until clearer data accumulated).

To repeat, I claim no special expertise, wisdom, or foresight on any of the issues reviewed in this chapter. They have been discussed here as examples; one can arrive at different conclusions about the facts involved; and the suggested emphasis is on the spirit of unbiased inquiry and open mindedness in confronting them. There are of course many other ideologically divisive issues about which I am even less qualified to express an opinion. One such highly significant controversy is over the reality and prospect of global warming—its causes, potential effects, and what practically can and should be done about it—which has similarly become an ideological battleground. Before the process of mutual radicalization and polarization continues to spiral, what I suggest in this chapter is that both sides should pause and ask themselves something like the following questions: after the partly necessary offensives and counteroffensives in the culture-ideological trench war, are they making any real progress, and are they likely to defeat the other? Having virtually fought each other to a standstill, is the stalemate producing much good? Is the mutually inflicted damage not too costly for the game to continue along the same lines? Is the current "crisis of democracy" not largely due to the ideological and political impasse?[34] Are there any prospects of a return to a more constructive bipartisan approach? Or are the sides' respective ideological fixations stronger than them both?

It is extremely difficult to compromise on what is most deeply regarded as sacred principles—to say nothing of vested interests and party political calculations, partly or fully standing behind the canons of faith. Furthermore, for many, ideological identity is not merely a vehicle for realizing just causes in the world, but also a source of existential meaning, something that elevates people above the difficulties and trivialities of daily life. Still, some hard look at the facts—often obscure and partly open to conflicting interpretations as they are—might perhaps help to overcome what appears to be almost impossible to overcome.

9

Conclusion

Ideological Fixation—Now and Ever

While the previous chapter has been offered as a positive exercise in open-mindedness and the avoidance of bias in the assessment of facts, this book was undertaken with an acute awareness of how much such a venture was a forlorn hope and, indeed, with a deep sense of wonderment about this.

To the surprise of many, ideological divides and tensions in the liberal democracies have resurfaced with renewed energy after the disintegration of the post-1945 consensus. In the United States, more than anywhere else in the developed world, the ideological divide has become particularly venomous and exclusionary. There are reasons, most of them quite familiar, why the United States stands out in this respect. Although, as we have seen, an American nation, whose existence is grounded in much more than "adherence to the Constitution", is very much a reality, the country is more heterogeneous ethnically and racially, and is therefore less cohesive than more traditional national states. "Identity politics" has greatly accentuated this state of affairs.[1] Another often-mentioned reason for the recent polarization of politics in the United Sates is the practice of "gerrymandering" and the winner-takes-all electoral system, which militate against centrist politics and the traditional practice of reaching bipartisan compromises across the aisle.

More recently and crucially, there has been the opening up of the media market to a great number of radio and television outlets, followed, even more revolutionarily, by the advent of digital social networks. Although these developments have not been unique to the United States, they have reinforced the above-mentioned factors. The results are well recognized: people are closed within their favorite media outlets and social media groups, and are only exposed to the opinions and polemics of like-minded people. Moreover, they draw confidence and vigor from this shared identity and group discourse. Additionally, whereas the traditional media—whatever its shortcomings and biases—imposed

Ideological Fixation. Azar Gat, Oxford University Press. © Oxford University Press 2022.
DOI: 10.1093/oso/9780197646700.003.0009

standards of reporting and civility and functioned as gatekeepers of the public debate, the gates have now swung wide open. The tone and content of public speech has become unrestrained, aggressive, and hostile; and the ability to distinguish between real information and "fake news" has been greatly eroded. The reality and prospect of censorship by the social media networks is no less alarming. Thus, what some academic political theorists during the 1980s and 1990s celebrated as a new age of "participatory democracy" might turn out to resemble more the crowd politics—easily swayed by demagogues—which the classical and early modern philosophers blamed for the failure of Athenian democracy.

In view of this ideological polarization, the last several chapters, dealing with ideological fixations prevailing in the liberal democracies, might be hard to swallow for many readers. Many of the ideological propositions discussed have become undisputable and sanctified axioms. Not only would it be difficult for their adherents to accept that such stock ideas and factual claims about the world are largely misguided; they might also charge that I reveal my true ideological colors in criticizing them. With living ideologies, it is close to impossible for people to step out of a view of the world in which they are totally immersed—to practically step out of their skin—compromise on their normative commitments, and override their emotional investment. All these constitute who they are, their self- and group-identity and loyalty within their community of the right and righteous. Their emotional mobilization is often scarcely less intense than that which marked the great religions of the past, with ideological disputes sometimes seemingly taking forms reminiscent of the wars of religion (blissfully, in developed liberal democracies, with little bloodshed). As I wrote in the Preface, the other side is widely viewed as malicious, irrational, or downright stupid and, often, as scarcely legitimate. And the prospects of bringing even the best and the brightest—particularly the best and the brightest—on either side of an ideological divide to critically examine their camp's dogmas or consider the possibility of an even partial validity of some of the other side's arguments are very slim indeed. "But the other side are *really* like this", is a most typical response (yes, some of them are, and on your side too). And I am not talking here about Nazism, but about the main ideological and political currents in today's liberal democracies. That those who express the opposite claims are progressives or conservatives is enough to close ears and minds on both sides. Again, in this dialogue of the deaf, the arguments simply do not register and are received with a mixture of contempt and rage.

To repeat, we focus here on the factual element of ideologies, on the validity of their claims about the world, not on their normative-value element. As we have maintained throughout, the latter represents largely subjective preferences rather than facts (though they may be affected by the presence of facts). Furthermore, the differences between such preferences are often irreconcilable. If their adherents cannot arrive at some common ground, bridge the divide, and accept mutual concessions, then they have little alternative to fighting out their convictions and preferences in the public and political arena. With respect to the factual element of ideology, it is by no means suggested here that both sides to an ideological dispute are *equally* right, and that the truth necessarily lies in the middle—certainly not in the "geometrical" middle. It is only submitted that there might be *some* important truths in the arguments of the other side—that they can be, say, 40 or 30 or even 20 percent right. If so, they still deserve serious attention, consideration, and, possibly, adjustments to our own views, even if they do not change our fundamental positions. Remember the Jewish joke from the first chapter about the rabbi and his wife? A rabbi receives two people for judgment over a dispute between them. After hearing one of them he says: you are right. After hearing the other, he says: you are also right. The rabbi's wife then tells him: how can they both be right? To which the rabbi replies: you are also right. The deep truth underlying this joke is that the rabbi's statements do not necessarily violate the law of non-contradiction. As we have seen, the conceptual frameworks through which we comprehend reality are necessarily partial; and although not all propositions capture truth in equal measure, or are true at all, many of them may incorporate kernels of truth, offer suggestive perspectives, and illuminate reality from neglected angles.

An often-made criticism is that every factual statement about the world is inevitably tied up with, and therefore shaped by, value preferences—that there is no such thing as objectivity about the facts. Some have called this the "Mannheim Paradox", after the important sociologist of knowledge and ideology. Any rejection of an ideological bias is supposedly grounded in the critic's own ideological perspective and bias. However, Mannheim himself did not subscribe to the paradox later coined after him. He indeed stressed the context-dependence of all observations about the world. He pointed out that facts are not understood in isolation but are viewed from within a particular social context and reflect values and impulses that shape the questions we ask and the perspectives through which we interpret the world. At the same time, he argued that awareness of this should make us more objective. Because every point of view is limited, he thought it best to consider and take into account as many conflicting perspectives as possible, and be flexible and dialectical rather than rigid and dogmatic. As he wrote: "a total view implies both assimilation and transcendence of the limitations of particular points of view."[2] "Total" was not the best choice of word, which I believe did not reflect Mannheim's actual meaning. The concept of absolute objectivity is as misleading as that of absolute truth; for although we cannot encompass the totality of the world, there is more or less objectivity in the same way that there is more or less truth to our comprehension of the world. Both truth and objectivity should not be viewed as absolutes but as a matter of degree, and what a difference there is between more or less of them.

I share Mannheim's attitude. I suspect that by now I might have irked not a few readers who may think that I hold a pretense to some superior knowledge, an Olympian perspective above that of the ideological crowds or an Archimedean point on which to rest my judgments. However, as you can learn from my discussion of truth, I hold no special pretense to it. Certainly, I have strong opinions about subjects I have studied in depth, and in general I do not lack opinions or normative preferences. At the same time, while not fully subscribing to Socrates' hyperbolic dictum "I know that I know nothing", which supposedly made him wiser than others, I identify with the sense of cognitive modesty that it implies. So what I actually claim is a considerable intellectual and emotional openness to often-conflicting arguments, together with an acute sensitivity to ideological biases—without any of this entailing a lack of strong intellectual and normative commitments on my part. You may be familiar with the famous Gestalt images where people can view, in the same picture—alternatingly, but not at the same time—a rabbit or a duck, a vase or human faces, a bearded man or a naked female beauty, a young woman or an old lady. I claim some ability to comprehend both images at the same time (not really, only metaphorically).

Of course, Mannheim was not alone in maintaining such an approach to reality. Here are some expressions of various aspects of such an approach. Johann Wolfgang Goethe (cited with approval by Mill) preached holism: "Let us be many-sided! Turnips are good, but they are best mixed with chestnuts. And these two noble products of the earth grow far apart."[3] As Scott Fitzgerald has put it: "The test of a first-rate intelligence is the ability to hold two opposed ideas in mind at the same time and still retain the ability to function." Amid the fury and zeal of the ideological debates that divided the Jewish community in pre-state Israel-Palestine of the 1930s and 1940s, Amos Oz's mother, Fania, he tells us in *A Tale of Love and Darkness*: "just sat silent, smiling faintly, as though she was trying to decipher from their argument why Mr. Zarchi maintained that particular view and Mr. Hanani the opposite one: would the argument be any different if they suddenly changed around, and each defended the other's position while attacking the one he had argued for previously?"

It is not that the profound ideological controversies that raged in pre-state Israel were of no consequence; on the contrary, they revolved around questions that had crucial bearings on the reality and on the future of the Zionist project. Some of them are still with us in today's Israel, and are equally fateful. At the same time, Fania Oz's partial detachment and natural openness may remind us of the great changes and shifts in both reality and doctrine that have affected all the ideologies involved (again, not necessarily in equal measure)—the undermining or demise of so many ideological certainties that were, in the spirit of the times, held to be beyond dispute among the adherents of the various creeds.

In his beautiful essay "Fathers and Children: Turgenev and the Liberal Predicament", the Oxford sage Isaiah Berlin describes Turgenev's mind as follows (Berlin just as well might have been writing about himself):

> was painfully preoccupied with the controversies, moral and polit-
> ical, social and personal, which divided the educated Russians of his
> day; in particular, the profound and bitter conflicts between Slavophil
> nationalists and admirers of the west, conservatives and liberals, liberals
> and radicals, moderates and fanatics, realists and visionaries, above all
> between old and young. He tried to stand aside and see the scene ob-
> jectively. He did not always succeed. But because he was an acute and
> responsive observer, self-critical and self-effacing both as a man and as
> a writer . . . he proved a better prophet than the two self-centred, angry
> literary giants [Tolstoy and Dostoevsky], with whom he is usually
> compared, and discerned the birth of social issues which have grown
> world-wide since his day.[4]

Note how relevant this remains: "Turgenev regarded [the radical and Slavophil criticism of Western civilization] . . . as a violent exaggeration. . . . Of course the Germans were pompous and ridiculous; Louis Napoleon and the profiteers of Paris were odious, but the civilisation of the west was not crumbling. It was the greatest achievement of mankind."[5] At the same time, " 'He felt and under-stood the opposite sides of life', said Henry James of him, 'our Anglo-Saxon, Protestant, moralistic conventional standards were far away from him. . . . half the charm of conversation with him was that one breathed an air in which cant phrases . . . simply sounded ridiculous.'"[6]

Turgenev deeply felt the plight of his native country, whose vast population of peasant-serfs was steeped in backwardness—hopeless in the foreseeable future—and whose rule by an oppressive autocracy, exploitative aristocratic es-tate owners, and corrupt bureaucracy was both a consequence and a cause of this condition. He identified with the strong moral impulse of the small and inef-fectual intellectual circles in Russia that aspired to revolutionize and redeem the country, either according to a liberal or socialist Western program or along some "Slavophil" lines. At the same time, he was painfully aware of the disconnect between the lofty ideals and depressing realities, and, moreover, of the dangers and calamities that this disconnect might bring if attempts were to be made to translate visions into reality. The tragic history of Russia since then, well into the present, is a dire testimony to this gap between compelling ideals and even more compelling realities. And yet, as we have seen, the same gap, and the terrible dangers and impossible choices it harbors, is still very much with us today with respect to parts of the developing world.

As Berlin writes: "The doubts Turgenev raised have not been stilled. The dilemma of morally sensitive, honest, and intellectually responsible men at a time of acute polarisation of opinion has, since his time, grown acute and worldwide."[7] Ideals and moral visions are capable of radically changing reality—and have done so throughout history. At the same time, some ideals might bring about disasters and human misery of horrendous proportions. This might be so either because of the nature of the ideals themselves, or because what otherwise may be considered worthy ideals might, in their clash with "objective conditions", produce results that are far worse than the existing situation.

The history of ideologies should teach modesty, or at least warn against fixations and biases. This does not exempt us from taking stands on current issues, some of them crucial and sometimes requiring a very firm stand. Moreover, the intrinsic tension between normative principles and the constraints of reality is very difficult to overcome. We think according to rule and principle, our magical cognitive device to distill both factual and normative simplicity and order from a complex reality. Moral clarity in particular, sticking to one's principles, is universally regarded as an admirable virtue. Furthermore, as we have seen, psychological research indicates that it is the morality of good intentions that guides our normative apparatus. By contrast, the morality of consequences—often conflicting with "good intentions", but sometimes being the approach that can guard against great humanitarian disasters—is far less natural to us, and requires a slow and difficult cognitive process to accept. This is why the notion that what is at stake is simply a matter of doing the right thing has such a strong appeal in people's minds. Hence the mood expressed in the once famous saying that "it is better to be wrong with Sartre than right with Aron". Indeed, partly because of the way our natural moral mechanism is built and the sense of moral purity, dedication, and vigor, everything went Sartre's way and that of the circle around him: the intellectual and social hype, the trendy coffeeshop gatherings, the fun parties, and the admiring attention of young women.

The Intellectuals' Occupational Hazard

On the face of it, intellectuals—people who are professionally engaged with abstract, general ideas about human affairs and the world—should be the most sensitive and most immune to ideological fixations and biases. After all, they are trained to detect and point them out; regularly do so in their historical and sociological analyses of class and privilege; are well versed in concepts such as "false consciousness" and the "Whig interpretation of history"; and are familiar with past certainties that achieved consensual status in their time but later were proven more fallible, as perspectives and intellectual fashions changed. And yet intellectuals—both inside and outside academia—appear to be particularly prone to ideological fixations and biases, while rarely ascribing them to, or suspecting them in, themselves. Indeed, ideological fixations seem to be their particular occupational hazard. Just consider the record described in the last chapters, and there is much more, of course. I am far from the first to make this point, which is rarely taken kindly by my fellow tradesmen. They often label it "anti-intellectualism", an assault on the very keepers of wisdom and truth. Many of those who regard it as their duty to express an opinion on and criticize everything under the sun are revealed to be incapable of taking criticism themselves, let alone taking it in. They tend to exhibit that most typical human bias toward the self, close ranks like any trade union, genuinely feel insulted and threatened, and vehemently express their indignation at the "slanders".

A sense of proportion and balance is called for in this regard as well. Scholars in all fields generate a huge amount of genuine information and constantly expand the frontiers of knowledge, a process without which modern developed civilization cannot be imagined—indeed, cannot exist. In the same way, the generation of ideas in the public and political field, many of which arise from a professional class of intellectuals, is crucial for the development of any civilization—our modern one in particular. Errors are inevitable in this process; and yet ideologically motivated fixations and biases are not simple errors. It should also be added that blatant ideological fixations and biases are probably exhibited mostly by a small, ideologically committed and vocal minority among intellectuals and academics. At the same time, as we have seen, its influence on entire fields and subjects of research, especially in the publicly and politically relevant humanities and social sciences, has often been sweeping and decisive. Although people's views are not immune to evidence, and individuals differ considerably in the extent of their ideological commitment, addiction, and zeal, the sway of ideology is tremendous.

There are some obvious reasons why intellectuals as a social category are particularly vulnerable to ideological fixations and biases: the habit of talking *ex-cathedra*, from the authority of their position, which might breed intellectual hubris; the feeling that their special professional knowledge and skills—even though it is usually limited to a particular and sometimes rather esoteric field of specialty—gives them a superior perspective on and special duty with respect to the major questions of the day; the considerable powers of articulation that often come with the trade; and, indeed, the fact that, as they say in German, *Papier ist geduldig*, paper is patient and tolerant—it offers little resistance. Dealing with ideas, which are manipulated so much more easily than reality, intellectuals are often tempted to dictate the rule to the world. Indeed, they tend to be isolated in their ivory towers and lack practical experience in the messy affairs of the world.

Of course, there are many first-rate, extremely smart minds around in academia and among intellectuals. At the same time, there is a great deal of mediocrity that can sometimes be sufficient for professional achievements in a chosen scholarly field. Furthermore, even the musings of brilliant scholars might prove embarrassing when they venture beyond their professional fields. Alas, this is my impression of much of what is going on—with the least bit of self-awareness—on the academic social networks to which I am subscribed by virtue of my profession. In a somewhat similar vein, I remember an episode from my early days in academia, when a senior member of my department told me about his impressions from the Friday evening social gatherings in his home of some very respected scholars at the time. In Israel it is quite common to talk politics in such social gatherings—politics is the national pastime. So what do they say, I asked. Nothing that is distinguishable from or more remarkable than the opinions you would otherwise hear in any such Friday evening social gathering, he wryly replied. Scholars who in their professional work may exhibit the greatest subtlety and discerning powers in analyzing currents and sub-currents in other periods and cultures are all too often reduced to shallow pamphlet-style opinions with respect to major questions of the day.

Again, I am not the first to note that intellectuals are particularly vulnerable to ideological fixations and biases of a fanciful nature. Probably the most striking criticism ever, compressed into one sentence, came from George Orwell: "There are some ideas so absurd that only an intellectual could believe them, no ordinary man could be such a fool." In his *The Opium of the Intellectuals* (1955), Raymond Aron criticized what he regarded as the mass craze for communist redemption and the justification of totalitarianism and its worst horrors that dominated the French intellectual scene at the time. He argued that the problem was in large part due to intellectuals' intrinsic conceit, alienation from the real world, addiction to half-baked visions of human salvation, and, not least, herd mentality. The last point strikingly clashes with their self-perception of fierce individuality. This dissonance finds expression in the quip: "why can't you be a nonconformist just like everybody else?"

Certainly, the question of intellectuals' active involvement in the great ideological issues of the day is a very serious one. The principle of *wertfrei* scholarship, scholarship that should be "value-free" and stick to the facts, guided the great German academic tradition of the nineteenth and early twentieth centuries. It has been blamed for the silence and docility of the German academic and intellectual establishment, most notably with respect to the rise of Nazism. Moreover, it has been regarded as a false pretense, as many in this establishment supported the nineteenth-century Prussian autocratic state or were in various degrees fellow-travelers of Nazism. Indeed, the scholarly claims of many of them, far from being "value-free", were closely affected by their ideological views.

In his iconic *The Betrayal of the Intellectuals* (1927), French thinker and novelist Julien Benda denounced what he saw as intellectuals' increased identification with the "passions" that engulf modern mass society. "And do not those who are subject to such emotions now all tend *to say the same thing?*", he wrote (emphases in the original). "Political passions, as passions, seem to have attained the habit of discipline. . . . It is easy to see what increased strength they [the intellectuals] acquired thereby."[8] Embracing ideologies such as nationalism, socialism, antisemitism, and fascism, intellectuals, who, according to Benda, had previously stood aloof from daily politics *"began to play the game of political passions."*[9] Benda was clearly naive about many things, including his idealized view of intellectuals in earlier history and the sharp distinction he drew between intellectuals and the masses. He was also naive in his belief in universal morality, purity, and spirituality that intellectuals should espouse, as opposed to particularistic doctrines he thought they should avoid. Indeed, while Benda was right in claiming that intellectuals often wander astray in succumbing to "passions", he is open to the criticism that intellectuals must get involved in the crucial affairs of the day. In the wake of Nazism and the struggle against racial segregation and discrimination in the United States from the 1950s and 1960s on, the view that intellectuals had a duty to take a public stand has gained the upper hand, and for very good reasons. Intellectuals have made major contributions to many important developments in the liberal democracies. At the same time, they have been responsible for some highly influential, often ideologically driven errors and missteps in the interpretation of reality, which, by shaping opinion, has greatly influenced reality itself.

Criticisms of the weaknesses and failings of the intellectual class have much increased over recent decades, some of which has been made by less eminent names than Orwell or Aron. While not rendering these criticisms any less valid, it has made them easier to ward off and dismiss. All the same, given the long and impressive catalogue of intellectuals' ideological fixations, biases, and errors of the kind described earlier in this book, this growing criticism was only to be expected. There has been a considerable loss of confidence in and growing skepticism of the authority and trustworthiness of their views, with some critics going as far as viewing the opinions of "eggheads" as particularly misleading. A typical saying that expresses this mood is that "soundness is more important than brilliance". There have been other contributing factors behind the diminishing stature of intellectuals in the public arena. Far more people now attend institutions of higher education than was the case until the 1960s and 1970s. While this has exposed college graduates more widely to the prevailing intellectual and ideological currents, it also has made them more confident in intellectual matters, previously completely dominated by the intellectual class. Additionally, this class itself has expanded from a relatively small group of intellectuals and professors to a numerically large category, with all the inflationary effects that this development has entailed.

There has been another side to the coin, of course. Criticism and distrust of intellectuals' irrational fixations, biases, and gross errors have bred—on the margins and then at the core of the public scene—a no less, indeed, a possibly greater problem: popular anti-rationalism. Boorish ignorance, the spread of wild conspiracy theories, and an offhand dismissal of relevant knowledge—with a strong backwind from the Oval Office—cannot be the right response to intellectual hubris. Reason—open-minded and self-critical—remains the key to our species' tremendous success.

Some Final Observations

Ideological clashes, antagonism, and fixations are as old as civilization. Is there a rationale that can explain when ideological divides become more prevalent and more acute? The states and rulers of premodern societies strove to monopolize the ideological scene that prescribed the nature of the cosmos and of the social order within it. However, not infrequently there were divisions within the elite, with the clergy, aristocracy, and literati developing competing ideologies and counter-ideologies. Of these, the literate religious ideologies were to become particularly powerful, eventually spreading across state lines and becoming major foci of identification. States strove to co-opt them, lived alongside them and other ideological brands in a somewhat uneasy coexistence, or sometimes violently clashed with them. The more authoritarian the regime, the more hegemonic ideologically it could be, but also the more intense the occasional eruptions of opposition, conflicts of interests, and ideological antagonisms might be. With modernity, the major, universal, ideologies or "secular religions" again extended across state borders, representing major alternative responses to the challenges of the industrial age. Whereas the new totalitarian regimes imposed unprecedented levels of ideological uniformity and conformity, in open liberal societies, ideological pluralism has become the norm. In general, the more divided a society along class and economic lines or in terms of identity, the more polarized ideologically it is likely to be.

Our interest in this book is the nature and deep roots of the ideological mode of thinking, with its resulting, no less intrinsic, ideological fixations and biases. Had this study been confined to the psychological discipline, we would have cited at much greater length the prolific and highly valuable literature on various aspects of the phenomenon: the evidence for cognitive closure, active reluctance to learn about the positions of the other side, and avoidance of cognitive dissonance;[10] the relation of ideological orientation to deep personality traits,[11] to different basic modes of comprehending the world, and, indeed, to satisfaction with life (conservatives tend to be more content[12]). Some of these traits have been found to have innate roots, which may be activated by particular issues and debates. Here, however, are some broader explanatory factors we have emphasized throughout this book.

Humans employ simplified conceptual frameworks and normative cues to make sense of and cope with the infinite complexity of the natural and social world. This is the magical devise that has made our species' amazing trajectory possible, and it relies on our unique capacity for social learning. It is patently impossible for any individual to generate all the knowledge and know-how of the world by him- or herself. One inevitably acquires and assimilates a vast amount of socially accumulated wisdom—stands on the shoulders of others, on a giant cultural and conceptual edifice. We adopt and conform to a cognitive and normative map that guides our interpretation of reality, and we work within genres and templates. As I have already suggested, the ideological mode of thinking may belong to a different category from the two Daniel Kahneman described as "fast" and "slow". It combines highly complex interpretations of and emotional-behavioral reactions to the world, for which we rely on acquired, ready-made, and deeply internalized templates to produce instant, reflex-like attitudes and propositions.

There is a strong intrinsic tension between the cognitive and normative aspects of ideology. Whereas some people are more attuned to the structure, constrains—and potentialities—of reality, others (and, indeed, whole disciplines) are more oriented toward principles and norms. More important, we tend to be highly biased toward what we desire and regard as desirable. As Marx, with only some exaggeration, has made us all very aware, ideological differences are not just an expression of disinterested cognition. They are more typically a rationalized product of "interest", and therefore represent "false consciousness"—"where you stand depends on where you sit".[13] This does not, however, mean that there is only "interest", and no factual truth and falsity, in ideological debates. As quite a few scholars, from Mannheim on, have pointed out—refining and amending Marx—ideologies are two-pronged: they often incorporate very significant truths about reality while, at the same time, being wholly harnessed to, and biased toward, their social mission to change the world in their image. This mission is their true yardstick, whose realization, however, is not entirely independent of their picture of reality. For obvious reasons, evolution has put the premium on the mobilization of every resource—including our very considerable powers of argumentation—to advance our cause in the never-ending game of social bargaining and resulting social bickering. Rallying around the flag and not giving up a single inch to the other side is often the most effective tactic in social bargaining, which is the reason this behavioral pattern is deeply embedded in us. In many cases, however, it creates a boomerang effect, as the other side might escalate its resistance, radicalize, and itself grow less compromising. Moreover, if our factual roadmap or manual for navigating reality is misleading, we may find that our social-normative objectives cannot be realized.

Still, the sense of shared communal identity and belonging, and the confidence in numbers, are major elements of the ideological phenomenon, even, or especially, if the group in question is a minority one. Closing ranks is both a key to success and product of the acquired nature of our ideological persuasions, as ideologies constitute an entire culture or sub-culture into which people are socialized. The culture's cognitive and normative scripts determine what is reasonable and acceptable in the social discourse and what should be fought against as evil, heretical, or blasphemous. This does not mean that people do not sometimes change persuasions, cultures, and ideological camps, as paradigmatic crises, collapses, and shifts occasionally occur. But, as a rule, people tend to be convinced, loyal, and emphatic captives of their ideological culture or sub-culture, and ideological clashes often take the form of full-scale culture wars. Each ideology projects its own particular mythology, sacred history, icons, prophets, heroes, saints, martyrs, villains, and demons. Not only do people close their ears to the opposite arguments; they are also prone to resort to smear, character assassination, and witch-hunt as their most authentic gut response. Reading comments sections in online newspapers, it never ceases to amaze me how this is many people's weapon of first resort. Again, the evolutionary logic behind ideological self-righteousness and stark antagonism is quite obvious. Robert Kurzban whimsically but all too accurately titled his book on this phenomenon: *Why Everyone (Else) Is a Hypocrite* (2010). Being aware of this syndrome typically offers very little help in this regard. Our intrinsic biases are stronger than us.

It is never redundant to repeat that all this does not imply that the issues that ideologies engage are not important. On the contrary, they often represent the starkest of normative choices and programs for the world that are of crucial significance for individual and social life. Ideologies are the powerful templates for shaping the societies we live in. At the same time, the long catalogue of past fixations and errors associated with what adherents to the creed used to hold as absolute and sacred certainties should teach caution, intellectual restraint, and constant self-examination in the light of experience. The problem is that distortions of reality that seem clearer in hindsight and in relation to bygone ideologies appear invisible in living ones. People within the mold are practically incapable of recognizing them. As in the stock market, the trend is stronger than everything. As in the fashion industry, only this year's style looks quite right. People tend to march along with the bandwagon, identifying themselves with the spirit of the time and mixing both conviction and commitment with prudent conformity in various and often indistinguishable measures. Ideologies are tsunami-like, and their massive waves tend to carry all before them.

Thus, an interest in breaking the mold of ideological fixation—to the extent that such an interest exists—encounters stupendous difficulties. It might be motivated by either a greater concern for the truth value of ideology or by the apprehension that misconceptions about reality might weaken the cause or lead to its failure. Illumination on both the huge problems and partial solutions involved is shed by the most rigorous large-scale study of people's ability to correctly predict major political events. It was conducted by political psychologist Philip Tetlock and his team over a long period of time, and its results are quite surprising and humbling. It found that experts fail to predict future events in their fields of specialty. Their rate of success is no greater than that of random probability, which is no different from the success rate of non-experts. There is, however, a more positive find, equally non-trivial. It turns out that there is a group in the population that stands out in its ability to forecast (short-term) future events, beating both random probability and everybody else. Tetlock calls them "superforecasters". The reasons he has found for both the failure and success of prediction are eye-opening. The evidence shows that experts typically fall victim to their preconceptions and overconfidence. More significant still, those who are captive of great ideas have been found to err the most. Furthermore, they tend not to admit their failure, deny they were wrong, and resist all change to their forecast, insisting that in the end they will prove right. By contrast, "the superforecasters"—ordinary people, not marked by particularly higher intelligence—typically exhibit intellectual openness, cautiousness, curiosity, and, above all, self-criticism. They are less emotionally invested in their assessments, less bound by ego, and have fewer problems changing their mind and admitting error. Finally (in the spirit of Goethe, Fitzgerald, and Mannheim), they tend to combine different perspectives and diverging points of view in their analyses of the situations at hand.[14] Indeed, both experts and ordinary people should draw a lesson from these findings. Reason is still our signature tool for coping with a complex reality, yet it is easily subverted by overconfidence, cognitive closure, and biases.

What else is there to add to these hard data–based findings? It is interesting to know to what extent the personality traits revealed in Tetlock's experiments are more innate or more learned. My guess is that the former is more significant, though the latter might have a contribution, and a process of self-education through life and strict self-discipline along these lines might help. Nonattachment to ego and identity in questions of fact and in admitting mistakes, as well as openness to the arguments of the other side, is crucial. Given the great difficulties of all this, we are exceedingly prone to ideological fixations, with intellectuals perhaps more vulnerable to them than other categories of the population. Many will not welcome this message, and, moreover, will probably charge that I, and the views expressed in this book, are every bit victims of the phenomenon of ideological fixation I pretend to lay bare. Maybe. Such criticism cannot be helped. After all, the message of this book is that the first (and often last), instinctive, question that people ask themselves is whether the person to whose views they are exposed belongs to our or the opposite camp. I leave the claim of my possible ideological fixations to the judgment of readers. Perhaps the ideas expressed in this book will strike a chord with some of them.

NOTES

Chapter 1

1. Thomas Nagel, *Mortal Questions* (Cambridge: Cambridge University Press, 1979), chap. 12.
2. The school's ideas have mainly survived in the work of the presumably second-century author Sextus Empiricus, *Outlines of Scepticism* (Cambridge: Cambridge University Press, 2000). Here see: bk. i, sections 49–78.
3. Aristotle, *Metaphysics* IV.1011b.
4. Plato, *Cratylus* 385b, *Sophist* 263b.
5. Plato, *The Republic*, Bk vii, sections 514a–520a.
6. René Descartes, *Meditations on First Philosophy* (Cambridge: Cambridge UP, 1996 [1641]).
7. George Berkeley, *A Treatise Concerning the Principles of Human Knowledge*, 1710.
8. James Boswell, *The Life of Samuel Johnson* (New York: John Dearborn, 1833 [1791]), i.209.
9. For Wilfrid Sellars's "the myth of the given", see his "Empiricism and the Philosophy of Mind", in his *Science, Perception and Reality* (Atascadero, CA: Ridgeview, 1991 [1963]), 127–196; also, John McDowell, *Mind and World* (Cambridge MA: Harvard University Press, 1996).
10. Sextus Empiricus, *Outlines of Scepticism*, i.178–179.
11. Marcus Aurelius, *Meditations* (London: Blackie, 1910), 2.15.
12. Willard Van Orman Quine, "Two Dogmas of Empiricism", *Philosophical Review* 60 (1951): 20–43, and *Word and Object* (Cambridge, MA: MIT Press, 1964); Quine and J. S. Ullian, *The Web of Belief* (New York: McGraw-Hill, 1978 [1970]); Sellars, *Science, Perception and Reality*; Donald Davidson, *Inquiries into Truth and Interpretation* (Oxford: Oxford University Press, 2001 [1984]), *Problems of Rationality* (Oxford: Oxford University Press, 2004), and *Truth, Language, and History* (Oxford: Oxford University Press, 2005); Hilary Putnam, *Reason, Truth and History* (Cambridge: Cambridge University Press, 1981). A first-class popular exposition is Sean Carroll, *The Big Picture: On the Origins of Life, Meaning, and the Universe Itself* (New York: Dutton, 2016). Some of the philosophical traditions synthesized into the above view include "holism" and "coherence"; see Harold Joachim, *The Nature of Truth* (Oxford: Oxford University Press, 1906), developing on the ideas of F. H. Bradley and the British idealist school.
13. Quoted in Plato, *Cratylus*, 402a.
14. Sextus Empiricus, *Outlines of Scepticism*, i.181–184.
15. Aristotle, *Metaphysics*, IV.1010a.
16. Putnam, *Reason, Truth and History*, 54–55.
17. See his collected articles in Max Weber, *The Methodology of the Social Sciences* (New York: Free Press, 1949).
18. Maudemarie Clark, *Nietzsche on Truth and Philosophy* (New York: Cambridge University Press, 1990), is one of the more recent attempts to make sense of this long-noted contradiction. She suggests that Nietzsche moved from a denial of both metaphysics and truth in his

early works to a more discerning view in his last works, which rejected only metaphysics while affirming a version of truth as perspectivist correspondence.

19. Friedrich Nietzsche, *The Will to Power* (London: Weidenfeld & Nicolson, 1967), §481.

20. Cf. Quine and Ullian, *The Web of Belief*, 5.

21. See note 12 above. In addition, see Ralph Walker, *The Coherence Theory of Truth: Realism, Anti-Realism, Idealism* (London: Routledge, 1989).

22. Terrence Deacon, *The Symbolic Species: The Co-Evolution of Language and the Brain* (New York: W. W. Norton, 1997), 434.

23. Weber, *The Methodology of the Social Sciences*.

24. Molière, *Le malade imaginaire*, Act III, Sc. iii.

25. Clare O'Farrell, *Michel Foucault* (London: Sage, 2005), 23.

26. Putnam, *Reason, Truth and History*, 54.

27. Charles Taylor, *A Secular Age* (Cambridge MA: Harvard University Press, 2007), is a most erudite study of this development by a prominent philosopher, who at same time seeks to salvage "transcendence" from the threat of naturalism.

28. Putnam, *Reason, Truth and History*, 156–158.

29. Michel Foucault, *History of Madness* (New York: Routledge, 2006 [1961]).

30. From Jacques Derrida's voluminous work see, for example, his *Of Grammatology* (Baltimore: Johns Hopkins University Press, 1976 [French original 1967]). Of the legion of his critics see John Ellis, *Against Deconstruction* (Princeton, NJ: Princeton University Press, 1989).

31. Although mathematics is definitely not my field, I tend to be in full agreement here with (indeed, was happy to discover) George Lakoff and Rafael Núñez, *Where Mathematics Comes From: How the Embodied Mind Brings Mathematics into Being* (New York: Basic Books, 2000), Introduction, 344–346, and *passim*.

32. Thomas Kuhn, *The Structure of Scientific Revolutions* (Chicago: University of Chicago Press, 1962); Paul Feyerabend, *Against Method* (New York: Verso, 1993 [1975]).

33. For this view, see most notably Richard Boyd, "Scientific Realism and Naturalistic Epistemology Source", *Proceedings of the Biennial Meeting of the Philosophy of Science Association* (1980), 2:613–662. Two collections of papers represent both sides of the debate: Jarrett Leplin, ed., *Scientific Realism* (Berkeley: University of California Press, 1984); Patrick Greenough and Michael Lynch, eds., *Truth and Realism* (Oxford: Oxford University Press, 2006).

34. See along these lines: Richard Rorty, *Consequences of Pragmatism: Essays 1972–1980* (Minneapolis: University of Minnesota Press, 1982); Larry Laudan, "A Confutation of Convergent Realism", in *Scientific Realism*, ed. Leplin, 218–249.

35. In Leplin, *Scientific Realism*, see especially: Ernan McMullin, "A Case for Scientific Realism", 8–40; and Jarrett Leplin, "Truth and Scientific Progress", 193–217. Also, Michael Devitt, "Scientific Realism", in *Truth and Realism*, ed. Greenough and Lynch, 100–124.

36. Rorty, *Consequences of Pragmatism*, 163.

37. Rorty, *Consequences of Pragmatism*, 163.

38. Richard Rorty, *Truth and Progress: Philosophical Papers* (Cambridge: Cambridge University Press, 1998), 3:74.

39. In addition to the collection of essays cited above, Rorty, *Philosophy and the Mirror of Nature* (Princeton, NJ: Princeton University Press, 1979), is the original and most elaborate, though perhaps less engaging, exposition of his views. See also R. B. Brandom, ed., *Rorty and His Critics* (Oxford: Blackwell, 2000).

40. The view of concepts in terms of linguistic conventions is traced back to philosopher John Austin and his criticism of the naive "isometric" view of correspondence propounded by Bertrand Russell and the early Wittgenstein. Richard Kirkham, *Theories of Truth: A Critical Introduction* (Cambridge, MA: MIT Press, 2001 [1992]), 119, 124, refers to these opposing views of correspondence as "correlation" vs. "congruence".

41. Cf. Putnam's critique in his *Reason, Truth and History*, chap. 5.

42. See very acutely: Kirkham, *Theories of Truth*.

43. Rorty, *Truth and Progress*, 20.

44. Ernst Cassirer, *An Essay on Man: An Introduction to a Philosophy of Human Culture* (Garden City, NY: Doubleday, n.d. [1944]), 35–37, 42, and 43 (quotation).

Chapter 2

1. Among Plato's dialogues, those mostly concerned with morality, knowledge as virtue, and reason leading the pleasures are: *Protagoras, Gorgias, The Republic,* and *Philebus*. For the immortal soul as reflecting the immutable *logos* of the world: *Phaedo, The Republic, Phaedrus,* and *Timaeus*.

2. Aristotle, Nicomachean *Ethics*, Bk I, articles 4–5, 13.

3. Plato, *The Republic*, I.338.

4. "The Principal Doctrines: Diogenes Laertius", 10.139–154, article 33; also 31, and 34–38, in *The Epicurus Reader: Selected Writings and Testimonia*, trans. and ed. B. Inwood and L. P. Gerson (Indianapolis: Hackett, 1994), 35–36.

5. Voltaire, "Epître à l'auteur du livre des *trois imposteurs*," in *Œuvres complètes de Voltaire* (Paris: Garnier, 1877–1885 [1768]), 10:402–405.

6. See A. J. Ayer, *Language, Truth and Logic* (London: Penguin, 1971 [1936]), chap. 6; Charles Stevenson, *Ethics and Language* (New Haven, CT: Yale University Press, 1944); R. M. Hare, *The Language of Morals* (Oxford: Oxford University Press, 1952).

7. David Hume, *A Treatise of Human Nature* (1739–1740), Bk I, Pt III, Section xiv.

8. David Hume, *An Inquiry Concerning the Principles of Morals* (1751), secs. 2–3.

9. Ibid., sec. iv, article 170.

10. Ibid., sec. v, article 173.

11. Ibid., sec. v, articles 174–79; appendix ii, articles 247–254.

12. Hume, *Treatise of Human Nature*, Bk III, Pt I, section i.

13. Hume, *Treatise of Human Nature*, Bk III, Pt I, section i; *Inquiry Concerning the Principles of Morals*, sec. i, articles 134–137; appendix i.

14. Hume, *Treatise of Human Nature*, Bk II, Pt III, section iii.

15. Ibid.

16. John Searle, "How to Derive 'Ought' from 'Is' ", *Philosophical Review* 73 (1964): 43–58. Also, Hilary Putnam, *Reason, Truth and History* (Cambridge: Cambridge University Press, 1981), chaps. 6 and 9; Donald Davidson, *Problems of Rationality* (Oxford: Oxford University Press, 2004), 16, 26.

17. Cf. Owen Flanagan, Aaron Ancell, Stephen Martin, and Gordon Steenbergen, "Empiricism and Normative Ethics: What Do the Biology and the Psychology of Morality Have to Do with Ethics?", in *Evolved Morality: The Biology and Philosophy of Human Conscience*, ed. F. De Waal, P. Smith, T. Pievani, and S. Parmigiani (Leiden: Brill, 2014), 73–92; Philip Kitcher, *The Ethical Project* (Cambridge, MA: Harvard University Press, 2011), chap. 7; also, ever sensible, Sean Carroll, *The Big Picture: On the Origins of Life, Meaning, and the Universe Itself* (New York: Dutton, 2016), chap. 46.

18. Again cf. Flanagan et al. in "Empiricism and Normative Ethics".

19. Hume, *Inquiry Concerning the Principles of Morals*, appendix ii, article 250; my emphasis.

20. Ibid., appendix ii, articles 250–251; also 252.

21. David Hume, *Dialogues Concerning Natural Religion* (1779). For a summary of the ancient Greek schools see Marcus Tullius Cicero, *De natura deorum* (On the Nature of the Gods), which influenced Hume.

22. Charles Darwin, *The Descent of Man and Selection in Relation to Sex* (Cambridge: Cambridge University Press, 2009 [1871]), 78.

23. Ibid., 71–72.

24. Ibid., 78.

25. See, for example, Steven Pinker, *The Blank Slate: The Modern Denial of Human Nature* (New York: Penguin, 2003).

26. John Mackie, *Ethics: Inventing Right and Wrong* (London: Pelican, 1977), 43.

27. Ibid., 192; also 113.

28. Notably, though, in a later, very insightful review of Dawkins's book and shortly before Mackie's death, he admirably kept abreast of this new line of investigation: John Mackie, "The Law of the Jungle: Moral Alternatives and Principles of Evolution", *Philosophy* 53, no. 206 (1978): 455–464.

29. Cited by P. Railton, "Moral Realism", *Philosophical Review* 95 (1986): 163–207, quote from 200.

30. For presentations of the various objectivist-realist positions see: David Sidorsky, "Incomplete Routes to Moral Objectivity: Four Variants of Naturalism", *Social Philosophy and Policy* 18, no. 2 (2001): 177–217; Russ Shafer-Landau, *Moral Realism: A Defence* (Oxford: Oxford University Press, 2003).

31. John Rawls, *A Theory of Justice* (Cambridge, MA: Harvard University Press, 1971); Davidson, *Problems of Rationality*, 47–52; Marc Hauser, *Moral Minds: The Nature of Right and Wrong* (New York: HarperCollins, 2006); John Mikhail, "Universal Moral Grammar: Theory, Evidence, and the Future", *Trends in Cognitive Science* 11 (2007): 143–152.

32. Noam Chomsky, *The Minimalist Program* (Cambridge, MA: MIT Press, 1995); Marc Hauser, Noam Chomsky, and W. Fitch, "The Faculty of Language: What Is It, Who Has It, and How Did It Evolve?", *Science* 298, no. 5598 (November 2002): 1569–1579.

33. Putnam, *Reason, Truth and History*, 147; John McDowell, "Values and Secondary Qualities", in *Essays on Moral Realism*, ed. G. Sayre-McCord (Ithaca: Cornell University Press, 1988), 166–180; Daniel Robinson, *Praise and Blame: Moral Realism and Its Applications* (Princeton, NJ: Princeton University Press, 2002).

34. Hume, *Treatise of Human Nature*, Bk IIII, Pt I, Section i.

35. Our greater disagreement on moral values was stressed by Gilbert Harman, *The Nature of Morality: An Introduction to Ethics* (Oxford: Oxford University Press, 1977). But for a fuller criticism of the difference here, similar to mine, see Michael Smith, *Ethics and the A Priori: Selected Essays on Moral Psychology and Meta-Ethics* (Cambridge: Cambridge University Press, 2004), chap. 12.

36. Cf. Shaun Nichols, *Sentimental Rules: On the Natural Foundations of Moral Judgment* (New York: Oxford University Press, 2004), chap. 3; Jesse Prinz, *The Emotional Construction of Morals* (New York: Oxford University Press, 2007), 42–47.

37. Putnam, *Reason, Truth and History*, 133–147; Putnam, *Ethics without Ontology* (Cambridge, MA: Harvard University Press, 2004), 71–78; Terence Cuneo, *The Normative Web: An Argument for Moral Realism* (Oxford: Oxford University Press, 2007).

38. Interestingly, it was Putnam's main partner in developing the philosophy of scientific realism, Richard Boyd, who has drawn attention to the problems that should be taken into account when considering the extension of the criteria of truth to morality: Richard Boyd, "How to Be a Moral Realist", in *Essays on Moral Realism*, ed. Sayre-McCord, chap. 9. In my view, Boyd has correctly noted the main issues, while not drawing the full conclusions from them.

39. David Bourget and David Chalmers, "What Do Philosophers Believe?", *Philosophical Studies* 170, no. 3 (2014): 465–500.

40. Simon Blackburn, *Ruling Passions: A Theory of Practical Reasoning* (New York: Oxford University Press, 1999), vi.

41. Here is a select reading list: W. D. Hamilton, "The Genetical Evolution of Social Behaviour", *Journal of Theoretical Biology* 7 (1964): 1–16, 17–52; Robert Trivers, "The Evolution of Reciprocal Altruism", *Quarterly Review of Biology* 46 (1971): 35–57; Trivers, "Parent-Offspring Conflict", *American Zoologist* 14 (1974): 249–264; E. O. Wilson, *Sociobiology: The New Synthesis* (Cambridge, MA: Harvard University Press, 1975); Wilson, *On Human Nature* (Cambridge, MA: Harvard University Press, 1979); Richard Dawkins, *The Selfish Gene* (Oxford: Oxford University Press, 1976); W. D. Hamilton and Robert Axelrod, *The Evolution of Cooperation* (New York: Basic Books, 1984); Richard Alexander, *The Biology of Moral Systems* (New York: Aldine, 1987); Robert Frank, *Passions within Reason: The Strategic Role of the Emotions* (New York: W. W. Norton, 1988); Daniel Dennett, *Darwin's Dangerous Idea: Evolution and the Meanings of Life* (New York: Simon & Schuster, 1995); Matt Ridley, *The Origins of Virtue: Human Instincts and the Evolution of Cooperation* (New York: Viking, 1996); Samuel Bowles and Herbert Gintis, *A Cooperative Species: Human Reciprocity and Its Evolution* (Princeton, NJ: Princeton University Press, 2011); Christopher Boehm, *Moral Origins: The Evolution of Virtue, Altruism, and Shame* (New York: Basic Books, 2012); Michael Tomasello, *A Natural History of Human Morality* (Cambridge, MA: Harvard University Press, 2016). The following are informed by the evolutionary logic in the field of cognitive moral psychology: Hauser, *Moral Minds*; Jonathan Haidt, *The Righteous Mind: Why Good People Are Divided by Politics and Religion* (New York: Pantheon, 2012); Joshua Greene, *Moral Tribes: Emotion, Reason, and the Gap between Us and Them* (New York: Penguin, 2013).

42. Hume, *Inquiry Concerning the Principles of Morals*, appendix ii, article 252.
43. Hume, *Treatise of Human Nature*, Bk III, Pt II, section xii; *Inquiry Concerning the Principles of Morals*, sec. iv, article 166.
44. Cf. Andrea Glenn and Adrian Raine, "The Immoral Brain", in *The Moral Brain: Essays on the Evolutionary and Neuroscientific Aspects of Morality*, ed. J. Verplaetse et al. (Springer: Heidelberg, 2009), 45–67.
45. Hauser, *Moral Minds*; Haidt, *The Righteous Mind*; and Greene, *Moral Tribes*, summarize the research.
46. Cicero made a similar claim with respect to the Epicurean pleasure principle: Marcus Tullius Cicero, *De finibus bonorum et malorum* (On the ends of good and evil) (London: Heinemann, 1914), Bk. I, article vii. See as an argument in Hubert Dreyfus and Charles Taylor, *Retrieving Realism* (Cambridge, MA: Harvard University Press, 2015), 26. Blackburn, not a Darwinist, cites this as one of the most persistent responses he encounters to his view that values are not "objective": *Ruling Passions*, vi.
47. Theodosius Dobzhansky, "Nothing in Biology Makes Sense Except in the Light of Evolution", *American Biology Teacher* 35, no. 3 (1973): 125–129.
48. See, for example, Frans de Waal, *Good Natured: The Origins of Right and Wrong in Humans and Other Animals* (Cambridge, MA: Harvard University Press, 1996).
49. The most comprehensive attempts, in several ways similar to mine, can be found in Nichols, *Sentimental Rules*; and Prinz, *The Emotional Construction of Morals*. For philosophers sympathetic to the evolutionary perspective, see n. 52 below.
50. David Lahti, "On the Partnership between Natural and Moral Philosophy", in *Understanding Moral Sentiments from a Darwinian Perspective*, ed. H. Putnam, S. Neiman and J. Schloss (New Brunswick, NJ: Transaction, 2014), 229–256; quotation from 229.
51. Ibid., 231.
52. For such exceptions among philosophers see most notably: Sharon Street, "A Darwinian Dilemma for Realist Theories of Value", *Philosophical Studies* 127, no. 1 (2006): 109–166, which has created quite a stir; Michael Ruse, "The Significance of Evolution", in *A Companion to Ethics*, ed. P. Singer (Oxford: Blackwell, 1991), 500–510; Ruse, *The Philosophy of Human Evolution* (Cambridge: Cambridge University Press, 2012), chap. 6; Richard Joyce, *The Evolution of Morality* (Cambridge, MA: MIT Press, 2006). Peter Singer, *Practical Ethics*, 3rd ed. (Princeton, NJ: Princeton University Press, 2011), is also positive, however one views his moral inferences from the evolutionary logic.
53. Putnam, "Not Very Much", in Putnam, Neiman and Schloss, *Understanding Moral Sentiments from a Darwinian Perspective*, 203–211.
54. Friedrich Nietzsche, *The Will to Power* (New York: Vintage, 1968 [originally composed 1883–1888]), notes 647–658, 684–685; also, his *Beyond Good and Evil* (Cambridge: Cambridge University Press, 2001 [1886]), sec. 253.
55. Putnam, *Ethics without Ontology*; Mark Timmons, *Morality without Foundations: A Defense of Ethical Contextualism* (Oxford: Oxford University Press, 1999).
56. For summaries of the experimental literature, see particularly: Hauser, *Moral Minds*; Haidt, *The Righteous Mind*; Greene, *Moral Tribes*.
57. Jeremy Bentham, *An Introduction to the Principles of Morals and Legislation* (1781); John Stuart Mill, *Utilitarianism* (1863). Also see pragmatist philosopher John Dewey, *Reconstruction in Philosophy* (New York: Holt, 1920); and today: Singer, *Practical Ethics*; Greene, *Moral Tribes*.
58. Cicero made this point in *De finibus bonorum et malorum*, Bk. II; the modern version is identified with the so-called open question posed by G. E. Moore in his *Principia Ethica* (1903), article 13.
59. See n. 56, above.
60. Marcus Tullius Cicero, *De Officiis* (On duties), is a major summary of the ancient Greek sources.
61. Mill, *Utilitarianism*, chap. 2.
62. Alasdair MacIntyre, *After Virtue: A Study in Moral Theory*, 3rd ed. (Notre Dame, IN: University of Notre Dame, 2007 [1981]), 219.
63. Ibid., 190–191, 219.
64. Aristotle, *Nicomachean Ethics*, Bk I, article 3.

65. Ibid., II, 2 and 6–9.

66. For example: MacIntyre, Putnam, Nagel, Blackburn, Timmons, and David Brink.

67. Cf. Ridley, *The Origins of Virtue*.

68. See Gilbert Harman, for example in his and Judith Thomson, *Moral Relativism and Moral Objectivity* (Oxford: Blackwell, 1996), where he argues that morality is relative to a frame of reference, none of which is more correct than another. At the same time, Harman does not really account for the common core beyond the moral conventions, and although familiar with the evolutionary explanation, thinks they may be just a habit. Philip Kitcher has put forward a naturalistic, non-metaphysical view, more or less similar to mine, of *The Ethical Project* (Cambridge, MA: Harvard University Press, 2011).

69. See Timmons, *Morality without Foundations*, defining himself as an irrealist.

70. John Maynard Keynes, *Two Memoirs* (London: Rupert Hart-Davis, 1949), 85.

71. The most famous response has been Robert Nozick's libertarian work *Anarchy, State, and Utopia* (New York: Basic Books, 1974).

72. Cf. Stevenson, *Ethics and Language*, chap. vi–vii; also MacIntyre, *After Virtue*, xii–xiv.

73. See, for example, Bernard Williams, *Morality: An Introduction to Ethics* (Cambridge: Cambridge University Press, 1993).

74. William Napier, *History of General Sir Charles Napier's Administration of Scinde* (London, Chapman, 1851), 35.

75. Joshua Halberstam, "From Kant to Auschwitz", *Social Theory and Practice* 14, no. 1 (1988): 41–54.

76. For example, Kant erred in giving the example of suicide as a behavior that one could not wish to make a universal law, or, as he added, a universal law of nature: *Groundwork of the Metaphysics of Morals*, 4:421–422. There is no obvious reason why not. This difficulty may be the reason Kant added "of nature" to his second formulation of the universal law. However, making life a principle of nature does not solve the problem, and, contrary to Kant's logic, only makes his principle naturalistic.

77. See my *War in Human Civilization* (Oxford: Oxford University Press, 2006); and my *The Causes of War and the Spread of Peace: But Will War Rebound?* (Oxford: Oxford University Press, 2017).

78. On this (as opposed to things in the world), I am in agreement with Richard Rorty, "Universality and Truth", in *Rorty and His Critics*, ed. R. B. Brandom (Oxford: Blackwell, 2000), 1–30, esp. 14.

79. Both Nichols, *Sentimental Rules*, chap. 7, and Prinz, *The Emotional Construction of Morals*, chap. 8, present an approach that is more or less similar to mine, although our development of the subject is somewhat different. See also my reservations in n. 90 and related text.

80. Again cf. Kitcher, *The Ethical Project*.

81. Aristotle, *Politics*, Bk ii, Pt 5; Hume, *Inquiry Concerning the Principles of Morals*, sec. iii, article 155–156.

82. Putnam, *Ethics without Ontology*, 72–75.

83. Bernard Williams, "Human Rights and Relativism", in his *In the Beginning Was the Deed: Realism and Moralism in Political Argument* (Princeton, NJ: Princeton University Press, 2005, 62–74); quotation from 65, 68; criticizes Nagel's moral universalism, 67.

84. Alasdair MacIntyre, *Dependent Rational Animals: Why Human Beings Need the Virtues* (Peru, IL: Open Court, 1999), especially ix–x, 11–13.

85. For the dismissal, see Simon Blackburn's otherwise admirable *Ethics: A Very Short Introduction* (Oxford: Oxford University Press, 2001), 33–38. Notably, in his "How to Be an Ethical Anti-Realist", in *Essays in Quasi-Realism* (New York: Oxford University Press, 1993), 165–181, which deals positively with naturalism, Blackburn mentions the evolutionary emergence of cooperation and altruism, citing Robert Axelrod's *The Evolution of Cooperation*, but not Darwin. And for the later citation: Blackburn, "Human Nature and Science: A Cautionary Essay", in *Evolved Morality*, ed. de Waal et al., 107.

86. Philosopher Thomas Nagel has written *Mind and Cosmos: Why the Materialist Neo-Darwinian Conception of Nature Is Almost Certainly False* (Oxford: Oxford UP, 2012), to defend the realist view of morality against the implications of evolutionary theory, whose validity he largely accepts. Nagel makes two main arguments. One is that the immanent course of evolution

in the cosmic order is such that it embodies morality as its ultimate *logos* and destination, an Aristotelian (or Hegelian) *telos* and teleology. Nagel states that he is not a creationist, and there is no God in his evolving cosmos. His concept is therefore less susceptible to the problems of the more common attempt to combine and reconcile a creator with evolution. Whether or not his view sits well with the cosmology in which human life is an infinitesimally small part of an infinitesimally huge cosmos, and what meaning his view of a conscious cosmos has in this context, is for anybody to decide.

Nagel's second argument, that "the materialist neo-Darwinian conception of nature is almost certainly false", evokes one of the oldest and deepest problems of modern philosophy. This is the schism that exists in our worldview between a materialist physical explanation of the world and the world of our consciousness, with its vivid sensations such as pain, pleasure, happiness, or sadness that are difficult to see emerging from inanimate matter. I entirely agree that, as of now, we simply do not have a convincing solution to the mind-matter problem, as it is known. Perhaps one day we will. Nagel is wrong, however, to hold that the validity of evolutionary theory hinges on the reduction of consciousness to inanimate matter. See also his student David Enoch, *Taking Morality Seriously: A Defense of Robust Realism* (Oxford: Oxford University Press, 2011); Dreyfus and Taylor, *Retrieving Realism*; Ronald Dworkin, *Justice for Hedgehogs* (Cambridge, MA: Harvard University Press, 2011); and Dworkin, *Religion without God*, Cambridge, MA: Harvard University Press, 2013.

87. For example, Katia Vavova, "Evolutionary Debunking of Moral Realism", *Philosophy Compass* 10, no. 2 (2015): 104–116; but see again, Prinz, *The Emotional Construction of Morals*.

88. C. J. Lumsden and E. O. Wilson, *Genes, Mind and Culture* (Cambridge, M: Harvard University Press, 1981); L. L. Cavalli-Sforza and M. W. Feldman, *Cultural Transmission and Evolution* (Princeton: Princeton University Press, 1981); Robert Boyd and Peter Richerson, *Culture and the Evolutionary Process* (Chicago: University of Chicago Press, 1985); W. H. Durham, *Coevolution: Genes, Culture, and Human Diversity* (Stanford, CA: Stanford University Press, 1991); Peter Richerson and Robert Boyd, *Not by Genes Alone* (Chicago: University of Chicago Press, 2005); Joseph Henrich, *The Secret of Our Success: How Culture Is Driving Human Evolution, Domesticating Our Species, and Making Us Smarter* (Princeton, NJ: Princeton University Press, 2016).

89. Richard Wrangham, *Catching Fire: How Cooking Made Us Human* (New York: Basic Books, 2009).

90. In his rejection of the relevance of the evolutionary perspective to morality, Putnam, "Not Very Much", 209, has contended that moral evolution is cultural rather than biological, and hence Lamarckian rather than Darwinian. Unfortunately, both Shaun Nichols and Jesse Prinz, philosophers who like me hold a naturalistic understanding of morality, have unnecessarily underscored this false dichotomy. The latter has gone so far as writing that "morality is artificial all the way down": Nichols, *Sentimental Rules*, chaps. 6–7; Prinz, *The Emotional Construction of Morals*, chaps. 6–7, quotation from 246. While the two works are remarkably similar to each other, Nichols's grasp of the evolutionary rationale seems at times to be somewhat shaky. He sets himself as being entirely opposed to the view that moral norms are evolutionary adaptations (they only partly are), and seems to suggest that the various evolutionary mechanisms for prosocial behavior are alternative rather than complementary to one another (120). He is more to the point, and more balanced than Prinz, in holding that morality is culturally elaborated from basic natural tendencies.

Chapter 3

1. Robert McCauley, *Religion Is Natural and Science Is Not* (New York: Oxford University Press, 2011); Justin Barrett, *Born Believers: The Science of Children's Religious Belief* (New York: Free Press 2012); and his more popular *Cognitive Science, Religion, and Theology: From Human Minds to Divine Minds* (West Conshohocken, PA.: Templeton, 2011).

2. For summaries of research see: Stuart Vyse, *Believing in Magic: The Psychology of Superstition* (New York: Oxford University Press, 1997); Michael Shermer, *The Believing Brain: From Ghosts and Gods to Politics and Conspiracies—How We Construct Beliefs and Reinforce Them as Truths* (New York: Holt, 2011), 7–8; McCauley, *Religion Is Natural and Science Is Not*; Barrett,

Born Believers, chap. 9; Michael Ruse, *Atheism: What Everyone Needs to Know* (Oxford: Oxford University Press, 2015), chap. 3; also Robert Hinde, *Why Gods Persist* (London: Routledge, 1999), 3–4. For various aspects of secularization see Talal Asad, *Formations of the Secular: Christianity, Islam, Modernity* (Stanford, CA: Stanford University Press, 2003).

3. Edward Tylor, *Primitive Culture* (London: John Murray, 1871), chaps. 11–19.

4. Most recently see Rob Iliffe, *Priest of Nature: The Religious Worlds of Isaac Newton* (Oxford: Oxford University Press, 2017).

5. McCauley, *Religion Is Natural and Science Is Not*, is a recent serious attempt to distinguish between religion, whose status as primitive, intuitive science whose cognitive patterns are natural to us the author underlines, and science per se. I agree with some, but not all, of his suggestions in this regard.

6. B. F. Skinner, "'Superstition' in the Pigeon", *Journal of Experimental Psychology* 38 (1948): 168–172.

7. Two otherwise rich and insightful works err on this: Pascal Boyer, *Religion Explained: The Evolutionary Origins of Religious Thought* (New York: Basic Books, 2001); and Scott Atran, *In Gods We Trust: The Evolutionary Landscape of Religion* (New York: Oxford University Press, 2002). Kierkegaard's view that religion means the embrace of the "absurd", which Atran cites in support of his argument, came only after the schism between religion and science had opened up during modern times. For the counterargument see McCauley, *Religion Is Natural and Science Is Not*.

8. Max Weber, *The Sociology of Religion* (London: Methuen, 1965), 1–2. And for the long line of scholars who have reached the same conclusion see: Charles Darwin, *The Descent of Man*, chap. iii. in *The Origin of the Species and the Descent of Man* (New York: Modern Library, n.d.); James Frazer, *The Golden Bough* (New York: Macmillan, 1922); R. Horton, "African Traditional Thought and Western Science", in *Rationality*, ed. B. Wilson (Oxford: Blackwell, 1970), 131–171; T. Luckmann, *The Invisible Religion* (New York: Macmillan, 1967); P. Berger, *The Social Reality of Religion* (Harmondsworth: Penguin, 1973). Emphasizing the manipulative element on top of the interpretative one are Émile Durkheim, *The Elementary Forms of Religious Life* (New York: Free Press, 1965), 165ff, 476–477, 463–464; Bronislav Malinovski, *The Foundations of Faith and Morals* (London: Oxford University Press, 1936); Malinovski, *Magic, Science and Religion* (New York: Doubleday Anchor, 1954); all in fact anticipated by Hobbes, *Leviathan*, chap. 12.

9. Stewart Guthrie, *Faces in the Clouds: A New Theory of Religion* (New York: Oxford University Press, 1993); McCauley, *Religion Is Natural and Science Is Not*. Barrett, who has conducted important psychological experiments in babies and small children, is also a believing Christian. See his *Cognitive Science, Religion, and Theology*, 149–156; and for more on the relevance of HADD to religious belief: Roger Trigg and Justin Barrett eds., *The Roots of Religion: Exploring the Cognitive Science of Religion* (Farnham: Ashgate, 2014).

10. Recently, see eminent scientist Stuart Kauffman, *Reinventing the Sacred: A New View of Science, Reason, and Religion* (New York: Basic Books, 2008), chaps. 12–13; also, James Fetzer, *Consciousness Evolving* (Amsterdam: John Benjamins, 2002).

11. Durkheim, *The Elementary Forms of Religious Life*; Malinovski, *The Foundation of Faith and Morals*; Malinovski, *Magic, Science and Religion*; A. R. Radcliffe-Brown, "Religion and Society", in his *Structure and Function in Primitive Society* (London: Cohen and West, 1952), 153–177; Brian Hayden, *A Prehistory of Religion: Shamans, Sorcerers and Saints* (Washington, DC: Smithsonian, 2003).

12. First phrased this way by Richard Dawkins, *The Selfish Gene* (Oxford: Oxford University Press, 1976); also, among many others: Boyer, *Religion Explained*; Daniel Dennett, *Breaking the Spell: Religion as a Natural Phenomenon* (New York: Penguin, 2007).

13. David Wilson, *Darwin's Cathedral: Evolution, Religion, and the Nature of Society* (Chicago: Chicago University Press, 2002), which, surprisingly gives little attention to the advantage in war. The whole subject involves a controversy over the existence of "group selection"; see Azar Gat, "Long Childhood, Family Networks, and Cultural Exclusivity: Missing Links in the Debate over Human Group Selection and Altruism", *Evolutionary Studies in Imaginative Culture* 2, no. 1 (2018): 49–58.

14. In my view, the most brilliant work is that by science writer Robert Wright, *The Evolution of God* (New York: Little, Brown, 2009). A recent comprehensive work by a leading sociologist of both early Christianity and religion in general, Rodney Stark, *Discovering God: The Origins of the Great Religions and the Evolution of Belief* (New York: HarperCollins, 2007), makes some strange historical claims, at least partly due to the author's special pleading for God in this book. Another recent work by a leading sociologist of religion, Robert Bellah, *Religion in Human Evolution: From the Paleolithic to the Axial Age* (Cambridge, MA: Harvard University Press, 2011), is very learned, but, in my view, swamped by largely irrelevant details.

15. See, for example: N. Wallin et al., eds., *The Origins of Music* (Cambridge, MA: MIT Press, 1999).

16. As well noted by Ara Norenzayan, *Big Gods: How Religion Transformed Cooperation and Conflict* (Princeton, NJ: Princeton University Press, 2013), 114–115.

17. As noted, Atran, *In Gods We Trust*, is rich and full of insights. I agree with some of them, such as the variety of cognitive and mental sources that feed the religious phenomena and its close correspondence to deep grooves in our psyche. At the same time, I think Atran is wrong about some of his main contentions, besides the counterintuitive nature of religion: religion was not costly, nor did it support morality, in the human state of nature. Much the same criticisms apply to Nicholas Wade's otherwise insightful *The Faith Instinct: How Religion Evolved and Why It Endures* (New York: Penguin, 2009); and Dominic Johnson, *God Is Watching You: How the Fear of God Makes Us Human* (New York: Oxford University Press, 2015).

18. Cf. Hayden, *A Prehistory of Religion*, 10. Indeed, all the anthropological evidence suggests as much.

19. I believed I was original in expressing this criticism until discovering that I had been preceded by Norenzayan's brilliant *Big Gods*, 135–137.

20. The term was coined by Karl Jaspers, *The Origin and Goal of History* (London: Routledge, 1953); also, Shmuel Eisenstadt, "The Axial Age: The Emergence of Transcendental Visions and the Rise of the Clerics", *Archives européennes de sociologie* 23 (1982): 294–314. The long-noted association of religion with morality since the "Axial Age" has recently been reconfirmed by large-scale empirical surveys: Benjamin Purzycki et al., "Moralistic Gods, Supernatural Punishment and the Expansion of Human Sociality", *Nature* 530 (February 18, 2016): 327–330; Harvey Whitehouse et al., "Complex Societies Precede Moralizing Gods throughout World History", *Nature* (March 20, 2019); also, Joseph Henrich et al., "Markets, Religion, Community Size, and the Evolution of Fairness and Punishment", *Science* 327 (2010): 1480–1484; Nicholas Baumard and Pascal Boyer, "Explaining Moral Religions", *Trends in Cognitive Science* 17 (2013): 272–280; Joseph Watts et al., "Broad Supernatural Punishment but Not Moralizing High Gods Precede the Evolution of Political Complexity in Austronesia", *Proceedings of the Royal Society B* (April 7, 2015); Ara Norenzayan et al., "The Cultural Evolution of Prosocial Religions", *Behavioral Brain Science* 39 (2016): e1.

21. J. H. Lesher, *Xenophanes of Colophon: Fragments* (Toronto: University of Toronto Press, 1992), frag. 11.

22. Plato, *The Republic*, Bk ii, sects. 364–365, 379–383.

23. For example, the two first-class works: Wright, *The Evolution of God*, and Norenzayan, *Big Gods*. While Norenzayan's book is superbly insightful and nuanced, he attributes the "big gods" phenomenon solely to their new function as watchful "big brothers" who impose morality. I suggest that the gods grew in size (with the monotheistic gods as a final stage in this development) also, perhaps primarily, in response to the progressive growth of the states themselves and of the authority and splendor of their kings, which the concept of the gods had to surpass.

24. Daniel Mullins et al., "A Systematic Assessment of 'Axial Age' Proposals Using Global Comparative Historical Evidence", *American Sociological Review* 83 (2018): 596–626, demystify the concept and, consequently, loosen its chronological and geographical scope, without invalidating it.

25. Plato, *The Republic*, Bk ii, sects. 364–365, 379–383; Aristotle, *Metaphysics*, Bk 11, chaps. 7–10. See also Epicurus' view of God as a perfect, non-interfering being: "Letter to Menoeceus", articles 123–124; "Letter to Herodotus", article 77, in Epicurus, *The Extant Remains* (Oxford: Oxford University Press, 1926).

26. Nicolas Baumard et al. argue that "Increased Affluence Explains the Emergence of Ascetic Wisdoms and Moralizing Religions", *Current Biology* 25 (2015): 10–15. While rejecting increased political complexity as the cause for this development, they fail to consider spreading literacy as a decisive factor.

27. Karl Marx, "A Contribution to the Critique of Hegel's Philosophy of Right" (1843), Introduction; also, "The German Ideology" (1845). For a collection in English: Karl Marx, *The Early Writings* (New York: Vintage, 1975).

28. For example, Ronald Dworkin, *Justice for Hedgehogs* (Cambridge, MA: Harvard University Press, 2011); Dworkin, *Religion without God* (Cambridge, MA: Harvard University Press, 2013).

29. Works on the narrative format are a legion. Among the most significant are Hayden White, "Interpretation in History", *New Literary History* 4, no. 2 (Winter 1973): 281–314; White, "The Value of Narrativity in the Representation of Reality", *Critical Inquiry* 7, no. 1 (Autumn 1980): 5–27; White, "The Question of Narrative in Contemporary Historical Theory", *History and Theory* 23, no. 1 (February 1984): 1–33. A first-class recent collection is Jonathan Gottschall, David Sloan Wilson, E. O. Wilson, and Frederick Crews, eds., *The Literary Animal: Evolution and the Nature of Narrative* (Evanston, IL: Northwestern University Press, 2005); and the best on the subject is Jonathan Gottschall, *The Storytelling Animal: How Stories Make Us Human* (New York: Houghton Mifflin Harcourt, 2012). On religion, see, for example: Hinde, *Why Gods Persist*, chap. 8; Terrence Deacon and Tyrone Cashman, "The Role of Symbolic Capacity in the Origin of Religion", *Journal for the Study of Religion, Nature and Culture* 3 (2009): 490–517; McCauley, *Religion Is Natural and Science Is Not*, 186–189.

30. Sigmund Freud, *Obsessive Actions and Religious Practices* (1907), *Totem and Taboo* (1913), *The Future of an Illusion* (1927), and *Moses and Monotheism* (1939).

31. See Clifford Geertz, *The Interpretation of Culture* (New York: Basic Books, 1973), chaps. 4–6.

32. Joseph Henrich, *The Secret of Our Success: How Culture Is Driving Human Evolution, Domesticating Our Species, and Making Us Smarter* (Princeton, NJ: Princeton University Press, 2016). See also Susan Blackmore, *The Meme Machine* (Oxford: Oxford University Press, 1999), which nicely develops Richard Dawkins's idea of memes.

33. Henrich, *The Secret of Our Success*.

34. This view was mainly associated with, and taken to fanciful length in, the many works of cultural anthropologist Marvin Harris, for example, *Good to Eat: Riddles of Food and Culture* (New York: Simon & Schuster, 1985).

35. Gat, "Long Childhood, Family Networks, and Cultural Exclusivity"; Azar Gat (with Alexander Yakobson), *Nations: The Long History and Deep Roots of Political Ethnicity and Nationalism* (Cambridge: Cambridge University Press, 2013).

36. Anthony Smith, *Chosen Peoples: Sacred Sources of National Identity* (Oxford: Oxford University Press, 2003); Gat, *Nations*.

37. Jonathan Swift, *Gulliver's Travels* (Oxford: Oxford University Press, 2005), 43.

38. Milman Parry, *The Making of Homeric Verse: The Collected Papers of Milman Parry* (Oxford: Oxford University Press, 1971), pioneered the study of the oral epic form; more recently see Walter Ong, *Orality and Literacy* (New York: Routledge, 2002).

39. Most famously see Leon Festinger, Henry Riecken, and Stanley Schachter, *When Prophecy Fails* (San Francisco: Harper & Row, 1956).

40. Lesher, *Xenophanes*, frags. 14, 16, 15, respectively.

41. A. J. Mattill Jr, *The Seven Mighty Blows to Traditional Beliefs* (Gordo, AL: Flatwoods, 1995), 32.

42. Charles Taylor, *A Secular Age* (Cambridge, MA: Harvard University Press, 2007), is a most erudite study by an eminent philosopher of religious leanings. Philip Kennedy, *A Modern Introduction to Theology: New Questions for Old Beliefs* (London: I. B. Tauris, 2006), is an introductory overview. Gareth Jones, ed., *The Blackwell Companion to Modern Theology* (Oxford: Blackwell, 2004), is a mixture of scholarly and theological essays, focusing somewhat narrowly on Christian doctrines; but chap. 32, "Science", in this book (512–556), by Robert John Russell and Kirk Wegter-McNelly, is a very comprehensive and well-informed overview of current questions and positions in the theological perspectives on science. P. Clayton and Z. Simpson, eds., *The Oxford Handbook of Religion and Science* (Oxford: Oxford

University Press, 2006), is wider in scope than the Blackwell collection and somewhat less theological.

43. Richard Dawkins, *The God Delusion* (New York: Houghton Mifflin, 2006); Christopher Hitchens, *God Is Not Great: How Religion Poisons Everything* (New York: Twelve, 2007); Dennett, *Breaking the Spell*; Sam Harris, *The End of Faith: Religion, Terror, and the Future of Reason* (New York: W. W. Norton, 2004).

44. Robert Putnam and David Campbell, *American Grace: How Religion Divides and Unites Us* (New York: Simon & Schuster, 2010), chap. 11.

45. A collection of scholarly papers is Mark Wrathall, ed., *Religion after Metaphysics* (Cambridge: Cambridge University Press, 2003). For one of the most radical modernists see Don Cupitt's many books, most notably his popular *The Sea of Faith* (London: BBC Books, 1984).

46. Friedrich Schleiermacher, *On Religion* (London: Kegan Paul, 1893 [German original 1799]). For a recent example, see John Hick, *God Has Many Names* (London: Palgrave, 1980); Hick, *The Rainbow of Faiths: Critical Dialogues in Religious Pluralism* (London: SCM, 1995). For a study of the historical transformation in the European consciousness, see Tomoko Masuzawa, *The Invention of World Religions: or, How European Universalism Was Preserved in the Language of Pluralism* (Chicago: University of Chicago Press, 2005).

47. Putnam and Campbell, *American Grace*, chap. 15. Even among Evangelicals, whose toleration levels are lower, such views are held by the majority.

48. Dawkins, *The God Delusion*, 36.

49. This factor has long been noted, but perhaps not sufficiently highlighted. See, for example: Putnam and Campbell, *American Grace*, chap. 9.

50. Summary of research in Hinde, *Why Gods Persist*, 4–5; Barrett, *Born Believers*, chap. 9; Ruse, *Atheism*, 64; Charles Murray, *Coming Apart: The State of White America 1960–2010* (New York: Crown, 2012), chap. 15.

51. Azar Gat, *War in Human Civilization* (Oxford: Oxford University Press, 2006), esp. 431–436; supported by the statistical data in Norenzayan, *Big Gods*, 157.

52. Buster Smith and Rodney Stark, "Religious Attendance Relates to Generosity Worldwide: Religious and the Secular More Charitable If They Attend Services", *Gallup News*, September 4, 2009; also Putnam and Campbell, *American Grace*, chap. 13.

53. Deborah Hall, David Matz, and Wendy Wood, "Why Don't We Practice What We Preach? A Meta-Analytic Review of Religious Racism", *Personality and Social Psychology Review* 14, no. 1 (2010): 126–139; Putnam and Campbell, *American Grace*, chap. 13.

54. *Yedioth Ahronoth*, September 22, 2015.

55. For example, Gordon Kaufman, *In Face of Mystery: A Constructive Theology* (Cambridge, MA: Harvard University Press, 1993); Paul Brockelman, *Cosmology and Creation: The Spiritual Significance of Contemporary Cosmology* (Oxford: Oxford University Press, 1999).

56. Bertrand Russell, "Is There a God?" (1952), in *The Collected Papers of Bertrand Russell*, ed. J. Slater, vol. 11 (London: Routledge, 1997), 542–548; there is also the more handy *Russell on Religion: Selections from the Writings of Bertrand Russell* (London: Routledge, 1999); Dawkins, *The God Delusion*, 53.

57. Cited by Stark, *Discovering God*, 7.

58. Rosamond Sprague, ed., *The Older Sophists* (Indianapolis: Hackett, 2001), 20.

59. For a recent return to this subject by neuroscientists who are also practicing Christians, see Malcolm Jeeves and Warren Brown, *Neuroscience, Psychology, and Religion* (West Conshohocken, PA, Templeton, 2009).

60. Cf. Dawkins, *The God Delusion*, 50–54.

61. Barrett, *Cognitive Science, Religion, and Theology*, esp. chaps. 8–9. See also n. 9 above.

62. See, for example, philosopher Alvin Plantinga and his critics: J. Beilby, ed., *Naturalism Defeated?: Essays on Plantinga's Evolutionary Argument against Naturalism* (Ithaca NY: Cornell University Press, 2002).

63. For a review of some of the statistics see, for example, Ruse, *Atheism*, chap. 3, and p. 158. The United States and the post-communist countries diverge in being more and less religious, respectively, than the general trend, but the correlation is still significant *within* the United States.

64. Putnam and Campbell, *American Grace*, chap. 13.
65. See Ronald Inglehart and Christian Welzel, *Modernization, Cultural Change, and Democracy: The Human Development Sequence* (New York: Cambridge University Press, 2005). McCauley, *Religion Is Natural and Science Is Not*, importantly underlining the innateness of key religious features in our psyche and, hence, the likely endurance of the religion, does not give sufficient account to these quantitative and qualitative changes.

Chapter 4

1. Edward Shils, "The End of Ideology?", *Encounter* 5 (November 1955): 52–58, reporting on this view among distinguished sociologists and economists; Seymour Lipset, "The End of Ideology?", in his *Political Man* (New York: Anchor, 1963), 403–417; Daniel Bell, *The End of Ideology: On the Exhaustion of Political Ideas in the Fifties* (New York: Collier, 1962), esp. 13–17, 393–407. A collection of these and many other contributions is Chaim Waxman, ed., *The End of Ideology Debate* (New York: Simon & Schuster, 1968).
2. Francis Fukuyama, *The End of History and the Last Man* (New York: Free Press, 1992).
3. The following is a select list of general surveys, all covering a more or less similar ground: R. Eatwell and A. Wright, eds., *Contemporary Political Ideologies* (London: Pinter, 1993); Robert Eccleshall et al., *Political Ideologies: An Introduction* (New York: Routledge, 2003); Andrew Vincent, *Modern Political Ideologies* (Oxford: Blackwell, 2009); Lyman Sargent, *Contemporary Political Ideologies: A Comparative Analysis* (Belmont, CA: Wadsworth, 2009); Terrence Ball, Richard Dagger, and Daniel O'Neill, *Political Ideologies and the Democratic Ideal* (Boston: Pearson, 2014); Andrew Heywood, *Political Ideologies: An Introduction* (London: Palgrave, 2017).
4. Marx developed his concept and critique of ideology in his early writings: his "Critique of Hegel's Philosophy of Right" (1843), "Economic and Philosophic Manuscripts" (1844), and, most notably, "The German Ideology" (1845). For a collection in English, see: Karl Marx, *The Early Writings* (New York: Vintage, 1975).
5. Engels to Franz Mehring, July 14, 1893, in *Marx and Engels Correspondence* (New York: International Publishers, 1968).
6. Antonio Gramsci, *Prison Notebooks* (New York: Columbia University Press, 2011 [1947]); Louis Althusser, *Essays on Ideology* (London: Verso, 1984).
7. There were many references to these concepts in more or less significant works that I shall not cite here. Hans Kelsen, *Secular Religion: A Polemic against the Misinterpretation of Modern Social Philosophy, Science and Politics as "New Religion"* (New York: Springer, 1964), while objecting to the concept, provides a long list of references from 1920 on in his Introduction and chap. 1. But see the much earlier pronouncements by Renan and Sorel cited in n. 38 below. Two comprehensive studies are: Ernest Koenker, *Secular Salvations: The Rites and Symbols of Political Religions* (Philadelphia: Fortress Press, 1965); and Emilio Gentile, *Politics as Religion* (Princeton, NJ: Princeton University Press, 2006).
8. Karl Mannheim, *Ideology and Utopia* (London: Routledge, 1954 [1936; original German 1929]); Clifford Geertz, "Ideology as a Cultural System", in his *The Interpretation of Culture* (New York: Basic Books, 1973), chap. 8, first published in David Apter, *Ideology and Discontent* (New York: Free Press, 1964), chap. 1; Michael Freeden, *Ideologies and Political Theory: A Conceptual Approach* (Oxford: Oxford University Press, 1996); Freeden, *Ideology: A Very Short Introduction* (Oxford: Oxford University Press, 2003); Jack Balkin, *Cultural Software: A Theory of Ideology* (New Haven, CT: Yale University Press, 1998). The same approach characterizes the literature cited in n. 3, above. Some other histories and analyses of the concept of ideology are: David McLellan, *Ideology* (Minneapolis: University of Minnesota Press, 1986); Ian Adams, *The Logic of Political Belief: A Philosophical Analysis of Ideology* (Hemel: Harvester, 1989); Jorge Larrain, *The Concept of Ideology* (London: Hutchinson, 1979); Raymond Boudon, *The Analysis of Ideology* (Chicago, University of Chicago Press, 1989); Bernard Susser, *The Grammar of Modern Ideology* (London: Routledge, 1988).
9. John Locke's *The Second Treatise of Civil Government* (1689), chaps. 2 and 5.

10. Karl Marx, *The Eighteenth Brumaire of Louis Bonaparte* (New York: Mondial, 2005), chap. 7; originally published in 1852.

11. According to Kevin Lockridge's assessments in his *Literacy in Colonial New England* (New York: W. W. Norton, 1974), literacy was practically full by the time of Independence. It was somewhat lower but still high among whites in the south.

12. Two classics, each in its time, are still relevant here: Alexis de Tocqueville, *Democracy in America* (New York: Harper, 2000 [French original 1835, 1840]), esp. vol. 1, chaps. 3 and 9; Barrington Moore, *Social Origins of Dictatorship and Democracy: Lord and Peasant in the Making of the Modern World* (Boston: Beacon, 1966).

13. Aristotle, *Politics* Bk IV, Pr 11.

14. Azar Gat, "The Arabs' 1848", *The National Interest*, April 20, 2014; reprinted in my *War and Strategy in the Modern World: From Blitzkrieg to Unconventional Terrorism* (Abingdon: Routledge, 2018), 122–130.

15. John Stuart Mill, *Autobiography* (n.p.: Floating Press, 2009 [1873]), chap. 5, citations from 162–163, 170.

16. John Stuart Mill, *On Representative Government* (London: The Electric Book, 2001 [1861]), chap. 8; Mill, *On Liberty* (New Haven, CT: Yale University Press, 2003 [1859]), 179–184.

17. Mill, *On Representative Government*, 136 n.

18. Mill, *On Liberty*, 113.

19. Herbert Butterfield, *The Whig Interpretation of History* (London: Bell, 1931).

20. Most recently, see Steven Pinker's excellent *Enlightenment Now: The Case for Reason, Science, Humanism, and Progress* (New York: Viking, 2018).

21. Most notably, Mill, *On Liberty*, chap. 4; generally, Peter Berkowitz, *Virtue and the Making of Modern Liberalism* (Princeton, NJ: Princeton University Press, 1999); and with respect to the American experience in the nineteenth century, Charles Murray, *Coming Apart: The State of White America 1960–2010* (New York: Crown, 2012), chap. 6.

22. Isaiah Berlin, "Two Concepts of Liberty", in his *Four Essays on Liberty* (Oxford: Oxford University Press, 1969), 118–172.

23. Karl Marx, *A Contribution to the Critique of Political Economy* (Moscow: Progress Publishers, 1977), Preface.

24. Marxists' haggling over this has been endless. But see most notably: Engels to J. Bloch, September 21, 1890, printed in *Historical Materialism (Marx, Engels, Lenin)* (Moscow: Progress Publishers, 1972), 294–296, on the WWW; Georg Lukács, *History and Class Consciousness: Studies in Marxist Dialectics* (Cambridge, MA: MIT, 1972 [1922]); and the most subtle and knowledgeable of the devout Marxists, Louis Althusser, *For Marx* (London: Penguin, 1969 [French orig. 1965]), 87–128.

25. Marx, *The Eighteenth Brumaire of Louis Bonaparte*, chap. 1.

26. Eduard Bernstein, *The Preconditions of Socialism* (Cambridge: Cambridge University Press, 1993 [1899]).

27. Aristotle, *Politics* Bk ii, Pt 5; Hume, *Inquiry Concerning the Principles of Morals*, sec. iii, article 155–156.

28. For a shortlist on fascism, see: Eugen Weber, *Varieties of Fascism* (Princeton, NJ: Princeton University Press, 1969); James Gregor, *The Ideology of Fascism* (New York: Free Press, 1969); Ernst Nolte, *Three Faces of Fascism* (New York: New American Library, 1969); Hugh Trevor-Roper, "The Phenomenon of Fascism", in *European Fascism*, ed. S. J. Woolf (New York: Vintage, 1969); George Mosse, *The Nationalization of the Masses* (New York: Fertig, 1975); H. Turner, ed., *Reappraisals of Fascism* (New York: Watts, 1975); Jeffrey Herf, *Reactionary Modernism* (Cambridge: Cambridge University Press, 1984); Stanley Payne, *Fascism* (Madison: University of Wisconsin Press, 1980); Payne, *A History of Fascism* (Madison: University of Wisconsin Press, 1995); Zeev Sternhell, *Neither Right nor Left* (Berkeley: University of California Press, 1986); Roger Griffin, *The Nature of Fascism* (London: Routledge, 1991); Griffin, *Modernism and Fascism* (New York: Palgrave, 2007); and my own *Fascist and Liberal Visions of War* (Oxford: Oxford University Press, 1998), part 1.

29. For a recent comprehensive study of this widely familiar subject see: Gentile, *Politics as Religion*; also Koenker, *Secular Salvations*.

30. For an academic argument along these lines, see Daniel A. Bell, *The China Model: Political Meritocracy and the Limits of Democracy—How China's Political Model Could Prove to Be a Viable Alternative to Western Democracy* (Princeton, NJ: Princeton University Press, 2015).

31. See n. 34, below.

32. For this school's most radical exponent see: Herbert Marcuse, *One-Dimensional Man: Studies in the Ideology of Advanced Industrial Society* (Boston: Beacon, 1964).

33. Lipset, *Political Man*; Fukuyama, *The End of History*; Michael Mandelbaum, *The Ideas That Conquered the World: Peace, Democracy, and Free Markets in the Twenty-first Century* (New York: Public Affairs, 2002); Mandelbaum, *Democracy's Good Name: The Rise and Risks of the World's Most Popular Form of Government* (New York: Public Affairs, 2007).

34. Gat, *War in Human Civilization*, 563–567, 620–621; Gat, "The Return of Authoritarian Great Powers", *Foreign Affairs* 86, no. 4 (2007): 59–69; Gat, "Which Way Is History Marching: Debating the Authoritarian Revival", *Foreign Affairs* 88, no. 4 (2009): 150–155; Gat, *Victorious and Vulnerable: Why Democracy Won in the 20th Century and How It Ss Still Imperiled* (Stanford, CA: Hoover/Rowman & Littlefield, 2010); Gat, *The Causes of War and the Spread of Peace: But Will War Rebound* (Oxford: Oxford University Press, 2017). For an opposite, one-directional view, see Ronald Inglehart, *Cultural Evolution* (Cambridge: Cambridge University Press, 2018).

35. Lipset, *Political Man*; Robert Dahl, *Polyarchy* (New Haven, CT: Yale University Press, 1971); Larry Diamond, "Economic Development and Democracy Reconsidered", in *Reexamining Democracy*, ed. G. Marks and L. Diamond (Newbury Park, CA: Sage, 1992), 93–139; Axel Hadenius, *Democracy and Development* (Cambridge: Cambridge University Press, 1992); Robert Barro, "Determinants of Economic Growth: A Cross-Country Empirical Study", *National Bureau of Economic Research Working Paper* 5698 (1996); Amartya Sen, *Development and Freedom* (New York: Knopf, 1999), which offers little historical perspective. Theoretically, see Mancur Olson, *Power and Prosperity: Outgrowing Communist and Capitalist Dictatorships* (New York: Basic Books, 2000). Ferguson, *The Cash Nexus*, 348–349, 363–369, is a good summary and analysis; also, Fukuyama, *The End of History*, 123. Two comprehensive studies are Adam Przeworski, Michael Alvarez, Jose Cheibub, and Fernando Limongi, *Democracy and Development* (Cambridge: Cambridge University Press, 2000); and Morton Halperin, Josef Siegle, and Michael Weinstein, *The Democracy Advantage: How Democracies Promote Prosperity and Peace* (New York: Routledge, 2005). The former is excellent, while the latter is more limited, but both fail to distinguish between capitalist and non-capitalist (including communist!) dictatorships, or to account for the staggering performance of the East Asian capitalist non-democratic economies.

36. See n. 34 above.

37. Max Weber, "Politics as a Vocation". Also, Mannheim, *Ideology and Utopia*, 84–86; Freeden, *Ideologies and Political Theory*, 259ff, 275.

38. Georges Sorel, *Reflections on Violence* (Cambridge: Cambridge University Press, 1999 [1908]), 30–31.

39. James Coleman, *Foundations of Social Theory* (Cambridge, MA: Harvard University Press, 1990), 495.

40. A lengthy study, more or less along similar lines, is Teun van Dijk, *Ideology: A Multidisciplinary Approach* (London: Sage, 1998).

41. The subject was initiated in the scholarly realm in relation to the United States by Robert Bellah, "Civil Religion in America", *Dædalus* 96, no. 1 (1967): 1–21, followed by his *The Broken Covenant: American Civil Religion in Time of Trial* (Chicago: University of Chicago Press, 1975). See also Koenker, *Secular Salvations*; Gentile, *Politics as Religion*, Introduction, with bibliographical references to the ensuing debate; Christopher Flood, *Political Myth* (London: Routledge, 2002).

42. See, most radically, Marcuse, *One-Dimensional Man*.

Chapter 5

1. Herbert Marcuse, *One-Dimensional Man: Studies in the Ideology of Advanced Industrial Society* (Boston: Beacon, 1964).

2. Ronald Inglehart and Christian Welzel, *Modernization, Cultural Change and Democracy* (Cambridge: Cambridge University Press, 2005).

3. Robert Hughes, *Culture of Complaint: The Fraying of America* (New York: Oxford University Press, 1993).

4. See most notably, from the left, Robert Putnam, *Bowling Alone: The Collapse and Revival of American Community* (New York: Simon & Schuster, 2000), and his *Our Kids: The American Dream in Crisis* (New York: Simon & Schuster, 2015); from the right, Charles Murray, *Coming Apart: The State of White America 1960–2010* (New York: Crown, 2012).

5. See, for example, the founder of modern American anthropology, Mead's teacher and researcher of the natives of the American Northwest and their ferocious warfare: Franz Boas, *Kuakiutl Ethnography* (Chicago: University of Chicago Press, 1966), 105–119. The seminal collection, R. Lee and I. DeVore, eds., *Man the Hunter* (Chicago: Aldine, 1968), still incorporates many reports of warfare, including Aboriginal Australia, our best, isolated laboratory, exclusively populated by hunter-gatherers. For my elaboration on the extensive Australian evidence, see my cited works in n. 10, below.

6. Margaret Mead, *Coming of Age in Samoa* (New York: Blue Ribbon, 1928), 198. For fighting in her other works on Samoa, see Derek Freeman, *Margaret Mead and Samoa: The Making and Unmaking of an Anthropological Myth* (Cambridge, MA: Harvard University Press, 1983), 89–90.

7. The term was coined by Elizabeth Thomas, *The Harmless People* (New York: Knopf, 1959). See Richard Lee, *The !Kung San* (New York: Cambridge University Press, 1979), 398; Lee, "Politics, Sexual and Non-Sexual, in Egalitarian Society," in *Politics and History in Band Societies*, ed. R. Lee and E. Leacock (New York: Cambridge University Press, 1982), 44; also Marshall Sahlins, "The Original Affluent Society", in Lee and DeVore, *Man the Hunter*.

8. Jean Briggs, *Never in Anger* (Cambridge, MA: Harvard University Press, 1970); Briggs, "'Why Don't You Kill Your Baby Brother?' The Dynamics of Peace in Canadian Inuit Camps", in *The Anthropology of Peace and Nonviolence*, ed. L. Sponsel and T. Gregor (London: Lynne Rienner, 1994), 156; J. Darwent and M. Christyann, "Scales of Violence across the North American Arctic", in *Violence and Warfare among Hunter-Gatherers*, ed. M. Allen and T. Jones (Walnut Creek, CA: Left Coast Press, 2014), 182–203.

9. Vicious allegations were raised, for example, against anthropologist Napoleon Chagnon, author of the seminal *Yanomamo: The Fierce People*, 2nd ed. (New York: Holt, 1977).

10. Lawrence Keeley, *War before Civilization: The Myth of the Peaceful Savage* (Oxford: Oxford University Press, 1996); Azar Gat, "The Pattern of Fighting in Simple, Small Scale, Pre-State Societies", *Journal of Anthropological Research* 55 (1999): 563–583, and "The Human Motivational Complex: Evolutionary Theory and the Causes of Hunter-Gatherer Fighting", *Anthropological Quarterly* 73:1–2 (2000): 20–34, 74–88 (both incorporated into my *War in Human Civilization* (Oxford: Oxford University Press, 2006); Steven LeBlanc with Katherine Register, *Constant Battles: The Myth of the Peaceful Noble Savage* (New York: St. Martin's, 2003); also J. Guilaine and J. Zammit, *The Origins of War: Violence in Prehistory* (Malden, MA: Blackwell, 2005). Steven Pinker, *The Better Angels of Our Nature: Why Violence Has Declined* (New York: Penguin, 2011), has drawn wider public attention to these finds. For the latest stages in the debate, see Gat, "Proving Communal Warfare among Hunter-Gatherers: The Quasi-Rousseauan Error", *Evolutionary Anthropology* 24 (2015): 111–126; incorporated as chap. 1 in my *The Causes of War and the Spread of Peace: But Will War Rebound?* (Oxford: Oxford University Press, 2017).

11. Patrick Kirch, *The Evolution of the Polynesian Chiefdoms* (Cambridge: Cambridge University Press, 1984); Irving Goldman, *Ancient Polynesian Society* (Chicago: University of Chicago Press, 1970); Timothy Earle, *How Chiefs Come to Power: The Political Economy in Prehistory* (Stanford, CA: Stanford University Press, 1997).

12. Freeman, *Margaret Mead and Samoa*; Freeman, *The Fateful Hoaxing of Margaret Mead* (Boulder, CO: Westview, 1999). For balance see: Martin Orans, *Not Even Wrong: Margaret Mead, Derek Freeman, and the Samoans* (Novato, CA: Chandler and Sharp, 1996); Paul Shenkman, *The Trashing of Margaret Mead* (Madison: University of Wisconsin Press, 2009).

13. See, most glaringly: Douglas Fry, *The Human Potential for Peace* (Oxford: Oxford University Press, 2006); Fry, ed., *War, Peace, and Human Nature*; Fry and Patrik Söderberg, "Lethal

Aggression in Mobile Forager Bands and Implications for the Origins of War", *Science* 341 (2013): 270–273. For my critique of his ideological bias in treating the evidence: Gat, "Proving Communal Warfare among Hunter-Gatherers", esp. 119–122.

14. A recent, authoritative, and balanced depiction is Jared Diamond, *The World until Yesterday: What Can We Learn from Traditional Societies?* (New York: Viking, 2012).

15. Gat, *War in Human Civilization*, with the subject expanded upon in my *The Causes of War*.

16. John Stuart Mill, *Principles of Political Economy* (New York: Kelley, 1961), bk. III, chap. xvii, sect. 5, p. 582.

17. Gat, *The Causes of War*, 138 (including the source material), and chap. 6 in general.

18. John Gallagher and Ronald Robinson, "The Imperialism of Free Trade", *Economic History Review* 4 (1953): 1–15; and their *Africa and the Victorians: The Climax of Imperialism* (Garden City, NY: Doubleday, 1968).

19. Lance Davis and Robert Huttenback, *Mammon and the Pursuit of Empire: The Political Economy of British Imperialism, 1860–1912* (Cambridge: Cambridge University Press, 1986), invalidates J. M. A. Hobson, *Imperialism: A Study* (Ann Arbor: University of Michigan Press, 1965 [1902]); and Vladimir Lenin, *Imperialism: The Highest Stage of Capitalism* (New York: Penguin, 2010 [1917]). See also D. K. Fieldhouse, *Economics and Empire 1830–1914* (Ithaca, NY: Cornell University Press, 1973); and on France, Henri Brunschwig, *French Colonialism 1871–1914: Myths and Realities* (New York: Praeger, 1966), 90–91, 96.

20. Daniel Headrick, *The Tools of Empire: Technology and European Imperialism in the Nineteenth Century* (New York: Oxford University Press, 1981).

21. See again Gat, *War in Human Civilization*, 542–557.

22. Cf. Dale Copeland, "Economic Interdependence and War: A Theory of Trade Expectations", *International Security* 20, no. 4 (1996): 5–41.

23. Gat, *War in Human Civilization*; Gat, "The Return of Authoritarian Great Powers", *Foreign Affairs* 86, no. 4 (2007): 59–69; Gat, "Which Way Is History Marching: Debating the Authoritarian Revival", *Foreign Affairs* 88, no. 4 (2009): 150–155; Gat, *Victorious and Vulnerable: Why Democracy Won in the 20th Century and How It Is Still Imperiled* (Stanford, CA: Hoover/Rowman & Littlefield, 2010); Gat, *The Causes of War and the Spread of Peace*.

24. Gil Merom, *How Democracies Lose Small Wars* (Cambridge: Cambridge University Press, 2003); Azar Gat and Gil Merom, "Why Counterinsurgency Fails", in Gat, *Victorious and Vulnerable*, chap. 7.

25. Ibid.

26. For opposite views here see: Elie Kedourie, "Introduction", to his (ed.) *Nationalism in Asia and Africa* (New York: New American Library, 1970); Azar Gat, with Alexander Yakobson, *Nations: The Long History and Deep Roots of Political Ethnicity and Nationalism* (Cambridge: Cambridge University Press, 2013), esp. 124–125, 226, 193.

27. Gat, *Nations*, 286–292.

28. Ibid., 52–53.

29. Max Gluckman, "The Kingdom of the Zulu of South Africa", in *African Political Systems*, ed. M. Fortes and E. Evans-Pritchard (Oxford: Oxford University Press, 1940), 25–55; Max Gluckman, "The Rise of the Zulu Empire", *Scientific American* 202 (1960): 157–168; Keith Otterbein, "The Evolution of Zulu Warfare" (1964), reprinted in his *Feuding and Warfare* (Longhorne, PA: Gordon & Breach, 1994), 25–32; Elman Service, *Origins of the State and Civilization* (New York: W. W. Norton, 1975), 104–116.

30. Karl Marx, "The Future Results of British Rule in India", *New York Daily Tribune*, August 8, 1853; reprinted in the *New-York Semi-Weekly Tribune*, No. 856, August 9, 1853; on the WWW.

31. "Address by Prime Minister Dr. Manmohan Singh in acceptance of Honorary Degree from Oxford University", July 8, 2005, on the WWW.

32. Niall Ferguson, *Empire: The Rise and Demise of the British World Order and the Lessons for Global Power* (New York: Basic Books, 2003). See also n. 64 below.

33. Jean-Paul Sartre, *The Communists and Peace, with A Reply to Claude Lefort* (New York: George Braziller, 1968), 201, emphasis in the original. The French original was published in article form in *Les temps modernes* in the years 1952–1954, and in book form in 1964.

34. "The Legitimacy of Violence as a Political Act? Noam Chomsky Debates with Hannah Arendt, Susan Sontag, et al.", December 15, 1967, on the WWW.

35. Noam Chomsky and Edward Herman, "Distortions at Fourth Hand", *The Nation*, June 6, 1977. For more on Chomsky's efforts in this regard, see Donald Beachler, "Arguing about Cambodia: Genocide and Political Interest", *Holocaust and Genocide Studies* 23, no. 2 (2009): 214–238, esp. 221–223.

36. From an interview that Foucault gave in September 1978, translated into English and reproduced in Janet Afary and Kevin Anderson, *Foucault and the Iranian Revolution: Gender and the Seductions of Islamism* (Chicago: University of Chicago Press, 2005). This book is the most comprehensive treatment of Foucault and the Iranian Revolution, and it includes an appendix with his entire corpus on the subject. For the quotation see 185.

37. Foucault, in *Le nouvel observateur*, October 16–22, 1978, in ibid., 206.

38. Edward Said, *Orientalism* (London: Penguin, 1995 [1978]), 4–5; my emphases.

39. Ibid., 48–49.

40. For Said's criticism of Lewis, see *Orientalism*, esp. 314–320, 342–346. From the other side, see among others, Bernard Lewis, "The Question of Orientalism", *New York Review of Books*, June 24, 1982. From among Lewis's many works on the state of the Arab Middle East, see, for example, his *What Went Wrong?* (New York: Oxford University Press, 2002).

41. Said, *Orientalism*, 204.

42. Ibid., 323–324; my emphasis.

43. Ibid., 331.

44. Justus Reid Weiner, " 'My Beautiful Old House' and Other Fabrications by Edward Said", *Commentary*, September 1999.

45. M. Finley, *Economy and Society in Ancient Greece* (London: Chatto & Windus, 1981), chaps. 6–9.

46. Michael Gomez, *Reversing Sail: A History of the African Diaspora* (Cambridge: Cambridge University Press, 2005), 35.

47. Suzanne Miers and Igor Kopytoff, eds., *Slavery in Africa: Historical and Anthropological Perspectives* (Madison: University of Wisconsin Press, 1979); Paul Lovejoy, *Transformations in Slavery: A History of Slavery in Africa* (Cambridge: Cambridge University Press, 2000); Robin Law, "Dahomey and the Slave Trade: Reflections on the Historiography of the Rise of Dahomey", *Journal of African History* 27, no. 2 (1986): 237–267; Seid Mohammed, "A Social Institution of Slavery and Slave Trade in Ethiopia: Revisited", *African Journal of History and Culture* 7, no. 3 (2015): 85–90; Giulia Bonacci and Alexander Meckelburg, "Revisiting Slavery and the Slave Trade in Ethiopia", *Northeast African Studies* 17, no. 2 (2017): 5–30.

48. Robert Davis, *Christian Slaves, Muslim Masters: White Slavery in the Mediterranean, the Barbary Coast and Italy, 1500–1800* (New York: Palgrave Macmillan, 2003).

49. Karl Marx, *Capital*, vol. i. (New York: Progress, 1995 [1867, 1887]), part viii, esp. chap. 31. The thesis was developed by Eric Williams, *Capitalism and Slavery* (Chapel Hill: University of North Carolina Press, 1944), which still retains its value. More recently see: Sven Beckert, *Empire of Cotton: A Global History* (New York: Knopf, 2014).

50. On the more minimalist side: Stanley Engerman, "The Slave Trade and British Capital Formation in the Eighteenth Century: A Comment on the Williams Thesis", *Business History Review* 46, no. 4 (1972): 430–443; David Richardson, "The British Empire and the Atlantic Slave Trade, 1660–1807", in *The Oxford History of the British Empire*, Vol. II: *The Eighteenth Century*, ed. P. Marshall (Oxford: Oxford University Press, 1998), 440–464, esp. 460–462. For the more maximalist position: Beckert, *Empire of Cotton*. Thomas Piketty, *Capital and Ideology* (Cambridge, MA: Harvard University Press, 2020), appeared after this chapter had already been written. While I am critical of many aspects of that book (see at the end of this chapter), its chap. 6 is very valuable on the subject.

51. Beckert, *Empire of Cotton*.

52. J. R. Ward, "The British West Indies in the Age of Abolition", in Marshall, *The Oxford History of the British Empire*, II, 415–439, esp. 424–428.

53. Henry Louis Gates Jr., based on The Trans-Atlantic Slave Database, edited by David Eltis and David Richardson (both on the WWW).

54. Samuel H. Williamson and Louis Cain, "Measuring Slavery in 2016 Dollars", MeasuringWorth, 2020 (on the WWW); Piketty, *Capital and Ideology*, chap. 6.

55. Jon Meacham, *Thomas Jefferson: The Art of Power* (New York: Random House, 2012).

56. Sean Wilentz, "A Matter of Facts: *The New York Times*' 1619 Project Launched with the Best of Intentions, but Has Been Undermined by Some of Its Claims", *The Atlantic*, January 22, 2020. The author, speaking for other historians as well, is a professor of history at Princeton University.

57. For a development of this notion, see again Williams, *Capitalism and Slavery*; Beckert, *Empire of Cotton*.

58. Williams, *Capitalism and Slavery*, 7.

59. The most extended argument along these lines has been made by historical sociologist Michael Mann, *The Dark Side of Democracy: Explaining Ethnic Cleansing* (Cambridge: Cambridge University Press, 2004). The following is based on my critique, first appearing in the *London Times' Literary Supplement* and republished, with minor modifications, in my *Victorious and Vulnerable*, chap. 8.

60. Jared Diamond, *Guns, Germs, and Steel: The Fates of Human Societies* (New York: W. W. Norton, 1997), is an enlightening survey of the phenomenon based on the scholarly litera-ture. William McNeill, *Plagues and Peoples* (New York: Anchor, 1976), all but established this field of research

61. Allan Bloom, *The Closing of the American Mind: How Higher Education Has Failed Democracy and Impoverished the Souls of Today's Students* (New York: Simon & Schuster, 1987), was a passionate and sensational pushback against the trend. I sympathize with some of its themes and take issue with others. Recently see: Stanley Kurtz, *The Lost History of Western Civilization* (New York: National Association of Scholars, 2020).

62. Steven Pinker, *Enlightenment Now: The Case for Reason, Science, Humanism, and Progress* (New York: Viking, 2018), 492. Also highly critical of the real harms done by radical intellectuals is Mark Lilla, *The Reckless Mind: Intellectuals in Politics* (New York: New York Review of Books, 2001).

63. Delivered on July 6, 2020; on the WWW.

64. The article has been reprinted in *Academic Questions*, Summer 2018; quotation from the pro-logue there. See also n. 32 and adjacent text above.

65. For such an intellectual development, see, for example: Irving Kristol, *Reflections of a Neo-Conservative* (New York: Basic Books, 1983).

66. "The Newest Moynihan", *New York Times*, August 7, 1994.

Chapter 6

1. For a tentative summary see: Donald Brown, *Human Universals* (New York: McGraw Hill, 1991).

2. The Standard Social Science Model has been seminally criticized by J. Barkow, L. Cosmides, and J. Tooby, *The Adapted Mind: Evolutionary Psychology and the Generation of Culture* (Oxford: Oxford University Press, 1992).

3. Ernest Gellner, *Nations and Nationalism* (Oxford: Blackwell, 1983), 34–35.

4. Linda Colley, *Britons: Forging the Nation 1707–1837* (New Haven, CT: Yale University Press, 1992).

5. John Stuart Mill, *Considerations on Government by Representatives* (New York: Harper, 1862), chap. 16, 310.

6. Yael Tamir, *Liberal Nationalism* (Princeton, NJ: Princeton University Press, 1993); David Miller, *On Nationality* (Oxford: Oxford University Press, 1995).

7. Ernest Gellner, *Nationalism* (London: Weidenfeld & Nicolson, 1997), ix.

8. Steven Pinker, *Enlightenment Now: The Case for Reason, Science, Humanism, and Progress* (New York: Viking, 2018), 450 and passim; my emphasis.

9. Adam Smith, *The Wealth of Nations*, IV.ii.23.

10. Other critics of modernism include Hugh Seton-Watson, *Nations and States: An Inquiry into the Origins of Nations and the Politics of Nationalism* (Boulder, CO: Westview, 1977); John Armstrong, *Nations before Nationalism* (Chapel Hill: University of North Carolina Press, 1982); Steven Grosby, *Biblical Ideas of Nationality: Ancient and Modern* (Winona Lake, IN: Eisenbrauns, 2002); Aviel Roshwald, *The Endurance of Nationalism* (New York: Cambridge University Press, 2006). Anthony Smith, *The Ethnic Origins of Nations* (Oxford: Blackwell,

1986), was a landmark; in some later of his many works, Smith came closer to recognizing the notion of premodern nations.

11. Freud, "Group Psychology and the Analysis of the Ego" (1921) and "Civilization and Its Discontents" (1930), in *The Complete Psychological Works*, vol. 18, 101–104, and vol. 21, 108–116, respectively. Freud confessed his puzzlement over the reasons for group ties in general. He tried to explain the "narcissism" as a bottled-up expression of an elementary aggressive drive, thus turning the matter on its head and denying it any logic, evolutionary or otherwise. In actuality, it is ethnic differences, even minor, that may trigger aggression, rather than the other way around.

12. L. L. Cavalli-Sforza, P. Menozzi, and A. Piazza, *The History and Geography of Human Genes* (Princeton, NJ: Princeton University Press, 1994), was seminal. But this monumental work has already been rendered obsolescent by fast improving techniques and a legion of specialized studies on specific populations.

13. Michael Billig, *Banal Nationalism* (London: Sage, 1995).

14. Jürgen Habermas, *The Postnational Constellation* (Cambridge: Polity, 2001), 74.

15. See, for example: Maurizio Virdi, *For Love of Country: An Essay on Patriotism and Nationalism* (Oxford: Oxford University Press, 1995).

16. This point has been picked up by Rich Lowry, *The Case for Nationalism: How It Made Us Powerful, United, and Free* (New York: Broadside Books, 2019). But it becomes much more prominent in his newspaper articles following the publication of his book.

17. Yossi Shain, *Marketing the American Creed Abroad: Diasporas in the US and Their Homelands* (New York: Cambridge University Press, 1999).

18. Herbert Gans, "Symbolic Ethnicity: The Future of Ethnic Groups and Cultures in America", in *Nationalism*, ed. J. Hutchinson and A. Smith (London: Routledge, 2000), vol. 4, 1217–1237.

19. For this misconception, see Thomas Sowell, *Ethnic America: A History* (New York: Basic Books, 1981), 4. The literature on American ethnicity and ethnic groups is legion. Lawrence Fuchs, *The American Kaleidoscope: Race, Ethnicity and the Civic Culture* (Lebanon, NH: University Press of New England, 1990), celebrates the history of American civic nationhood. By comparison, Rogers Smith, *Civic Ideals: Conflicting Visions of Citizenship in US History* (New Haven, CT: Yale University Press, 1997), dispels the notion of a civic nation by documenting the ethnic exclusionary element of American historical naturalization laws. However, Smith, too, regards only immigrants but not Americans as ethnic; that is, he is aware only of ethnic exclusion but not inclusion. This oversight is largely corrected in his later book, *Stories of Peoplehood* (Cambridge: Cambridge University Press, 2003). Noah Pickus, *True Faith and Allegiance: Immigration and American Civic Nationalism* (Princeton, NJ: Princeton University Press, 2005), advocating republican solidarity, is also oblivious to the unifying and nation-creating role of American culture. Thomas Archdeacon, *Becoming American: An Ethnic History* (New York: Free Press, 1983), is general and intelligent, while Roger Daniels, *Coming to America: A History of Immigration and Ethnicity in American Life* (New York: Harper, 1991), is conventional. Ronald Takaki, *A Different Mirror: A History of Multicultural America* (Boston: Little, Brown, 1993), focuses on the racial aspect. The best book on the historical transformations of American identity is, in my view: Michael Lind, *The Next American Nation* (New York: Free Press, 1995). Very important insights can be found in Eric Kaufmann, *Whiteshift: Populism, Immigration and the Future of White Majorities* (New York: Penguin, 2019). For more, see below.

20. Joel Perlmann and Mary Waters, "Intermarriage and Multiple Identities", in *The New Americans: A Guide to Immigration since 1965*, ed. M. Waters and R. Ueda (Cambridge, MA: Harvard University Press, 2007), 114; Jeffrey Passel, Wendy Wang, and Paul Taylor, "Marrying Out: One-in-Seven New US Marriages Is Interracial or Interethnic", Pew Research Center: A Social and Demographic Trends Report, 2010; also, Eric Kaufmann, *The Rise and Fall of Anglo-America* (Cambridge, MA: Harvard University Press, 2004), 236–238.

21. Will Herberg, *Protestant, Catholic, Jew* (Garden City, NY: Doubleday, 1955).

22. Richard Alba, *Ethnic Identity: The Transformation of White America* (New Haven, CT: Yale University Press, 1990), extensively documenting these processes, suggests that they have created a new European-American joint ethnic identity that largely replaces the old country-of-origin ethnic identity. Alba agrees that there is a large convergence between

European-American and what may simply be regarded as American ethnic identity (203, 312, 315). In his early book, *The Rise and Fall of Anglo-America*, Kaufmann held a similar view. He maintained that this American core ethnos, originally Anglo-Protestant and from the 1960s simply white, has been losing its dominance because of the recent arrival of non-white immigrants. However, in my view, while Americans of European descent happen to be the older waves of immigration, continuing similar processes of intermarriage and cultural integration within American society and into an all-American identity seem to be occurring also with the newer waves of arrival from East Asia and Latin America. In his recent book *Whiteshift*, Kaufmann apparently adopts a similar view.

23. Perlmann and Waters, "Intermarriage and Multiple Identities", 111.

24. Michael Walzer recognizes that in American history, immigrants' assimilation into American culture generally followed naturalization; yet he believes that with the ethnic resurgence this is no longer the case, nor should it be, because the state can and should be neutral about ethnicity: Walzer, "Pluralism in Political Perspective", in *The Politics of Ethnicity*, ed. M. Walzer et al. (Cambridge, MA: Harvard University Press, 1982), 1–28; Walzer, "Comment", in *Multiculturalism: Examining the Politics of Recognition*, ed. A. Gutmann (Princeton, NJ: Princeton University Press, 1994), 99–103; Walzer, *What It Means to Be an American* (Delhi: East-West Publishing, 1994). However, in response to Will Kymlicka's critique (see n. 27, below), Walzer has effectively conceded that the United States is not ethnically neutral, most conspicuously with respect to the English language. He claims, however (and Kymlicka agrees), that this ethnic element is thin in comparison with nonimmigrant countries: Michael Walzer, "Nation-States and Immigrant Societies", in *Can Liberal Pluralism be Exported?*, ed. W. Kymlicka and M. Opalski (Oxford: Oxford University Press, 2001), 150–153. Although this view is obviously true to a large degree, I believe it still overestimates the sometimes marked, yet mostly symbolic, significance of the ancestral ethnic identities in the United States; generalizes from particularly strong cases of such identity (e.g., Jewish); and underestimates the depth of American culture and the degree of cultural integration and intermarriage over the generations.

25. Although her approach is different to mine, see: Elizabeth Theiss-Morse, *Who Counts as an American?* (Cambridge: Cambridge University Press, 2009).

26. For some more on Canada, Australia, and New Zealand, including references, see Azar Gat (with Alexander Yakobson), *Nations: The Long History and Deep Roots of Political Ethnicity and Nationalism* (Cambridge: Cambridge University Press, 2013), 277–279.

27. Will Kymlicka, *Politics in the Vernacular: Nationalism, Multiculturalism, and Citizenship* (Oxford: Oxford University Press, 2001), 23–26.

28. Pew Research Center, "More Say Immigrants Strengthen U.S. as the Partisan Divide Grows", October 4, 2017, on the WWW; Adam Przeworski, *Crises of Democracy* (New York: Cambridge University Press, 2019), 115.

29. For counterarguments, especially regarding the degree of the immigrants' integration into American society and culture, see: Rodolfo de la Garza et al., *Latino Voices: Mexican, Puerto Rican, and Cuban Perspectives on American Politics* (Boulder, CO: Westview, 1992); Rodolfo de la Garza, Angelo Falcon, and F. Chris Garcia, "Will the Real Americans Please Stand Up: Anglo and Mexican-American Support of Core American Political Values", *American Journal of Political Science* 40, no. 2 (1996): 335–351; David Lopez and Vanessa Estrada, "Language", in Waters and Ueda, *The New Americans: A Guide to Immigration since 1965*, 228–242, esp. 233, 237, 239, 240–241; Richard Alba and Victor Nee, *Remaking the American Mainstream: Assimilation and Contemporary Immigration* (Cambridge, MA: Harvard University Press, 2003).

30. A recent analysis, and critique, is Douglas Murray, *The Strange Death of Europe: Immigration, Identity, Islam* (London: Bloomsbury, 2017).

31. Liav Orgad, *The Cultural Defense of Nations: A Liberal Theory of Majority Rights* (Oxford: Oxford University Press, 2015).

32. See an overview of the literature in K. Banting and W. Kymlicka, eds., *Multiculturalism and the Welfare State: Recognition and Redistribution in Contemporary Democracies* (Oxford: Oxford University Press, 2006), 11–12, 93–94.

33. Rounded figures for the years 2000 and 1998, respectively: Alberto Alesina and Edward Glaeser, *Fighting Poverty in the US and Europe: A World of Difference* (Oxford: Oxford University Press, 2004), 17, 19.

34. Ibid., 133–134, 145.

35. Ibid., 146–166.

36. Ibid., 41. Other researchers make similar claims in different contexts: Daniel Béland and Andre Lécours, *Nationalism and Social Policy: The Politics of Territorial Solidarity* (Oxford: Oxford University Press, 2008). In the study by Alesina and Glaeser, Japan appears as an outlier in being one of the most ethnically homogeneous countries in the world, while ranking only on the middle of the scale in terms of government expenditure and income inequality. However, in the UN Human Development Report for 2009, Japan ranks with the Scandinavian countries among the most equal societies in the world, with a Gini coefficient of .25. This fits Japanese's self-perception of their people as being both close kin and middle class.

37. For a different view, see most notably the studies in Banting and Kymlicka, *Multiculturalism and the Welfare State*. However, the book is more concerned with refuting the claim that social solidarity and wealth redistribution are adversely affected by multiculturalist policies, rather than by ethnic heterogeneity in general.

38. Keith Banting, Richard Johnston, Will Kymlicka, and Stuart Soroka, "Do Multiculturalism Policies Erode the Welfare State", in Banting and Kymlicka, *Multiculturalism and the Welfare State*, chap. 2, especially 83.

39. Yoram Hazony, *The Virtue of Nationalism* (New York: Basic Books, 2018); for the scant reference to the value of international cooperation, see 135.

40. Again, I have written extensively on this subject: Azar Gat, "The Human Motivational Complex: Evolutionary Theory and the Causes of Hunter-Gatherer Fighting", *Anthropological Quarterly* 73, no. 1–2 (2000): 20–34, 74–88, incorporated into my *War in Human Civilization* (Oxford: Oxford University Press, 2006); adapted to students of international relations: Gat, "So Why Do People Fight: Evolutionary Theory and the Causes of War", *European Journal of International Relations* 15 (2009): 571–599; and my *The Causes of War and the Spread of Peace: But Will War Rebound?* (Oxford: Oxford University Press, 2017), chaps. 2 and 3; also my "Is War in Our Nature: What Is Right and What Is Wrong about the Seville Statement on Violence", *Human Nature* 30, no. 2 (2019): 149–154.

41. In addition to Freud's latter-day theorizing about a death drive or instinct, see most notably: Konrad Lorenz, *On Aggression* (London: Methuen, 1966); Robert Ardrey, *The Territorial Imperative: A Personal Inquiry into the Animal Origins of Property and Nations* (New York: Atheneum, 1966); and Desmond Morris, *The Naked Ape: A Zoologist's Study of the Human Animal* (London: Jonathan Cape, 1967). Unfortunately, something like this is at least implied by leading evolutionary biologist E. O. Wilson, "Is War Inevitable?", *Discover*, June 12, 2012, excerpted from his *The Social Conquest of Earth* (New York: W. W. Norton, 2012).

42. Margaret Mead, "Warfare Is Only an Invention—Not a Biological Necessity", *Asia* 40, no. 8 (1940): 402–405.

43. Georg Simmel, *Conflict: The Web of Group Affiliations* (Glencoe, IL: Free Press, 1955).

44. The Statement can be found on the WWW. It has been criticized as an example of false-consciousness and the subordination of scholarly integrity to an ideological cause, for example by J. H. Manson and R. W. Wrangham, "Is Human Aggression Nonbiological? Problems with the Statement on Violence", *Human Ethnology Newsletter* (1987); G. Beroldi, "Critique of the Seville Statement on Violence", *American Psychologist* 49, no. 10 (1994): 847–848; Steven Pinker, *How the Mind Works* (New York: W. W. Norton, 1997).

45. Robert Kagan, *The Jungle Grows Back: America and Our Imperiled World* (New York: Knopf, 2018), 12, and repeatedly thereafter.

46. Ibid., 105–106.

Chapter 7

1. In the psychological research this attitude dominated Eleanor Maccoby, ed., *The Development of Sex Differences* (Stanford: Stanford University Press, 1966).

2. Simone de Beauvoir, *The Second Sex* (New York: Vintage 2011 [French original 1949]), 330.
3. Steven Pinker, *The Blank Slate: The Modern Denial of Human Nature* (New York: Penguin, 2002), 344–345. See most notably: David Geary, *Male, Female: The Evolution of Human Sex Differences* (Washington, DC: American Psychological Association, 1998); Doreen Kimura, *Sex and Cognition* (Cambridge, MA: MIT Press, 1999); Diane Halpern, *Sex Differences in Cognitive Abilities*, 4th ed. (New York: Psychology Press, 2012). For more see below.
4. Mary Anne Baker, ed., *Sex Differences in Human Performance* (Chichester: Wiley, 1987), esp. 109–110, 117, 127, 136–137, 180.
5. Richard Lee, "Politics, Sexual and Non-Sexual, in Egalitarian Society," in *Politics and History in Band Societies*, ed. R. Lee and E. Leacock (New York: Cambridge University Press, 1982), 44.
6. Marshall Segal, "Cultural Factored Biology and Human Aggression", in *Aggression and War*, ed. J. Groebel and R. A. Hinde (Cambridge: Cambridge University Press, 1989), 177–178; Matt Ridley, *The Red Queen: Sex and the Evolution of Human Nature* (New York: Macmillan, 1994), 252; Richard Wrangham and Dale Peterson, *Demonic Males: Apes and the Origins of Human Violence* (London: Bloomsbury, 1997), 113, 115.
7. Martin Daly and Margo Wilson, *Homicide* (New York: Aldin, 1988), 147–148. Denmark is the exception, with 85 percent for the males, but after omitting infanticide the figure rises to 100 percent.
8. K. Bjorkqvist and P. Niemela, eds., *Of Mice and Women: Aspects of Female Aggression* (Orlando, FL: Academic Press, 1992); Kirsti Lagerspetz and Kaj Björkqvist, "Indirect Aggression in Boys and Girls", in *Aggressive Behavior: Current Perspectives*, ed. L. R. Huesmann (New York: Plenum Press, 1994), 131–150.
9. Lise Eliot, *Pink Brain, Blue Brain: How Small Differences Grow Into Troublesome Gaps—And What We Can Do about It* (Boston: Houghton, 2009), 270.
10. Lisa Brandes, "Public Opinion, International Security and Gender: The United States and Great Britain since 1945", unpublished doctoral dissertation, Yale University, 1994; Mark Tessler and Ira Warriner, "Gender, Feminism, and Attitudes towards International Conflict", *World Politics* 49 (1997): 250–281.
11. In addition to n. 8, earlier studies include: R. M. Rose et al., "Androgens and Aggression: A Review of Recent Findings in Primates", in *Primate Aggression, Territoriality, and Xenophobia*, ed. Ralph Holloway (New York: Academic Press, 1974), 276–304; E. E. Maccoby and C. N. Jacklin, *The Psychology of Sex Differences* (Palo Alto, CA: Stanford University Press, 1974); Luigi Valzelli, *Psychobiology of Aggression and Violence* (New York: Raven Press, 1981), 116–121; Anne Moir and David Jessel, *Brain Sex: The Real Difference between Men and Women* (New York: Lyle Stuart, 1991); M. Daly and M. Wilson, *Sex Evolution and Behavior* (Belmont, CA: Wadsworth, 1983); Felicity Huntingford and Angela Turner, *Animal Conflict* (London: Chapman, 1987), 95–128, 339–341; J. Herbert, "The Physiology of Aggression", and Segal, "Cultural Factored Biology and Human Aggression", in Groebel and Hinde, *Aggression and War*, 58–71, 173–185; Ridley, *The Red Queen*, 247–263.
12. Pinker, *The Blank Slate*, 338.
13. A wealth of data and illuminating graphs are assembled by Esteban Ortiz-Ospina, Sandra Tzvetkova, and Max Rosner, "Women's Employment", in *Our World in Data*, Oxford University Martin School (on the www).
14. Tatiana Zerjal, Yali Xue, Giorgio Bertorelle, et al., "The Genetic Legacy of the Mongols", *American Journal of Human Genetics* 72 (2003): 717–721.
15. Donald Symons's pioneering *The Evolution of Human Sexuality* (New York: Oxford University Press, 1979), retains its value. David Buss, *The Evolution of Desire: Strategies of Human Mating* (New York: Basic Books, 2003 [1994]), is the most comprehensive survey of the research. Sarah Hrdy, *The Woman That Never Evolved* (Cambridge, MA: Harvard University Press, 1999 [1981]), was groundbreaking in bringing to the fore the active role of females in the "battle of the sexes" and the evolutionary logic behind it. Nancy Etcoff, *Survival of the Prettiest: The Science of Beauty* (New York: Anchor, 2000), is particularly good on beauty.
16. Literature summarized in Buss, *The Evolution of Desire*, chap. 4.
17. Kathryn Walter, Daniel Conroy-Beam, David Buss, et al. (seventy-five contributors), "Sex Differences in Mate Preferences across 45 Countries: A Large-Scale Replication", *Psychological Science* 31, no. 4 (2020): 408–423.

18. Reported in the memoirs book by Lydia Chukovskaya, Akhmatova's "Boswell"; courtesy of Alex Yakobson.

19. Andrea Dworkin, *Intercourse* (New York: Free Press, 1987), 154–155.

20. Betty Friedan, *The Second Stage* (Cambridge, MA: Harvard University Press, 1998 [1981]), 35–36.

21. Ibid., 41, my emphasis.

22. Radical author Naomi Wolf's *The Beauty Myth: How Images of Beauty Are Used against Women* (New York: William Morrow, 1991), is typical in regarding the "myth" as a pure invention of patriarchy in bourgeois society. The only valuable point in the book is its warning against the health hazards of the excessive pursuit of the beauty ideal, such as eating disorders and much else.

23. Russell Clark and Elaine Hatfield, "Gender Differences in Receptivity to Sexual Offers", *Journal of Psychology and Human Sexuality* 2 (1989): 39–55. For their story of the article's difficult road to publication and the stormy reactions it received, see: Clark and Hatfield, "Love in the Afternoon", *Psychological Inquiry* 14, no. 3–4 (2003): 227–231.

24. Pinker, *The Blank Slate*, 359–371.

25. Ibid., 362.

26. This applies also to scholarly works, such as Simon Baron-Cohen, *The Essential Difference: The Truth about the Male and Female Brain* (New York: Basic Books, 2003). While citing many correct and familiar differences, his dichotomous framing of them is off the mark.

27. For a recent broad survey: Patrick Heck, Daniel Simons, and Christopher Chabris, "65% of Americans Believe They Are above Average in Intelligence: Results of Two Nationally Representative Surveys", *PLOS One*, July 3, 2018.

28. For a summary of studies see: "Why Women Are Better at Investing?", *Forbes*, December 29, 2018.

29. Buss, *The Evolution of Desire*, 81.

30. Jonathan Haidt and Matthew Hersh, "Sexual Morality: The Cultures and Emotions of Conservatives and Liberals", *Journal of Applied Social Psychology* 31, no. 1 (2001): 191–221; Jonathan Haidt, *The Righteous Mind: Why Good People Are Divided by Politics and Religion* (New York, Pantheon, 2012), chap. 2.

31. Astrid Elkjaer Sørensen, "Gender Segregation in the Nordic Labour Market", *Nordics.Info*, February 22, 2019, Aarhus University; on the WWW.

32. Annemiek Bolscher and Ine Megens, "The Netherlands", in *Women and the Military System*, ed. Eva Isakson (New York: Palgrave Macmillan, 1988), 359–369.

33. Ellen Elster, "Norway", in ibid., 371–373.

34. Barbara Seitz, Linda Lobao, and Ellen Treadway, "No Going Back: Women's Participation in the Nicaraguan Revolution and in Postrevolutionary Movements", in *Women and the Use of Military Force*, ed. R. Howes and M. Stevenson (Boulder, CO, and London: Lynne Rienner, 1993), 167–183.

35. Larry Hedges and Amy Nowell, "Sex Differences in Mental Test Scores, Variability, and Numbers of High-Scoring Individuals", *Science* 269 (1995): 41–45; quotation from 44.

36. Joel's scholarly work is presented to the public in a more accessible book form: Daphna Joel and Luba Wikhanski, *Gender Mosaic: Beyond the Myth of the Male and Female Brain* (New York: Little, Brown Spark, 2019).

37. Daphna Joel et al., "Analysis of Human Brain Structure Reveals That the Brain 'Types' Typical of Males are also Typical of Females, and Vice Versa", *Frontiers in Human Neuroscience* 12 (October 2018): 1–18, citation from 16. For several striking criticisms of her conclusions and framing of the question, see: *Proceedings of the National Academy of Sciences* 113, no. 14 (2016): 1965–1971.

38. Cordelia Fine, John Dupré, and Daphna Joel, "Opinion: Sex-Linked Behavior: Evolution, Stability, and Variability", *Trends in Cognitive Sciences* 21, no. 9 (2017): 666–673, argue that in the balance and interaction between genetic-evolutionary and environmental factors in human behavior, including the sexual, the latter is underappreciated. They conclude: an "important point of difference between ourselves and other species is our capacity to transform our material and cultural developmental systems. As history has shown, sufficient cultural change can produce remarkable changes in sex-linked patterns" (672). I cannot agree

more, while still holding that they err in the opposite direction and underplay the genetic-evolutionary factor.

39. Gina Rippon, *The Gendered Brain: The New Neuroscience That Shatters the Myth of the Female Brain* (New York: Random House, 2019), 308. See also, albeit much more balanced: Rebecca Jordan-Young, *Brain Storm: The Flaws in the Science of Sex Differences* (Cambridge, MA: Harvard University Press, 2010).

40. Eliot, *Pink Brain, Blue Brain*, 212; my emphasis.

41. Ibid., 252.

42. Arieh O'Sullivan, "IDF Soldiers In for a Close Shave", *Jerusalem Post*, November 16, 2001.

43. Sigmund Freud, "Why War" (1933), in *The Complete Psychological Works of Sigmund Freud* (London: Hogarth, 1953–1974), vol. 22, 203–215, especially 210–211.

44. Jonathan Gottschall, "Introduction", to the ground-breaking *The Literary Animal: Evolution and the Nature of Narrative*, ed. J. Gottschall and D. S. Wilson (Evanston, IL: Northwestern University Press, 2005), xix–xx. See also his *The Storytelling Animal: How Stories Make Us Human* (Boston: Houghton Mifflin Harcourt, 2012).

Chapter 8

1. Vito Tanzi and Ludger Schuknecht, *Public Spending in the 20th Century: A Global Perspective* (Cambridge: Cambridge University Press, 2000).

2. John Cogan, *The High Cost of Good Intentions: A History of U.S. Federal Entitlement Programs* (Stanford, CA: Stanford University Press, 2017).

3. Whatever the merit of many of his other arguments, such one-sidedness is demonstrated, for example, by progressive author and economics Nobel laureate: Joseph Stiglitz, *The Great Divide: Unequal Societies and What We Can Do about Them* (New York: W. W. Norton, 2015); Joseph Stiglitz et al., *Rewriting the Rules of the American Economy: An Agenda for Growth and Shared Prosperity* (New York: W. W. Norton, 2016).

4. Thomas Piketty, *Capital and Ideology* (Cambridge, MA: Harvard University Press, 2020), 448; quotation from Binyamin Appelbaum, *The Economists' Hour: How the False Prophets of Free Markets Fractured Our Society* (New York: Little Brown, 2019), 106.

5. Thomas Piketty, *Capital in the Twenty-First Century* (Cambridge, MA: Harvard University Press, 2014), 291, 261, 260, respectively; Thomas Piketty, Emmanuel Saez, and Gabriel Zucman, "Distributional National Accounts: Methods and Estimates for the United States", *Quarterly Journal of Economics* 133, no. 2 (2018): 553–609.

6. Gerald Auten and David Splinter, "Income Inequality in the United States: Using Tax Data to Measure Long-term Trends", *Journal of Economic Literature* (December 20, 2019): 1–43; Congressional Budget Office, "The Distribution of Household Income, 2016", on the WWW. See also Piketty, Saez, and Zucman, "Distributional National Accounts", 582, 587; Stephen Rose, *Squeezing the Middle Class: Income Trajectories from 1967 to 2016* (Washington, DC: Brookings Institution, 2020).

7. Credit Suisse, *Global Wealth Report 2021*, 12; on the WWW.

8. Piketty, *Capital in the Twenty-First Century*, 293 and 484 (quotation).

9. Again the most impressive general studies are: more left-leaning, Robert Putnam, *Bowling Alone: The Collapse and Revival of American Community* (New York: Simon & Schuster, 2000); Putnam, *Our Kids: The American Dream in Crisis* (New York: Simon & Schuster, 2015); and from the right, Charles Murray, *Coming Apart: The State of White America 1960–2010* (New York: Crown, 2012). For scholarly articles see: Miles Corak, "Income Inequality, Equality of Opportunity, and Intergenerational Mobility", *Journal of Economic Perspectives* 27, no. 3 (2013): 79–102; J. Blanden, "Cross-Country Rankings in Intergenerational Mobility: A Comparison of Approaches from Economics and Sociology", *Journal of Economic Surveys* 27 (2013): 38–73.

10. Drew DeSilver, "High-Income Americans Pay Most Income Taxes, but Enough to Be 'Fair'"? Pew Research Center (2016). Data for 2014.

11. Andrea Coombes, "Taxes—Who Really Is Paying Up", *Wall Street Journal*, April 15, 2012; also Piketty, Saez, and Zucman, "Distributional National Accounts", 599; Piketty, *Capital and Ideology*, 453.

12. Emmanuel Saez and Gabriel Zucman, *The Triumph of Injustice: How the Rich Dodge Taxes and How to Make Them Pay* (New York: W. W. Norton, 2019).

13. The classical work in this genre is Robert Nozick, *Anarchy, State and Utopia* (New York: Basic Books, 1974).

14. Robert Kurzban and Jason Weeden, *The Hidden Agenda of the Political Mind: How Self-Interest Shapes Our Opinions and Why We Won't Admit It* (Princeton, NJ: Princeton University Press, 2015).

15. Whatever one thinks of his prescriptions, see, for example: Ronald Dworkin, *Sovereign Virtue: The Theory and Practice of Equality* (Cambridge, MA: Harvard University Press, 2000).

16. George Will, *The Conservative Sensibility* (New York: Hachette, 2019), 279.

17. For example: Sara Solnick and David Hemenway, "Is More Always Better? A Survey on Positional Concerns", *Journal of Economic Behavior & Organization* 37 (1998): 373–383.

18. Anne Case and Angus Deaton, *Deaths of Despair and the Future of Capitalism* (Princeton, NJ: Princeton University Press, 2020).

19. This applies to the books by both Robert Putnam and Charles Murray, and the criticism has been made with respect to Piketty's two major books.

20. Putnam, *Our Kids*, 19.

21. Piketty, *Capital and Ideology*, chap. 17. He does not address the "moral hazards" of idleness and lack of incentive in his projected society. And against current experience—even between the member states of the European Union—he appears to be very hopeful about the prospect of international cooperation in the cause of socialism and global equality. Indeed, only his great awareness of fierce public opposition (which he is barely able to resist calling "racism") prevents Piketty from openly advocating a complete opening of borders to immigration.

22. "More Say Immigrants Strengthen U.S. as the Partisan Divide Grows", Pew Research Center, October 4, 2017; on the WWW.

23. Edward Schlosser, *Vox*, June 3, 2015.

24. Daniel Bell, *The Cultural Contradictions of Capitalism* (New York: HarperCollins, 1976); David Brooks, *Bobos in Paradise: The New Upper Class and How They Got There* (New York: Simon & Schuster, 2000).

25. For such critiques see, for example: Mark Lilla, *The Once and Future Liberal: After Identity Politics* (New York: Harper, 2017); also, Adam Gopnik, *A Thousand Small Sanities: The Moral Adventure of Liberalism* (New York: Basic Books, 2019); and chap. 11 of Francis Fukuyama's otherwise semi-metaphysical and disappointingly ahistorical *The Demand for Dignity and the Politics of Resentment* (New York: Farrar, Straus & Giroux), 2018. For more data-based studies, see: Eric Kaufmann, *Whiteshift: Populism, Immigration and the Future of White Majorities* (New York: Penguin, 2019); and Piketty, *Capitalism and Ideology*, chaps. 14–16.

26. David Brooks returned to the subject in his "How the Bobos Broke America: The Creative Class Was Supposed to Foster Progressive Values and Economic Growth. Instead We Got Resentment, Alienation, and Endless Political Dysfunction", *The Atlantic*, August 2021. Both he and his conservative critic Peter Berkowitz, "David Brooks Reproaches Elites, Recycles Clichés about the People", *RealClearPolitics*, August 22, 2021, both highlighting *mentalité* and social attitudes, neglect to mention the crucial taxation "paradox".

27. Peter Berkowitz, *Constitutional Conservatism: Liberty, Self-Government, and Political Moderation* (Stanford, CA: Hoover, 2013), chap. 5.

28. Laura Bronner, "Why Statistics Don't Capture the Full Extent of the Systemic Bias in Policing", *FiveThirtyEight*, June 25, 2020.

29. "Homicide Trends in the United States, 1980–2008", U.S. Department of Justice, Bureau of Justice Statistics, November 2011; Uniform Crime Reports (UCR), Crime in the United States 2013, "Murder Offenders by Age, Sex, Race and Ethnicity", on the WWW.

30. Lydia Saad, "Black Americans Want Police to Retain Local Presence", August 5, 2020, on the WWW.

31. The main source for the data is the National Vital Statistics Reports on births, issued by the Centers for Disease Control and Prevention (CDC). See also, for poor whites: Murray, *Coming Apart*, chap. 6.

32. Thomas Sowell, "A Painful Anniversary", on the WWW.

33. Mill, *On Liberty* (New Haven, CT: Yale University Press, 2003 [1859]), 113.

34. Adam Przeworski, *Crises of Democracy* (New York: Cambridge University Press, 2019), is a good one here.

Chapter 9

1. Recently, see, for example, Ezra Klein, *Why We're Polarized* (New York: Simon & Schuster, 2020).

2. Karl Mannheim, *Ideology and Utopia* (London: Routledge, 1954 [1936; original German, 1929]), particularly 4–5, 71–80, 88, 91; quotation from 94. See also: Paul Ricoeur, *Lectures on Ideology and Utopia* (New York: Columbia University Press, 1986), 9 and chap. 10; I do not agree with Ricoeur that Mannheim ultimately succumbed to the paradox.

3. Johann Wolfgang von Goethe, *The Maxims and Reflections of Goethe* (New York: Macmillan, 1906), 177.

4. Isaiah Berlin, "Fathers and Children: Turgenev and the Liberal Predicament", in his *Russian Thinkers* (London: Penguin 1994), 261–305; quotation from 263.

5. Ibid., 270.

6. Ibid., 272.

7. Ibid., 303.

8. Julien Benda, *The Betrayal of the Intellectuals* (Boston: Beacon, 1955 [original French, 1927]), 3–4.

9. Ibid., 31.

10. Leon Festinger, *A Theory of Cognitive Dissonance* (Stanford, CA: Stanford University Press, 1957); C. Lord, L. Ross, and M. Lepper, "Biased Assimilation and Attitude Polarization: The Effects of Prior Theories on Subsequently Considered Evidence", *Journal of Personality and Social Psychology* 37, no. 11 (1979): 2098–2109; H. Tajfel and J. Turner, "The Social Identity Theory of Intergroup Behavior", in *Psychology of Intergroup Relations*, ed. S. Worchel and W. Austin (Chicago: Nelson Hall, 1985), 7–24; G. Cohen, "Party over Policy: The Dominating Impact of Group Influence on Political Beliefs", *Journal of Personality and Social Psychology* 85, no. 5 (2003): 808–822; C. Taber and M. Lodge, "Motivated Skepticism in the Evaluation of Political Beliefs", *American Journal of Political Science* 50 (2006): 755–769; J. Frimer, L. Skitka, and M. Motyl, "Liberals and Conservatives Are Similarly Motivated to Avoid Exposure to One Another's Opinions", *Journal of Experimental Social Psychology* 72 (2017): 1–12.

11. T. Adorno, E. Frenkel-Brunsivik, D. Levinson, and N. Sanford, *The Authoritarian Personality* (New York: Harper, 1950), was a landmark in the empirical study of personality and political orientation, though its theoretical claims now seem quite ridiculous and thoroughly biased. For more recent studies see: J. Alford, C. Funk, and J. Hibbing, "Are Political Orientations Genetically Transmitted?", *American Political Science Review* 99, no. 2 (2005): 153–167(yes, as one among several factors); J. Alford and J. Hibbing, "Personal, Interpersonal, and Political Temperaments", *The ANNALS of the American Academy of Political and Social Science* 614, no. 1 (2007): 196–212 (skeptical); D. Carney, J. Jost, S. Gosling, and J. Potter, "The Secret Lives of Liberals and Conservatives: Personality Profiles, Interaction Styles, and the Things They Leave Behind", *Political Psychology* 29, no. 6 (2008): 807–840 (yes). Three recent books are: John Hibbing, Kevin Smith, and John Alford, *Predisposed: Liberals, Conservatives, and the Biology of Political Differences* (New York: Routledge, 2013); Christopher Johnston, Howard Lavine, and Christopher Federico, *Open versus Closed: Personality, Identity, and the Politics of Redistribution* (Cambridge: Cambridge University Press, 2017); Marc Hetherington and Jonathan Weiler, *Prius or Pickup?: How the Answers to Four Simple Questions Explain America's Great Divide* (New York: Houghton Mifflin Harcourt, 2018).

12. J. Napier and J. Jost, "Why Are Conservatives Happier Than Liberals?", *Psychological Science* 19 (2008): 565–572.

13. For an interesting recent demonstration as applied to the current American scene, see again: Kurzban and Weeden, *The Hidden Agenda of the Political Mind*.

14. Philip Tetlock, *Expert Political Judgment: How Good Is It? How Can We Know?* (Princeton, NJ: Princeton University Press, 2006); Philip Tetlock and Dan Gardner, *Superforecasting: The Art and Science of Prediction* (New York: Crown, 2015). See also Adam Grant's penetrating and lively *Think Again* (New York: Viking, 2021).

INDEX

For the benefit of digital users, indexed terms that span two pages (e.g., 52–53) may, on occasion, appear on only one of those pages.